Your All-in-One Resource

On the CD that accompanies this book, you'll find additional resources to extend your learning.

The reference library includes the following fully searchable titles:

- *Microsoft Computer Dictionary*, 5th ed.
- *First Look 2007 Microsoft Office System* by Katherine Murray
- Windows Vista Product Guide

Also provided are a sample chapter and poster from *Look Both Ways: Help Protect Your Family on the Internet* by Linda Criddle

The CD interface has a new look. You can use the tabs for an assortment of tasks:

- Check for book updates (if you have Internet access)
- Install the book's practice file
- Go online for product support or CD support
- Send us feedback

The following screen shot gives you a glimpse of the new interface.

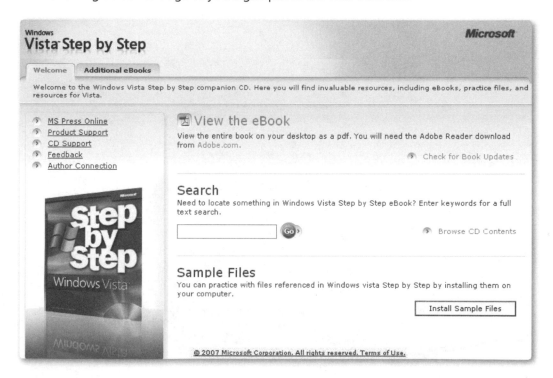

Microsoft® Office® Home and Student Step by Step

Joan Preppernau
Joyce Cox
Curtis Frye

PUBLISHED BY
Microsoft Press
A Division of Microsoft Corporation
One Microsoft Way
Redmond, Washington 98052-6399

Library of Congress Control Number: 2007938164

Printed and bound in the United States of America.

4 5 6 7 8 9   QWT   2 1 0 9 8

Distributed in Canada by H.B. Fenn and Company Ltd.

A CIP catalogue record for this book is available from the British Library.

Microsoft Press books are available through booksellers and distributors worldwide. For further information about international editions, contact your local Microsoft Corporation office or contact Microsoft Press International directly at fax (425) 936-7329. Visit our Web site at www.microsoft.com/mspress. Send comments to mspinput@microsoft.com.

Acquisitions Editor: Juliana Aldous Atkinson
Developmental Editor: Sandra Haynes
Project Editor: Rosemary Caperton
Editorial Production: Online Training Solutions, Inc.

Body Part No. X14-17390

Contents

Part I   Microsoft Office Word 2007

What do you think of this book? We want to hear from you!

Microsoft is interested in hearing your feedback so we can continually improve our books and learning resources for you. To participate in a brief online survey, please visit:

www.microsoft.com/learning/booksurvey/

Part II   Microsoft Office Excel 2007

Introducing the 2007 Microsoft Office System

The 2007 Microsoft Office system is a comprehensive system of programs, servers, services, and solutions. The 2007 Microsoft Office suites include more than a dozen desktop productivity programs. To meet the varying needs of individuals and organizations, Microsoft offers eight different suites of the most common desktop programs.

Microsoft Office Home and Student 2007

Office Home and Student 2007 includes the following programs:

- **Microsoft Office Word 2007.** A sophisticated word-processing program with which you can quickly and effiiciently author and format documents.
- **Microsoft Office Excel 2007.** A powerful spreadsheet program with which you can analyze, communicate, and manage information.
- **Microsoft Office PowerPoint 2007.** A full-featured program with which you can develop and present dynamic, professional-looking presentations.
- **Microsoft Office OneNote 2007.** A digital notebook program in which you can collect and organize many types of electronic information, and quickly locate information when you need it.

The Microsoft Office Fluent User Interface

Many of the programs in the 2007 Office system feature a new look and feel, as well as a new way of interacting with the program that is designed to make the commands you need, in the context of the task you are currently performing, easily available. This new feature set is named the *Microsoft Office Fluent user interface*.

In the Home and Student Edition, the Microsoft Office Fluent user interface is available in Word, Excel, and PowerPoint. (OneNote has the classic Office interface in which commands are presented on menus and toolbars.)

Special features of the Microsoft Office Fluent user interface include:

- **The Office menu.** This menu, which appears when you click the Microsoft Office Button located in the upper-left corner of the program window, contains commands related to working with entire documents (rather than the document content).

- **The Office Fluent Ribbon.** Probably the most visible element of the Office Fluent user interface, the Ribbon replaces the menus and toolbars found in earlier versions of Office. Commands are arranged on the Ribbon on task-specific tabs.

- **The Office Fluent Quick Access Toolbar.** This toolbar provides easy access to the commands you use most frequently. You can change its position, add and remove commands, and create custom command groups for specific documents.

- **Contextual command availability.** Infrequently used commands, such as those specific to working with a table, a graphic, and headers and footers, appear only when you select one of those elements. A Mini Toolbar displaying formatting commands appears when you select text.

- **Office Fluent Live Preview.** See the effect of a formatting change on selected text without applying the format.

- **Quick Styles, Layouts, and Formats.** These features provide professionally designed color palettes, themes, and graphic effects.

- **SmartArt graphics.** These graphics and new styles and formatting methods greatly simplify the process of creating and formatting a variety of documents.

- **Document inspection and finishing tools.** This collection of tools provides a way to safely share information with other people.

Certification

Desktop computing proficiency is becomingly increasingly imoprtant in today's business world. As a result, when screening, hiring, and training employees, more employers are relying on the objectivity and consistency of technology certification to ensure the competence of their workforce. As an employee or job seeker, you can use technology certification to prove that you already have the skills you need to succeed.

A Microsoft Certified Application Specialist (MCAS) is an individual who has demonstrated worldwide skill standards through a certification exam in Windows Vista or in one or more of the 2007 Microsoft Office programs, including Word, Excel, PowerPoint, Microsoft Office Outlook 2007, or Microsoft Office Access 2007. To learn more about the MCAS program, visit

www.microsoft.com/learning/mcp/mcas/

Information for Readers Running Windows XP

The graphics and operating system–related instructions in this book reflect the Windows Vista user interface. However, Windows Vista is not required; you can also use a computer running Windows XP.

Most of the differences you will encounter when working through the exercises in this book on a computer running Windows XP center around appearance rather than functionality. For example, the Windows Vista Start button is round rather than rectangular and is not labeled with the word *Start*; window frames and window-management buttons look different; and if your system supports Windows Aero, the window frames might be transparent.

In this section, we provide steps for navigating to or through menus and dialog boxes in Windows XP that differ from those provided in the exercises in this book. For the most part, these differences are small enough that you will have no difficulty in completing the exercises.

Managing the Practice Files

The instructions given in the "Using the Book's CD" section are specific to Windows Vista. On a computer running Windows Vista, the default installation location of the practice files is *Documents\Microsoft Press\2007OfficeSBS_HomeStudent*. On a computer running Windows XP, the default installation location is *My Documents\Microsoft Press\ 2007OfficeSBS_HomeStudent*. If your computer is running Windows XP, whenever an exercise tells you to navigate to your *Documents* folder, you should instead go to your *My Documents* folder.

To uninstall the practice files from a computer running Windows XP, follow this procedure:

1. On the Windows taskbar, click the **Start** button, and then click **Control Panel**.
2. In **Control Panel**, click (or in Classic view, double-click) **Add or Remove Programs**.
3. In the **Add or Remove Programs** window, click **Microsoft Office Home and Student 2007 Step by Step**, and then click **Remove**.
4. In the **Add or Remove Programs** message box asking you to confirm the deletion, click **Yes**.

> **Important** If you need help installing or uninstalling the practice files, please see the "Getting Help" section later in this book. Microsoft Product Support Services does not provide support for this book or its companion CD.

Using the Start Menu

Follow this procedure to start a program, such as Microsoft Office Word, on a computer running Windows XP:

→ Click the **Start** button, point to **All Programs**, click **Microsoft Office**, and then click **Microsoft Office Word 2007**.

Folders on the Windows Vista Start menu expand vertically. Folders on the Windows XP Start menu expand horizontally. .

Navigating Dialog Boxes

On a computer running Windows XP, some of the dialog boxes you will work with in the exercises not only look different from the graphics shown in this book but also work differently. These dialog boxes are primarily those that act as an interface between Office and the operating system, including any dialog box in which you navigate to a specific location.

To navigate to the *WordExploring* folder in Windows Vista:

→ In the **Favorite Links** pane, click **Documents**. Then in the folder content pane, double-click **Microsoft Press**, **2007OfficeSBS_HomeStudent**, and **WordExploring**.

To move back to the *2007OfficeSBS_HomeStudent* folder in Windows Vista:

Back

→ In the upper-left corner of the dialog box, click the **Back** button.

To navigate to the *WordExploring* folder in Windows XP:

→ On the **Places** bar, click **My Documents**. Then in the folder content pane, double-click **Microsoft Press**, double-click **2007OfficeSBS_HomeStudent**, and then double-click **WordExploring**.

To move back to the *2007OfficeSBS_HomeStudent* folder in Windows XP:

Up One Level

→ On the toolbar, click the **Up One Level** button.

Features and Conventions of This Book

This book has been designed to lead you step by step through some of the tasks you are most likely to want to perform in the programs included with Home and Student Edition of the 2007 Microsoft Office system: Microsoft Office Word 2007, Microsoft Office Excel 2007, Microsoft Office PowerPoint 2007, and Microsoft Office OneNote 2007. If, after completing the exercises, you later need help remembering how to perform a procedure, the following features of this book will help you locate specific information:

- **Detailed table of contents.** A listing of the topics and sidebars within each chapter.
- **Chapter thumb tabs.** Easily locate the beginning of the chapter you want.
- **Topic-specific running heads.** Within a chapter, quickly locate the topic you want by looking at the running head of odd-numbered pages.
- **Quick Reference.** General instructions for each procedure covered in specific detail elsewhere in the book. Refresh your memory about a task while working with your own documents.
- **Detailed index.** Look up specific tasks and features and general concepts in the index, which has been carefully crafted with the reader in mind.
- **Companion CD.** Contains the practice files needed for the step-by-step exercises, as well as a fully searchable electronic version of this book and other useful resources.

In addition, we provide a glossary of terms for those times when you need to look up the meaning of a word or the definition of a concept.

You can save time when you use this book by understanding how the *Step by Step* series shows special instructions, keys to press, buttons to click, and so on.

Convention	Meaning
(CD icon)	This icon at the end of a chapter introduction indicates information about the practice files provided on the companion CD for use in the chapter.
USE	This paragraph preceding a step-by-step exercise indicates the practice files that you will use when working through the exercise.
BE SURE TO	This paragraph preceding or following an exercise indicates any require-ments you should attend to before beginning the exercise or actions you should take to restore your system after completing the exercise.
OPEN	This paragraph preceding a step-by-step exercise indicates files that you should open before beginning the exercise.
CLOSE	This paragraph following a step-by-step exercise provides instructions for closing open files or programs before moving on to another topic.
1 **2**	Blue numbered steps guide you through step-by-step exercises and Quick Reference versions of procedures.
1 2	Black numbered steps guide you through procedures in sidebars and expository text.
→	An arrow indicates a procedure that has only one step.
See Also	These paragraphs direct you to more information about a given topic in this book or elsewhere.
Troubleshooting	These paragraphs explain how to fix a common problem that might prevent you from continuing with an exercise.
Tip	These paragraphs provide a helpful hint or shortcut that makes working through a task easier, or information about other available options.
Important	These paragraphs point out information that you need to know to complete a procedure.
(Save button) Save	The first time you are told to click a button in an exercise, a picture of the button appears in the left margin. If the name of the button does not appear on the button itself, it appears under the picture.
Enter	In step-by-step exercises, keys you must press appear as they would on a keyboard.
Ctrl + Home	A plus sign (+) between two key names means that you must hold down the first key while you press the second key. For example, "press Ctrl + Home" means "hold down the Ctrl key while you press the Home key."
Program interface elements	In steps, the names of program elements, such as buttons, commands, and dialog boxes, are shown in black bold characters.
User input	Anything you are supposed to type appears in blue bold characters.
Glossary terms	Terms that are explained in the glossary at the end of the book are shown in blue italic characters in the chapters.

Using the Book's CD

The companion CD included with this book contains practice files you can use as you work through the book's exercises. By using practice files, you won't waste time creating samples and typing large amounts of data. Instead, you can jump right in and concentrate on learning how to use the programs.

What's on the CD?

The following table lists the practice files supplied on the book's CD.

Chapter	Folder\File
Chapter 1: Exploring Word 2007	WordExploring\Opening.docx
	WordExploring\Printing.docx
	WordExploring\Viewing1.docx
	WordExploring\Viewing2.docx
Chapter 2: Editing and Proofreading Documents	WordEditing\Changes.docx
	WordEditing\Finalizing.docx
	WordEditing\FindingText.docx
	WordEditing\FindingWord.docx
	WordEditing\Outline.docx
	WordEditing\SavedText.docx
	WordEditing\Spelling.docx
Chapter 3: Changing the Look of Text	WordFormatting\Characters.docx
	WordFormatting\Lists.docx
	WordFormatting\Paragraphs.docx
	WordFormatting\QuickFormatting.docx
Chapter 4: Presenting Information in Columns and Tables	WordPresenting\Calculations.docx
	WordPresenting\Columns.docx
	WordPresenting\Loan.xlsx
	WordPresenting\LoanData.xlsx
	WordPresenting\Memo.docx
	WordPresenting\Table.docx
	WordPresenting\TableAsLayout.docx
	WordPresenting\TabularList.docx

Chapter	Folder\File
Chapter 5: Setting Up a Workbook	ExcelCreating\Exception Summary.xlsx ExcelCreating\Route Volume.xlsx
Chapter 6: Working with Data and Data Tables	ExcelData\2007Q1ShipmentsByCategory.xlsx ExcelData\Average Deliveries.xlsx ExcelData\Driver Sort Times.xlsx ExcelData\Series.xlsx ExcelData\Service Levels.xlsx
Chapter 7: Performing Calculations on Data	ExcelFormulas\ConveyerBid.xlsx ExcelFormulas\ITExpenses.xlsx ExcelFormulas\PackagingCosts.xlsx ExcelFormulas\VehicleMiles.xlsx
Chapter 8: Changing Workbook Appearance	ExcelAppearance\acbluprt.jpg ExcelAppearance\callcenter.jpg ExcelAppearance\CallCenter.xlsx ExcelAppearance\Dashboard.xlsx ExcelAppearance\ExecutiveSearch.xlsx ExcelAppearance\HourlyExceptions.xlsx ExcelAppearance\HourlyTracking.xlsx ExcelAppearance\VehicleMileSummary.xlsx
Chapter 9: Starting a New Presentation	PptStarting\Converting.docx PptStarting\Creating.pptx PptStarting\Reusing1.pptx PptStarting\Reusing2.pptx
Chapter 10: Working with Slide Text	PptWorking\Changing.pptx PptWorking\Correcting.pptx PptWorking\Editing.pptx PptWorking\Finding.pptx PptWorking\Spelling.pptx PptWorking\TextBoxes.pptx
Chapter 11: Adjusting the Layout, Order, and Look of Slides	PptAdjusting\Background.pptx PptAdjusting\ColorScheme.pptx PptAdjusting\Layout.pptx PptAdjusting\OtherColors.pptx PptAdjusting\Rearranging.pptx PptAdjusting\Theme1.pptx PptAdjusting\Theme2.pptx

Chapter	Folder\File
Chapter 12: Delivering a Presentation Electronically	*PptDelivering\Adapting.pptx* *PptDelivering\NotesHandouts.pptx* *PptDelivering\Rehearsing.pptx* *PptDelivering\Showing.pptx* *PptDelivering\Travel.pptx* *PptDelivering\YinYang.png*
Chapter 13: Getting Started with OneNote	None
Chapter 14: Creating and Configuring Notebooks	*OneCreating\SBS Sections* notebook
Chapter 15: Collecting Information in a Notebook	*OneCollecting\Arizona01.jpg–Arizona03.jpg* *OneCollecting\Logo_ADatum.jpg* *OneCollecting\Organization101.pptx* *OneCollecting\SBS Collecting* notebook
Chapter 16: Organizing and Locating Information	*OneOrganizing\SBS Moving* notebook

In addition to the practice files, the CD contains some exciting resources that will really enhance your ability to get the most out of using this book and the 2007 Microsoft Office system, including the following:

- *Microsoft Office Home and Student 2007 Step by Step* in eBook format
- *Microsoft Computer Dictionary*, 5th ed. eBook
- Sample chapter and poster from *Look Both Ways: Help Protect Your Family on the Internet* (Linda Criddle, 2007)
- Windows Vista Product Guide
- Microsoft Office Fluent Ribbon Quick Reference

> **Important** The companion CD for this book does not contain the 2007 Office system software. You should purchase and install that program before using this book.

Minimum System Requirements

The Home and Student Edition of the 2007 Microsoft Office system includes the following programs:

- Microsoft Office Word 2007
- Microsoft Office Excel 2007
- Microsoft Office PowerPoint 2007
- Microsoft Office OneNote 2007

Additional programs are available with other editions and separately.

To install and run these programs, your computer needs to meet the following minimum requirements:

- 500 megahertz (MHz) processor
- 256 megabytes (MB) RAM
- CD or DVD drive
- 2 gigabytes (GB) available hard disk space; a portion of this disk space will be freed if you select the option to delete the installation files

> **Tip** Hard disk requirements will vary depending on configuration; custom installation choices might require more or less hard disk space.

- Monitor with 800×600 screen resolution; 1024×768 or higher recommended
- Keyboard and mouse or compatible pointing device
- Internet connection, 128 kilobits per second (Kbps) or greater, for download and activation of products, accessing Microsoft Office Online and online Help topics, and any other Internet-dependent processes
- Windows Vista or later, Microsoft Windows XP with Service Pack 2 (SP2), or Windows Server 2003 or later
- Windows Internet Explorer 7 or Microsoft Internet Explorer 6 with service packs

In addition to the hardware, software, and connections required to run the 2007 Office system, you will need the following to successfully complete the exercises in this book:

- Word 2007, Excel 2007, PowerPoint 2007, and OneNote 2007
- Access to a printer
- 360 MB of available hard disk space for the practice files

Installing the Practice Files

You need to install the practice files in the correct location on your hard disk before you can use them in the exercises. Follow these steps:

1. Remove the companion CD from the envelope at the back of the book, and insert it into the CD drive of your computer.

   The Step By Step Companion CD License Terms appear. Follow the on-screen directions. To use the practice files, you must accept the terms of the license agreement. After you accept the license agreement, a menu screen appears.

   > **Important** If the menu screen does not appear, click the Start button and then click Computer. Display the Folders list in the Navigation pane, click the icon for your CD drive, and then in the right pane, double-click the StartCD executable file.

2. Click **Install Practice Files**.

3. Click **Next** on the first screen, and then click **Next** to accept the terms of the license agreement on the next screen.

4. If you want to install the practice files to a location other than the default folder (*Documents\Microsoft Press\2007OfficeSBS_HomeStudent*), click the **Change** button, select the new drive and path, and then click **OK**.

   > **Important** If you install the practice files to a location other than the default, you will need to substitute that path within the exercises.

5. Click **Next** on the **Choose Destination Location** screen, and then click **Install** on the **Ready to Install the Program** screen to install the selected practice files.

6. After the practice files have been installed, click **Finish**.

7. Close the **Step by Step Companion CD** window, remove the companion CD from the CD drive, and return it to the envelope at the back of the book.

Using the Practice Files

When you install the practice files from the companion CD that accompanies this book, the files are stored on your hard disk in chapter-specific subfolders under *Documents\ Microsoft Press\2007OfficeSBS_HomeStudent* unless you specify a different location during installation. Each exercise is preceded by one or more paragraphs listing the files needed for that exercise and explaining any preparations needed before you start working through the exercise. Here is an example:

> **USE** the *Worksheets* presentation and the *Costs* workbook. These practice files are located in the *DocumentsMicrosoft Press\2007OfficeSBS_HomeStudent\PptWorking* folder.
>
> **BE SURE TO** start PowerPoint before beginning this exercise.
>
> **OPEN** the *Worksheets* presentation.

You can display the practice file folder in Windows Explorer by following these steps:

Start

● On the Windows taskbar, click the **Start** button, point to **All Programs**, point to **Microsoft Press**, and then click **Office Home and Student 2007 SBS**.

You can browse to the practice files from a dialog box by following these steps:

1. In the **Favorite Links** pane of the dialog box, click **Documents**.

2. In your *Documents* folder, double-click **Microsoft Press**, double-click **2007OfficeSBS_HomeStudent**, and then double-click the specified chapter folder.

Removing and Uninstalling the Practice Files

You can free up hard disk space by uninstalling the practice files that were installed from the companion CD. The uninstall process deletes any files that you created in the *Documents\Microsoft Press\2007OfficeSBS_HomeStudent* chapter-specific folders while working through the exercises. Follow these steps:

Start

1. On the Windows taskbar, click the **Start** button, and then click **Control Panel**.

2. In **Control Panel**, under **Programs**, click the **Uninstall a program** task.

3. If the **Programs and Features** message box appears, asking you to confirm the deletion, click **Yes**.

> **Important** Microsoft Product Support Services does not provide support for this book or its companion CD.

Getting Help

Every effort has been made to ensure the accuracy of this book and the contents of its companion CD. If you do run into problems, please contact the sources listed in the following sections for assistance.

Getting Help with This Book and Its Companion CD

If your question or issue concerns the content of this book or its companion CD, please first search the online Microsoft Press Knowledge Base, which provides support information for known errors in or corrections to this book, at the following Web site:

www.microsoft.com/mspress/support/search.asp

If you do not find your answer at the online Knowledge Base, send your comments or questions to Microsoft Press Technical Support at:

mspinput@microsoft.com

Getting Help with an Office Program

If your question is about a specific application, and not about the content of this book, your first recourse is the Office Help system. This system is a combination of tools and files stored on your computer when you installed the 2007 Microsoft Office system and, if your computer is connected to the Internet, information available from Microsoft Office Online. There are several ways to find general or specific Help information:

- To find out about an item on the screen, you can display a *ScreenTip*. For example, to display a ScreenTip for a button, point to the button without clicking it. The ScreenTip gives the button's name, the associated keyboard shortcut if there is one, and unless you specify otherwise, a description of the associated action.

Help

- You can click the Help button at the right end of the program window Microsoft Office Fluent Ribbon to display the Help window.

- In a dialog box, you can click the Help button at the right end of the dialog box title bar to display the Help window with topics related to the functions of that dialog box already identified.

To practice getting help in an Office application, using Microsoft Office PowerPoint 2007 as an example, you can work through the following exercise.

 BE SURE TO start PowerPoint before beginning this exercise.

Help

1. At the right end of the Office Fluent Ribbon, click the **Help** button.

   The PowerPoint Help window opens.

2. In the list of topics in the **PowerPoint Help** window, click **Activating PowerPoint**.

   PowerPoint Help displays a list of topics related to activating Microsoft Office system programs.

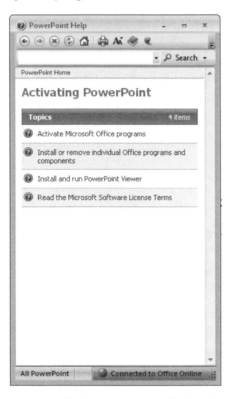

You can click any topic to display the corresponding information.

Show Table of
Contents

3. On the toolbar, click the **Show Table of Contents** button.

The Table Of Contents appears in the left pane, organized by category, like the table of contents in a book.

Clicking any category (represented by a book icon) displays that category's topics (represented by help icons) as well as any available online training (represented by training icons).

Category Topic Online training

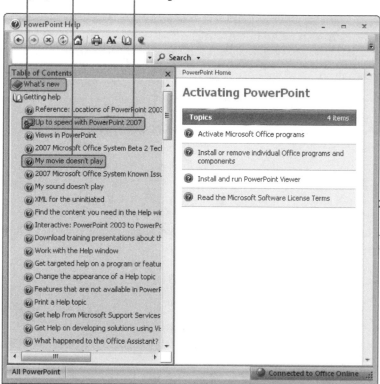

If you're connected to the Internet, PowerPoint displays topics and training available from the Office Online Web site, as well as topics stored on your computer.

4. In the **Table of Contents**, click a few categories and topics, and then click the **Back** and **Forward** buttons to move among the topics you have already viewed.

Close

5. At the right end of the **Table of Contents** title bar, click the **Close** button.

6. At the top of the **PowerPoint Help** window, click the **Type word to search for** box, type Help window, and then press the [Enter] key.

The PowerPoint Help window displays topics related to the words you typed.

7. In the results list, click **Print a Help topic**.

The selected topic appears in the PowerPoint Help window, explaining that you can click the Print button on the toolbar to print any topic.

8. Below the title at the top of the topic, click **Show All**.

PowerPoint displays any hidden auxiliary information available in the topic and changes the Show All button to Hide All. You can display or hide an individual item by clicking it. When you click the Print button, PowerPoint will print all displayed information.

 CLOSE the PowerPoint Help window.

More Information

If your question is about a Microsoft software product and you cannot find the answer in the product's Help system, please search the appropriate product solution center or the Microsoft Knowledge Base at:

support.microsoft.com

In the United States, Microsoft software product support issues not covered by the Microsoft Knowledge Base are addressed by Microsoft Product Support Services. Location-specific software support options are available from:

support.microsoft.com/gp/selfoverview/

About the Authors

Joyce Cox

Joyce has more than 25 years' experience in the development of training materials about technical subjects for non-technical audiences, and is the author of dozens of books about Office and Windows technologies. She is the Vice President of Online Training Solutions, Inc. (OTSI). She was President of and principal author for Online Press, where she developed the *Quick Course* series of computer training books for beginning and intermediate adult learners. She was also the first managing editor of Microsoft Press, an editor for Sybex, and an editor for the University of California. Joyce and her husband Ted live in downtown Bellevue, Washington, and escape as often as they can to their tiny, offline cabin in the Cascade foothills.

Curtis Frye

Curt is a freelance writer and Microsoft Most Valuable Professional for Microsoft Office Excel. He lives in Portland, Oregon, and is the author of eight books from Microsoft Press. He has also written numerous articles for the Microsoft Work Essentials Web site. Before beginning his writing career in June 1995, Curt spent four years with The MITRE Corporation as a defense trade analyst and one year as Director of Sales and Marketing for Digital Gateway Systems, an Internet service provider. Curt graduated from Syracuse University in 1990 with an honors degree in political science. When he's not writing, Curt is a professional improvisational comedian with ComedySportz Portland.

Joan Preppernau

Joan has worked in the training and certification industry for more than 10 years. As president of Online Training Solutions, Inc. (OTSI), Joan is responsible for guiding the translation of technical information and requirements into useful, relevant, and measurable training, learning, and certification deliverables. Joan is a Microsoft Certified Professional, and the author of more than a dozen books about Windows operating systems and Microsoft Office. Joan and her family live in San Diego, California.

Online Training Solutions, Inc. (OTSI)

OTSI specializes in the design, creation, and production of Office and Windows training products for information workers and home computer users.

The OTSI publishing team includes the following outstanding professionals:

Susie Bayers

Jan Bednarczuk

R.J. Cadranell

Jeanne Craver

Marlene Lambert

Jaime Odell

Barry Preppernau

Jean Trenary

Lisa Van Every

For more information about OTSI, visit *www.otsi.com*.

Quick Reference

1 Exploring Word 2007

To start Word

→ On the **Start** menu, point to **All Programs**, click **Microsoft Office**, and then click **Microsoft Office Word 2007**.

To open an existing file

→ On the **Office** menu, click **Open**. In the **Open** dialog box, navigate to the folder that contains the file you want to open, and then double-click the file.

To move the insertion point to the beginning or end of the document

→ Press `Ctrl` + `Home` or `Ctrl` + `End`.

To convert a document created in an earlier version of Word

→ On the **Office** menu, click **Convert**.

To view multiple pages

→ On the **View** toolbar, click the **Zoom** button. In the **Zoom** dialog box, click the **Many pages** arrow, select the number of pages, and then click **OK**.

To adjust the magnification of a document

→ On the **View** toolbar, click the **Zoom** button. In the **Zoom** dialog box, click a **Zoom to** percentage or type an amount in the **Percent** box, and then click **OK**.

To display the Document Map

→ On the **View** tab, in the **Show/Hide** group, select the **Document Map** check box.

To display thumbnails of pages

→ On the **View** tab, in the **Show/Hide** group, select the **Thumbnails** check box.

To display or hide non-printing characters

→ On the **Home** tab, in the **Paragraph** group, click the **Show/Hide ¶** button.

To display a document in a different view

→ On the **View** tab, in the **Document Views** group, click the button for the desired view.

→ Click a view button on the **View** toolbar at the right end of the status bar.

To switch among open documents

→ On the **View** tab, in the **Window** group, click the **Switch Windows** button, and then click the name of the document you want to switch to.

To view multiple open documents

→ On the **View** tab, in the **Window** group, click the **Arrange All** button.

To open a new document

→ On the **Office** menu, click **New**, and then in the **New Document** window, double-click **Blank document**.

To save a document for the first time

1. On the **Quick Access Toolbar**, click the **Save** button; or click **Save As** on the **Office** menu.

2. Navigate to the location where you want to save the file, type a name for the document in the **File name** box, and then click **Save**.

To create a new folder while saving a document

1. In the **Save As** dialog box, click the **New Folder** button.

2. Type the name of the new folder, press ⌨ Enter , and then click **Open**.

To preview how a document will look when printed

→ On the **Office** menu, point to **Print**, and then click **Print Preview**.

To print a document with the default settings

→ On the **Office** menu, point to **Print**, and then click **Quick Print**.

To print a document with custom settings

→ On the **Office** menu, click **Print**. Modify the print settings as needed, and click **OK**.

2   Editing and Proofreading Documents

To select text

- Word: Double-click the word.
- Sentence: Click in the sentence while holding down the ⌨ Ctrl key.
- Paragraph: Triple-click in the paragraph, or double-click in the selection area to the left of the paragraph.
- Block: Click to the left of the first word, hold down the ⌨ Shift key, and then click immediately to the right of the last word or punctuation mark.
- Line: Click in the selection area to the left of the line.
- Document: Triple-click in the selection area.

To delete selected text

→ Press `Del` or `Backspace`.

To copy or cut and paste selected text

1. On the **Home** tab, in the **Clipboard** group, click the **Copy** or **Cut** button.

2. Click where you want to paste the text, and then in the **Clipboard** group, click the **Paste** button.

To undo an action

→ On the **Quick Access Toolbar**, click the **Undo** button.

To save selected text as a building block

1. On the **Insert** tab, in the **Text** group, click the **Quick Parts** button, and then click **Save Selection to Quick Part Gallery**.

2. In the **Create New Building Block** dialog box, type a name for the building block, make any necessary changes to the settings, and then click **OK**.

To insert a building block in a document

→ Click where you want to insert the building block. Then either type the name of the building block, and press `F3`.

→ On the **Insert** tab, in the **Text** group, click the **Quick Parts** button, and select the building block from the **Quick Part** gallery.

To insert the date and time

1. Click where you want the date or time to appear, and then on the **Insert** tab, in the **Text** group, click the **Date & Time** button.

2. In the **Date and Time** dialog box, under **Available formats**, click the format you want, and then click **OK**.

To use the Thesaurus

1. Double-click the word you want to replace, and then on the **Review** tab, in the **Proofing** group, click the **Thesaurus** button.

2. In the **Research** task pane, point to the word you want to insert in place of the selected word, click the arrow that appears, and then click **Insert**.

To research information

1. On the **Review** tab, in the **Proofing** group, click **Research**.

2. In the **Research** task pane, in the **Search for** box, type the research topic.

3. Click the arrow of the box below the **Search for** box, click the resource you want to use, and then in the results list, click a source to view its information.

To translate a selected word or phrase into another language

1. On the **Review** tab, in the **Proofing** group, click the **Translate** button.
2. In the **Translation** area of the **Research** task pane, select the desired languages in the **From** and **To** boxes to display the translation.

To display a document in Outline view

→ On the **View** toolbar, click the **Outline** button.

To display specific heading levels in Outline view

→ On the **Outlining** tab, in the **Outline Tools** group, click the **Show Level** arrow, and then in the list, click a heading level.

To collapse or expand heading levels in Outline view

→ Click anywhere in the heading to be collapsed or expanded. Then on the **Outlining** tab, in the **Outline Tools** group, click the **Collapse** or **Expand** button.

To demote or promote headings in Outline view

→ Click the heading to be demoted or promoted. Then on the **Outlining** tab, in the **Outline Tools** group, click the **Demote** or **Promote** button.

To move content in Outline view

→ Collapse the heading whose text you want to move. Then on the **Outlining** tab, in the **Outline Tools** group, click the **Move Up** or **Move Down** button.

To find text

1. On the **Home** tab, in the **Editing** group, click the **Find** button.
2. On the **Find** tab of the **Find and Replace** dialog box, specify the text you want to find, and then click **Find Next**.

To replace text

1. On the **Home** tab, in the **Editing** group, click the **Replace** button.
2. On the **Replace** tab of the **Find and Replace** dialog box, specify the text you want to find and the text you want to replace it with, and then click **Find Next**.
3. Click **Replace** to replace the first instance of the text, **Replace All** to replace all instances, or **Find Next** to leave that instance unchanged and move to the next one.

To check spelling and grammar

1. On the **Review** tab, in the **Proofing** group, click the **Spelling & Grammar** button.
2. In the **Spelling and Grammar** dialog box, click the appropriate buttons to correct the errors Word finds or to add words to the custom dictionary or AutoCorrect list.

To remove personal information from a document

1. On the **Office** menu, point to **Prepare**, and then click **Inspect Document**.

2. In the **Document Inspector** dialog box, select the items you want checked, and then click **Inspect**.

3. In the **Document Inspector** summary, click the **Remove All** button to the right of any items you want removed, and then close the **Document Inspector** dialog box.

To mark a document as final

1. On the **Office** menu, point to **Prepare**, and then click **Mark as Final**.

2. Click **OK** in the message box, click **Save**, then click **OK** in the finalization message.

3 Changing the Look of Text

To preview and apply styles to selected text

→ On the **Home** tab, in the **Styles** group, display the **Styles** gallery, point to the thumbnail of the style you want to preview, and then click the thumbnail of the style you want to apply.

To change the style set

→ On the **Home** tab, in the **Styles** group, click the **Change Styles** button, click **Style Set**, and then click the set you want to use.

To apply character formatting to selected text

→ On the **Home** tab, in the **Font** group (or on the **Mini toolbar** that appears), click the button of the formatting you want to apply.

To copy formatting of selected text

→ On the **Home** tab, in the **Clipboard** group (or on the **Mini toolbar** that appears), click the **Format Painter** button, and select the text to which you want to apply the copied formatting.

To clear formatting from selected text

→ On the **Home** tab, in the **Font** group, click the **Clear Formatting** button.

To change the font of selected text

→ On the **Home** tab, in the **Font** group, click the **Font** arrow, and then in the list, click the font you want.

To change the font size of selected text

→ On the **Home** tab, in the **Font** group, click the **Font Size** arrow, and then in the list, click the font size you want.

To apply text effects to selected text

1. On the **Home** tab, click the **Font** Dialog Box Launcher.
2. In the **Font** dialog box, under **Effects**, select the check box for the effect you want, and then click **OK**.

To change the color of selected text

→ On the **Home** tab, in the **Font** group, click the **Font Color** arrow, and in the color palette, click the color you want.

To highlight selected text with a color

→ On the **Home** tab, in the **Font** group, click the **Highlight** arrow, and click the color you want.

To select all text with the same formatting

→ Click the formatted text. Then on the **Home** tab, in the **Editing** group, click the **Select** button, and click **Select Text With Similar Formatting**.

To insert a line break

→ Click at the right end of the text where you want the line break to appear. Then on the **Page Layout** tab, in the **Page Setup** group, click the **Breaks** button, and click **Text Wrapping**.

To align paragraphs

→ Click the paragraph, or select multiple paragraphs. Then on the **Home** tab, in the **Paragraph** group, click the **Align Left**, **Center**, **Align Right**, or **Justify** button.

To indent the first line of a paragraph

→ Click the paragraph. Then on the horizontal ruler, drag the **First Line Indent** marker to the location of the indent.

To indent an entire paragraph

→ Click the paragraph, or select multiple paragraphs. Then on the horizontal ruler, drag the **Left Indent** or **Right Indent** marker to the location of the indent.

To increase or decrease indenting

→ Click the paragraph, or select multiple paragraphs. Then in the **Paragraph** group, click the **Increase Indent** or **Decrease Indent** button.

To set a tab stop

→ Click the paragraph, or select multiple paragraphs. Then click the **Tab** button until it displays the type of tab you want, and click the horizontal ruler where you want to set the tab stop for the selected paragraph(s).

To change the position of a tab stop

→ Click the paragraph, or select multiple paragraphs. Then on the horizontal ruler, drag the tab stop to the new mark.

To add a border or shading to a selected paragraph

1. On the **Home** tab, in the **Paragraph** group, click the **Borders and Shading** arrow, and click **Borders and Shading**.

2. In the **Borders and Shading** dialog box, on the **Borders** tab, click the icon of the border style you want to apply, and then click **OK**.

3. In the **Borders and Shading** dialog box, on the **Shading** tab, click the **Fill** arrow, click the shading color you want, and then click **OK**.

To format selected paragraphs as a list

→ On the **Home** tab, in the **Paragraph** group, click the **Bullets** or **Numbering** button.

To change the style of selected list paragraphs

1. On the **Home** tab, in the **Paragraph** group, click the **Bullets** or **Numbering** arrow.

2. In the **Bullets Library** or **Numbering Library**, click the bullet or number style you want to use.

To change the indent level of selected list paragraphs

→ On the **Home** tab, in the **Paragraph** group, click the **Decrease Indent** or **Increase Indent** button.

To sort items in a selected list

1. On the **Home** tab, in the **Paragraph** group, click the **Sort** button.

2. In the **Sort Text** dialog box, in the **Type** list, click the type of text by which to sort.

3. Select **Ascending** or **Descending**, and then click **OK**.

To create a multilevel list

1. Click where you want to create the list. Then on the **Home** tab, in the **Paragraph** group, click the **Multilevel List** button.

2. In the **Multilevel List** gallery, click the thumbnail of the multilevel list style you want to use.

3. Type the text of the list, pressing `Enter` to create another item at the same level, pressing `Enter` and then `Tab` to create a subordinate item, or pressing `Enter` and then `Shift` + `Tab` to create a higher-level item.

4   Presenting Information in Columns and Tables

To format selected text in multiple columns

→ On the **Page Layout** tab, in the **Page Setup** group, click the **Columns** button, and click the number of columns you want.

To change the width or spacing of columns

1. Click anywhere in the column you want to change. Then on the **Page Layout** tab, in the **Page Setup** group, click the **Columns** button, and then click **More Columns**.

2. In the **Columns** dialog box, under **Width and spacing**, change the setting in the **Width** column or the **Spacing** column, and then click **OK**.

To hyphenate text automatically

→ On the **Page Layout** tab, in the **Page Setup** group, click the **Hyphenation** button, and then click **Automatic**.

To insert a column break

→ On the **Page Layout** tab, in the **Page Setup** group, click the **Breaks** button, and then click **Column**.

To create a tabular list

1. Type the text of the list, pressing ⟦Tab⟧ between each item on a line and pressing ⟦Enter⟧ at the end of each line.

2. Select the lines of the list, change the **Tab** button to the type of tab stop you want, and then click the horizontal ruler where you want to set tab stops that will line up the items in columns.

To insert a table

1. On the **Insert** tab, in the **Tables** group, click the **Table** button.

2. In the grid, point to the upper-left cell, move the pointer across and down to select the number of columns and rows you want, and click the lower-right cell in the selection.

To add rows to a table

→ Click in the row above or below which you want to add a single row, and then on the **Layout** tab, in the **Rows & Columns** group, click the **Insert Above** or **Insert Below** button.

→ Select the number of rows you want to insert, and then in the **Rows & Columns** group, click the **Insert Above** or **Insert Below** button.

To merge selected table cells

→ On the **Layout** contextual tab, in the **Merge** group, click the **Merge Cells** button.

To convert selected text to a table

1. On the **Insert** tab, in the **Tables** group, click the **Table** button, and then click **Convert Text to Table**.

2. In the **Convert Text to Table** dialog box, enter the dimensions of the table in the **Number of columns** and **Number of Rows** boxes, select the type of text separator, and then click **OK**.

To insert a Quick Table

1. Click where you want to insert the table. Then on the **Insert** tab, in the **Tables** group, click the **Table** button, and then point to **Quick Tables**.

2. In the **Quick Tables** gallery, click the table style you want.

To apply a table style

→ Click the table whose style you want to change. Then on the **Design** contextual tab, in the **Table Styles** group, click the style you want in the **Table Styles** gallery.

To total a column of values in a table

1. Click the cell in the table where you want the total to appear.

2. On the **Layout** contextual tab, in the **Data** group, click the **Formula** button.

3. With the SUM formula in the **Formula** box, click **OK** to total the values.

To draw a table

1. Click where you want to draw the table. Then on the **Insert** tab, in the **Tables** group, click the **Table** button, and then click **Draw Table**.

2. Drag the pointer (which has become a pencil) across and down to create a cell.

3. Point to the upper-right corner of the cell, and drag to create another cell, or draw column and row boundaries inside the first cell.

To insert an Excel worksheet

→ Click where you want to insert the worksheet, and then on the **Insert** tab, in the **Tables** group, click the **Table** button, and click **Excel Spreadsheet**.

→ Copy the worksheet data in Excel, and then in Word, click where you want to insert the copied data, and on the **Home** tab, in the **Clipboard** group, click the **Paste** button.

Or

1. In Excel, copy the worksheet data. Then in Word, click where you want to insert the copied data, and on the **Home** tab, in the **Clipboard** group, click the **Paste** arrow, and click **Paste Special**.

2. In the **Paste Special** dialog box, in the **As** list, click **Microsoft Office Excel Worksheet Object**, select the **Paste link** option, and then click **OK**.

5   Setting Up a Workbook

To open a workbook

1. On the **Office** menu, click **Open**.

2. Navigate to the workbook you want to open, and then click **Open**.

To create a new workbook

→ On the **Office** menu, click **New**, and then click **Blank Workbook**.

To save a workbook

1. On the **Quick Access Toolbar**, click the **Save** button.

2. Type a name for the file, and then click **Save**.

To set file properties

1. On the **Office** menu, point to **Finish**, and then click **Properties**.

2. Add information describing your file.

To define custom properties

1. On the **Office** menu, point to **Finish**, and then click **Properties**.

2. In the **Property Views and Options** list, click **Advanced**.

3. On the **Custom** tab, type a property name, select the type of data contained in the property, and type a value for the property.

4. Click **Add**, and then click **OK**.

To display a worksheet

→ Click the sheet tab of the worksheet you want to display.

To create a new worksheet

→ Right-click the sheet tab of the worksheet that follows the location where you want to insert a worksheet, click **Insert**, and then double-click **Worksheet**.

To change the order of worksheets in a workbook

→ Drag the sheet tab of the worksheet you want to move.

To copy a worksheet to another workbook

1. Open the target workbook,and then switch to the source workbook..

2. Hold down the Ctrl key, and click the sheet tabs of the worksheets you want to copy.

3. Right-click the selection, and then click **Move Or Copy**.

4. Select the **Create A Copy** check box. In the **To Book** list, click the workbook to which you want to copy the worksheet(s). Then click **OK**.

To rename a worksheet

1. Double-click the sheet tab of the worksheet you want to rename.

2. Type the new name of the worksheet, and then press Enter.

To hide a worksheet

1. Hold down the Ctrl key, and then click the sheet tabs of the worksheets you want to hide.

2. Right-click any selected worksheet tab, and then click **Hide**.

To unhide a worksheet

1. Right-click any worksheet tab, and then click **Unhide**.

2. Click the worksheet you want to unhide, and then click **OK**.

To delete a worksheet

1. Hold down the Ctrl key, and then click the sheet tabs of the worksheets you want to delete.

2. Right-click the selection, and then click **Delete**.

To change a row's height or column's width

1. Select the rows and columns you want to resize.

2. Drag a row or column border until it is the desired size.

To insert a column or row

→ Right-click the column header to the right of, or the row header below, where you want the new column or row to appear, and then click **Insert**.

To delete a selected column or row

→ Right-click the column or row, and then click **Delete**.

To hide a selected column or row

→ Right-click the column or row, and then click **Hide**.

To unhide a column or row

1. Click the row or column header of the row above or the column to the left of the rows or columns you want to unhide.

2. Hold down the [Shift] key, and click the row or column header of the row or column below or to the right of the rows or columns you want to unhide.

3. Right-click the selection, and then click **Unhide**.

To insert a cell

1. Select the cells in the location where you want to insert new cells.

2. On the **Home** tab, in the **Cells** group, click the **Insert** arrow, and then in the list, click **Insert Cells**.

3. Click the option representing how you want to move the existing cells to make room for the inserted cells, and then click **OK**.

To delete selected cells

1. On the **Home** tab, in the **Cells** group, in the **Delete** list, click **Delete Cells**.

2. Click the option representing how you want the remaining cells to fill the deleted space, and then click **OK**.

To zoom in or out on a worksheet

→ Click the **Zoom In** control to make your window's contents 10 percent larger per click.

→ Click the **Zoom Out** control to make your window's contents 10 percent smaller per click.

→ Drag the **Zoom** slider control to the left to zoom out, or to the right to zoom in.

To zoom in or out to a specific zoom level

1. On the **View** tab, in the **Zoom** group, click **Zoom**.

2. Click **Custom**, type a new zoom level in the **Custom** field, and then click **OK**.

To change to another open workbook

1. On the **View** tab, in the **Window** group, click **Switch Windows**.

2. Click the name of the workbook you want to display.

To arrange all open workbooks in the program window

1. On the **View** tab, in the **Window** group, click **Arrange All**.

2. Select the arrangement you want, and then click **OK**.

To remove a button from the Quick Access Toolbar

→ Right-click the button, and then click **Remove from Quick Access Toolbar**.

To add a button to the Quick Access Toolbar

1. Click the **Customize Quick Access Toolbar** button, and then click **More Commands**.

2. In the **Choose Commands From** list, click the command category you want.

3. Click the command you want to add, click **Add**, and then click **OK**.

To move a button on the Quick Access Toolbar

1. Click the **Customize Quick Access Toolbar** button, and then click **More Commands**.

2. Click the command you want to move.

3. Click the **Move Up** button or the **Move Down** button.

6   Working with Data and Data Tables

To enter a data series using AutoFill

1. Type the first label or value for your list.

2. Drag the fill handle to the cell containing the last label or value in the series.

To change how dragging the fill handle extends a series

1. Type the first label or value for your list.

2. Hold down the `Ctrl` key, and drag the fill handle to the cell containing the last label or value in the series.

To enter data by using AutoComplete

1. Type the beginning of an entry.

2. Press `Tab` to accept the AutoComplete value.

To enter data by picking from a list

1. Right-click a cell in a column with existing values, and then click **Pick from Drop-down List**.

2. Click the item in the list you want to enter.

To copy and paste selected cells

1. On the **Home** tab, in the **Clipboard** group, click **Copy**.

2. Click the destination cells. Then in the **Clipboard** group, click **Paste**.

To copy and paste a selected row or column

1. On the **Home** tab, in the **Clipboard** group, click **Copy**.

2. Click the header of the row or column into which you want to paste the values. Then in the **Clipboard** group, click **Paste**.

To find data within a worksheet

1. On the **Home** tab, in the **Editing** group, click **Find and Select**, and then click **Find**.

2. Type the text you want to find, and then click **Find Next**.

To replace a value with another value within a worksheet

1. On the **Home** tab, in the **Editing** group, click **Find and Select**, and then click **Replace**.

2. Type the text you want to replace, and the text you want to take the place of the existing text.

3. Click **Find Next**. Follow any of these steps:

    ● Click **Replace** to replace the text.

    ● Click **Find Next** to skip this instance of the text and move to the next time it occurs.

    ● Click **Replace All** to replace every instance of the text.

To edit a cell's contents by hand

1. Click the cell you want to edit.

2. In the **Formula Bar**, make the changes you want, and then press ⎡Enter⎤.

To check spelling

1. On the **Review** tab, in the **Proofing** group, click **Spelling**. If you are asked whether you want to save your work, do so.

2. Follow any of these steps:

    ● Click **Ignore Once** to ignore the current misspelling.

    ● Click **Ignore All** to ignore all instances of the misspelled word.

    ● Click **Add to Dictionary** to add the current word to the dictionary.

    ● Click the correct spelling, and then click **Change** to replace the current misspelling with the correct word.

    ● Click the correct spelling, and then click **Change All** to replace all instances of the current misspelling with the correct word.

    ● Click **Cancel** to stop checking spelling.

3. Click OK to clear the dialog box that appears after the spelling check is complete.

To look up a selected word in the Thesaurus

→ On the **Review** tab, in the **Proofing** group, click **Thesaurus**.

To translate a selected word to another language

→ On the **Review** tab, in the **Proofing** group, click **Translate**.

To create a data table

1. Click any cell in the range from which you want to create a table.

2. On the **Home** tab, in the **Styles** group, click **Format as Table**.

3. Click the table style you want, and verify that Excel identified the data range correctly.

4. If your table has headers, select the **My table has headers** check box. Then click **OK**.

To add rows to a data table

→ Click the cell in the lower-right corner of the data table, and then press Tab to create a new table row.

→ Type data in the cell below the lower-left corner of the data table, and then press Tab.

To resize a table

→ Click any cell in the table, and then drag the resize handle to expand or contract the table.

To add a Total row to a table

1. Click any cell in the table.

2. On the **Design** tab, in the **Table Style Options** group, click **Total Row**.

To change the Total row summary function

→ Click any cell in the table's **Total** row, click the arrow that appears, and then click the desired summary function.

To rename a table

1. Click any cell in the table.

2. On the **Design** tab, in the **Properties** group, type a new value in the **Table Name** box.

7 Performing Calculations on Data

To create a named range from selected cells

1. On the **Formula Bar**, click the **Name Box**.

2. Type the name you want for the range, and then press Enter.

To create a named range from a selection including the name

1. Select the cells you want to name as a range. Be sure either the first or last cell contains the name for the range.

2. On the **Formulas** tab, in the **Defined Names** group, click **Create from Selection**.

3. Select the check box for the cell that contains the name you want. Then click **OK**.

To display the Name Manager

→ On the **Formulas** tab, in the **Defined Names** group, click **Name Manager**.

To edit a named range

1. On the **Formulas** tab, in the **Defined Names** group, click **Name Manager**.

2. Click the named range you want to edit, and then click the **Edit** button.

3. Click the **Collapse Dialog** button, select the cells you want in the range, and then click **Close**.

To create a formula

1. Click the cell into which you want to enter a formula.

2. Type =.

3. Type the expression representing the calculation you want to perform.

4. Press Enter.

To create a formula by using the Insert Function dialog box

1. On the **Formulas** tab, in the **Function Library** group, click **Insert Function**.

2. Select the function you want to use, and then click **OK**.

3. Fill in the **Function Arguments** dialog box, and then click **OK**.

To refer to a table column or row in a formula

1. Click the cell in which you want to create the formula.

2. Type =, followed by the function to include in the formula and a left parenthesis, for example, =SUM(.

3. Move the mouse pointer over the header of the table column you want to use in the formula. When the mouse pointer changes to a black, downward-pointing arrow, click the column header.

4. Type a right parenthesis, and then press Enter.

To create a formula that doesn't change when copied between cells

→ Precede all column and row references with a dollar sign, for example, $C$4.

To create a conditional formula

1. Click the cell in which you want to enter an IF function.

2. On the **Formulas** tab, in the **Function Library** group, click **Logical**, and then click **IF**.

3. Type a conditional statement that evaluates to true or false. Type the text you want to appear if the condition is true, and the text you want to appear if the condition is false. Then click **OK**.

To display cells that provide values for a formula

1. Click the cell you want to track.

2. On the **Formulas** tab, in the **Formula Auditing** group, click the **Trace Precedents** button.

To display formulas that use a cell's contents

1. Click the cell you want to track.

2. On the **Formulas** tab, in the **Formula Auditing** group, click the **Trace Dependents** button.

To remove tracer arrows

1. Click the cell you want to track.

2. On the **Formulas** tab, in the **Formula Auditing** group, click the **Remove Arrows** button.

To locate errors in a worksheet

1. On the **Formulas** tab, in the **Formula Auditing** group, click the **Error Checking** button.

2. Click the **Edit in Formula Bar** button.

3. Edit the formula.

4. Click the **Next** button to view the next error.

To step through a formula to locate an error

1. Click the cell with the formula you want to evaluate.

2. On the **Formulas** tab, in the **Formula Auditing** group, click **Evaluate Formula**.

3. Click **Evaluate** (one or more times) to move through the formula's elements.

To watch a value in a cell

1. On the **Formulas** tab, in the **Formula Auditing** group, click **Watch Window**.

2. Click **Add Watch,** select the cells you want to watch, and then click **Add**.

3. Click **Watch Window**.

To delete a watch

1. On the **Formulas** tab, in the **Formula Auditing** group, click **Watch Window**.
2. Click the watch you want to delete, and then click **Delete Watch**.

8   Changing Workbook Appearance

To change a cell's font, font style, font color, or background color

1. Select the cells you want to change.
2. On the **Home** tab, use the controls in the **Font** group to format the cells.

To add a border to a selected cell or cells

→ On the **Home** tab, in the **Font** group, click the **Border** arrow, and then in the list, click the type of border you want to apply.

To apply a style to a selected cell or cells

1. On the **Home** tab, in the **Styles** group, click **Cell Styles**.
2. Click a style.

To create a new style

1. On the **Home** tab, in the **Styles** group, click **Cell Styles**.
2. Click **New Cell Style**, and then type a new style name.
3. Click **Format,** specify the formatting you want the style to apply, and then click **OK** twice.

To delete a style

1. On the **Home** tab, in the **Styles** group, click **Cell Styles**.
2. Right-click the style you want to delete, and then click **Delete**.

To copy a cell's formatting onto another cell

1. Click the cell that contains the format you want to apply to another cell.
2. On the **Home** tab, in the **Clipboard** group, click the **Format Painter** button.
3. Select the cells to which you want to apply the formatting.

To change theme fonts, colors, and graphic effects

Using the **Controls** on the **Page Layout** tab, in the **Themes** group, follow one of these steps:

- Click the **Fonts** button, and then select a new font.
- Click the **Colors** button, and then select a new color set.
- Click the **Effects** button, and then select a new default effect.

To apply a workbook theme

1. On the **Page Layout** tab, in the **Themes** group, click **Themes**.
2. Click the theme you want to apply.

To save a workbook's format as a new theme

1. Format your worksheet using the colors, fonts, and effects you want to include in your theme.
2. On the **Page Layout** tab, in the **Themes** group, click **Themes**.
3. Click **Save Current Theme**.
4. Type a name for your theme.
5. Click **Save**.

To create a new table style

1. On the **Home** tab, in the **Styles** group, click **Format as Table**, and then click **New Table Style**.
2. In the **Name** field, type a name for the table style.
3. In the **Table Element** list, click the element you want to format.
4. Click **Format**, and use the controls in the **Format** dialog box to format the table element. Then click **OK**.
5. Repeat as desired to format other elements, and then click **OK**.

To format a cell value as a phone number

1. On the **Home** tab, click the **Number** Dialog Box Launcher.
2. Click **Special**, click **Phone Number**, and then click **OK**.

To format cell data as a currency value

→ On the **Home** tab, in the **Number** group, click the **Accounting Number Format** button.

To select a foreign currency symbol

→ On the **Home** tab, in the **Number** group, click the **Accounting Number Format** arrow, and then in the list, click the currency symbol you want to apply.

To add words to a cell's value

1. On the **Home** tab, click the **Number** Dialog Box Launcher.
2. Click **Custom**, and then click the format to serve as the base for your custom format.
3. Type the text to appear in the cell, enclosed in quotes, for example, "cases," and then click **OK**.

To apply a conditional format to selected cells

1. On the **Home** tab, in the **Styles** group, click **Conditional Formatting**.

2. Click **New Rule**.

3. Click **Format Only Cells That Contain**. In the **Comparison Phrase** list, click the comparison phrase you want. Then type the constant values or formulas you want evaluated.

4. Click **Format**, specify the formatting you want, and then click **OK** twice.

To edit a conditional formatting rule

1. Select the cells that contain the rule you want to edit.

2. On the **Home** tab, in the **Styles** group, click **Conditional Formatting**.

3. Click **Manage Rules**, click the rule you want to change, and then click **Edit Rule**.

4. Make your changes, and then click **OK** twice to save them.

To delete a conditional formatting rule

1. Select the cells that contain the rule you want to delete.

2. On the **Home** tab, in the **Styles** group, click **Conditional Formatting**.

3. Click **Manage Rules**, click the rule you want to delete, click **Delete Rule**, and then click **OK**.

To display data bars in selected cells

1. On the **Home** tab, in the **Styles** group, click **Conditional Formatting**.

2. Point to **Data Bars**, and then click the data bar option you want to apply.

To display a color scale in selected cells

1. On the **Home** tab, in the **Styles** group, click **Conditional Formatting**.

2. Point to **Color Scales**, and then click the color scale pattern you want to apply.

To display icon sets in selected cells

1. On the **Home** tab, in the **Styles** group, click **Conditional Formatting**.

2. Point to **Icon Sets**, and then click the icon set you want to apply.

To add a picture to a worksheet

1. On the **Insert** tab, in the **Illustrations** group, click **Picture**.

2. Navigate to and double-click the picture you want to insert.

To change thea selected picture's characteristics

→ Use the controls on the **Format** tab to edit the picture.

9   Starting a New Presentation

To base a presentation on an example from Office Online

1. On the **Office** menu, click **New**.
2. In the left pane, under **Microsoft Office Online**, click **Presentations**.
3. Scroll the center pane until you find the presentation you want, and then click **Download**.

To base a presentation on an existing presentation

1. On the **Office** menu, click **New**.
2. In the left pane, under **Templates**, click **New from existing**.
3. Navigate to the folder containing the presentation on which you want to base the new one, and then double-click that presentation.

To base a presentation on a design template

1. On the **Office** menu, click **New**.
2. In the left pane, under **Microsoft Office Online**, click **Design slides**.
3. In the **Design slides** category list, click the category that you want.
4. Scroll the center pane until you find the template you want, and then click **Download**.

To add a new slide with the default layout

→ On the **Home** tab, in the **Slides** group, click the **New Slide** button.

To add slides with other layouts

→ On the **Home** tab, in the **Slides** group, click the **New Slide** arrow, and then in the list, click the layout you want.

To delete a slide

→ At the top of the **Overview** pane, on the **Slides** tab, right-click the slide, and then click **Delete Slide**.

To convert a Microsoft Office Word outline into a presentation

1. On the **Home** tab, in the **Slides** group, click the **New Slide** arrow, and then click **Slides from Outline**.
2. Navigate to the folder containing the Word outline, and then double-click the Word document.

To save a presentation as an outline

1. On the **Office** menu, click **Save As**.
2. In the **File name** box, enter the name of the outline file.
3. In the **Save as type** list, click **Outline/RTF**.
4. Navigate to the folder where you want to store the outline, and then click **Save**.

To insert a slide from another presentation

1. Click the slide after which you want to insert the slide.
2. On the **Home** tab, in the **Slides** group, click the **New Slide** arrow, and then in the list, click **Reuse Slides**.
3. In the **Reuse Slides** task pane, click the **Open a PowerPoint File** link.
4. Navigate to the folder containing the presentation with the slide you want to reuse, and double-click the presentation.
5. In the task pane, click the slide you want to reuse.

10 Working with Slide Text

To create slides, bullet points, and subpoints on the Outline tab

● Click to the right of a slide title, and then press `Enter` to create a new slide.
● With the insertion point in a slide title, press `Tab` to convert it to a bullet point.
● With the insertion point in a bullet point, press `Shift`+`Tab` to convert it to a slide.
● With the insertion point in the bullet point, press `Tab` to convert it to a subpoint.

To delete or replace a word

→ Double-click the word to select it, and then press `Del` or `Backspace`.
→ Double-click the word, and then type a different word.

To move selected text

→ On the **Outline** tab or the slide, drag the selection to the desired location.
  Or
1. On the **Home** tab, in the **Clipboard** group, click the **Cut** button.
2. Click where you want to insert the text, and then click the **Paste** button.

To undo or redo editing actions

→ On the **Quick Access Toolbar**, click the **Undo** or **Redo** button.

To select an entire placeholder

→ Point to the border of the placeholder, and when the pointer changes to a four-headed arrow, click the mouse button once.

To create a text box

→ On the **Insert** tab, in the **Text** group, click the **Text Box** button, click the slide, and then type the text.

To rotate a selected text box

→ Drag the green rotating handle in the direction you want.

To move a selected text box

→ Point to the border of the box (not to a handle), and then drag the box to the location you want.

To size a selected text box

→ Point to one of the square or round handles around its frame, and drag the handle until the box is the size you want.

To add a solid border to a text box

1. Right-click the border of the text box, and then click **Format Shape**.

2. In the **Format Shape** dialog box, click **Line Color**, click the line option you want, select appropriate options, and then click **Close**.

To change the default settings of a text box

1. Format the text and the text box the way you want all the text boxes you create from now on in this presentation to be.

2. Right-click the border of the text box, and then click **Set as Default Text Box**.

To add an AutoCorrect entry

1. On the **Office** menu, click **PowerPoint Options**, click **Proofing**, and then click **AutoCorrect Options**.

2. In the **Replace** box above the table in the dialog box, type a word you commonly misspell, and then press Tab.

3. In the **With** box, type the correct spelling of the word, click **Add**, and then click **OK** twice to close the dialog box and PowerPoint Options window.

To correct a word flagged as a misspelling

→ Right-click the word, and on the context menu, click the correct spelling.

To mark a non-English word

1. With the insertion point in the word, on the **Review** tab, in the **Proofing** group, click the **Language** button.

2. In the **Language** dialog box, click the language, and then click **OK**.

To check the spelling of an entire presentation

1. With the first slide displayed, on the **Review** tab, in the **Proofing** group, click the **Spelling** button.

2. If the **Spelling** dialog box appears, click the appropriate buttons to correct the errors PowerPoint finds or to add words to the custom dictionary or AutoCorrect list.

3. Click **OK** when PowerPoint reaches the end of the spelling check, and then click **Close**.

To find a synonym for a selected word

1. On the **Review** tab, in the **Proofing** group, click the **Thesaurus** button.

2. Point to the word you want to substitute for the selection, click the arrow that appears, and then click **Insert**.

To find and replace a word

1. On the **Home** tab, in the **Editing** group, click the **Replace** button.

2. In the **Find what** box, type the word you want to replace, and in the **Replace with** box, type the replacement text.

3. If necessary, select the **Match case** or **Find whole words only** check box.

4. Click **Find Next**, and then click **Replace** or **Replace All**.

To find and replace a font

1. On the **Home** tab, in the **Editing** group, click the **Replace** arrow, and then in the list, click **Replace Fonts**.

2. In the **Replace** list, click the font you want to replace. In the **With** list, click the re-placement font. Then click **Replace**.

To hide or display an object on a slide

1. On the **Home** tab, in the **Editing** group, click the **Select** button, and then click **Selection Pane**.

2. Under **Shapes on this Slide** in the task pane, click the box to the right of the object to hide or display it.

To change the font size

→ On the **Home** tab, in the **Font** group, click the **Decrease Font Size** or **Increase Font Size** button.

→ In the **Font Size** list, click the desired size.

To change the size of a placeholder

➔ Point to one of the placeholder's handles, and when the pointer changes to a two-headed arrow, drag to increase or decrease the size.

To size a placeholder to fit its text

1. Right-click the placeholder's border, and then click **Format Shape**.
2. Click **Text Box**, select the **Resize shape to fit text** option, and then click **Close**.

To change text alignment

➔ With the insertion point in the text you want to align, on the **Home** tab, in the **Paragraph** group, click the **Left**, **Center**, **Right**, or **Justify** button.

To adjust line spacing

➔ Click the paragraph. Then on the **Home** tab, in the **Paragraph** group, click the **Line Spacing** button, and click the spacing you'd like to use.

   Or

1. Click the paragraph, and then click the **Paragraph** Dialog Box Launcher.
2. Under **Spacing**, in the **Paragraph** dialog box, adjust the **Line Spacing** setting, and then click **OK**.

To change the text case

➔ On the **Home** tab, in the **Font** group, click the **Change Case** arrow, and then in the list, click the option you want.

To apply bold or italic formatting to text

➔ On the **Home** tab, in the **Font** group, click the **Bold** or **Italic** button.

➔ On the **Mini toolbar**, click the **Bold** or **Italic** button.

To change the color of text

➔ On the **Home** tab, in the **Font** group, click the **Font Color** arrow, and click the color you want.

11   Adjusting the Layout, Order, and Look of Slides

To change the layout of a slide

➔ On the **Home** tab, in the **Slides** group, click the **Layout** button. Then in the **Layout** gallery, click the layout you want.

To restore the default layout after making changes

➔ On the **Home** tab, in the **Slides** group, click the **Reset** button.

To collapse bullet points under slide titles

➜ On the **Outline** tab of the **Overview** pane, double-click the title of the slide whose bullet points you want to hide. Double-click again to redisplay them.

To expand or collapse the entire presentation outline

➜ On the **Outline** tab of the **Overview** pane, right-click the title of a slide, point to **Expand** or **Collapse**, and then click **Expand All** or **Collapse All**.

To arrange slides in a presentation

➜ On the **Slides** tab of the **Overview** pane, drag slide thumbnails to new positions.

➜ On the **View** toolbar, click the **Slide Sorter** button, and then drag slide thumbnails to new positions.

To move slides from one open presentation to another

1. Open two or more presentations in Slide Sorter view, and then on the **View** tab, in the **Window** group, click the **Arrange All** button.

2. Drag slides from one presentation window to another.

To change the theme

➜ On the **Design** tab, in the **Themes** group, click the **More** button to display the Themes gallery, and then click the theme you want.

To change the color scheme

1. On the **Design** tab, in the **Themes** group, click the **Colors** button.

2. In the **Colors** gallery, click the color scheme you want.

To create your own color scheme

1. On the **Design** tab, in the **Themes** group, click the **Colors** button, and then click **Create New Theme Colors**.

2. In the **Create New Theme Colors** dialog box, select the colors you want, and then click **Save**.

To change the color scheme of the current slide

➜ On the **Design** tab, in the **Themes** group, click the **Colors** button. Then right-click the color scheme you want, and click **Apply to Selected Slides**.

To change a theme's fonts and effects

➜ On the **Design** tab, in the **Themes** group, click the **Fonts** button, and then click the font combination you want.

➜ On the **Design** tab, in the **Themes** group, click the **Effects** button, and then click the effect combination you want.

To create a custom font combination

1. On the **Design** tab, in the **Themes** group, click the **Fonts** button, and then click **Create New Theme Fonts**.

2. In the **Create New Theme Fonts** dialog box, specify the font combination you want, and then click **Save**.

To add a picture to the slide background

1. On the **Design** tab, in the **Background** group, click the **Background Styles** button, and then in the list, click **Format Background**.

2. In the **Format Background** dialog box, click **Picture or texture fill**.

3. Click **File**, navigate to the folder containing the picture you want to use, and then double-click the picture you want.

4. To make the picture fill the entire slide, select the **Tile picture as texture** check box.

5. To use the picture in the background of the current slide, click **Close**, or to use it in the background of all slides, click **Apply to All**.

To add a shade or texture to the slide background

→ On the **Design** tab, in the **Background** group, click the **Background Styles** button, and then click a shade.

→ On the **Design** tab, in the **Background** group, click **Format Background**, and specify a shade or texture in the **Format Background** dialog box.

12   Delivering a Presentation Electronically

To create a custom slide show

1. On the **Slide Show** tab, in the **Start Slide Show** group, click the **Custom Slide Show** button, and then click **Custom Shows**.

2. In the **Custom Shows** dialog box, click **New**.

3. In the **Slide show name** box of the **Define Custom Show** dialog box, type a name for the custom show.

4. In the **Slides in presentation** list, click the slides you want, and then click **Add**.

To start a custom show

→ Display the **Custom Shows** dialog box, select the custom show, and then click **Show**.

To hide a slide

→ In the **Overview** pane, on the **Slides** tab, right-click the slide, and then click **Hide Slide**.

To display a hidden slide while delivering a presentation

➔ Right-click the screen, point to **Go to Slide**, and then click the hidden slide.

To apply slide timings to all the slides

1. On the **Animations** tab, in the **Transition to This Slide** group, under **Advance Slide**, select the **Automatically After** check box, and then type or select the time you want the current slide to appear on the screen.

2. On the **Animations** tab, in the **Transition to This Slide** group, click the **Apply To All** button.

To rehearse a presentation and apply slide timings

1. With Slide 1 displayed, on the **Slide Show** tab, in the **Set Up** group, click the **Rehearse Timings** button.

2. Rehearse the presentation, clicking **Next** to move to the next slide. To repeat the rehearsal for a particular slide, on the **Rehearsal** toolbar, click the **Repeat** button to reset the time for that slide to 0:00:00.

3. At the end of the slide show, click **Yes** to apply the recorded slide timings to the slides.

To set up a self-running presentation

1. On the **Slide Show** tab, in the **Set Up** group, click the **Set Up Slide Show** button.

2. In the **Show type** area of the **Set Up Show** dialog box, click **Browsed at a kiosk (full screen)**, and select or clear the **Show without narration** and the **Show without animation** check boxes. Then click **OK**.

To enter speaker notes

➔ With a slide selected, in the **Notes** pane, click the **Click to add notes** placeholder, type your note, and then press <kbd>Enter</kbd>.

To insert a graphic, table, or other object in a note

1. On the **View** tab, in the **Presentations Views** group, click the **Notes Pages** button.

2. Insert the object the way you would insert it on a slide.

To customize the layout of speaker notes

➔ On the **View** tab, in the **Presentation Views** group, click the **Notes Master** button. Then adjust the layout the way you would adjust the layout of a slide master.

To print speaker notes or handouts

1. On the **Office** menu, click **Print**.

2. In the **Print** dialog box, in the **Print what** list, click **Notes Pages** or **Handouts**.

To prepare a presentation for travel

1. On the **Office** menu, point to **Publish**, and then click **Package for CD**. Click **OK** in the message box that appears.

2. In the **Name the CD** box of the **Package for CD** dialog box, type the name you want.

3. To include embedded fonts, click **Options**. Then under **Include these files**, select the **Embedded TrueType fonts** check box, and click **OK**.

4. Insert a blank CD in your CD burner, and then click **Copy to CD**, or click **Copy to Folder**, and then select the folder in which you want to store the package.

5. When PowerPoint asks you to verify that you want to include linked content, click **Yes**.

To run a presentation in the PowerPoint Viewer

- If you're running your presentation from a CD, insert the CD into the CD burner, and then in the list of file and folder names, double-click the presentation name.

- If you're running the presentation from your computer, navigate to the folder where the package is stored, and double-click the package folder. Then double-click **PPTVIEW** to start the Presentation Viewer.

To navigate by using the keyboard

- To move to the next slide, press `Space`, the `↓` key, or the `→` key.
- To move to the previous slide, press the `Page Up` key or the `←` key.
- To end the presentation, press the `Esc` key.

To end a presentation without a black screen

1. On the **Office** menu, click **PowerPoint Options**, and then click **Advanced**.

2. In the **Slide Show** area, clear the **End with Black Slide** check box, and then click **OK**.

To navigate by using the onscreen toolbar

- To move to the next slide, click the **Next** button.

- To move to the previous slide, click the **Previous** button.

- To jump to a slide out of sequence (even if it is hidden), click the **Navigation** button, click **Go To Slide**, and then click the slide.

- To display the slides in a custom slide show, click the **Navigation** button, click **Custom Show**, and then click the show.

- To display keyboard shortcuts for slide show tasks, click the **Navigation** button, and then click **Help**.

- To end the presentation, click the **Navigation** button, and then click **End Show**.

To use a pen tool to mark up slides

→ Right-click the screen, point to **Pointer Options**, click a pen style, and then use the pen pointer to mark slides. (Change the pointer option to **Arrow** to turn off the pen.)

To erase all markup from a slide

→ Right-click the screen, point to **Pointer Options**, and then click **Erase All Ink on Slide**.

13   Getting Started with OneNote

To start OneNote

→ On the **Start** menu, point to **All Programs**, click **Microsoft Office**, and then click **Microsoft Office OneNote 2007**.

To open a notebook

1. On the **File** menu, point to **Open**, and then click **Notebook**.

2. Browse to the *Documents\OneNote Notebooks* folder.

3. Click (don't double-click) the folder representing the notebook you want to open, and then click **Open**.

To close a notebook

→ On the **Navigation Bar**, right-click the button of the notebook you want to close, and then click **Close this Notebook**.

→ On the **File** menu, click **Close this Notebook** to close the active notebook.

To display or hide toolbars

→ Right-click anywhere in the toolbar area. On the context menu that appears, select the toolbars you want and clear those you don't.

To display a selected page with only the Full Page View toolbar and scroll bar visible

→ At the right end of the menu bar, click the **Full Page View** button.

To display additional commands for the Full Page View toolbar

→ At the right end of the Full Page View toolbar, click the **Toolbar Options** button.

To add commands to or remove commands from the Full Page View toolbar menu

1. On the **Toolbar Options** menu, point to **Add or Remove Buttons**, and then point to **Full Page View**.

2. Scroll the list by pointing to the arrow at the bottom of the list, and select or clear the commands you want.

To rename a section

→ On the **Navigation Bar**, right-click the button of the notebook you want to rename, and then click **Rename**.

To exit OneNote

→ Click the **Close** button in the upper-right corner of the OneNote program window.

→ On the **File** menu, click **Exit**.

14 Creating and Configuring Notebooks

To create a notebook for use on only one computer

1. On the **File** menu, point to **New**, and then click **Notebook**.

2. On the first page of the **New Notebook Wizard**, click the type of notebook you want to create. In the **Name** box, type a name for your notebook. In the **Color** palette, click the color you want. Then click **Next**.

3. On the **Who will use this Notebook page**, click **I will use it on this computer**, and then click **Next**.

4. On the **Confirm Notebook Location** page, confirm that the **Path** box specifies the folder in which you want to save the notebook. Then click **Create**.

To create a notebook that you can access from multiple computers

1. On the **File** menu, point to **New**, and then click **Notebook**.

2. On the first page of the **New Notebook Wizard**, click the type of notebook you want to create. In the **Name** box, type a name for your notebook. In the **Color** palette, click the color you want. Then click **Next**.

3. On the **Who will use this notebook** page, click **I will use it on multiple computers**, and then click **Next**.

4. On the **Confirm notebook location** page, enter the shared location in the **Path** box; or click the **Browse** button, navigate to the shared location where you want to store the notebook, and then click **Select**.

5. If Microsoft Office Outlook or another e-mail program is installed and configured on your computer, leave the **Send me a link** check box selected; otherwise, clear the check box. Then click **Create**.

6. If you are prompted to enter credentials to access the shared location, do so.

7. If your e-mail program opens an e-mail message window, address the e-mail message to yourself, and then send it.

To share a notebook from its original location (on a computer running Windows Vista)

1. Close the notebook. Then in Windows Explorer, open the folder that contains the notebook folder (by default, your *Documents\OneNote Notebooks* folder).

2. Click the notebook folder, and then on the toolbar, click **Share**.

3. In the **File Sharing** window, click the user list arrow, click **Everyone**, and then click **Add**. In the **Everyone** row of the user list, click the **Permission Level** arrow, and then click **Contributor**.

4. In the **File Sharing** window, click **Share**.

To move a notebook to a shared location

1. Close the notebook. Then in Windows Explorer, open the folder that contains the notebook folder (by default, your *Documents\OneNote Notebooks* folder).

2. In a second instance of Windows Explorer, navigate to the shared location.

3. Point to the notebook folder, hold down the right mouse button, and drag the folder from its original location to the shared location. When you release the mouse button, click **Move**.

To generate an e-mail message containing connection information to a shared notebook

1. In OneNote, on the **File** menu, point to **Open**, and then click **Notebook**.

2. In the **Open Notebook** dialog box, browse to the shared location, click the notebook folder, and then click **Open**.

3. On the **Share** menu, click **Send Shared Notebook Link to Others**.

To add a page to a notebook

→ On the Standard toolbar, click the **New** arrow, and then in the list, click **Page**.

→ In the **Page Tabs** area, click the **New Page** button.

To apply a template to a page

→ In the **Page Tabs** area, click the **New Page** arrow, and then in the list, click the template you want to apply.

To name a page

→ In the page title box, type the name you want.

To add a subpage to a section

→ In the **New Page** list, click **New Subpage**.

To move a section to a section group

→ On the **Navigation Bar**, drag the section to the section group.

To add a section to a notebook and name the section

1. On the Standard toolbar, click the **New Section** button.

2. With the section name selected, type the section name you want, and then press `Enter`.

To add a section group to a notebook and name the section group

1. On the Standard toolbar, in the **New** list, click **Section Group**.

2. With the section name selected, type the section name you want, and then press `Enter`.

15 Collecting Information in a Notebook

To change the paragraph indentation for the purpose of assigning a level

1. Click to position the insertion point at the beginning of the paragraph.

2. Press the `Tab` key to increase the level, or press the `Backspace` key or `Shift` + `Tab` to decrease the level.

To hide one or more levels of text within a note

→ Right-click the note container header, point to **Hide Levels Below**, and then click the lowest level you want visible.

To enter text in a notebook page

→ Click to position the insertion point on the page, and then type what you want.

To insert the content of an Office document

1. On the **Insert** menu, click **Files as Printouts**.

2. In the **Choose Document to Insert** dialog box, browse to the file you want, and then click **Insert**.

To insert a picture

1. On the **Insert** menu, point to **Pictures**, and then click **From Files**.

2. In the **Insert Picture** dialog box, browse to the picture you want, and click **Insert**.

To resize an inserted image

1. Point to the edge of the image so that a dashed outline appears. When the pointer changes to a four-headed arrow, click the image outline.

2. Drag a sizing handle to resize the image.

3. Right-click the image to display additional options.

To create a handwritten note

1. Display the Writing Tools toolbar.
2. On the Writing Tools toolbar, in the **Pen** list, click the option you want.
3. Point to the notebook page, and drag the pen on the notebook page to draw or write what you want.

To insert clip art from another program

1. In Word (or another program that supports clip art), click the **Clip Art** button in the **Illustrations** group on the **Insert** menu.
2. In the **Clip Art** task pane, locate the clip art you want.
3. Point to the clip art, click the arrow that appears, and then click **Copy**.
4. Switch to OneNote, and paste the clip art from the Clipboard onto the page.

To insert clip art from the Clip Organizer

1. On the **Start** menu, click **All Programs**, click **Microsoft Office**, click **Microsoft Office Tools**, and then click **Microsoft Clip Organizer**.
2. In the **Clip Organizer**, locate the clip art you want.
3. Point to the clip art, click the arrow that appears, and then click **Copy**.
4. Switch to OneNote, and paste the clip art from the Clipboard onto the page.

To start the Screen Clipper

→ If your keyboard has a Windows logo key, press ⊞ + [Space].
→ Right-click the OneNote icon in the notification area of the taskbar, and then click **Create Screen Clipping**.
→ In the OneNote program window, click the **Clip** button on the Standard toolbar, or click **Screen Clipping** on the **Insert** menu.

To capture a Web note

1. Display the Web page you want to send to OneNote.
2. On the **Tools** menu, click **Send to OneNote**.

To capture a screen clipping

1. Display the content you want to capture.
2. If your keyboard has a Windows logo key, press ⊞ + [Space]; or in the notification area at the right end of the taskbar, right-click the **OneNote** icon, and then click **Create Screen Clipping**.
3. Drag to select the area that you want to clip.

To delete all the notes from a section

→ In the **Page Tabs** area, click the active page tab, and press Ctrl + Del to select all the pages in the section. Then press Del.

To create an audio recording

1. Ensure that your computer system includes a microphone. If necessary, run the **Tuning Wizard** to configure the microphone input levels.

2. Display the page on which you want to insert the audio clip.

3. On the **Insert** menu, click **Audio Recording**.

4. Speak, sing, or otherwise deliver the audio content you want to record. When you finish, click the **Stop** button on the Audio And Video Recording toolbar.

To create a video recording

1. Ensure that your computer system includes a video camera.

2. Display the page on which you want to insert the video clip.

3. On the **Insert** menu, click **Video Recording**.

4. Deliver the video content you want to record. When you finish, click the **Stop** button on the Audio And Video Recording toolbar.

To play back a recording

→ Double-click the **Audio Clips** or **Video Clips** icon on the notebook page.

To manually install OneNote Mobile

1. Start OneNote, and connect your mobile device to the computer.

2. On the **Tools** menu, click **Options**.

3. In the **Category** list, click **OneNote Mobile**.

4. Click the **Install OneNote Mobile** button, and follow the instructions in the setup program.

To turn on the OneNote icon in the notification area

1. In OneNote, click **Options** on the **Tools** menu.

2. In the **Options** window, in the **Category** list, click **Other**.

3. Select the **Place OneNote icon in the notification area of the taskbar** check box, and then click **OK**.

To change what happens when you click the OneNote icon

→ Right-click the **OneNote** icon, point to **Options**, point to **OneNote Icon Defaults**, and then click the action you want.

To unhide the OneNote icon in the notification area

1. Right-click a blank area of the taskbar or notification area, or of the Windows **Start** button, and then click **Properties**.

2. In the **Taskbar and Start Menu Properties** dialog box, display the **Notification Area** tab.

3. In the **Icons** area, click **Customize**.

4. In the **Icon** list, locate the **One Note** icon (the label will vary depending on the action assigned to it). Click the corresponding behavior, and then in the list, click **Show**.

5. Click **OK** twice to close the dialog boxes and save your changes.

16   Organizing and Locating Information

To manipulate objects on a page

→ Drag the note by its header.

→ Select the note, and then when the pointer changes to a four-headed arrow, drag it by any part.

→ Right-click the note, click **Move**, and then press the arrow keys (or hold down the `Ctrl` key and press the arrow keys to move in smaller increments).

→ Right-click the note header, click **Cut**, right-click the new note location, and then click **Paste**.

To merge the contents of two note containers

→ Hold down the `Shift` key while dragging one note container by its move handle to the other note container.

To split one note container into two containers

→ Drag the object selector of any paragraph or object away from the note container to a different location on the page.

Or

1. On the **Insert** menu, click **Extra Writing Space**, or on the **Writing Tools** toolbar, click **Insert or Remove Extra Writing Space**.

2. Point to the place in the note container where you want to separate the information. When the pointer changes to a downward-pointing arrow accompanied by a heavy blue horizontal line, drag downward until the content is separated into two containers.

To move a page between sections

→ Click the tab of the page you want to move, and then drag it to the section you want, releasing it when the pointer changes to an arrow with a dotted box under it.

To move a note between pages

→ Right-click the note container, and click **Cut**. Then right-click the tab of the page you want to move the note to, and click **Paste**.

To create a hyperlink to a note

1. Right-click any part of the note container you want to link to, and then click **Copy Hyperlink to this Paragraph**.

2. On the page where you want to include the link to the note, right-click near the location you want, and then click **Paste**.

To delete an object from a page

→ Point to the object, and click the dashed line that appears. Then press the ⌈Del⌋ key.

To open multiple concurrent sessions of a notebook

→ On the **Window** menu, click **New Window**.

To tag a specific paragraph within a note

→ Place the insertion point anywhere in the paragraph (or select it). Then apply the tag.

To tag all the first-level (non-indented) paragraphs in a note

→ Select the note container. Then apply the tag.

To apply a tag after indicating the content you want to tag

→ On the Standard toolbar, click the **Tag** button to apply the currently selected tag (the tag used most recently).

→ In the **Tag** list, click the tag you want to apply.

→ Press one of the nine key combinations to apply the tag assigned to that combination.

To view your tagged notes

→ In the **Tag** list, click **Show All Tagged Notes**.

To generate a summary page of your tagged notes

→ At the bottom of the **Tags Summary** task pane, click the **Create Summary Page** button.

To enable Audio Search

1. On the **Tools** menu, click **Options**.

2. In the **Options** window, display the **Audio and Video** page.

3. Under **Audio Search**, select the **Enable searching audio and video recordings for words** check box.

4. In the **Did you know about audio search?** window, click the **Enable Audio Search** button, and then in the **Options** window, click **OK**.

Microsoft Office Word 2007

Chapter at a Glance

Work in the Word environment, **page 4**

Display different views of a document, **page 17**

Preview and print a document, **page 29**

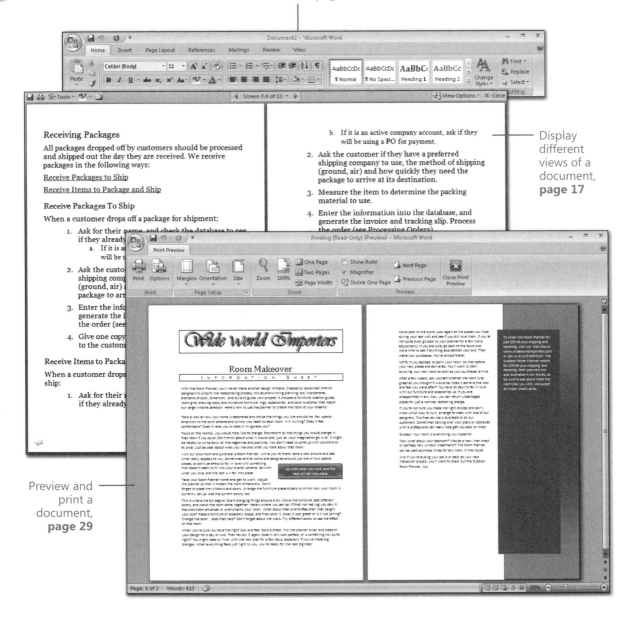

1 Exploring Word 2007

In this chapter, you will learn to:

- ✔ Work in the Word environment.
- ✔ Open, move around in, and close a document.
- ✔ Display different views of a document.
- ✔ Create and save a document.
- ✔ Preview and print a document.

When you use a computer program to create, edit, and produce text documents, you are *word processing*. Microsoft Office Word 2007 is one of the most sophisticated word-processing programs available today. With Word 2007, it is easier than ever to efficiently create a wide range of business and personal documents, from the simplest letter to the most complex report. Word includes many *desktop publishing* features that you can use to enhance the appearance of documents so that they are appealing and easy to read. The program has been completely redesigned to make these and other powerful features more accessible. As a result, even novice users will be able to work productively in Word after only a brief introduction.

In this chapter, you will first familiarize yourself with the Word working environment. Then you will open an existing Word document, learn ways of moving around in it, and close it. You will explore various ways of viewing documents so that you know which view to use for different tasks and how to tailor the program window to meet your needs. You will create and save a new document and then save an existing document in a different location. Finally, you will preview and print a document.

See Also Do you need only a quick refresher on the topics in this chapter? See the Quick Reference entries at the beginning of this book.

Important Before you can use the practice files in this chapter, you need to install them from the book's companion CD to their default location. See "Using the Book's CD" at the beginning of this book for more information.

> **Troubleshooting** Graphics and operating system–related instructions in this book reflect the Windows Vista user interface. If your computer is running Windows XP and you experience trouble following the instructions as written, please refer to the "Information for Readers Running Windows XP" section at the beginning of this book.

Working in the Word Environment

As with all programs in the 2007 Microsoft Office release, the most common way to start Word is from the Start menu displayed when you click the Start button at the left end of the Microsoft Windows taskbar. If Word is the first program in the 2007 Office system that you have used, you are in for a surprise! The look of the program window has changed radically from previous versions.

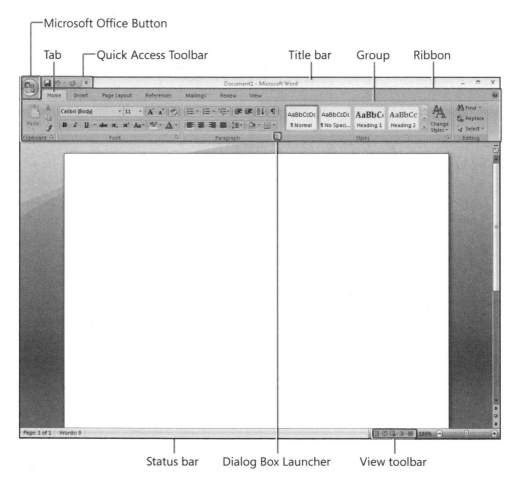

> **Tip** What you see on your screen might not match the graphics in this book exactly. The screens in this book were captured on a monitor set to a resolution of 1024 by 768 pixels with the Windows taskbar is hidden to increase the display space.

The new Word environment is designed to more closely reflect the way people generally work with the program. When you first start Word, this environment consists of the following elements:

Microsoft Office
Button

- Commands related to managing Word and Word documents as a whole (rather than document content) are gathered together on a menu that is displayed when you click the *Microsoft Office Button*.

- Commands can be represented as buttons on the *Quick Access Toolbar* to the right of the Microsoft Office Button. By default, this toolbar displays the Save, Undo, and Repeat buttons, but you can customize the toolbar to include any command that you use frequently.

- The *title bar* displays the name of the active document. At the right end of the title bar are the three familiar buttons that have the same function in all Windows programs. You can temporarily hide the Word window by clicking the Minimize button, adjust the size of the window with the Restore Down/Maximize button, and close the active document or quit Word with the Close button.

- Below the title bar is the *Ribbon*, which makes all the capabilities of Word available in a single area so that you can work efficiently with the program.

- Commands related to working with document content are represented as buttons on the *tabs* that make up the Ribbon. The Home tab is active by default. Clicking one of the other tabs, such as Insert, displays that tab's buttons.

> **Tip** If Microsoft Outlook with Business Contact Manager is installed on your computer, you will have a Business Tools tab in addition to those shown in our graphics.

- On each tab, buttons are organized into *groups*. Depending on the size of the program window, in some groups the button you are likely to use most often is bigger than the rest.

> **Tip** Depending on your screen resolution and the size of the program window, a tab might not have enough room to display all of its groups. In that case, the name of the group resembles a button, and clicking the button displays the group's commands.

Dialog Box
Launcher

● Related but less common commands are not represented as buttons in the group. Instead they are available in a dialog box, which you can display by clicking the *Dialog Box Launcher* at the right end of the group's title bar.

● Some button names are displayed and some aren't. Pausing the mouse pointer over any button for a few seconds (called *hovering*) displays a *ScreenTip* with not only the button's name but also its function.

● Some buttons have arrows, but not all arrows are alike. If you point to a button and both the button and its arrow are in the same box and are the same color, clicking the button will display options for refining the action of the button. If you point to a button and the button is in one box and its arrow is in a different box with a different shade, clicking the button will carry out that action with the button's current settings. If you want to change those settings, you need to click the arrow to see the available options.

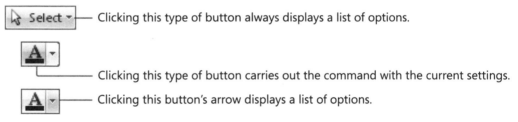

Clicking this type of button always displays a list of options.

Clicking this type of button carries out the command with the current settings.

Clicking this button's arrow displays a list of options.

● The *Microsoft Office Word Help button* appears at the right end of the Ribbon.

● You create a document in the *document window*. When more than one document is open, each document has its own window.

● Across the bottom of the program window, the *status bar* gives you information about the current document. You can turn off the display of an item of information by right-clicking the status bar and then clicking that item.

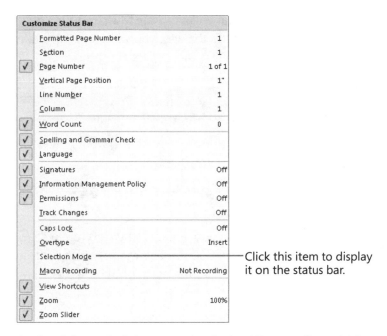

Click this item to display it on the status bar.

● At the right end of the status bar is the *View toolbar*, which provides tools for adjusting the view of document content.

See Also For information about adjusting the view of a document, see "Displaying Different Views of a Document" later in this chapter.

The goal of the redesigned environment is to make working on a document more intuitive. Commands for tasks you perform often are no longer hidden on menus and in dialog boxes, and features that you might not have discovered before are now more visible.

For example, when a formatting option has several choices available, they are often displayed in a *gallery* of *thumbnails*. These galleries give you an at-a-glance picture of each choice. If you point to a thumbnail in a gallery, an awesome new feature called *live preview* shows you what that choice will look like if you apply it to your document.

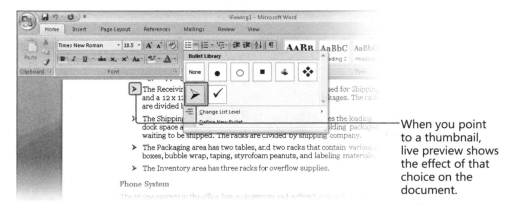

When you point to a thumbnail, live preview shows the effect of that choice on the document.

In this exercise, you will start Word and explore the Microsoft Office Button and the tabs and groups on the Ribbon. Along the way, you will see how to take advantage of galleries and live preview. There are no practice files for this exercise.

> **BE SURE TO** start your computer, but don't start Word yet.

Start

Microsoft Office
Button

1. On the taskbar, click the **Start** button, click **All Programs**, click **Microsoft Office**, and then click **Microsoft Office Word 2007**.

   The Word program window opens, displaying a blank document.

2. Click the **Microsoft Office Button**.

   Commands related to managing documents (such as creating, saving, and printing) are available from the menu that opens. This menu, which we refer to throughout this book as the *Office menu*, takes the place of the File menu that appeared in previous versions of Word.

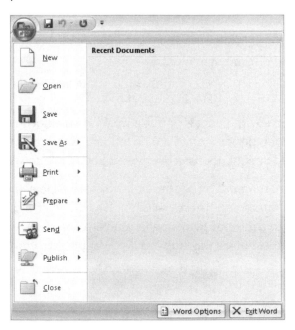

The commands on the left are for tasks related to the document as a whole. After you have worked with a document, its name appears in the Recent Documents list so that you can quickly open it again. At the bottom of the menu are buttons for changing program options and for exiting Word.

3. Press the Esc key to close the menu.

On the Ribbon, the Home tab is active. Buttons related to working with document content are organized on this tab in five groups: Clipboard, Font, Paragraph, Styles, and Editing. Only the buttons representing commands that can be performed on the currently selected document element are active.

4. Hover the mouse pointer over the active buttons on this tab to display the ScreenTips that name them and describe their functions.

> **Important** Depending on your screen resolution and the size of the program window, you might see more or fewer buttons in each of the groups, or the buttons you see might be represented by larger or smaller icons than those shown in this book. Experiment with the size of the program window to understand the effect on the appearance of the tabs.

5. Click the **Insert** tab, and then explore its buttons.

Buttons related to all the items you can insert are organized on this tab in seven groups: Pages, Tables, Illustrations, Links, Header & Footer, Text, and Symbols.

6. Click the **Page Layout** tab, and then explore its buttons.

Buttons related to the appearance of your document are organized on this tab in five groups: Themes, Page Setup, Page Background, Paragraph, and Arrange.

Margins

Dialog Box
Launcher

7. In the **Page Setup** group, display the ScreenTip for the **Margins** button.

The ScreenTip tells you how you can adjust the margins.

8. At the right end of the **Page Setup** group's title bar, click the **Page Setup** Dialog Box Launcher.

The Page Setup dialog box opens.

The dialog box provides a single location where you can set the margins and orientation, and specify the setup of a multi-page document. You can preview the results of your changes before applying them.

9. Click **Cancel** to close the dialog box.

10. In the **Themes** group, click the **Themes** button.

Themes

You see a gallery of thumbnails of the available themes.

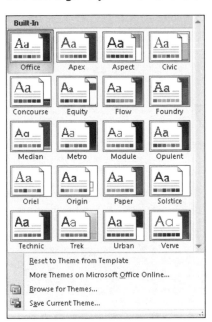

11. Press Esc to close the gallery without making a selection.

12. In the **Page Background** group, click the **Page Color** button, and then in the top row of the **Theme Colors** palette, point to each box in turn.

The blank document page shows a live preview of what it will look like if you click the color you are pointing to. You can see the effect of the selection without actually applying it.

13. Press Esc to close the palette without making a selection.

14. Click the **References** tab, and then explore its buttons.

Buttons related to items you can add to long documents, such as reports, are organized on this tab in six groups: Table Of Contents, Footnotes, Citations & Bibliography, Captions, Index, and Table Of Authorities.

15. Click the **Mailings** tab, and then explore its buttons.

    Buttons related to creating mass mailings are organized on this tab in five groups: Create, Start Mail Merge, Write & Insert Fields, Preview Results, and Finish.

16. Click the **Review** tab, and then explore its buttons.

    Buttons related to proofing, commenting, and changing documents are organized on this tab in six groups: Proofing, Comments, Tracking, Changes, Compare, and Protect.

17. Click the **View** tab, and then explore its buttons.

    Buttons related to changing the view or the display of documents are organized on this tab in five groups: Document Views, Show/Hide, Zoom, Window, and Macros.

Opening, Moving Around in, and Closing a Document

To open an existing document, you click the Microsoft Office Button and then click Open to display the Open dialog box. The first time you use this command, the dialog box displays the contents of your *Documents* folder. If you display the dialog box again in the same Word session, it displays the contents of whatever folder you last used. To see the contents of a different folder, you use standard Windows techniques. After you locate the file you want to work with, you can double-click it to open it.

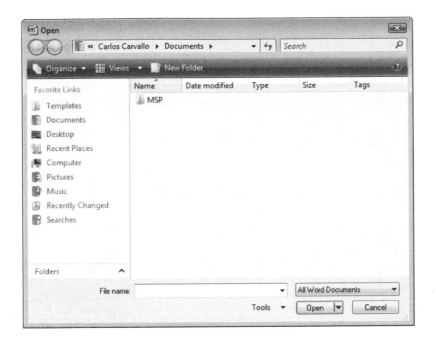

> **Tip** Clicking a file name and then clicking the Open arrow in the lower-right corner of the Open dialog box displays a list of alternative ways in which you can open the file. To look through the document without making any inadvertent changes, you can open the file as *read-only*, or you can open an independent copy of the file. You can open an file in a Web browser, or open an XML file with a transform. In the event of a computer crash or other similar incident, you can tell Word to open the file and attempt to repair any damage. And you can display earlier versions of the file.

To move around in an open document without changing the location of the insertion point, you can use the vertical and horizontal scroll bars in the following ways:

- Click the scroll arrows to move the document window up or down by a line, or left or right by a few characters.

- Click above or below the vertical scroll box to move up or down one windowful, or to the left or right of the horizontal scroll box to move left or right one windowful.

- Drag the scroll box on the scroll bar to display the part of the document corresponding to the location of the scroll box. For example, dragging the scroll box to the middle of the scroll bar displays the middle of the document.

You can also move around in a document in ways that do move the insertion point. To place the insertion point at a particular location, you simply click there. To move the insertion point back or forward a page, you can click the Previous Page and Next Page buttons below the vertical scroll bar.

You can also press a key or a *key combination* on the keyboard to move the insertion point. For example, you can press the Home key to move the insertion point to the left end of a line or press Ctrl+Home to move it to the beginning of the document.

> **Tip** The location of the insertion point is displayed on the status bar. By default, the status bar tells you which page the insertion point is on, but you can also display its location by section, line, and column, and in inches from the top of the page. Simply right-click the status bar, and then click the option you want to display.

This table lists ways to use your keyboard to move the insertion point.

To move the insertion point...	Press...
Left one character	Left Arrow
Right one character	Right Arrow
Down one line	Down Arrow
Up one line	Up Arrow
Left one word	Ctrl+Left Arrow
Right one word	Ctrl+Right Arrow
To the beginning of the current line	Home
To the end of the current line	End
To the beginning of the document	Ctrl+End
To the beginning of the previous page	Ctrl+Page Up
To the beginning of the next page	Ctrl+Page Down
Up one screen	Page Down
Down one screen	Page Up

In a long document, you might want to move quickly among elements of a certain type; for example, from graphic to graphic. You can click the Select Browse Object button at the bottom of the vertical scroll bar and then make a choice in the palette of browsing options that appears, such as Browse by Page or Browse by Graphic.

If more than one document is open, you can close it by clicking the Close button at the right end of the title bar. If only one document is open, clicking the Close button closes the document and also quits Word. If you want to close the document but leave Word open, you must click the Microsoft Office Button and then click Close.

In this exercise, you will open an existing document and explore various ways of moving around in it. Then you will close the document.

USE the *Opening* document. This practice file is located in the *Documents\Microsoft Press\ 2007OfficeSBS_HomeStudent\WordExploring* folder.

Microsoft Office Button

1. Click the **Microsoft Office Button**, and then click **Open**.

The Open dialog box opens, showing the contents of the folder you used for your last open or save action.

2. If the contents of the *Documents* folder are not displayed, in the **Navigation Pane**, click **Documents**.

3. Double-click the **Microsoft Press** folder, double-click the **2007OfficeSBS_ HomeStudent** folder, and then double-click the **WordExploring** folder.

4. Click the *Opening* document, and then click the **Open** button.

The *Opening* document opens in the Word program window.

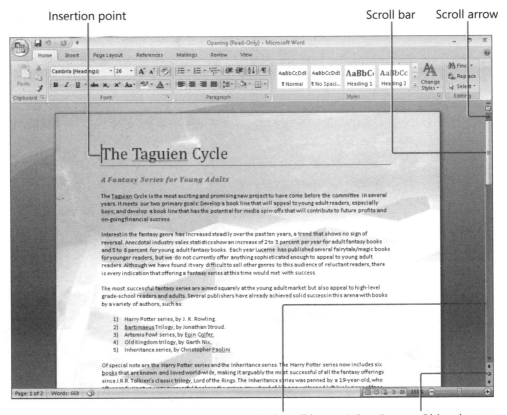

Insertion point   Scroll bar   Scroll arrow

Vertical scroll bar   Select Browse Object button

5. In the second line of the document title, click at the end of the paragraph to position the insertion point.

6. Press the ⬚Home⬚ key to move the insertion point to the beginning of the line.

7. Press the ⬚→⬚ key two times to move the insertion point to the beginning of the word *Fantasy* in the heading.

8. Press the ⬚End⬚ key to move the insertion point to the end of the line.

9. Press ⬚Ctrl⬚+⬚End⬚ to move the insertion point to the end of the document.

10. Press ⬚Ctrl⬚+⬚Home⬚ to move the insertion point to the beginning of the document.

Next Page

11. At the bottom of the vertical scroll bar, click the **Next Page** button.

12. Click above the vertical scroll box to change the view of the document by one windowful.

13. Drag the vertical scroll box to the top of the vertical scroll bar.

    The beginning of the document comes into view. Note that the location of the insertion point has not changed—just the view of the document.

Select Browse Object

14. Click to the left of the title to place the insertion point at the top of the document, and then at the bottom of the vertical scroll bar, click the **Select Browse Object** button.

    A palette of browse choices opens.

15. Move the pointer over the buttons representing the objects you can browse among.

    As you point to each button, the name of the object appears at the top of the palette.

Browse by Page

16. Click the **Browse by Page** button.

    The insertion point moves from the beginning of Page 1 to the beginning of Page 2.

17. Click the **Microsoft Office Button**, and then click **Close**.

> **Troubleshooting** If you click the Close button at the right end of the title bar instead of clicking the Microsoft Office Button and then clicking Close, you will close the open Word document and quit the Word program. To continue working, start Word again.

Compatibility with Earlier Versions

Word 2007 uses a different file format than previous versions of the program. You can open a document created with previous versions, but the new features of Word 2007 will not be available. The name of the document appears in the title bar with [Compatibility Mode] to its right. You can work in Compatibility Mode, or you can convert the document to the Word 2007 file format by clicking the Microsoft Office Button, and clicking Convert. You can then click the Save button on the Quick Access Toolbar to overwrite the existing document, or click Save As on the Office menu to save the document in the new format as a different file.

You cannot open a Word 2007 document in a previous version of Word unless you install the Compatibility Pack for the 2007 Office system, which is available for free download from Microsoft Office Online. After installing the Compatibility Pack, you can open and work with Word 2007 documents, but you cannot open Word 2007 templates.

Displaying Different Views of a Document

In Word, you can view a document in a variety of ways:

- *Print Layout view*. This view displays a document on the screen the way it will look when printed. You can see elements such as margins, page breaks, headers and footers, and watermarks.

- *Full Screen Reading view*. This view displays as much of the content of the document as will fit on the screen at a size that is comfortable for reading. In this view, the Ribbon is replaced by a single toolbar at the top of the screen with buttons that you can use to save and print the document, access references and other tools, highlight text, and make comments. You can also move from page to page and adjust the view.

- *Web Layout view*. This view displays a document on the screen the way it will look when viewed in a Web browser. You can see backgrounds, AutoShapes, and other effects. You can also see how text wraps to fit the window and how graphics are positioned.

- *Outline view*. This view displays the structure of a document as nested levels of headings and body text, and provides tools for viewing and changing its hierarchy.

See Also For information about outlining, see "Reorganizing a Document Outline" in Chapter 2, "Editing and Proofreading Documents."

- *Draft view.* This view displays the content of a document with a simplified layout so that you can type and edit quickly. You cannot see layout elements such as headers and footers.

You switch among views by using buttons in the Document Views group on the View tab or by using the buttons on the View toolbar in the lower-right corner of the window.

You can use other buttons on the View tab to do the following:

- Display rulers and gridlines to help you position and align elements
- Display a separate pane containing the *Document Map*—a list of the headings that make up the structure of the document—while viewing and editing its text.
- Display a separate pane containing *thumbnails* of the document's pages.
- Arrange and work with windows.
- Change the magnification of the document.

You can also adjust the magnification of the document by using tools on the View toolbar at the right end of the status bar. You can click the Zoom button and select (or type) a percentage; drag the slider to the left or right; or click the Zoom Out or Zoom In button at either end of the slider.

When you are creating more complex documents, it is easier to place elements exactly if you turn on the display of non-printing characters. These characters fall into two categories: those that control the layout of your document and those that provide the structure for behind-the-scenes processes such as indexing. You can turn the display of non-printing characters on and off by clicking the Show/Hide ¶ button in the Paragraph group on the Home tab.

> **Tip** You can hide any text by selecting it, clicking the Font Dialog Box Launcher at the right end of the Font group's title bar on the Home tab, selecting the Hidden check box, and clicking OK. When the Show/Hide ¶ button is turned on, hidden text is visible and is identified in the document by a dotted underline.

In this exercise, you will first explore various ways that you can customize Print Layout view to make the work of developing documents more efficient. You will turn white space on and off, zoom in and out, display the rulers and Document Map, and view non-printing characters and text. Then you will switch to other views, noticing the differences so that you have an idea of which one is most appropriate for which task. Finally, you will switch between open documents and view documents in more than one window at the same time.

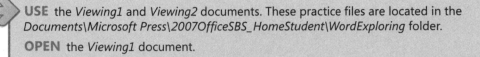

USE the *Viewing1* and *Viewing2* documents. These practice files are located in the *Documents\Microsoft Press\2007OfficeSBS_HomeStudent\WordExploring* folder.
OPEN the *Viewing1* document.

1. In Print Layout view, scroll through the document.

    As you can see, on all pages but the first, the printed document will have the title in the header at the top of the page, the page number in the right margin, and the date in the footer at the bottom of each page.

2. Point to the gap between any two pages, and when the pointer changes to two opposing arrows, double-click the mouse button. Then scroll through the document again.

    The white space at the top and bottom of each page and the gray space between pages is now hidden.

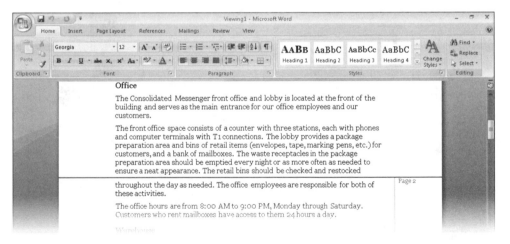

3. Restore the white space by pointing to the black line that separates one page from the next, double-clicking the mouse button.

4. Press `Ctrl` + `Home` to move to the top of the document, and then on the **View** toolbar, click the **Zoom** button.

100%

Zoom

The Zoom dialog box opens.

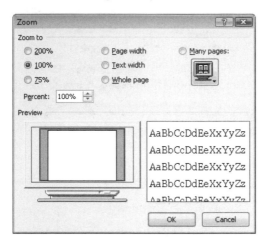

5. Under **Many pages**, click the monitor button, click the second page thumbnail in the top row, and then click **OK**.

The magnification changes so that you can see two pages side by side.

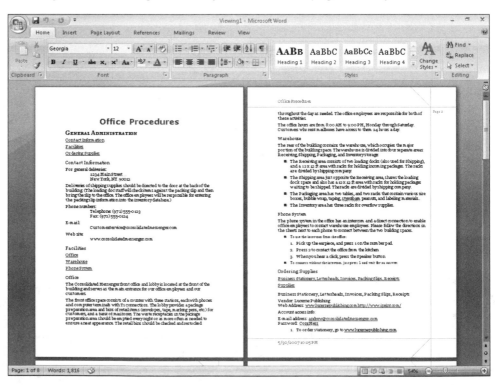

Next Page

6. Below the vertical scroll bar, click the **Next Page** button to display the third and fourth pages of the document.

7. On the **View** toolbar, click the **Zoom** button. Then in the **Zoom** dialog box, click **75%**, and click **OK**.

Notice that the Zoom slider position is adjusted to reflect the new setting.

Zoom Out

8. At the left end of the **Zoom** slider, click the **Zoom Out** button a couple of times.

As you click the button, the slider moves to the left and the Zoom percentage decreases.

Zoom In

9. At the right end of the **Zoom** slider, click the **Zoom In** button until the magnification is 100%.

10. On the **View** tab, in the **Show/Hide** group, select the **Ruler** check box.

Horizontal and vertical rulers appear above and to the left of the page. On the rulers, the active area of the page is white and the margins are blue.

11. In the **Show/Hide** group, click the **Document Map** check box.

A pane opens on the left side of the screen, displaying an outline of the headings in the document. The heading of the active section is highlighted.

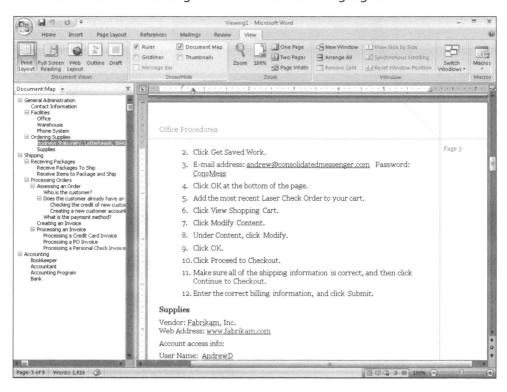

12. In the **Document Map**, click the **Shipping** heading.

Word displays the page containing the selected heading.

13. In the **Show/Hide** group, click the **Thumbnails** check box, and then scroll the **Thumbnails** pane, and click Page **5**.

Close

14. In the **Thumbnails** pane, click the **Close** button.

The pane on the left closes.

Show/Hide ¶

15. On the **Home** tab, in the **Paragraph** group, click the **Show/Hide ¶** button.

You can now see non-printing characters such as spaces, tabs, and paragraph marks.

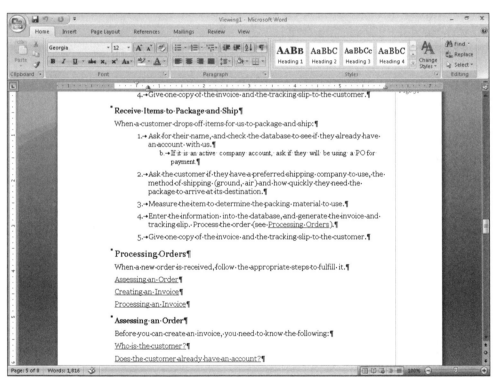

Full Screen
Reading

16. On the **View** tab, in the **Document Views** group, click the **Full Screen Reading** button.

The screen changes to display the document in a format that makes it easy to read.

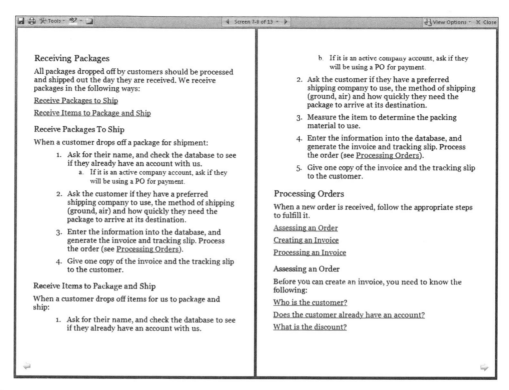

Next Screen

17. At the top of the screen, click the **Next Screen** button.

You move to the next two screens of information.

18. Explore the other buttons at the top of the Full Screen Reading view, and then click the **Close** button to return to Print Layout view.

19. Press ⌃Ctrl+Home. Then on the **View** toolbar, click the **Web Layout** button, and scroll through the document.

In a Web browser, the text column will fill the window and there will be no page breaks.

Outline

20. Press ⌃Ctrl+Home, and then on the **View** toolbar, click the **Outline** button.

The screen changes to show the document's hierarchical structure, and the Outlining tab appears at the left end of the Ribbon.

21. On the **Outlining** tab, in the **Outline Tools** group, click the **Show Level** arrow, and in the list, click **Level 2**.

The document collapses to display only the Level 1 and Level 2 headings.

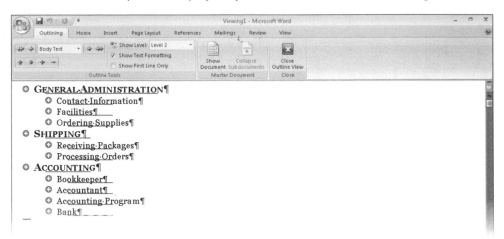

Draft

22. On the **View** toolbar, click the **Draft** button, and then scroll through the document.

You can see the basic content of the document without any extraneous elements, such as margins and headers and footers. The active area on the ruler indicates the width of the text column, dotted lines indicate page breaks, and scrolling is quick and easy.

23. Click the **Microsoft Office Button**, click **Open**, and then in the **Open** dialog box, double-click *Viewing2*.

The *Viewing2* document opens in Print Layout view in its own document window. Notice that the telephone number in the body of the memo has a dotted under-line because it is formatted as hidden.

24. On the **Home** tab, in the **Paragraph** group, click the **Show/Hide ¶** button to turn it off.

Non-printing characters and hidden text are no longer visible.

Switch Windows ▾

25. On the **View** tab, in the **Window** group, click **Switch Windows**, and then click *Viewing1*.

The other open document is displayed in Draft view, with non-printing characters visible.

26. On the **View** tab, in the **Window** group, click the **Arrange All** button.

The two document windows are sized and stacked one above the other. Each window has a Ribbon, so you can work with each document independently.

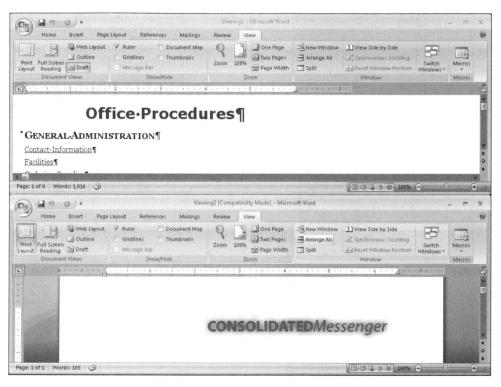

Close

27. At the right end of the *Viewing1* window's title bar, click the **Close** button.

Clicking the Close button does not quit Word because more than one document is open.

Maximize

28. At the right end of the *Viewing2* window's title bar, click the **Maximize** button.

The document window expands to fill the screen.

29. On the **View** tab, in the **Show/Hide** group, clear the **Ruler** check box to turn off the rulers.

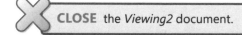 **CLOSE** the *Viewing2* document.

Creating and Saving a Document

To create a Word document, you simply open a new blank document and type your content. The blinking insertion point shows where the next character you type will appear. When the insertion point reaches the right margin, the word you are typing moves to the next line. Because of this *word wrap* feature, which is common in word-processing and desktop-publishing programs, you press Enter only to start a new paragraph, not a new line.

Each document you create is temporary unless you save it as a file with a unique name or location. To save a document for the first time, you click the Save button on the Quick Access Toolbar or click the Microsoft Office Button and then click Save. Either action displays the Save As dialog box, where you can assign the name and storage location.

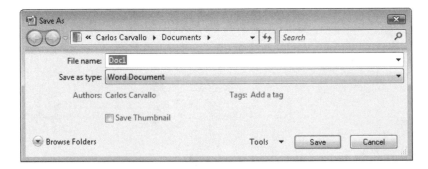

If you want to save the document in a folder other than the one shown in the Address bar, you can click the chevrons to the left of the current folder name and then navigate to the folder you want. You can also click Browse Folders to display the Navigation Pane and a toolbar. If you want to create a new folder in which to store the file, you can click the New Folder button on this toolbar.

After you save a document the first time, you can save changes simply by clicking the Save button. The new version of the document then overwrites the previous version. If you want to keep both the new version and the previous version, click Save As on the Office menu, and then save the new version with a different name in the same location or with the same name in a different location. (You cannot store two files with the same name in the same folder.)

In this exercise, you will enter text in a new document, and you will save the document in a folder that you create. There are no practice files for this exercise.

> **BE SURE TO** close any open documents before beginning this exercise.

Microsoft Office
Button

1. Click the **Microsoft Office Button**, click **New**, and then in the **New Document** window, double-click **Blank Document**.

   A new document window opens in Print Layout view.

2. With the insertion point at the beginning of the new document, type Decorators, Get Ready for Change!, and then press ⌷Enter⌷.

The text appears in the new document.

3. Type With spring just around the corner, let's start making those home decor changes you've been thinking about all winter. Let's introduce fresh new color. Let's add some accessories. Let's come up with a great plan for a room to love.

Notice that you did not need to press Enter when the insertion point reached the right margin because the text wrapped to the next line.

> Decorators, Get Ready for Change!
>
> With spring just around the corner, let's start making those home décor changes you've been thinking about all winter. Let's introduce fresh new color. Let's add some accessories. Let's come up with a great plan for a room to love.|

> **Tip** If a red wavy line appears under a word or phrase, Word is flagging a possible error. For now, ignore any errors.

4. Press ⌷Enter⌷, and then type Here at Wide World Importers, we realize that you need to have the right tools to guarantee a successful room makeover. And with that in mind, we are proud to present the latest addition to our line of decorating tools, the Room Planner.

Save

5. On the **Quick Access Toolbar**, click the **Save** button.

The Save As dialog box opens, displaying the contents of the *Documents* folder. In the File Name box, Word suggests *Decorators*, the first word in the document, as a possible name for this file.

6. In the lower-left corner of the dialog box, click Browse Folders.

The dialog box expands to show the Navigation Pane and a toolbar.

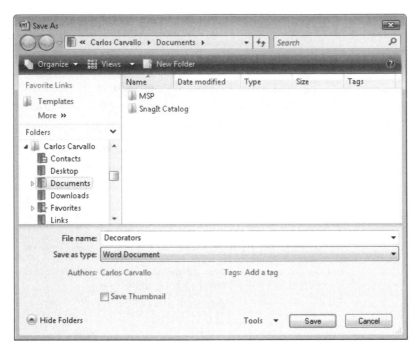

7. Double-click **Microsoft Press**, double-click **2007OfficeSBS_HomeStudent**, and double-click **WordExploring**.

8. On the dialog box's toolbar, click the **New Folder** button, type My New Documents as the name of the new folder, and then press Enter.

   My New Documents is now the current folder in the Save As dialog box.

9. In the **File name** box, double-click the existing entry, and then type My Announcement.

> **Troubleshooting** Programs that run on the Windows operating systems use file name extensions to identify different types of files. For example, the extension *.docx* identifies Word 2007 documents. Windows Vista programs do not display these extensions by default, and you shouldn't type them in the Save As dialog box. When you save a file, Word automatically adds whatever extension is associated with the type of file selected in the Save As Type box.

10. Click **Save**.

    The Save As dialog box closes, Word saves the *My Announcement* file in the *My New Documents* folder, and the name of the document, *My Announcement*, appears on the program window's title bar.

11. Click the **Microsoft Office Button**, and then click **Save As**.

The Save As dialog box opens, displaying the contents of the *My New Documents* folder.

12. In the Address bar in the **Save As** dialog box, click the chevrons to the left of *My New Documents*, and then in the list, click **WordExploring**.

The dialog box now displays the contents of the *My New Documents* folder's *parent folder*, *WordExploring*.

13. Click **Save**.

Word saves the *My Announcement* file in the *WordExploring* folder. You now have two versions of the document saved with the same name but in different folders.

 CLOSE the *My Announcement* file.

> **Tip** By default, Word periodically saves the document you are working on in case the program stops responding or you lose electrical power. To adjust the time interval between saves, click the Microsoft Office Button, click Word Options, click Save in the left pane of the Word Options window, and specify the period of time in the box to the right of the Save AutoRecover Information Every check box. Then click OK.

Previewing and Printing a Document

When you are ready to print a document, you can click the Microsoft Office Button, point to Print, and then click Quick Print. Word then uses your computer's default printer and the settings specified in the Print dialog box. To use a different printer or change the print settings, you click the Microsoft Office Button, and then click Print to open the Print dialog box. You can then specify which printer to use, what to print, and how many copies, and you can make other changes to the settings.

Before you print a document, you almost always want to check how it will look on paper by previewing it. Previewing is essential for multi-page documents but is helpful even for one-page documents. To preview a document, you click the Microsoft Office Button, point to Print, and then click Print Preview. This view shows exactly how each page of the document will look when printed. Word displays a Print Preview tab on the Ribbon to provide tools for checking each page and making adjustments if you don't like what you see.

By using the buttons in the Page Setup group on the Print Preview tab, you can make three types of changes.

- Change the margins of the document to fit more or less information on a page or to control where the information appears. You define the size of the top, bottom, left, and right margins by clicking the Margins button and making a selection from the Margins gallery, or by clicking Custom Margins and specifying settings on the Margins tab of the Page Setup dialog box.

- Switch the *orientation* (the direction in which a page is laid out on the paper). The default orientation is *portrait*, in which the page is taller than it is wide. You can set the orientation to *landscape*, in which the page is wider than it is tall, by clicking the Orientation button and selecting that option.

> **Tip** The pages of a document all have the same margins and are oriented the same way unless you divide your document into sections. Then each section can have independent margin and orientation settings.

- Select the paper size you want to use by clicking the Size button and making a selection in the Paper Size gallery.

You can click buttons in other groups to change the printer options, change the view of the document, and change the mouse pointer so that you can edit the text.

In this exercise, you will preview a document, adjust the margins, change the orientation, and select a new printer before sending the document to be printed.

> **USE** the *Printing* document. This practice file is located in the *Documents\Microsoft Press\2007OfficeSBS_HomeStudent\WordExploring* folder.
> **BE SURE TO** install a printer and turn it on before starting this exercise.
> **OPEN** the *Printing* document.

Microsoft Office
Button

1. Click the **Microsoft Office Button**, point to the **Print** arrow, and then click **Print Preview**.

The window's title bar now indicates that you are viewing a preview of the document, and the Print Preview tab appears on the Ribbon.

2. On the **Print Preview** tab, in the **Zoom** group, click the **Two Pages** button.

Word displays the two pages of the document side by side.

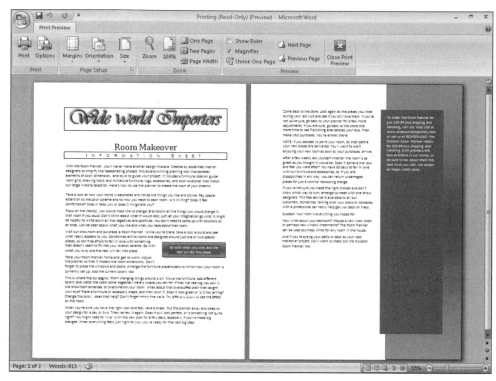

3. In the **Page Setup** group, click the **Margins** button.

The Margins gallery appears.

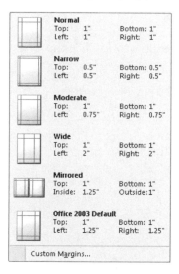

4. In the gallery, click **Wide**.

The text rewraps within the new margins, and the left end of the status bar indicates that the document now has 3 pages.

5. In the **Preview** group, click the **Next Page** button to see the last page of the document.

Dialog Box Launcher

6. Click the **Page Setup** Dialog Box Launcher.

   The Page Setup dialog box opens, displaying the Margins tab.

7. Under **Margins**, replace the value in the **Left** box by typing 1". Then replace the value in the **Right** box with 1", and click **OK**.

   The width of the margins decreases, and the text rewraps to fill 2 pages.

Orientation

8. In the **Page Setup** group, click the **Orientation** button, and then click **Landscape**.

   The pages of the document are now wider than they are tall.

9. Point to the top of the first page of the document so that the pointer becomes a magnifying glass, and then click.

   The first page is magnified. Notice that the Zoom box at the right end of the status bar now displays 100%.

10. Click near the top of the document.

   The Zoom percentage changes, and you now see both pages at the same time.

Close Print Preview

11. In the **Preview** group, click the **Close Print Preview** button.

   You don't have to be in Print Preview to change the orientation of a document. You can do it in Print Layout view.

12. On the **Page Layout** tab, in the **Page Setup** group, click the **Orientation** button, and then click **Portrait**.

13. Click the **Microsoft Office Button**, and then click **Print**.

> **Tip** You can click the Microsoft Office Button, point to Print, and then click Quick Print to print the document without first viewing the settings.

The Print dialog box opens.

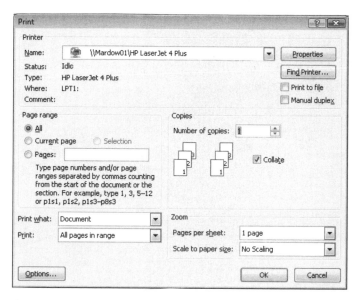

14. If you have more than one printer available and you want to switch printers, click the **Name** arrow, and in the list, click the printer you want.

15. Under **Page Range**, click **Current Page**.

16. Under **Copies**, change the **Number of copies** setting to 2, and then click **OK**.

Word prints two copies of the first page on the designated printer.

CLOSE the *Printing* document without saving your changes, and if you are not continuing directly on to the next chapter, exit Word.

Key Points

- You can open more than one Word document, and you can view more than one document at a time, but only one document can be active at a time.

- You create Word documents by typing text at the insertion point. It's easy to move the insertion point by clicking in the text or pressing keys and key combinations.

- When you save a Word document, you specify its name, location, and file format in the Save As dialog box.

- You can view a document in a variety of ways, depending on your needs as you create the document and on the purpose for which you are creating it.

Chapter at a Glance

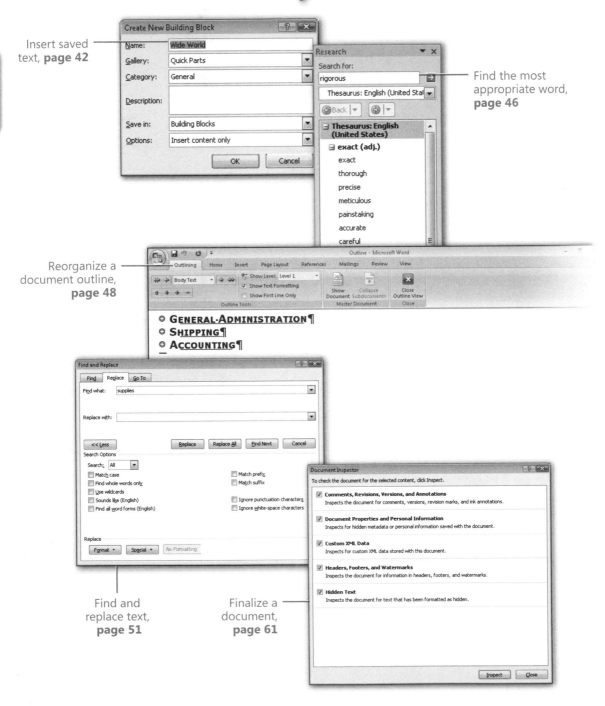

Insert saved text, **page 42**

Find the most appropriate word, **page 46**

Reorganize a document outline, **page 48**

Find and replace text, **page 51**

Finalize a document, **page 61**

2 Editing and Proofreading Documents

In this chapter, you will learn to:
- ✔ Make changes to a document.
- ✔ Insert saved text.
- ✔ Find the most appropriate word.
- ✔ Reorganize a document outline.
- ✔ Find and replace text.
- ✔ Correct spelling and grammatical errors.
- ✔ Finalize a document.

Unless the documents you create are intended for no one's eyes but your own, you need to ensure that they are correct, logical, and persuasive. Whether you are a novice writer or an experienced writer, Microsoft Office Word 2007 has several tools that make creating professional documents easy and efficient:

- Editing tools provide quick-selection techniques and drag-and-drop editing to make it easy to move and copy text anywhere you want it.

- The building blocks feature can be used to save and recall specialized terms or standard paragraphs.

- Reference and research tools include a thesaurus that makes it easy to track down synonyms and research services that provide access to a variety of Web-based reference materials.

- Outlining tools allow easy rearranging of headings and text to ensure that your argument is logical.

- Search tools can be used to locate and replace words and phrases, either one at a time or throughout a document.

- The AutoCorrect and Spelling And Grammar features make it easy to correct typos and grammatical errors before you share a document with others.

- Finalizing tools ensure that a document is ready for distribution.

In this chapter, you will edit the text in a document by inserting and deleting text, copying and pasting a phrase, and moving a paragraph. You will save a couple of building blocks, and you'll rearrange a document in Outline view. You will find a phrase and replace one phrase with another throughout the entire document. You'll change an AutoCorrect setting and add a misspelled word to its list. You'll check the spelling and grammar in a document and add a term to the custom dictionary. Finally, you'll inspect a document for inappropriate information and mark it as final.

See Also Do you need only a quick refresher on the topics in this chapter? See the Quick Reference entries at the beginning of this book.

Important Before you can use the practice files in this chapter, you need to install them from the book's companion CD to their default location. See "Using the Book's CD" at the beginning of this book for more information.

Troubleshooting Graphics and operating system–related instructions in this book reflect the Windows Vista user interface. If your computer is running Windows XP and you experience trouble following the instructions as written, please refer to the "Information for Readers Running Windows XP" section at the beginning of this book.

Making Changes to a Document

You will rarely write a perfect document that doesn't require any editing. You will almost always want to insert a word or two, change a phrase, or move text from one place to another. You can edit a document as you create it, or you can write it first and then revise it. Or you might want to edit a document that you created for one purpose so that it will serve a different purpose. For example, a letter from last year's marketing campaign might be edited to create a new letter for this year's campaign.

Inserting text is easy; you click to position the insertion point and simply begin typing. Any existing text to the right of the insertion point moves to make room for the new text.

What Happened to Overtype?

By default, Word is in Insert mode. In previous versions of Word, it was possible to accidentally switch to Overtype mode by inadvertently pressing the Insert key. In Overtype mode, existing text does not move to the right when you type new text; instead, each character you type replaces an existing character.

In Word 2007, you must deliberately switch to Overtype mode if you want to use it. Here's how:

1. Right-click the status bar, and then click **Overtype** to display the Insert mode status at the left end of the status bar.

2. Click **Insert** on the status bar.

   The word *Overtype* then replaces *Insert*. You can click the word to switch back to Insert mode when you have finished overtyping.

By default, pressing the Insert key has no effect on the mode. If you want the Insert key to turn Overtype mode on and off, follow these steps:

1. Click the **Microsoft Office Button**, and then click **Word Options**.

2. In the **Word Options** dialog box, click **Advanced** in the left pane, and then under **Editing options**, select the **Use the Insert key to control overtype mode** check box.

3. Click **OK**.

Deleting text is equally easy. If you want to delete only one or a few characters, you can simply position the insertion point and then press the Backspace or Delete key until the characters are all gone. Pressing Backspace deletes the character to the left of the insertion point; pressing Delete deletes the character to the right of the insertion point.

To delete more than a few characters efficiently, you need to know how to *select* the text. Selected text appears highlighted on the screen. You can select specific items as follows:

- To select a word, double-click it. Word selects the word and the space following it. It does not select punctuation following a word.

- To select a sentence, click anywhere in the sentence while holding down the Ctrl key. Word selects all the characters in the sentence, from the first character through the space following the ending punctuation mark.

- To select a paragraph, triple-click it.

You can select adjacent words, lines, or paragraphs by positioning the insertion point at the beginning of the text you want to select, holding down the Shift key, and then pressing the Arrow keys or clicking at the end of the text that you want to select. If you want to select words, lines, or paragraphs that are not adjacent, you make the first selection and then hold down the Ctrl key while selecting the next block.

As an alternative, you can use the *selection area* to quickly select various items. This is an invisible area in the document's left margin, where the pointer becomes a hollow right-pointing arrow. You can use the selection area as follows:

● To select a line, click the selection area to the left of the line.

● To select a paragraph, double-click the selection area to the left of the paragraph.

● To select an entire document, triple-click the selection area.

Selection Area

After selecting the text you want to work with, simply press the Backspace or Delete key.

Tip To deselect text, click anywhere in the document window except the selection area.

After selecting text, you can move or copy it in the following ways:

● Use the *Clipboard* when you need to move or copy text between two locations that you cannot see at the same time—for example, between pages or between documents. The Clipboard is a temporary storage area in your computer's memory. Select the text, and then click the Cut or Copy button in the Clipboard group on the Home tab. Then reposition the insertion point and click the Paste button to insert the selection in its new location. When you cut text, it is removed from its original location, and when you copy text, it remains in its original location.

See Also For more information, see the sidebar entitled "About the Clipboard" later in this topic.

● Use *drag-and-drop editing* (frequently referred to simply as *dragging*) when you need to move or copy text only a short distance—for example, within a paragraph or line. Dragging does not involve the Clipboard. Start by selecting the text. Then hold down the mouse button, drag the text to its new location, and release the mouse button. To copy the selection, hold down the Ctrl key while you drag.

If you make a change to a document and then realize that you made a mistake, you can easily reverse the change. You can undo your last editing action by clicking the Undo button on the Quick Access Toolbar. To undo an earlier action, click the Undo arrow and then click that actions in the list.

> **Tip** Clicking an action in the Undo list undoes that action and all the editing actions you performed after that one. You cannot undo a single action except the last one you performed.

If you undo an action and then change your mind, you can click the Redo button on the Quick Access Toolbar. You can redo only the last action that you undid.

In this exercise, you will edit the text in a document. You'll insert and delete text, undo the deletion, copy and paste a phrase, and move a paragraph.

USE the *Changes* document. This practice file is located in the *Documents\Microsoft Press\ 2007OfficeSBS_HomeStudent\WordEditing* folder.
BE SURE TO start Word before beginning this exercise.
OPEN the *Changes* document.

Show/Hide ¶

1. If non-printing characters are not visible in the document, on the **Home** tab, in the **Paragraph** group, click the **Show/Hide ¶** button.

2. In the third sentence of the first paragraph, click immediately to the left of the word **between**, hold down the ⌈ Shift ⌉ key, and then click immediately to the right of the word **fifteen** (and to the left of the comma that follows it).

Word selects the text between the two clicks.

¶

The Taguien Cycle¶
A Fantasy Series for Young Adults¶

¶

The Taguien Cycle is the most exciting and promising new book project to have come before the committee in several years. It meets our two principal goals: Develop a book line that will appeal to young adult readers between the ages of twelve to fifteen, especially boys, and develop a book line that has the potential for media spin-offs that will contribute to future profits and on-going financial success.¶

¶

Each year Lucerne has published several fairytale/magic books for younger readers, but we do not currently offer anything sophisticated enough to appeal to young adult readers. Although we have found it very difficult to sell other genres to this audience of reluctant readers, there is every indication that offering a fantasy series at this time would meet with success.¶

¶

Interest in the fantasy genre has increased steadily over the past ten years, a trend that shows no sign of reversal. Anecdotal industry sales statistics show an increase of 2 to 3 percent per year for adult fantasy books and 5 to 6 percent for young adult fantasy books.¶

3. Press the ⌨Del key to delete the selection.

Word also deletes the space before the selection.

4. Select the word **book** in the first sentence of the first paragraph by double-clicking it, and then press the ⌨Backspace key.

5. Double-click the word **principal** in the same paragraph, and then replace it by typing primary.

Notice that you don't have to type a space after *primary*. Word inserts the space for you.

> **Tip** Word inserts and deletes spaces because the Use Smart Cut And Paste check box is selected on the Advanced page of the Word Options dialog box. If you want to be able to control the spacing yourself, click the Microsoft Office Button, click Word Options, click Advanced, clear this check box, and click OK.

6. Position the mouse pointer in the selection area to the left of the phrase *A Fantasy Series for Young Adults*, and then click once to select the entire line of text.

Copy

7. On the **Home** tab, in the **Clipboard** group, click the **Copy** button.

The selection is copied to the Clipboard.

Paste

8. Click the Next Page button below the vertical scroll bar to move to the beginning of the next page, press the ⌨↓ key, and then in the **Clipboard** group, click the **Paste** button (not its arrow).

The Paste Options button appears below and to the right of the insertion. You can click this button if you want to change Word's default way of pasting, but in this case, you can just ignore it.

9. Return to Page 1, and then in the numbered list, triple-click anywhere in the *Bartimaeus Trilogy* paragraph to select the entire paragraph.

Cut

10. In the **Clipboard** group, click the **Cut** button.

11. Press the ⬆ key to move to the beginning of the *Harry Potter series* paragraph, and then in the **Clipboard** group, click the **Paste** button.

The two paragraphs have effectively switched places and the list has been renumbered.

See Also For more information about numbered lists, see "Creating and Modifying Lists" in Chapter 3, "Changing the Look of Text."

Undo

12. On the **Quick Access Toolbar**, click the **Undo** arrow, and in the list, click the third action (**Paste**).

Word undoes the previous cut-and-paste operation and the pasting of the copied text.

13. Press Ctrl + Home to move to the top of the document. Then move the pointer into the selection area adjacent to the paragraph that begins *Interest in the fantasy genre*, and double-click to select the paragraph.

14. Point to the selection, hold down the mouse button, and then drag the paragraph up to the beginning of the paragraph above it.

When you release the mouse, the text appears in its new location.

15. With the text still selected, press the End key.

Word releases the selection and moves the insertion point to the end of the paragraph.

16. Press Space , and then press Del.

Word deletes the paragraph mark, and the two paragraphs are now one paragraph.

¶

The·Taguien··Cycle¶
A·Fantasy·Series·for·Young··Adults¶

¶
The·Taguien··Cycle··is·the·most·exciting··and·promising··new·project·to·have··come·before·the·
committee··in·several··years.··It·meets·our·two·primary··goals:··Develop··a·book·line··that·will·
appeal·to·young··adult·readers,·especially··boys;··and·develop··a·book·line··that·has·the·potential·
for·media··spin-offs··that·will··contribute··to·future··profits··and·on-going··financial··success.¶
¶
Interest·in·the·fantasy··genre··has·increased··steadily··over·the·past·ten·years,·a·trend·that·shows·no·
sign··of·reversal.··Anecdotal··industry··sales·statistics··show·an·increase··of·2·to·3·percent·per·year·
for·adult·fantasy··books·and·5·to·6·percent·for·young··adult·fantasy··books.·Each·year·Lucerne·has·
published··several··fairytale/magic··books·for·younger··readers,·but·we·do·not·currently··offer·
anything··sophisticated··enough··to·appeal·to·young··adult·readers.··Although··we·have·found·it·
very·difficult··to·sell··other·genres·to·this··audience··of·reluctant··readers,·there·is·every·indication·
that·offering··a·fantasy··series··at·this··time··would··meet·with··success.¶
¶
¶

17. In the selection area, click adjacent to the paragraph mark below the combined paragraph, and then press ⌈Del⌉.

 CLOSE the *Changes* document without saving your changes.

About the Clipboard

You can view the items that have been cut and copied to the Clipboard by clicking the Clipboard Dialog Box Launcher to open the Clipboard task pane, which displays up to 24 cut or copied items.

To paste an individual item at the insertion point, you simply click the item. To paste all the items, click the Paste All button. You can point to an item, click the arrow that appears, and then click Delete to remove it from the Clipboard, or you can remove all the items by clicking the Clear All button.

You can control the behavior of the Clipboard task pane by clicking Options at the bottom of the pane. You can choose to have the Clipboard task pane appear when you cut or copy a single item or multiple items. You can also choose to display the Clipboard icon in the status area of the taskbar when the Clipboard task pane is displayed.

To close the Clipboard task pane, click the Close button at the right end of its title bar.

Inserting Saved Text

To save time and ensure consistency in your documents, you can save any text you use frequently as a *building block*. You do this by selecting the text, clicking Quick Parts in the Text group on the Insert tab, clicking Save Selection To Quick Part Gallery, and assigning the text a name. It then appears under its assigned name in the Quick Parts gallery.

After you have saved the text, you can insert it at any time by clicking Quick Parts to display its gallery and then clicking the building block you want.

Tip You can also type the name of the building block and then press the F3 key to insert it at the insertion point.

In this exercise, you will save the names of a company and a product as building blocks so that you can insert them elsewhere in a document.

USE the *SavedText* document. This practice file is located in the *Documents\Microsoft Press\2007OfficeSBS_HomeStudent\WordEditing* folder.

OPEN the *SavedText* document.

1. Toward the end of the first paragraph of the document, select **Wide World Importers**.

2. On the **Insert** tab, in the **Text** group, click the **Quick Parts** button, and then click **Save Selection to Quick Part Gallery**.

   The Create New Building Block dialog box opens.

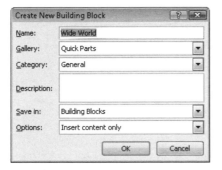

3. In the **Name** box, type www, and then click **OK**.

   Word saves the selection in the Quick Parts gallery.

4. In the third paragraph of the document, select **chimonobambusa marmorea**, and then in the **Text** group, click the **Quick Parts** button.

   Notice that the company name now appears as a building block in the Quick Parts gallery.

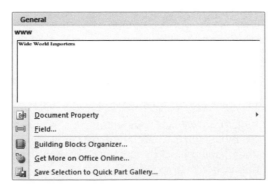

5. Click **Save Selection to Quick Part Gallery**, and save the selected text with the name cm.

6. Press `Ctrl`+`End` to move the insertion point to the end of the document, and then press `Space`.

7. Type In particular and a space. Then in the **Text** group, click the **Quick Parts** button, and in the gallery, click the **www** entry.

   The company name appears at the insertion point.

8. Type a space followed by recommends cm.

9. Press the `F3` key, and then type a period.

   Word replaces *cm* with its building block, *chimonobambusa marmorea*.

about anyone who wishes to grow one in their backyard. Some dwarf species include chimonobambusa marmorea, indocalamus tessellatus, and pleioblastus chino vaginatus. Also suitable for the personal garden are those categorized as mid size. Examples of these types of plants are bambusa glaucophylla and otatea acuminata aztectorum. Plant starts and seeds are easier to find than ever, being available at nurseries and through mail order. ¶
¶
Bamboo is quickly becoming an important economic factor in many developing nations. A 60-foot tree cut for marketing can take up to 60 years to replace, whereas a 60-foot bamboo can take as little as 60 days to reach marketability. And the majority of bamboo destined for the world market is harvested by women and children, most of who live at or below subsistence levels in poor nations. So as production increases, so does support for the economies of those countries that produce it. ¶
¶
Choosing bamboo as part of home or garden design makes sense on many levels. Not only does it have an appealing look, but it supports the environment as well as the countries that produce it. In particular Wide World Importers recommends chimonobambusa marmorea. ¶

www   cm

Troubleshooting Pressing the F3 key substitutes the corresponding building block only if the name you type contains no spaces. There must be a space to its left, and the insertion point must be to its right.

CLOSE the *SavedText* document without saving your changes.

Important When you quit Word, you will be asked whether you want to save the Building Blocks template, which by default is where your custom building blocks are saved. If you want to discard the building blocks you have created in this Word session, click No. If you want to save them, click Yes.

Inserting the Date and Time

One of the easiest ways to insert today's date or the current time in a document is to use the Insert Date And Time button in the Text group on the Insert tab. After you specify the format you want to use, Word retrieves the date or time from your computer's internal calendar or clock. You can insert the information as regular text or as a *field*. A field is a placeholder that tells Word to supply the specified information in the specified way. The advantage of using a field is that it can be updated with the click of a button.

Here are the steps for inserting the date or time:

1. With the insertion point located where you want the date or time to appear, on the **Insert** tab, in the **Text** group, click the **Date & Time** button.

   The Date And Time dialog box opens.

2. Under **Available formats**, click the date and/or time format you want.

3. If you want to insert a date or time field, select the **Update automatically** check box.

4. Click **OK**.

If you selected Update Automatically, Word inserts a Date or Time field depending on the format you selected. When you point to the field, it is highlighted as a unit. You can click the field to select it, and you can click the Update button that appears above it to update the field with the most current information. If you right-click the field, you can click Toggle Field Codes to see the codes that control the field; click the command again to redisplay the date or time information.

You can insert other types of date and time fields, such as a PrintDate field or an EditTime field. Insert a Date or Time field in the usual way, right-click the field, and then click Edit Field. In the Field dialog box, change the setting in the Categories box to Date And Time, and in the Field Names list, click the field you want. When you click OK, the information corresponding to the field type you specified is shown in the document.

Translating Text

Word now comes with built-in dictionaries for many common languages, so you can easily translate words and phrases from one language to another.

To translate a word into another language:

1. Select the word, and then on the **Review** tab, in the **Proofing** group, click the **Translate** button.

   The Research task pane opens with boxes in which you can specify the source language and the translation language.

2. Under **Translation** in the **Research** task pane, change the settings in the **From** and **To** boxes as necessary.

   The translated text appears under Bilingual Dictionary.

To translate a different word or phrase, you can type it in the Search For box and then click the Start Searching button to the right.

To view the translation of any word you point to, click the Translation ScreenTip button in the Proofing group on the Review tab, and then select the language you want to see. You can then point to any word in a document to display the equivalent word in the language you selected. Click the button again, and then click Turn Off Translation ScreenTip to turn off the translation display.

Finding the Most Appropriate Word

Language is often contextual—you use different words and phrases in a marketing brochure, in a letter requesting immediate payment of an invoice, and in an informal memo about a social gathering after work. To help you ensure that you are using the words that best convey your meaning in any given context, Word provides a *Thesaurus* where you can look up synonyms (alternative words) for a selected word. The Thesaurus is one of a set of Research services provided by Word.

To look up alternatives for a word in the Thesaurus, you select the word and then click the Thesaurus button in the Proofing group on the Review tab. The Research task pane opens, displaying a list of synonyms. You then click the synonym that you want to replace the selected word.

In this exercise, you'll use the Thesaurus to replace one word with another.

> **USE** the *FindingWord* document. This practice file is located in the *Documents\Microsoft Press\2007OfficeSBS_HomeStudent\WordEditing* folder.
>
> **OPEN** the *FindingWord* document.

1. Double-click the word **rigorous** in the last line of the first paragraph of the letter.

2. On the **Review** tab, in the **Proofing** group, click the **Thesaurus** button.

   The Research task pane opens, listing synonyms for the word *rigorous*.

3. In the task pane, under **exact**, click **meticulous**.

   The word *meticulous* replaces *rigorous* in the Search For box at the top of the task pane, and synonyms for *meticulous* are now listed in the task pane.

4. Point to the word **thorough**, click the arrow that appears, and then click **Insert**.

   The word *thorough* replaces *rigorous* in the document.

5. Close the **Research** task pane.

> **CLOSE** the *FindingWord* document without saving your changes.

Researching Information

In addition to the Thesaurus, the Research task pane provides access to a variety of informational resources from within Word. You can enter a topic in the Search For box and specify in the box below which resource Word should use to look for information about that topic. By clicking Research Options at the bottom of the Research task pane, you can specify which of a predefined list of reference materials, such as Microsoft Encarta and various Internet resources, will be available from a list, and you can add your own reference-material sources.

To research information:

1. On the **Review** tab, in the **Proofing** group, click the **Research** button to display the Research task pane.

2. In the **Search for** box, type the topic you are interested in researching.

   For example, you might type *bamboo*.

3. Click the arrow to the right of the box below the Search For box, and then in the list, click the resource you want to use to search for information.

   For example, you might click MSN Search. When you have made your selection, the Start Searching button to the right of the Search For box flashes, and seconds later, the search results are displayed in the task pane.

4. Click any information sources that interest you.

   You can click a hyperlink to a Web address to go to the Web to track down further information. You can also select part of a topic, right-click the selection, click Copy, and then paste the selection into your document. Or you can click right-click the selection and click Look Up to research information about the selection.

Reorganizing a Document Outline

If you are creating a document that contains headings, you can format it with built-in heading styles that include outline levels. Then it is easy to view and organize the document in Outline view. In this view, you can hide all the body text and display only the headings at and above a particular level. You can then rearrange the sections of a document by moving their headings.

To view a document in Outline view, click the Outline button in the Document Views group on the View tab, or click the Outline button on the View toolbar. The document is then displayed with a hierarchical structure, and the Outlining tab appears on the Ribbon.

The Outline Tools group on this tab includes buttons you can click to display only the headings at a specific level and above, to *promote* or *demote* headings or body text by changing their level, and to move headings and their text up or down in the document. The indentations and symbols used in Outline view to indicate the level of a heading or paragraph in the document's structure do not appear in the document in other views or when you print it.

> **Tip** You can click the buttons in the Master Document group to create a master document with subdocuments that you can then display and hide. The topic of master documents and subdocuments is beyond the scope of this book. For more information, see Word Help.

In this exercise, you'll switch to Outline view, promote and demote headings, move headings, and expand and collapse the outline.

> **USE** the *Outline* document. This practice file is located in the *Documents\Microsoft Press\2007OfficeSBS_HomeStudent\WordEditing* folder.
> **OPEN** the *Outline* document.

Outline

1. In the lower-right corner of the window, on the **View** toolbar, click the **Outline** button.

   The screen changes to display the document in Outline view, and the Outlining tab appears at the left end of the Ribbon.

2. On the **Outlining** tab, in the **Outline Tools** group, click the **Show Level** arrow, and in the list, click **Level 1**.

The document collapses to display only level-1 headings.

⊕ **GENERAL-ADMINISTRATION¶**
⊕ **SHIPPING¶**
⊕ **ACCOUNTING¶**

Expand

Demote

Undo

Collapse

3. Click anywhere in the **Accounting** heading.

4. In the **Outline Tools** group, click the **Expand** button.

   Word expands the *Accounting* section to display its level-2 headings.

5. In the **Outline Tools** group, click the **Demote** button.

   The *Accounting* heading changes to a level-2 heading.

6. On the **Quick Access Toolbar**, click the **Undo** button.

   The *Accounting* heading changes back to a level-1 heading.

7. In the **Outline Tools** group, click the **Collapse** button.

8. Click the **Demote** button.

   Again, the *Accounting* heading changes to a level-2 heading.

9. Click the **Expand** button.

   Because the subheadings were hidden under *Accounting* when you demoted the heading, all the subheadings have been demoted to level 3 to maintain the hierarchy of the section.

Promote

10. Click the **Collapse** button, and then in the **Outline Tools** group, click the **Promote** button.

    The *Accounting* heading is now a level-1 heading again.

11. Press Ctrl + Home to move to the top of the document, and then in the **Outline Tools** group, in the **Show Level** list, click **Level 2**.

    The outline shows all the level-1 and level-2 headings.

Move Up

12. Click the plus sign to the left of the *Accounting* heading, and then in the **Outline Tools** group, click the **Move Up** button three times.

The *Accounting* heading and all its subheadings move above the *Shipping* heading.

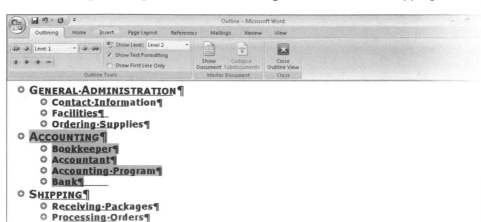

13. In the **Outline Tools** group, in the **Show Level** list, click **All Levels**.

    You can now scroll through the document to see the effects of the reorganization.

14. In the **Close** group, click the **Close Outline View** button.

    Word displays the reorganized document in Print Layout view.

CLOSE the *Outline* document without saving your changes.

Finding and Replacing Text

One way to ensure that the text in your documents is consistent and accurate is to use the Find feature of Word to search for every instance of a particular word or phrase. For example, if you were responsible for advertising a trademarked product, you would probably want to search your marketing materials to check that every instance of the product's name was correctly identified as a trademark.

Clicking the Find button in the Editing group on the Home tab displays the Find tab of the Find And Replace dialog box. After you enter the text you want to find in the Find What box, you can do the following:

● Click Find Next to select the first occurrence of that text.

● In the Reading Highlight list, click Highlight All to highlight all occurrences.

If you find an error in the document while conducting a search, you can make editing changes on the fly without closing the Find And Replace dialog box. Simply click the document, make the change, and then click the Find And Replace dialog box to make it active again.

If you know that you want to substitute one word or phrase for another, you can use the Replace feature to find each occurrence of the text you want to change and re-place it with different text. Clicking the Replace button in the Editing group displays the Replace tab of the Find And Replace dialog box, which is similar to the Find tab. On the Replace tab, you can do the following:

- Click Replace to replace the selected occurrence with the text in the Replace With box and move to the next occurrence.
- Click Replace All to replace all occurrences with the text in the Replace With box.
- Click Find Next to leave the selected occurrence as it is and locate the next one.

You can use other options in the Find And Replace dialog box to carry out more com-plicated searches and replaces. Clicking More expands the box to make these additional options available.

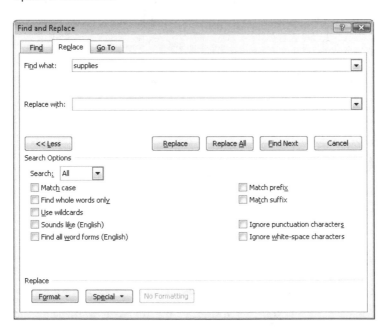

You can make a selection from the Search list to guide the direction of the search. You can select the Match Case check box to match capitalization and select the Find Whole Words Only check box to find only whole-word occurrences of the Find What text. If you want to check that your usage of two similar words, such as *effect* and *affect*, is correct, you can select the Use Wildcards check box and then enter a *wildcard character* in the Find What box to locate variable information. The two most common wildcard characters are:

- The ? wildcard stands for any single character in this location in the Find What text.
- The * wildcard stands for any number of characters in this location in the Find What text.

> **Tip** To see a list of the other available wildcards, use Help to search for wildcards.

Selecting the Sounds Like check box finds occurrences of the search text that sound the same but are spelled differently, such as *there* and *their*. Selecting the Find All Word Forms check box finds occurrences of a particular word in any form, such as *plan*, *planned*, and *planning*. You can match a prefix or a suffix, and you can ignore punctuation and white space. Finally, you can locate formatting, such as bold, or special characters, such as tabs, by selecting them from the Format or Special list.

In this exercise, you will find a phrase and make a correction to the document. Then you'll replace one phrase with another throughout the entire document.

> **USE** the *FindingText* document. This practice file is located in the *Documents\Microsoft Press\2007OfficeSBS_HomeStudent\WordEditing* folder.
> **OPEN** the *FindingText* document.

 1. With the insertion point at the beginning of the document, on the **Home** tab, in the **Editing** group, click the **Find** button.

The Find And Replace dialog box opens, displaying the Find tab.

2. In the **Find what** box, type The Taguien Cycle, click **Reading Highlight**, and then in the list, click **Highlight All**.

3. Scroll to Page 2.

Word has found and selected all the occurrences of *The Taguien Cycle* in the document. (We dragged the title bar of the dialog box to move it to the side.)

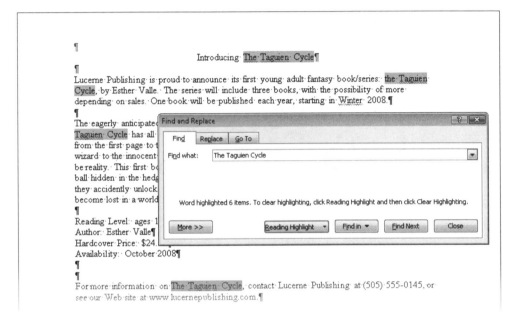

4. Click the document behind the **Find and Replace** dialog box, double-click the word **the** in *the Taguien Cycle* in the first paragraph (not the title) on Page 2, and then type The to correct the capitalization.

5. Press Ctrl + Home to move the insertion point to the beginning of the document.

6. Click the title bar of the **Find and Replace** dialog box, and then click the **Replace** tab.

The Find What box retains the entry from the previous search.

7. Click the **Replace with** box, type The Taguien Cycle, and then click the **More** button.

8. At the bottom of the expanded dialog box, click the **Format** button, and then click **Font**.

The Replace Font dialog box opens.

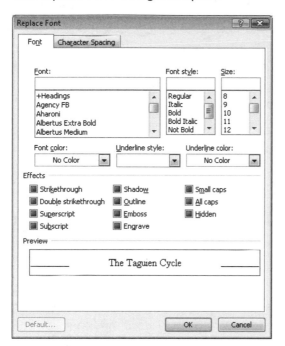

9. Under **Font Style**, click **Italic**, and then click **OK**.

10. Click **Find Next**, and then click **Replace**.

The selected plain text title is replaced with italicized text, and the next occurrence of *The Taguien Cycle* is selected.

11. Click **Replace All**.

Word displays a message box indicating that six replacements were made.

12. Click **OK** to close the message box, and then in the **Find and Replace** dialog box, click the **Find** tab.

13. In the **Find what** box, click **Reading Highlight**, and then in the list, click **Highlight All**.

Word highlights six occurrences of the Find What text.

14. Click **Reading Highlight**, and then in the list, click **Clear Highlighting**.

 CLOSE the Find And Replace dialog box, and then close the *FindingText* document without saving your changes.

Correcting Spelling and Grammatical Errors

In the days of handwritten and typewritten documents, people might have tolerated a typographical or grammatical error or two because correcting such errors without creating a mess was difficult. Word processors like Word have built-in spelling and grammar checkers, so now documents that contain these types of errors are likely to reflect badly on their creators.

> **Tip** Although Word can help you eliminate misspellings and grammatical errors, its tools are not infallible. You should always read through your documents to catch the problems that the Word tools can't detect.

Word provides two tools to help you with the chore of eliminating spelling and grammar errors: the AutoCorrect and Spelling And Grammar features.

Have you noticed that Word automatically corrects some misspellings as you type them? This is the work of the AutoCorrect feature. AutoCorrect corrects commonly misspelled words, such as *adn* to *and*, so that you don't have to correct them yourself. AutoCorrect comes with a long list of frequently misspelled words and their correct spellings. If you frequently misspell a word that AutoCorrect doesn't change, you can add it to the list in the AutoCorrect dialog box.

If you deliberately mistype a word and don't want to accept the AutoCorrect change, you can reverse it by clicking the Undo button on the Quick Access Toolbar before you type anything else.

Although AutoCorrect ensures that your documents are free of common misspellings, it doesn't detect random typographical and grammatical errors. For those types of errors, you can turn to the Spelling And Grammar feature for help. You might have noticed that as you type, Word underlines potential spelling errors with red wavy underlines and grammatical errors with green wavy underlines. You can right-click an underlined word or phrase to display suggested corrections.

If you want to check the spelling or grammar of the entire document, it is easier to click the Spelling & Grammar button in the Proofing group on the Review tab than to deal with underlined words and phrases individually. Word then works its way through the document from the insertion point and displays the Spelling And Grammar dialog box if it encounters a potential error. If the error is a misspelling, the Spelling And Grammar dialog box suggests corrections; if the error is a breach of grammar, the Spelling And Grammar dialog box tells you which rule you have broken as well as suggesting corrections. The buttons available in the Spelling And Grammar dialog box are dynamic and change to those most appropriate for fixing the error. For example, for a grammatical error, you are given the opportunity to ignore the rule you have broken throughout the document.

In this exercise, you'll change an AutoCorrect setting and add a misspelled word to its list. You'll check the spelling in the document and add terms to the custom dictionary, and you'll find, review, and correct a grammatical error.

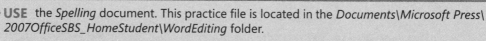

USE the *Spelling* document. This practice file is located in the *Documents\Microsoft Press\ 2007OfficeSBS_HomeStudent\WordEditing* folder.

OPEN the *Spelling* document.

1. Click at the end of the first paragraph in the letter, press [Space], and then type in your reserch, followed by a period.

As soon as you type the period, AutoCorrect changes *reserch* to *research*.

Microsoft Office Button

2. Click the **Microsoft Office Button**, and then click **Word Options**.

3. In the left pane of the **Word Options** window, click **Proofing**, and then on the Proofing page, click **AutoCorrect Options**.

The AutoCorrect dialog box opens, displaying the AutoCorrect tab.

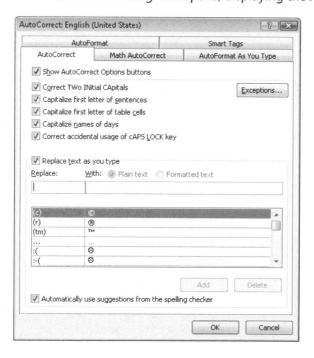

Notice the corrections that AutoCorrect will make. You can clear the check box of any item you don't want corrected. For example, if you don't want AutoCorrect to capitalize a lowercase letter or word that follows a period, clear the Capitalize First Letter Of Sentences check box.

4. Click in the **Replace** box, and then type avalable.

   Word scrolls the list below to show the entry that is closest to what you typed.

5. Press the ⌗Tab⌗ key to move the insertion point to the **With** box, and then type available.

6. Click **Add** to add the entry to the correction list, and then click **OK**.

7. Click **OK** to close the Word Options window.

8. Press ⌗Ctrl⌗+⌗End⌗ to move to the end of the document, and then in the paragraph that begins *Thank you for your* interest, position the insertion point to the right of the period at the end of the third sentence.

9. Press ⌗Space⌗, and then type Shelly will not be avalable May 10-15 followed by a period.

   The word *avalable* changes to *available*.

10. Press ⌗Ctrl⌗+⌗Home⌗ to move to the top of the document, and then right-click *sorces*, the first word with a red wavy underline.

    Word lists possible correct spellings for this word, as well as actions you might want to carry out.

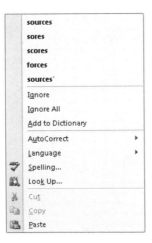

11. In the list, click **sources**.

Word removes the red wavy underline and inserts the correction.

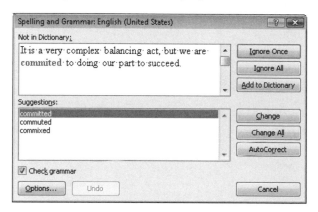

12. Press [Ctrl]+[Home] again, and then on the **Review** tab, in the **Proofing** group, click the **Spelling & Grammar** button.

The Spelling And Grammar dialog box opens, with the first word that Word does not recognize, *commited*, displayed in red in the Not In Dictionary box.

13. With **committed** selected in the **Suggestions** box, click **AutoCorrect**.

Word adds the misspelling and the selected correction to the AutoCorrect list, so that the next time you type *commited* by mistake, the spelling will be corrected for you as you type. Word then flags *Dyck* as the next possible misspelling.

> **Troubleshooting** If the errors we mention don't appear to be in the practice file, click Options at the bottom of the Spelling And Grammar dialog box. Then in the Word Options window, under When Correcting Spelling And Grammar In Word, click Recheck Document, click Yes to reset the checkers, and then click OK.

14. Click **Ignore All**.

Word will now skip over this and any other occurrences of this proper noun. It moves on to highlight the duplicate word *for*.

15. Click **Delete**.

Word deletes the second *for* and then flags a possible grammatical error.

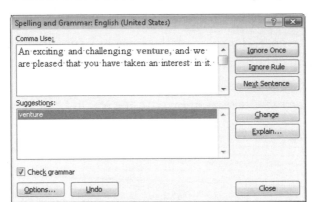

This grammatical error is identified as incorrect use of a comma. You need to read the sentence and then decide whether and how to correct it. In this case, the error is not related to the comma after *venture* but to the fact that there is no verb in the first half of the sentence.

> **Tip** Word's grammar checker helps identify phrases and clauses that do not follow traditional grammatical rules, but it is not always accurate. It is easy to get in the habit of ignoring green wavy underlines. However, it is wise to scrutinize them all to be sure that your documents don't contain any embarrassing mistakes.

16. Behind the **Spelling and Grammar** dialog box, click the document, double-click the word **An** at the beginning of the sentence with the error, and then type The import business is an.

17. Click the title bar of the **Spelling and Grammar** dialog box, and then click **Resume**.

    Word flags *Florian* as a word that it doesn't recognize. *Florian* is a proper noun and is spelled correctly. By adding words like this one to the custom dictionary, you can prevent Word from continuing to flag them.

18. Click **Add to Dictionary**.

    Word displays a message, indicating that it has finished checking the spelling and grammar of the document.

19. Click **OK** to close the message box.

 CLOSE the *Spelling* document without saving your changes.

Viewing Document Statistics

As you type, Word keeps track of the number of pages and words in your document, displaying this information at the left end of the status bar. To see the number of words in only part of the document, such as a few paragraphs, simply select that part. The status bar then displays the number of words in the selection, expressed as a fraction of the total, such as 250/800.

To see more statistics, you can open the Word Count dialog box by clicking the Word Count button in the Proofing group on the Review tab. In addition to the count of pages and words, the Word Count dialog box displays the number of characters, paragraphs, and lines. It also gives you the option of including or excluding words in text boxes, footnotes, and endnotes.

Finalizing a Document

When a document is complete and ready for distribution, you typically perform several final tasks. These might include inspecting the document for any remaining private or inappropriate information, restricting access, or adding a digital signature.

Many documents go through several revisions, and some are scrutinized by multiple reviewers. During this development process, documents can accumulate information that you might not want in the final version, such as the names of people who worked on the document, comments that reviewers have added to the file, or hidden text about status and assumptions. This extraneous information is not a concern if the final version is to be delivered as a printout. However, these days more and more files are delivered electronically, making this information available to anyone who wants to read it.

Word 2007 includes a tool called the Document Inspector, which finds and removes all extraneous and potentially confidential information. You can instruct the Document Inspector to look for comments, revisions, and annotations; for any personal information saved with the document; and for hidden text. The Document Inspector displays a summary of its findings and gives you the option of removing anything it finds.

Word also includes another finalizing tool called the Compatibility Checker, which checks for the use of features not supported in previous versions of Word.

After you handle extraneous information and compatibility issues, you can mark a document as final, which make the file read-only so that other people know that they should not make changes to this released document.

In this exercise, you will inspect a document for inappropriate information and mark it as final.

USE the *Finalizing* document. This practice file is located in the *Documents\Microsoft Press\ 2007OfficeSBS_HomeStudent\WordEditing* folder.

OPEN the *Finalizing* document.

Microsoft Office
Button

1. Click the **Microsoft Office Button**, point to **Prepare**, and then click **Properties**.

   The Document Information Panel opens above the document, showing the identifying information saved with the file. Some information, including the name of the author, was attached to the file by Word. Other information was added by a user.

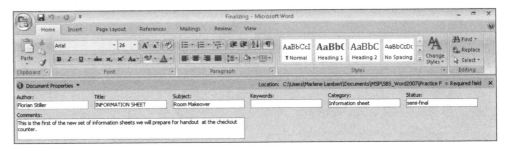

2. In the upper-left corner of the **Document Information Panel**, click the **Document Properties** arrow, and then in the list, click **Advanced Properties**.

   The Properties dialog box opens.

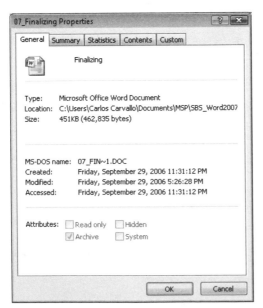

Close

3. In turn, click the **Summary** and **Statistics** tabs, noticing that additional identifying information is displayed there.

4. Click **Cancel** to close the **Properties** dialog box, and then in the upper-right corner of the **Document Information Panel**, click the **Close** button.

5. Save the document in the *WordEditing* folder with the name My Information Sheet.

6. Click the **Microsoft Office Button**, point to **Prepare**, and then click **Inspect Document**.

The Document Inspector dialog box opens, listing the items that will be checked.

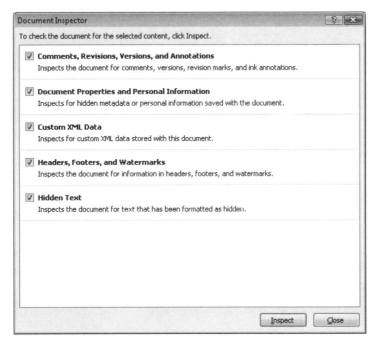

7. Without changing the default selections in the **Document Inspector** dialog box, click **Inspect**.

The Document Inspector reports the presence of the document properties and personal information that you viewed earlier in this exercise, as well as some custom XML data.

8. To the right of **Document Properties and Personal Information**, click **Remove All**.

Word removes the document properties and personal information.

9. To the right of **Custom XML Data**, click **Remove All**.

10. In the **Document Inspector** dialog box, click **Close**.

11. Click the **Microsoft Office Button**, point to **Prepare**, and then click **Mark As Final**.

A message tells you that the document will be marked as final and then saved.

12. Click **OK** to complete the process.

A message tells you that the document has been marked as final and that typing, editing commands, and proofing marks are turned off.

13. Click **OK** to close the message, and then click the **Insert** tab.

Most of the buttons are inactive, indicating that you cannot make changes to the document.

CLOSE the *My Information Sheet* document, and if you are not continuing directly on to the next chapter, exit Word.

Adding a Digital Signature

When you create a document that will be circulated to other people via e-mail or the Web, you might want to attach a *digital signature*, which is an electronic stamp of authentication. The digital signature confirms the origin of the document and indicates that no one has tampered with the document since it was signed.

To add a digital signature to a Word document, you must first obtain a digital ID. Certified digital IDs can be obtained from companies such as IntelliSafe Technologies and Comodo Inc. You can obtain the ID and attach it to a document by clicking the Microsoft Office Button, pointing to Prepare, clicking Add A Digital Signature, and then following the instructions.

Key Points

- You can cut or copy text and paste it elsewhere in the same document or in a different document. Cut and copied text is stored on the Clipboard.

- Made a mistake? No problem! You can undo a single action or the last several actions you performed by clicking the Undo button (or its arrow) on the Quick Access Toolbar. You can even redo an action if you change you mind again.

- You don't have to type the same text over and over again. Instead, save the text as a Quick Part and insert it with a few mouse clicks.

- Need a more precise word to get your point across? You can use the Thesaurus to look up synonyms for a selected word, and use the Research service to access specialized reference materials and online resources.

- If you take the time to apply heading styles to a document, you can use the outline to rearrange the document.

- You can find each occurrence of a word or phrase and replace it with another.

- You can rely on AutoCorrect to correct common misspellings. Correct other spelling and grammatical errors individually as you type or by checking the entire document in one pass.

- Before you distribute an electronic document, you can remove any information you don't want people to be able to see.

Chapter at a Glance

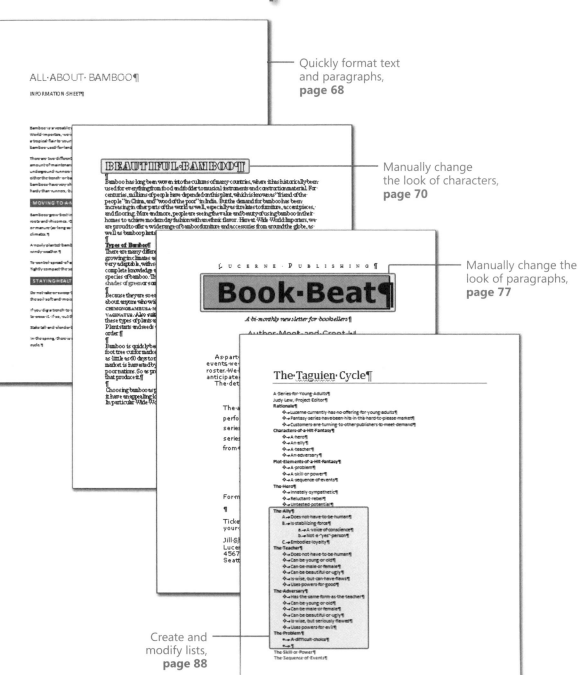

Quickly format text and paragraphs, **page 68**

Manually change the look of characters, **page 70**

Manually change the look of paragraphs, **page 77**

Create and modify lists, **page 88**

3 Changing the Look of Text

In this chapter, you will learn to:

✔ Quickly format text and paragraphs.

✔ Manually change the look of characters.

✔ Manually change the look of paragraphs.

✔ Create and modify lists.

The appearance of your documents helps to convey their message. Microsoft Office Word 2007 can help you develop professional-looking documents whose appearance is appropriate to their contents. You can easily format your text so that key points stand out and your arguments are easy to grasp.

In this chapter, you will experiment with Quick Styles and then change the look of individual words. Then you'll indent paragraphs, change paragraph alignment and spacing, set tab stops, modify line spacing, and add borders and shading. Finally, you'll create and format both bulleted and numbered lists.

See Also Do you need only a quick refresher on the topics in this chapter? See the Quick Reference entries at the beginning of this book.

> **Important** Before you can use the practice files in this chapter, you need to install them from the book's companion CD to their default location. See "Using the Book's CD" at the beginning of this book for more information.

> **Troubleshooting** Graphics and operating system–related instructions in this book reflect the Windows Vista user interface. If your computer is running Windows XP and you experience trouble following the instructions as written, please refer to the "Information for Readers Running Windows XP" section at the beginning of this book.

Quickly Formatting Text and Paragraphs

Word 2007 includes a number of new features, as well as enhancements to existing features, that make the process of formatting content effortless. For example, buttons for changing the font size, color, and other character attributes have been gathered in the Font group on the Home tab so that they are all easily accessible. And many common formatting buttons are available on the Mini toolbar that appears when you point to selected text.

See Also For information about changing character attributes, see "Manually Changing the Look of Characters" later in this chapter.

However, you don't have to apply attributes one at a time. You can easily change several attributes at once with a couple of mouse clicks by using *Quick Styles*. This powerful tool is available in the Styles group on the Home tab. Quick Styles are galleries consisting of the following:

- *Paragraph styles.* You can use these styles to apply a consistent look to different types of paragraphs, such as headings, body text, captions, quotations, and list paragraphs.

- *Character styles.* You can use these styles to change the appearance of selected words.

All of the Quick Styles in a particular gallery coordinate with each other, lending a clean, consistent, professional look to your documents. You can switch from one set of styles to another by selecting from Quick Styles galleries with names like Traditional, Distinctive, Modern, and Elegant. To help you choose the style you want, you can point to the name of the set to see a live preview of how your document will look with a particular set of Quick Styles applied to it. After you have applied one set of Quick Styles, you can easily change the look of the entire document by selecting a different set of Quick Styles from the Change Styles list.

In this exercise, you will experiment with Quick Styles.

> **USE** the *QuickFormatting* document. This practice file is located in the *Documents\Microsoft Press\2007OfficeSBS_HomeStudent\WordFormatting* folder.
> **BE SURE TO** start Word before beginning this exercise.
> **OPEN** the *QuickFormatting* document.

1. With the insertion point at the top of the document, on the **Home** tab, in the **Styles** group, move the pointer over each thumbnail in the displayed row of the **Quick Styles** gallery.

The formatting of the heading changes to show you a live preview of how the heading will look if you click the style you are pointing to. You don't have to actually apply the formatting to see its effect.

Down

2. Without making a selection, click the **Down** arrow to the right of the gallery.

> **Tip** This arrow has a dynamic ScreenTip that currently reads *Row 1 of 5*.

The next row of the Quick Styles gallery scrolls into view.

3. Move the pointer over each thumbnail in this row of the **Quick Styles** gallery.

More

4. In the **Styles** group, click the **More** button.

Word displays the entire Quick Styles gallery. The style applied to the paragraph containing the insertion point is surrounded by a border.

5. In the gallery, click the **Title** thumbnail to apply that style to the paragraph containing the insertion point.

6. Click anywhere in the **Information Sheet** heading, and then in the **Styles** group, click the **Subtitle** thumbnail.

> **Troubleshooting** If you select text and then apply a paragraph style, only the selected text takes on the formatting of the style. You can simply click again in the paragraph and reapply the style.

Up

7. Click anywhere in the **Moving to a New Home** heading, and then in the **Styles** group, click the **Up** arrow, and click the **Heading 1** thumbnail.

8. Apply the **Heading 1** style to the **Staying Healthy** and **Keeping Bugs at Bay** headings.

9. Apply the **Heading 3** style to the **Mites** and **Mealy Bugs** headings.

10. In the **Styles** group, click the **Change Styles** button, click **Style Set**, and then point to each set name in turn, watching the effect on the document.

11. When you have finished exploring, click **Modern**.

    The formatting of the document changes and the headings and text take on the look assigned to this set of styles.

CLOSE the *QuickFormatting* document without saving your changes.

Manually Changing the Look of Characters

When you type text in a document, it is displayed in a particular font. Each *font* consists of 256 alphabetic characters, numbers, and symbols that share a common design. By default the font used for text in a new Word document is Calibri, but you can change the font at any time. The available fonts vary from one computer to another, depending on the programs installed. Common fonts include Arial, Verdana, and Times New Roman.

You can vary the look of a font by changing the following *attributes*:

- Almost every font comes in a range of *font sizes*, which are measured in *points* from the top of letters that have parts that stick up (ascenders), such as *h*, to the bottom of letters that have parts that drop down (descenders), such as *p*. A point is approximately 1/72 of an inch.

- Almost every font comes in a range of *font styles*. The most common are regular (or plain), italic, bold, and bold italic.

- Fonts can be enhanced by applying *font effects*, such as underlining, small capital letters (small caps), or shadows.

- A palette of harmonious *font colors* is available, and you can also specify custom colors.

- You can alter the *character spacing* by pushing characters apart or squeezing them together.

After you have selected an appropriate font for a document, you can use these attributes to achieve different effects. Although some attributes might cancel each other out, they are usually cumulative. For example, you might use a bold font in various sizes and various shades of green to make different heading levels stand out in a newsletter. Collectively, the font and its attributes are called *character formatting*.

In this exercise, you will format the text in a document by changing its font, font style, size, color, and character spacing.

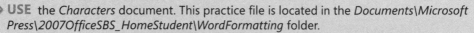

USE the *Characters* document. This practice file is located in the *Documents\Microsoft Press\2007OfficeSBS_HomeStudent\WordFormatting* folder.
OPEN the *Characters* document.

1. In the *Beautiful Bamboo* heading, click anywhere in the word **Beautiful**.

2. On the **Home** tab, in the **Font** group, click the **Underline** button.

Underline

> **Tip** If you click the Underline arrow, you can choose a style from the Underline gallery. You can also change the underline color.

The word containing the insertion point is now underlined. Notice that you did not have to select the entire word.

Repeat

3. In the same heading, click anywhere in the word **Bamboo**, and then on the **Quick Access Toolbar**, click the **Repeat** button.

The last formatting command is repeated. Again, although you did not select the entire word, it is now underlined.

4. In the selection area, click adjacent to *Beautiful Bamboo* to select the entire heading.

Word displays a Mini toolbar of buttons that you can use to quickly change the look of the selection.

B

Bold

5. On the **Mini toolbar**, click the **Bold** button.

The heading is now bold. The active buttons on the Mini toolbar and in the Font group on the Home tab indicate the attributes that you applied to the selection.

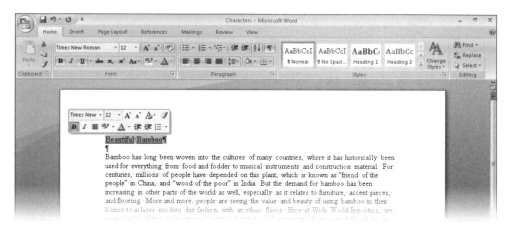

See Also For more information about the use of character formatting, see the sidebar "More About Case and Character Formatting" later in this chapter.

Format Painter

6. On the **Mini toolbar**, click the **Format Painter** button, and then click in the selection area adjacent to the *Types of Bamboo* heading.

   Word "paints" the formatting of *Beautiful Bamboo* onto *Types of Bamboo*.

> **Tip** The Format Painter button is also available in the Clipboard group on the Home tab.

7. Select **Beautiful Bamboo**, and then on the **Home** tab, in the **Font** group, click the **Font** arrow, scroll the list of available fonts, and then click **Stencil**.

> **Troubleshooting** If Stencil is not available, select any heavy font that catches your attention.

The heading at the top of the document now appears in the new font.

Font Size

8. In the **Font** group, click the **Font Size** arrow, and then in the list, click **26**.

   The size of the heading text increases to 26 points.

> **Tip** You can increase or decrease the font size in set increments by clicking the Grow Font and Shrink Font buttons in the Font group, or by clicking the same buttons on the Mini toolbar that appears when you select text.

Dialog Box
Launcher

9. In the **Font** group, click the **Dialog Box Launcher**.

   The Font dialog box opens.

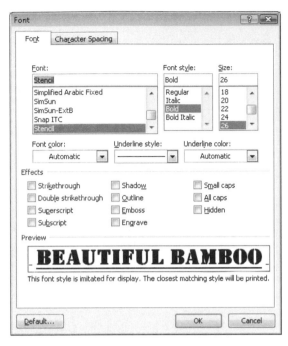

10. Click the Underline style arrow, and then in the list, click **(none)**.

11. Under **Effects**, select the **Outline** check box.

12. Click the **Character Spacing** tab.

13. Click the **Spacing** arrow, and then in the list, click **Expanded**.

14. To the right, click the **By** up arrow until the spacing is expanded by **2 pt** (points), and then click **OK**.

    The selected text appears with an outline effect and with the spacing between the characters expanded by 2 points.

Clear Formatting

15. On the **Home** tab, in the **Font** group, click the **Clear Formatting** button.

    The formatting of the selected text is removed.

Undo

16. On the **Quick Access Toolbar**, click the **Undo** button.

    The formatting of the selected text is restored.

17. In the last sentence of the second paragraph, select the words **light green**.

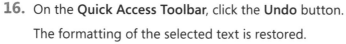

Font Color

18. On the **Home** tab, in the **Font** group, click the **Font Color** arrow, and then under **Standard Colors** in the palette, click the light green box.

    The selected words are now light green. (To see the color, clear the selection by clicking a blank area of the document.)

> **Tip** If you want to apply the Font Color button's current color, you can simply click the button (not the arrow).

19. In the same sentence, select **dark, rich shades of green**, click the **Font Color** arrow, and then below the palette, click **More Colors**.

    The Colors dialog box opens.

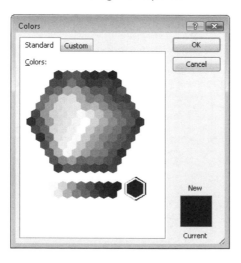

20. In the **Colors** wheel on the **Standard** tab, click one of the dark green shades on the left, and then click **OK**.

The selection is now dark green.

Highlight

21. Select the phrase **supports the environment** in the second sentence of the last paragraph. Then in the **Font** group, click the **Highlight** arrow, and under **Recent Colors** in the palette, click the green box.

This is the same green that you selected in step 20. After you select a custom color in one palette, it is available in all the palettes. The highlighted phrase now stands out from the rest of the text.

> **Tip** If you click the Highlight button without first making a selection, the mouse pointer becomes a highlighter that you can drag across text. Click the Highlight button again or press Esc to turn off the highlighter.

22. In the paragraph that begins *Because they are so easy to grow*, select the bamboo species name **chimonobambusa marmorea**. Then hold down the $\boxed{\text{Ctrl}}$ key while selecting **indocalamus tessellatus**, **pleioblastus chino vaginatus**, **bambusa glaucophylla**, and **otatea acuminata aztectorum**.

23. In the **Font** group, click the **Dialog Box Launcher**.

24. In the **Font** dialog box, click the **Font** tab, and under **Effects**, select the **Small caps** check box. Then click **OK**.

The lowercase letters in the species names now appear in small capital letters, making those names easy to find in the text.

25. Click anywhere in the first species name. Then on the **Home** tab, in the **Editing** group, click the **Select** button, and click **Select Text with Similar Formatting**.

All the species names that have been formatted in small caps are selected.

26. In the **Font** group, click the **Bold** button, and then click away from the selection.

The species names are now both small caps and bold.

Types of Bamboo¶
There are many different sizes and varieties of bamboo. It is both tropical and subtropical, growing in climates as diverse as jungles and mountainsides. Actually giant, woody grasses, it is very adaptable, with some species deciduous and others evergreen. Although there isn't yet a complete knowledge about this plant, there are believed to be between 1100 and 1500 different species of bamboo. The color range is from light green leaves and culms (stems) to dark, rich shades of green or some combination thereof.¶
¶
Because they are so easy to grow in such a variety of climates, there is a plant available for just about anyone who wishes to grow one in their backyard. Some dwarf species include **CHIMONOBAMBUSA MARMOREA**, **INDOCALAMUS TESSELLATUS**, and **PLEIOBLASTUS CHINO VAGINATUS**. Also suitable for the personal garden are those categorized as mid size. Examples of these types of plants are **BAMBUSA GLAUCOPHYLLA** and **OTATEA ACUMINATA AZTECTORUM**. Plant starts and seeds are easier to find than ever, being available at nurseries and through mail order.¶
¶
Bamboo is quickly becoming an important economic factor in many developing nations. A 60-foot tree cut for marketing can take up to 60 years to replace, whereas a 60-foot bamboo can take as little as 60 days to reach marketability. And the majority of bamboo destined for the world market is harvested by women and children, most of who live at or below subsistence levels in poor nations. So as production increases, so does support for the economies of those countries that produce it.¶
¶
Choosing bamboo as part of home or garden design makes sense on many levels. Not only does it have an appealing look, but it supports the environment as well as the countries that produce it. In particular Wide World Importers recommends chimonobambusa marmoreal.¶

CLOSE the *Characters* document without saving your changes.

More About Case and Character Formatting

The way you use case and character formatting in a document can influence its visual impact on your readers. Used judiciously, case and character formatting can make a plain document look attractive and professional, but excessive use can make it look amateurish and detract from the message. For example, using too many fonts in the same document is the mark of inexperience, so don't use more than two or three.

Bear in mind that lowercase letters tend to recede, so using all uppercase letters (capitals) can be useful for titles and headings or for certain kinds of emphasis. However, large blocks of uppercase letters are tiring to the eye.

Where do the terms uppercase and lowercase come from? Until the advent of computers, individual characters were assembled to form the words that would appear on a printed page. The characters were stored alphabetically in cases, with the capital letters in the upper case and the small letters in the lower case.

> **Tip** If you want to see a summary of the formatting applied to a selection, you can display the Style Inspector pane by clicking the Styles Dialog Box Launcher and then clicking the Style Inspector button (the middle button at the bottom of the Styles task pane). You can then click anywhere in the document to see a formatting summary of the word containing the insertion point. To see details about the formatting, you can click the Reveal Formatting button at the bottom of the Style Inspector pane to open the Reveal Formatting task pane.

Manually Changing the Look of Paragraphs

As you know, you create a *paragraph* by typing text and then pressing the Enter key. The paragraph can be a single word, a single sentence, or multiple sentences. You can change the look of a paragraph by changing its alignment, its line spacing, and the space before and after it. You can also put borders around it and shade its background. Collectively, the settings you use to vary the look of a paragraph are called *paragraph formatting*.

In Word, you don't define the width of paragraphs and the length of pages by defining the area occupied by the text; instead you define the size of the white space—the left, right, top, and bottom *margins*—around the text. You use the Margins button in the Page Setup group on the Page Layout tab to define these margins, either for the whole document or for sections of the document.

See Also For information about setting margins, see "Previewing and Printing a Document" in Chapter 1, "Exploring Word 2007."

Although the left and right margins are set for a whole document or section, you can vary the p osition of the text between the margins. The easiest way to do this is by moving controls on the horizontal ruler. You can indent paragraphs from the left and right margins, as well as specify where the first line of a paragraph begins and where the second and subsequent lines begin.

Setting a right indent indicates where all the lines in a paragraph should end, but sometimes you might want to specify where only a single line should end. For example, you might want to break a title after a particular word to make it look balanced on the page. You can end an individual line by inserting a *text wrapping break* or *line break*. After positioning the insertion point where you want the break to occur, you click the Breaks button in the Page Setup group on the Page Layout tab, and then click Text Wrapping. Word indicates the line break with a bent arrow. Inserting a line break does not start a new paragraph, so when you apply paragraph formatting to a line of text that ends with a line break, the formatting is applied to the entire paragraph, not just that line.

> **Tip** You can also press Shift+Enter to insert a line break.

You can align lines of text in different locations across the page by using *tab stops*. The easiest way to set tab stops is to use the horizontal ruler. By default, Word sets left-aligned tab stops every half-inch, as indicated by gray marks below this ruler. To set a custom tab stop, you start by clicking the Tab button located at the left end of the ruler until the type of tab stop you want appears. You have the following options:

- **Left Tab.** Aligns the left end of the text with the stop.
- **Center Tab.** Aligns the center of the text with the stop.
- **Right Tab.** Aligns the right end of the text with the stop.
- **Decimal Tab.** Aligns the decimal point in the text with the stop.
- **Bar Tab.** Draws a vertical bar aligned with the stop down the paragraph containing the insertion point.

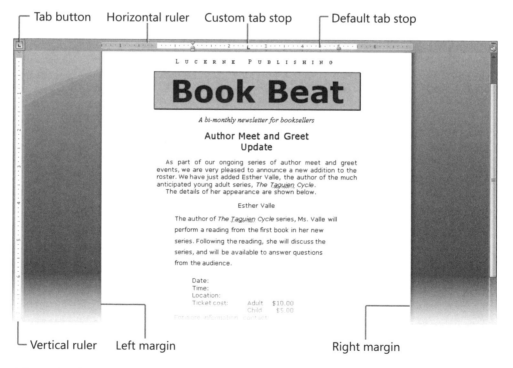

Tab button   Horizontal ruler   Custom tab stop   Default tab stop

Vertical ruler   Left margin   Right margin

After selecting the type of tab stop, you simply click the ruler where you want the tab stop to be. Word then removes any default tab stops to the left of the one you set. To change the position of an existing custom tab stop, you drag it to the left or right on the ruler. To delete a custom tab stop, you drag it away from the ruler.

To move the text to the right of the insertion point to the next tab stop, you press the Tab key. The text is then aligned on the tab stop according to its type. For example, if you set a center tab stop, pressing Tab moves the text so that its center is aligned with the tab stop.

> **Tip** When you want to fine-tune the position of tab stops, click the Paragraph Dialog Box Launcher on either the Home or Page Layout tab. In the Paragraph dialog box, click the Tabs button to display the Tabs dialog box. You might also open this dialog box if you want to use *tab leaders*—visible marks such as dots or dashes connecting the text before the tab with the text after it. For example, tab leaders are useful in a table of contents to carry the eye from the text to the page number.

In addition to tab stops, the horizontal ruler also displays *indent markers* that are used to control where each line of text starts and ends. You use these markers to indent text from the left or right margins as follows:

- **First Line Indent.** Begins a paragraph's first line of text at this marker.
- **Hanging Indent.** Begins a paragraph's second and subsequent lines of text at this marker.
- **Left Indent.** Indents the text to this marker.
- **Right Indent.** Wraps the text when it reaches this marker.

You can also determine the positioning of a paragraph between the left and right margins by changing its alignment. You can click buttons in the Paragraph group on the Home tab to align paragraphs as follows:

- **Align Left.** Aligns each line of the paragraph at the left margin, with a ragged right edge.
- **Align Right.** Aligns each line of the paragraph at the right margin, with a ragged left edge.
- **Center.** Aligns the center of each line in the paragraph between the left and right margins, with ragged left and right edges.
- **Justify.** Aligns each line between the margins, creating even left and right edges.

> **Tip** If you know that you want to type a centered paragraph, you don't have to type it and then format it as centered. You can use the *Click and Type* feature to create appropriately aligned text. Move the pointer to the center of a blank area of the page, and when the pointer's shape changes to an I-beam with centered text attached, double-click to create an insertion point that is ready to enter centered text. Similarly, you can double-click at the left edge of the page to enter left-aligned text and at the right edge to enter right-aligned text.

To make it obvious where one paragraph ends and another begins, you can add space between them by adjusting the Spacing After and Spacing Before settings in the Paragraph group on the Page Layout tab. You can adjust the spacing between the lines in a paragraph by clicking the Line Spacing button in the Paragraph group on the Home tab.

When you want to make several adjustments to the alignment, indentation, and spacing of selected paragraphs, it is sometimes quicker to use the Paragraph dialog box than to click buttons and drag markers. Click the Paragraph Dialog Box Launcher on either the Home or Page Layout tab to open the Paragraph dialog box.

To make a paragraph really stand out, you can put a border around it or shade its background. For real drama, you can do both.

> **Tip** A paragraph's formatting is stored in its paragraph mark. If you delete the paragraph mark, thereby making it part of the following paragraph, its text takes on the formatting of that paragraph. If you position the insertion point anywhere in the paragraph and press Enter to create a new one, the new paragraph takes on the existing paragraph's formatting.

In this exercise, you'll change text alignment and indentation, insert and modify tab stops, modify paragraph and line spacing, and add borders and shading around paragraphs to change their appearance.

USE the *Paragraphs* document. This practice file is located in the *Documents\Microsoft Press\2007OfficeSBS_HomeStudent\WordFormatting* folder.

BE SURE TO turn on the display of non-printing characters for this exercise. Also display the rulers.

OPEN the *Paragraphs* document.

Zoom Out

1. In the lower-right corner of the document window, click the **Zoom Out** button twice to set the zoom percentage to 80%.

   You can now see all the text of the document.

2. In the fourth line of the document, click to the left of *Update*, and then on the **Page Layout** tab, in the **Page Setup** group, click the **Breaks** button, and then click **Text Wrapping**.

Word inserts a line break character and moves the part of the paragraph that follows that character to the next line.

See Also For information about column breaks, see "Presenting Information in Columns" in Chapter 4, "Presenting Information in Columns and Tables."

Center

3. Select the first four lines of the document, and then on the **Home** tab, in the **Paragraph** group, click the **Center** button.

The lines are now centered between the margins. Notice that even though you did not select the fifth line, it is also centered because it is part of the *Author Meet and Greet* paragraph.

Text wrapping line break

Justify

4. Select the next two paragraphs, and then in the **Paragraph** group, click the **Justify** button.

The edges of the first paragraph are now flush against both the left and right margins. The second paragraph doesn't change because it is less than a line long.

First Line Indent

5. With both paragraphs still selected, on the horizontal ruler, drag the **First Line Indent** marker to the 0.25-inch mark.

The first line of each paragraph is now indented a quarter inch from the left margin.

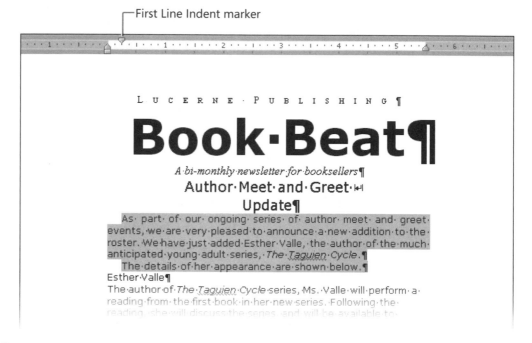

First Line Indent marker

6. Click anywhere in the *Esther Valle* paragraph, and then in the **Paragraph** group, click the **Center** button.

> **Tip** When applying paragraph formatting, you don't have to select the entire paragraph.

Left Indent

7. Select all the paragraphs below *Esther Valle*, and then on the horizontal ruler, drag the **Left Indent** marker to the 0.5-inch mark.

   The First Line Indent and Hanging Indent markers move with the Left Indent marker, and all the selected paragraphs are now indented a half inch from the left margin.

Right Indent

8. Drag the **Right Indent** marker to the 5-inch mark.

   The paragraphs are now indented from the right margin as well.

Left Indent marker   Right Indent marker

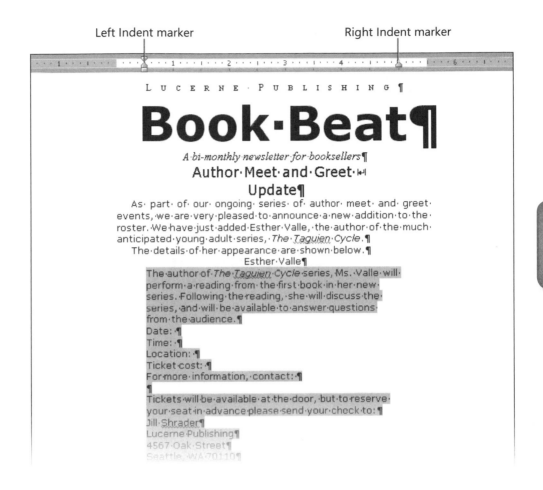

Increase Indent

9. Select the **Date:**, **Time:**, **Location:**, and **Ticket cost:** paragraphs, and then in the **Paragraph** group, click the **Increase Indent** button.

These four paragraphs are now indented to the 1-inch mark.

Left Tab

10. Without changing the selection, make sure the **Left Tab** button at the junction of the horizontal and vertical rulers is active, and then click the ruler at the 2.5-inch mark to set a left tab stop.

11. Click at the right end of the *Date:* paragraph to position the insertion point before the paragraph mark, and then press the [Tab] key.

Word will left-align any text you type after the tab character at the new tab stop.

12. Press the [↓] key, and then press [Tab].

13. Repeat step 12 for the *Location* and *Ticket cost* paragraphs.

All four paragraphs now have tabs that are aligned with the tab stop at the 2.5-inch mark.

Left-aligned tab stop

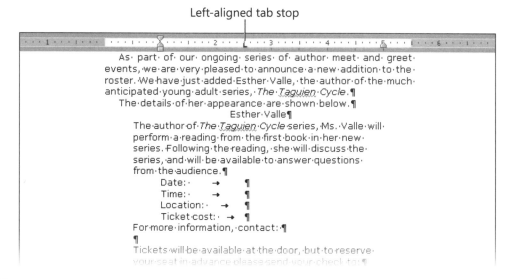

14. Without moving the insertion point, type **Adult**, and then press [Tab].

Decimal Tab

15. Click the **Tab** button three times to activate a decimal tab, and then click the 4-inch mark on the horizontal ruler.

16. Type **$10.00**, press [Enter], press [Tab] type **Child**, press [Tab] again, and then type **$5.00**.

The new paragraph takes on the same paragraph formatting as the *Ticket cost* paragraph, and the dollar amounts are aligned on their decimal points.

Decimal-aligned tab stop

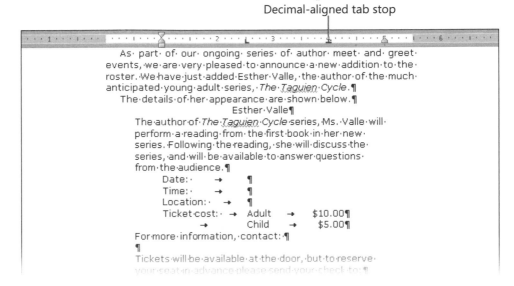

17. Drag through any part of the two paragraphs with dollar amounts, and then on the horizontal ruler, drag the decimal tab stop from the 4-inch mark to the 3.5-inch mark.

18. On the **Home** tab, in the **Editing** group, click the **Select** button, and then click **Select All**.

19. On the **Page Layout** tab, in the **Paragraph** group, change the **Spacing After** setting to **12 pt**.

    Word inserts 12 points of space after every paragraph in the document.

Line Spacing

20. Click anywhere in the paragraph that begins *As part of*, and then on the **Home** tab, in the **Paragraph** group, click the **Line Spacing** button, and then click **Remove Space After Paragraph**.

21. Select the **Date:**, **Time:**, **Location:**, and **Ticket cost:** paragraphs, and then repeat step 20.

22. Select the **Jill Shrader**, **Lucerne Publishing**, and **4567 Oak Street** paragraphs, and then repeat step 20 again.

23. Click anywhere in the paragraph that begins *The author of*, click the **Line Spacing** button again, and then click **1.5**.

You have adjusted both the paragraph and line spacing of the document.

Borders

24. Click the *Book Beat* paragraph. Then on the **Home** tab, in the **Paragraph** group, click the **Borders** arrow, and at the bottom of the list, click **Borders and Shading**.

The Borders And Shading dialog box opens.

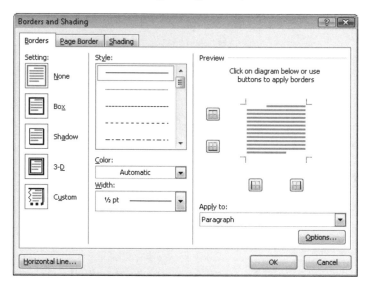

25. Under **Setting**, click the **Shadow** icon to select that border style.

> **Tip** You can change the settings in the Style, Color, and Width boxes to create the kind of border you want. If you want only one, two, or three sides of the selected paragraphs to have a border, click the buttons surrounding the image in the Preview area.

26. Click the **Shading** tab.

You can use the options on this tab to format the background of the selected paragraph.

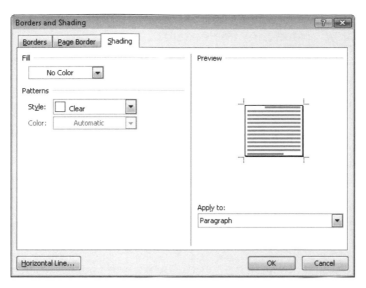

27. Click the **Fill** arrow, and under **Theme Colors**, click the second lightest purple box (**Purple, Accent 4, Lighter 60%**). Then click **OK** to close the **Borders and Shading** dialog box.

A border with a shadow surrounds the text, and the background color is light purple.

BE SURE TO change the Zoom percentage back to 100% before moving on to the next exercise, and if you want, turn off the rulers.

CLOSE the *Paragraphs* document without saving your changes.

Finding and Replacing Formatting

In addition to searching for words and phrases, you can use the Find And Replace dialog box to search for a specific format and replace it with a different format.

To search for a specific format and replace it with a different format:

1. On the **Home** tab, in the **Editing** group, click the **Replace** button.

   The Find And Replace dialog box opens, displaying the Replace tab.

2. Click **More** to expand the dialog box, click **Format**, and then click **Font** or **Paragraph**.

   The Find Font or Find Paragraph dialog box opens. (You can also click Style to search for paragraph styles or character styles.)

3. In the dialog box, click the format you want to find, and then click **OK**.

4. Click the **Replace with** text box, click **Format**, click **Font** or **Paragraph**, click the format you want to substitute for the Find What format, and then click **OK**.

5. Click **Find Next** to search for the first occurrence of the format, and then click **Replace** to replace that one instance or **Replace All** to replace every instance.

Creating and Modifying Lists

When you want to present a list of items in a document, you will usually want to put each item on its own line rather than burying the items in a paragraph. When the order of items is not important—for example, for a list of items needed to carry out a task—use a bulleted list. When the order is important—for example, for the steps in a procedure—use a numbered list.

With Word, you start a bulleted or numbered list as follows:

- To create a bulleted list, type * (an asterisk) at the beginning of a paragraph, and then press the Spacebar or the Tab key.

- To create a numbered list, type 1. (the numeral 1 followed by a period) at the beginning of a paragraph, and then press the Spacebar or the Tab key.

In either case, you then type the first item in the list and press Enter. Word starts the new paragraph with a bullet or 2 followed by a period and formats the first and second paragraphs as a numbered list. Typing items and pressing Enter adds subsequent bulleted or numbered items. To end the list, press Enter twice, or press Enter and then Backspace.

> **Troubleshooting** If you want to start a paragraph with an asterisk or number but don't want the paragraph to be formatted as a bulleted or numbered list, click the AutoCorrect Options button that appears after Word changes the formatting, and then click Undo.

After you create a list, you can modify, format, and customize the list as follows:

- You can move items around in a list, insert new items, or delete unwanted items. If the list is numbered, Word automatically updates the numbers.

- You can sort items in a bulleted list into ascending or descending order by clicking the Sort button in the Paragraph group on the Home tab.

- For a bulleted list, you can change the bullet symbol by clicking the Bullets arrow in the Paragraph group and making a selection from the Bullet Library. You can also define a custom bullet by clicking the Bullets arrow and then clicking Define New Bullet.

- For a numbered list, you can change the number style by clicking the Numbering arrow in the Paragraph group and making a selection from the Numbering Library. You can also define a custom style by clicking the Numbering arrow and then clicking Define New Number Format.

- You can create a multilevel bulleted list, numbered list, or outline by clicking the Multilevel List button in the Paragraph group, selecting a style from the List Library, and then typing the list. You press Enter to create a new item at the same level, the Tab key to move down a level, and the Backspace key to move up a level.

  See Also For information about another way to create an outline, see "Reorganizing a Document Outline" in Chapter 2, "Editing and Proofreading Documents."

- You can modify the indentation of the list by dragging the indent markers on the horizontal ruler. Lists are set up with the first line "outdented" to the left from the other lines, and you can change both the overall indentation of the list and the relationship of the first line to the other lines.

In this exercise, you will create a bulleted list and a numbered list and then modify lists in various ways. You will then create a multilevel list with letters instead of numbers.

USE the *Lists* document. This practice file is located in the *Documents\Microsoft Press\2007OfficeSBS_HomeStudent\WordFormatting* folder.

OPEN the *Lists* document.

Bullets

1. Select the three paragraphs under *Rationale*, and then on the **Home** tab, in the **Paragraph** group, click the **Bullets** button.

The selected paragraphs are reformatted as a bulleted list.

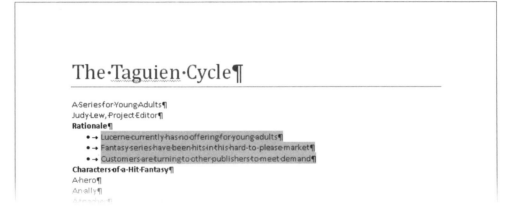

2. With the three paragraphs still selected, in the **Paragraph** group, click the **Bullets** arrow.

The Bullet Library appears.

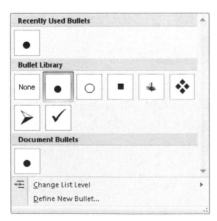

3. In the gallery, click the bullet composed of four diamonds.

   The bullet character in the selected list changes.

4. Select the four paragraphs under *Characters of a Hit Fantasy*, and then in the **Paragraph** group, click the **Bullets** button.

   The new list has the bullet character you selected for the previous list. This character will be the default until you change it.

5. Select the paragraphs under each of the bold headings, and then in the **Paragraph** group, click the **Bullets** button.

6. Scroll to the bottom of the page, select the four paragraphs under *The Sequence of Events*, and then in the **Paragraph** group, in the **Bullets Library**, click **None**.

   The bulleted paragraphs revert to normal paragraphs.

Numbering

7. With the paragraphs still selected, on the **Home** tab, in the **Paragraph** group, click the **Numbering** button.

   The selected paragraphs are reformatted as a numbered list.

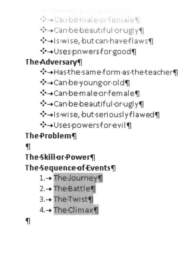

8. In the **Paragraph** group, click the **Numbering** arrow.

The Numbering Library appears.

Recently Used Number Formats
1. ————
2. ————
3. ————

Numbering Library

None	1. ———— 2. ———— 3. ————	1) ———— 2) ———— 3) ————
I. ———— II. ———— III. ————	A. ———— B. ———— C. ————	a) ———— b) ———— c) ————
a. ———— b. ———— c. ————	i. ———— ii. ———— iii. ————	

Document Number Formats
1. ————
2. ————
3. ————

⇥ Change List Level ▸
Define New Number Format...
✎ Set Numbering Value...

9. In the gallery, click the **A. B. C.** box.

The numbers change to capital letters.

Decrease Indent

10. With the numbered paragraphs still selected, in the **Paragraph** group, click the **Decrease Indent** button.

The numbered list moves to the left margin.

Increase Indent

11. In the **Paragraph** group, click the **Increase Indent** button to move the list back to its original indent.

> **Tip** You can also adjust the indent level of a bulleted list by selecting its paragraphs, and on the horizontal ruler, dragging the Left Indent marker to the left or right. The First Line Indent and Hanging Indent markers move with the Left Indent marker. You can move just the Hanging Indent marker to adjust the space between the bullets and their text.

Sort

12. Scroll the document until you can see the bulleted list under *The Hero*, select the three bulleted paragraphs, and then on the **Home** tab, in the **Paragraph** group, click the **Sort** button.

The Sort Text dialog box opens.

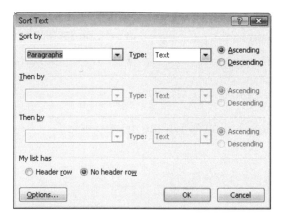

13. With **Ascending** clicked, click **OK**.

The order of the bulleted items changes to ascending alphabetical order.

Multilevel List

14. Click the blank paragraph under *The Ally*, and then on the **Home** tab, in the **Paragraph** group, click the **Multilevel List** button.

The List Library appears.

15. In the gallery, click the thumbnail under **Current List**.

The first item in the new numbered list will have a capital letter as its numbering style.

16. Type Does not have to be human, press [Enter], type Is a stabilizing force, press [Enter], and then press [Tab].

The new item is indented to the next level and assigned a different number style.

17. Type A voice of conscience, press [Enter], type Not a "yes" person, press [Enter], and then press [Shift]+[Tab].

18. Type Embodies loyalty.

Word takes care of all the formatting of the multilevel list.

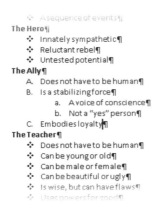

19. Under *The Problem*, click to the left of the blank paragraph mark, type * (an asterisk), press [Tab], type A difficult choice, and then press [Enter].

Word converts the asterisk into a bullet and formats the next paragraph as a bulleted item.

20. Type An injustice, press [Enter], and then type A quest.

CLOSE the *Lists* document without saving your changes. If you are not proceeding directly to the next chapter, exit Word.

Formatting Text as You Type

The Word list formatting capabilities are just one example of the program's ability to intuit how you want to format an element based on what you type. You can learn more about these and other AutoFormatting options by exploring the AutoCorrect dialog box. To open this dialog box, click the Microsoft Office Button, click Word Options, click Proofing in the left pane of the Word Options window, and then click AutoCorrect Options in the right pane.

On the AutoFormat As You Type tab, you can see the options that Word implements by default, including bulleted and numbered lists. You can select and clear options to control Word's AutoFormatting behavior.

One interesting option is Border Lines. When this check box is selected, you can type three consecutive hyphens (-) and press Enter to have Word draw a single line across the page. Or you can type three consecutive equal signs (=) and press Enter to have Word draw a double line.

Key Points

- Quick Styles are a great way to apply combinations of formatting to give your documents a professional look.

- You can format characters with an almost limitless number of combinations of font, size, style, and effect—but for best results, resist the temptation to use more than a handful of combinations.

- You can change the look of paragraphs by varying their indentation, spacing, and alignment and by setting tab stops. Use these formatting options judiciously to create documents with a balanced, uncluttered look.

- Bulleted and numbered lists are a great way to present information in an easy to read, easy to understand format. If the built-in bulleted and numbered list styles don't provide what you need, you can define your own styles.

Chapter at a Glance

Present information in a table, **page 104**

Present information in columns, **page 98**

Perform calculations in a table, **page 116**

Use a table to control page layout, **page 124**

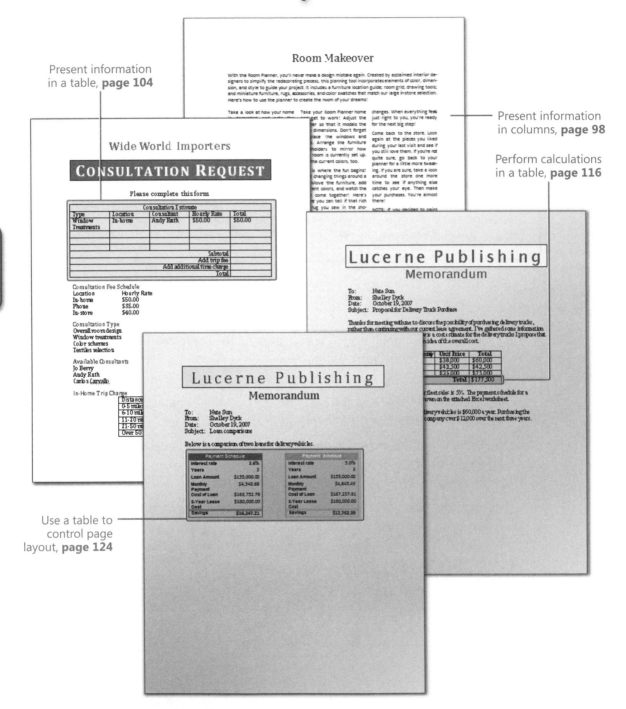

4 Presenting Information in Columns and Tables

In this chapter, you will learn to:

✔ Present information in columns.

✔ Create a tabular list.

✔ Present information in a table.

✔ Format table information.

✔ Perform calculations in a table.

✔ Use a table to control page layout.

When creating a Microsoft Office Word 2007 document, you might find it useful to organize certain information into columns or tables. Flowing text in multiple columns is common practice in newsletters, flyers, and brochures. After you specify the number of columns, Word flows the text from one column to the next. You can also manually end one column and move subsequent text to the next column.

It is often more efficient to present numeric data in a table than to explain it in a paragraph of text. Tables make the data easier to read and understand. Small amounts of data can be displayed in simple columns separated by left, right, centered, or decimal tab stops to create a tabular list. Larger amounts or more complex data is better presented in a Word table that includes a structure of rows and columns, frequently with row and column headings.

A Word table is useful not only for presenting data but also for providing the structure for complex document layouts. For example, you can set up a table with two columns and two rows to present a set of four paragraphs, four bulleted lists, or four tables in a format in which they can be easily compared.

In this chapter, you will create and modify columns of text, create a simple tabular list, create tables from scratch and from existing text, format a table in various ways, and perform calculations within a table. You will copy and paste worksheet data, link to worksheet data, and create a Microsoft Office Excel 2007 object. And finally, you will create a table for the purpose of displaying two other tables side by side.

See Also Do you need only a quick refresher on the topics in this chapter? See the Quick Reference entries at the beginning of this book.

Important Before you can use the practice files in this chapter, you need to install them from the book's companion CD to their default location. See "Using the Book's CD" at the beginning of this book for more information.

Troubleshooting Graphics and operating system–related instructions in this book reflect the Windows Vista user interface. If your computer is running Windows XP and you experience trouble following the instructions as written, please refer to the "Information for Readers Running Windows XP" section at the beginning of this book.

Presenting Information in Columns

By default, Word displays text in one *column*, but you can specify that text be displayed in two, three, or more columns to create layouts like those used in newspapers and magazines. When you format text to *flow* in columns, the text fills the first column and then moves to the top of the next column. You can insert a *column break* to move to the next column before the current column is full.

Word provides several standard options for dividing text into columns. You have the choice of one, two, or three equal columns, or two other two-column formats: one with a narrow left column and the other with a narrow right column. No matter how you set up the columns initially, you can change the layout or column widths at any time.

You can format the text in columns the same way you would any text. If you *justify* the columns for a neater look, you might want to have Word hyphenate the text to ensure that there are no large gaps between words.

In this exercise, you will divide part of a document into three columns. You will then justify the columns, change the column spacing, hyphenate the text, and indent a couple of paragraphs. You'll also break a column at a specific location instead of allowing the text to flow naturally from one column to the next.

> **USE** the *Columns* document. This practice file is located in the *Documents\Microsoft Press\2007OfficeSBS_HomeStudent\WordPresenting* folder.
>
> **BE SURE TO** display the rulers and non-printing characters before starting this exercise.
>
> **OPEN** the *Columns* document.

1. Click just to the left of the paragraph that begins *Take a look* (do not click in the selection area). Then scroll the end of the document into view, hold down the `Shift` key, and click just to the right of the period after *credit cards*.

   Word selects the text from the *Take a look* paragraph through the end of the document.

   > **Tip** If you want to format an entire document with the same number of columns, you can simply click anywhere in the document—you don't have to select the text.

2. On the **Page Layout** tab, in the **Page Setup** group, click the **Columns** button, and then click **Three**.

3. Press `Ctrl`+`Home` to move to the top of the document.

   Word has inserted a section break above the selection and formatted the text after the section break into three columns.

Room·Makeover¶

With·the·Room·Planner,·you'll·never·make·a·design·mistake·again.·Created·by·acclaimed·interior·designers·to·simplify·the·redecorating·process,·this·planning·tool·incorporates·elements·of·color,·dimension,·and·style·to·guide·your·project.·It·includes·a·furniture·location·guide;·room·grid;·drawing·tools;·and·miniature·furniture,·rugs,·accessories,·and·color·swatches·that·match·our·large·in·store·selection.·Here's·how·to·use·the·planner·to·create·the·room·of·your·dreams!¶

¶ ═══════════════════ Section·Break·(Continuous) ═══════════════════

Take·a·look·at·how·your·home·is·decorated·and·note·the·things·you·like·and·dislike.·Pay·special·attention·to·the·color·scheme·and·to·how·each·room·"feels"·to·you.·Is·it·inviting?·Does·it·feel·comfortable?·Does·it·relax·you·or·does·it·invigorate·you?¶

love,·and·the·rest·will·fall·into·place.¶

Take·your·Room·Planner·home·and·get·to·work!·Adjust·the·planner·so·that·it·models·the·room·dimensions.·Don't·forget·to·place·the·windows·and·doors.·Arrange·the·furniture·placeholders·to·mirror·how·

design·for·a·day·or·two.·Then·review·it·again.·Does·it·still·look·perfect,·or·is·something·not·quite·right?·You·might·need·to·"live"·with·the·new·plan·for·a·few·days,·especially·if·you've·made·big·changes.·When·everything·feels·just·right·to·you,·you're·ready·for·the·next·big·step!¶

4. On the **Home** tab, in the **Editing** group, click the **Select** button, and then click **Select All**.

Justify

5. In the **Paragraph** group, click the **Justify** button.

The spacing of the text within the paragraphs changes so the right edge of the paragraph is straight.

Center

6. Press Ctrl + Home to deselect the text and move to the top of the document, and then in the **Paragraph** group, click the **Center** button to center the title.

7. At the right end of the status bar, click the **Zoom** button. Then in the **Zoom** dialog box, click **75%**, and click **OK**.

You can now see about two-thirds of the first page of the document.

8. Click anywhere in the first column.

On the horizontal ruler, Word indicates the margins of the columns.

9. On the **Page Layout** tab, in the **Page Setup** group, click the **Columns** button, and then click **More Columns**.

The Columns dialog box opens. Because the Equal Column Width check box is selected, you can adjust the width and spacing of only the first column.

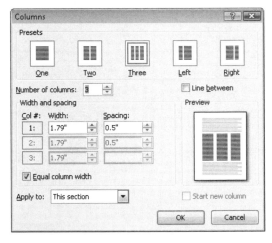

10. Under **Width and spacing**, in the **Spacing** column, click the down arrow until the setting is **0.2"**.

Word changes the measurement in the box below and widens all the columns to reflect the new setting.

11. Click **OK**.

Word reflows the columns to fit their new margins.

Room·Makeover¶

With·the·Room·Planner,·you'll·never·make·a·design·mistake·again.·Created·by·acclaimed·interior· designers·to·simplify·the·redecorating·process,·this·planning·tool·incorporates·elements·of·color,· dimension,·and·style·to·guide·your·project.·It·includes·a·furniture·location·guide;·room·grid;·drawing· tools;·and·miniature·furniture,·rugs,·accessories,·and·color·swatches·that·match·our·large·in-store· selection.·Here's·how·to·use·the·planner·to·create·the·room·of·your·dreams!·¶
¶··················Section·Break·(Continuous)··················

Take·a·look·at·how·your·home· is· decorated· and· note· the· things·you·like·and·dislike.·Pay· special· attention· to·the·color· scheme·and·to·how·each·room· "feels"· to· you.· Is· it· inviting?· Does·it·feel·comfortable?·Does· it·relax·you·or·does·it·invigorate· you?·¶

Focus· on· the· room(s)· you· would· most· like· to· change.· Brainstorm· all·the·things·you· would·change·in·that·room·if· you·could.·Don't·give·a·thought· to·any·financial·considerations;· just·let·your·imagine·go·wild!·It· might·be·helpful·to·write·down· all·the·negatives·and·positives.· You·don't·need·to·come·up·with·

planner·so· that· it·models·the· room·dimensions.·Don't·forget· to· place· the· windows· and· doors.· Arrange· the· furniture· placeholders· to· mirror· how· your·room·is·currently·set·up.· Add·the·current·colors,·too.·¶

This· is·where·the·fun·begins!· Start·changing·things·around·a· bit.· Move· the· furniture,· add· different·colors,·and·watch·the· room· come· together!· Here's· where·you·can·tell·if·that·rich· red· rug· you· saw· in· the· showroom· enhances· or· overwhelms·your·room.·What· about· that· overstuffed· chair· that·caught·your·eye?·Place·a· furniture· or· accessory·shape,·

just·right·to·you,·you're·ready· for·the·next·big·step!·¶

Come·back·to·the·store.·Look· again· at·the·pieces·you·liked· during·your·last·visit·and·see·if· you·still·love·them.·If·you're·not· quite· sure,· go· back· to· your· planner· for· a· little· more· tweaking.·If·you·are·sure,·take·a· look·around·the·store·one·more· time· to· see· if· anything· else· catches· your·eye.·Then·make· your·purchases.·You're·almost· there!·¶

NOTE:· If·you·decided·to·paint· your·room,·do·that·before·your· new·pieces·are·delivered.·You'll· want·to·start·enjoying·your·new· room·as·soon·as·your·purchases·

12. Click immediately to the left of *Take a look*. Then in the **Page Setup** group, click the **Hyphenation** button, and click **Automatic**.

Word hyphenates the text of the document, which fills in some of the large gaps between words.

13. Click anywhere in the *NOTE* paragraph in the third column.

14. On the horizontal ruler, in the third column, drag the **Hanging Indent** marker 0.25 inch (two marks) to the right.

All the lines in the *NOTE* paragraph except the first are now indented, offsetting the note from the paragraphs above and below it.

15. Click just to the left of *Take your Room Planner home* at the bottom of the first column on page 1. Then in the **Page Setup** group, click the **Breaks** button, and click **Column**.

The text that follows the column break moves to the top of the second column.

Repeat Insertion

16. Click just to the left of *If you're not sure* at the bottom of the third column on page 1, and then on the **Quick Access Toolbar**, click the **Repeat Insertion** button to insert another column break.

The text that follows the column break moves to the top of the first column on page 2.

CLOSE the *Columns* document without saving your changes.

Creating a Tabular List

If you have a relatively small amount of data to present in a table, you might choose to display it in a *tabular list*, which arranges text in simple columns separated by left, right, centered, or decimal tab stops.

See Also For more information about setting tab stops, see "Manually Changing the Look of Paragraphs" in Chapter 3, "Changing the Look of Text."

When entering text in a tabular list, people have a tendency to press the Tab key multiple times to align the columns of the list. If you do this, you have no control over the column widths. To be able to fine-tune the columns, you need to set custom tab stops rather than relying on the default ones. When you want to set up a tabular list, you should press Tab only once between the items that you want to appear in separate columns. You can then apply any necessary formatting and set the tabs in order from left to right so that you can see how everything lines up.

> **Tip** In addition to left, right, centered, and decimal tabs, you can set a bar tab. This type of tab does not align text like the others, but instead adds a vertical line to selected paragraphs. This bar can be used to further distinguish the columns in a tabular list.

In this exercise, you will create a tabular list. First you'll enter text separated by tabs, and then you'll format the text and set custom tab stops.

USE the *TabularList* document. This practice file is located in the *Documents\Microsoft Press\2007OfficeSBS_HomeStudent\WordPresenting* folder.
BE SURE TO display the rulers and non-printing characters before starting this exercise.
OPEN the *TabularList* document.

1. Scroll down to the bottom of the document, click to the left of the paragraph mark at the end of *The Skill or Power*, and then press ⌈ Enter ⌋.

2. Type Self, press `Tab`, type Other People, press `Tab`, type Nature, and then press `Enter`.

3. Add three more lines to the list by typing the following text. Press `Tab` once between each item in a line, and press `Enter` at the end of each line except the last.

Transformation `Tab` *Life/death* `Tab` *Weather*

Time travel `Tab` *Telepathy* `Tab` *Oceans*

Visible/invisible `Tab` *Mind control* `Tab` *Animals*

The tab characters push the items to the next default tab stop, but because some items are longer than others, they do not line up.

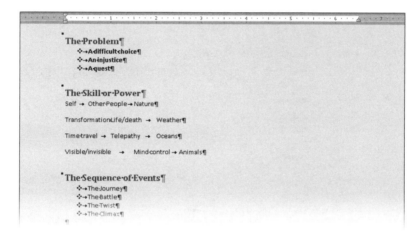

See Also For information about tab stops, see "Manually Changing the Look of Paragraphs" in Chapter 3, "Changing the Look of Text."

Bold

4. Select the first line of the tabular list, and then on the **Mini toolbar** that appears, click the **Bold** button.

> **Troubleshooting** If the Mini toolbar doesn't appear, click the Bold button in the Font group on the Home tab.

Increase
Indent

5. Select all four lines of the tabular list, and then on the **Mini toolbar**, click the **Increase Indent** button.

6. With the lines still selected, on the **Page Layout** tab, in the **Paragraph** group, under **Spacing**, change the **After** setting to 0 pt.

Left Tab

7. Without changing the selection, verify that the **Tab** button at the junction of the horizontal and vertical rulers shows a Left Tab stop (an L), and then click the 2-inch mark on the horizontal ruler.

   Word displays a Left Tab stop on the ruler, and the items in the second column of all the selected lines left-align themselves at that position.

8. Click the **Tab** button twice.

   The icon on the button changes to a Right Tab stop (a backward L), indicating that clicking the ruler now will set a right-aligned tab.

9. Click the horizontal ruler at the 4-inch mark.

   Word displays a Right Tab stop on the ruler, and the items in the third column of the selected lines jump to right-align themselves at that position.

Show/Hide ¶

10. On the **Home** tab, in the **Paragraph** group, click the **Show/Hide ¶** button to hide non-printing characters. Then click away from the tabular list to see the results.

    The tabular list resembles a simple table.

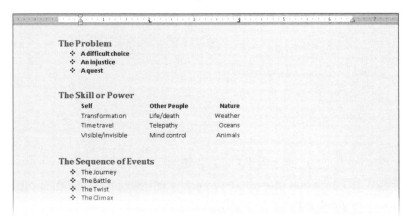

CLOSE the *TabularList* document without saving your changes.

Presenting Information in a Table

Creating a Word table is a simple matter of clicking the Table button and selecting the number of rows and columns you want from a grid. You can then enter text, numbers, and graphics into the table's *cells*, which are the boxes at the intersections of a row and a column. At any time, you can change the table's size; insert and delete columns, rows, and cells; and format individual entries or the entire table. You can sort the information in a logical order and perform calculations on the numbers in a column or row.

Clicking the Table button creates a table with the number of columns and rows you select from the grid, with all the cells of equal size. You can click Insert Table below the grid to open the Insert Table dialog box, where you can specify the number of rows and columns as well as their sizes. You can also create a table by drawing cells the size you want. If the text you want to appear in a table already exists in the document, you can convert the text to a table.

See Also For information about drawing tables, see "Using a Table to Control Page Layout" later in this chapter.

A new table appears in the document as a set of blank cells surrounded by *gridlines*. Each cell has an end-of-cell marker, and each row has an end-of-row marker. When the pointer is over the table, the table has a move handle in its upper-left corner and a size handle in its lower-right corner. While the insertion point is in the table, Word displays two Table Tools contextual tabs, Design and Layout.

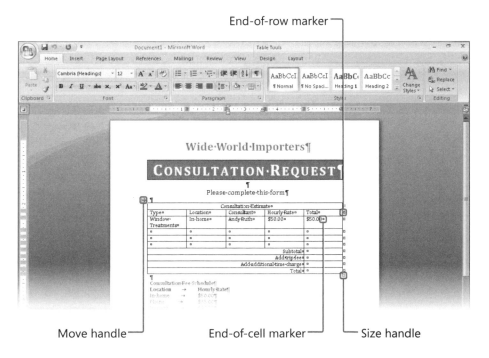

End-of-row marker

Move handle — End-of-cell marker — Size handle

Tip You cannot see the move handle and size handle in Draft view.

After you create a table, you can type text or numbers into cells and press the Tab key to move the insertion point from cell to cell. Pressing Tab when the insertion point is in the last cell in the last row adds a new row to the bottom of the table. In addition to the Tab key, you can use the Arrow keys to position the insertion point, or you can simply click any cell.

You can modify a table's structure at any time. To change the structure, you often need to select the entire table or specific rows or columns, by using the following methods:

- **Select a table.** Click anywhere in the table. Then on the Layout contextual tab, in the Table group, click the Select button, and click Select Table.

- **Select a column.** Point to the top border of the column. When the pointer changes to a black, down-pointing arrow, click once.

- **Select a row.** Point to the left border of the row. When the pointer changes to a white, right-pointing arrow, click once.

- **Select a cell.** Triple-click the cell or click its left border.

- **Select multiple cells.** Click the first cell, hold down the Shift key, and press the arrow keys to select adjacent cells in a column or row.

The basic methods for manipulating tables are as follows:

- **Insert a row or column.** Click anywhere in a row or column adjacent to where you want to make the insertion. Then on the Layout tab, in the Rows & Columns group, click the Insert Above, Insert Below, Insert Left, or Insert Right button. Selecting more than one row or column before you click an Insert button inserts that number of rows or columns in the table.

> **Tip** You can insert cells by clicking the Rows & Columns Dialog Box Launcher and specifying in the Insert Cells dialog box how adjacent cells should be moved to accommodate the new cells.

- **Delete a row or column.** Click anywhere in the row or column, and in the Rows & Columns group, click the Delete button. Then click Delete Cells, Delete Columns, Delete Rows, or Delete Table.

- **Size an entire table.** Drag the size handle.

- **Size a single column or row.** Drag a column's right border to the left or right. Drag a row's bottom border up or down.

- **Merge cells.** Create cells that span columns by selecting the cells you want to merge and clicking the Merge Cells button in the Merge group on the Layout tab. For example, to center a title in the first row of a table, you can create one merged cell that spans the table's width.

- **Split cells.** Divide a merged cell into its component cells by clicking Split Cells in the Merge group on the Layout tab.

- **Move a table.** Point to the table, and then drag the move handle that appears in its upper-left corner to a new location. Or use the Cut and Paste buttons in the Clipboard group on the Home tab to move the table.

- **Sort information.** Use the Sort button in the Data group on the Layout tab to sort the rows in ascending or descending order by the data in any column. For example, you can sort a table that has the column headings Name, Address, ZIP Code, and Phone Number on any one of those columns to arrange the information in alphabetical or numerical order.

In this exercise, you will work with two tables. First you'll create a table, enter text, align text in the cells, add rows, and merge cells. Then you'll create a second table by converting existing tabbed text, you'll size a column, and you'll size the entire table.

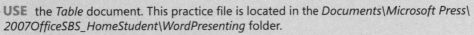

USE the *Table* document. This practice file is located in the *Documents\Microsoft Press\2007OfficeSBS_HomeStudent\WordPresenting* folder.

OPEN the *Table* document.

1. Click in the second blank line below *Please complete this form.*

2. On the **Insert** tab, in the **Tables** group, click the **Table** button, point to the upper-left cell, and move the pointer across five columns and down five rows.

   Word highlights the cells as you drag across them and creates a temporary table in the document to show you what the selection will look like.

3. Click the lower-right cell in the selection.

Word creates a blank table with five columns and five rows. The insertion point is located in the first cell. Because the table is active, Word displays the Table Tools Design and Layout contextual tabs.

4. In the selection area, point to the first row, and then click to select the row.

5. On the **Layout** contextual tab, in the **Merge** group, click the **Merge Cells** button.

Word combines the five cells in the first row into one cell.

Align Center

6. With the merged cell selected, in the **Alignment** group, click the **Align Center** button.

The end-of-cell marker moves to the center of the merged cell to indicate that anything you type there will be centered.

7. Type **Consultation Estimate**.

The table now has a title.

8. Click the first cell in the second row, type **Type**, and then press `Tab`.

9. Type **Location**, **Consultant**, **Hourly Rate**, and **Total**, pressing [Tab] after each entry.

The table now has a row of column headings. Pressing Tab after the *Total* heading moves the insertion point to the first cell of the third row.

10. Type **Window Treatments**, **In-home**, **Andy Ruth**, **$50.00**, and **$50.00**, pressing [Tab] after each entry.

You have entered a complete row of data.

Wide·World·Importers¶

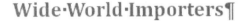

¶
Please·complete·this·form¶

¶

Consultation·Estimate◻					◻
Type◻	Location◻	Consultant◻	Hourly Rate◻	Total◻	◻
Window· Treatments◻	In-home◻	Andy Ruth◻	$50.00◻	$50.00◻	◻
◻	◻	◻	◻	◻	◻
◻	◻	◻	◻	◻	◻

¶

11. Select the last two rows, and then on the **Layout** tab, in the **Rows & Columns** group, click the **Insert Below** button.

Insert Below

Word adds two new rows and selects them.

12. In the last row, click the first cell, hold down the [Shift] key, and then press the [→] key four times to select the first four cells in the row.

13. In the **Merge** group, click the **Merge Cells** button.

Word combines the selected cells into one cell.

14. In the **Alignment** group, click the **Align Center Right** button.

Align Center
Right

15. Type Subtotal, and then press [Tab] twice.

Word adds a new row with the same structure to the bottom of the table.

16. Type Add trip fee, press [Tab] twice to add a new row, and then type Add additional time charge.

17. Press [Tab] twice to add a new row, and then type Total.

18. Scroll to the bottom of the document, and select the rows of the tabular list beginning with *Distance* and ending with *$20.00*.

19. On the **Insert** tab, in the **Tables** group, click the **Table** button, and then click **Convert Text to Table**.

The Convert Text To Table dialog box opens.

> **Tip** To convert a table to text, select the table, and then click the Convert To Text button in the Data group on the Layout tab.

20. Verify that the **Number of columns** box displays **2**, and then click **OK**.

The selected text appears in a table with two columns and six rows.

21. Click anywhere in the table to release the selection, and point to the right border of the table. When the pointer changes to two opposing arrows, double-click the right border.

Word adjusts the width of the right column so that it is exactly wide enough to contain its longest line of text.

Jo Berry¶
Andy Ruth¶
Carlos Carvallo¶

In-Home Trip Charge¶

Distance□	Fee□	□
0-5 miles□	No charge□	□
6-10 miles□	$5.50□	□
11-20 miles□	$7.00□	□
21-50 miles□	$10.00□	□
Over 50 miles□	$20.00□	□

¶

22. Point to the In-Home Trip Charge table.

Word displays the move handle in the upper-left corner and the size handle in the lower-right corner.

23. Drag the size handle to the right, releasing the mouse button when the right edge of the table aligns approximately with the 4-inch mark on the horizontal ruler.

CLOSE the *Table* document without saving your changes.

Other Layout Options

You can control many aspects of a table by clicking Properties in the Table group on the Layout tab to display the Table Properties dialog box. You can then set the following options:

- On the Table tab, you can specify the preferred width of the entire table, as well as the way it interacts with the surrounding text.

- On the Row tab, you can specify the height of each row, whether a row is allowed to break across pages, and whether a row of column headings should be repeated at the top of each page.

> **Tip** The Repeat As Header Row option is available only if the insertion point is in the top row of the table.

- On the Column tab, you can set the width of each column.

- On the Cell tab, you can set the preferred width of cells and the vertical alignment of text within them.

> **Tip** You can also control the widths of selected cells by using the buttons in the Cell Size group on the Layout contextual tab.

- You can control the margins of cells (how close text comes to the cell border) by clicking the Options button on either the Table or Cell tab.

> **Tip** You can also control the margins by clicking the Cell Margins button in the Alignment group on the Layout contextual tab.

If the first row of your table has several long headings that make it difficult to fit the table on one page, you can turn the headings sideways. Simply select the heading row and click the Text Direction button in the Alignment group on the Layout tab.

Formatting Table Information

Formatting a table to best convey its data is often a process of trial and error. With Word 2007, you can quickly get started by creating a *quick table*, a preformatted table with sample data that you can customize. You can then apply one of the *table styles* available on the Design contextual tab, which include a variety of borders, colors, and other attributes to give the table a professional look.

To customize the appearance of a quick table or a table you have created from scratch, you can use the buttons on the Design and Layout contextual tabs. You can also use buttons in the Paragraph group on the Home tab to change alignment and spacing. You can format the text by using the buttons in the Font group, just as you would to format any text in a Word document. You can also apply character formatting from the Styles gallery.

In this exercise, you will create a quick table and then apply a table style to it. You will then change some of the text attributes and modify the borders and shading in various cells to make the formatting suit the table's data. There are no practice files for this exercise.

> **BE SURE TO** display non-printing characters before starting this exercise.
>
> **OPEN** a new, blank document.

1. With the Zoom level at 100%, on the **Insert** tab, in the **Tables** group, click the **Table** button, and then point to **Quick Tables**.

   The Quick Tables gallery opens.

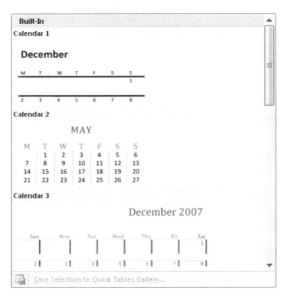

2. Scroll through the gallery, noticing the types of tables that are available, and then click **Matrix**.

   Word inserts the selected table and displays the Design contextual tab . Notice that the table data includes headings across the top and down the left column. Some of the cells are blank, and obviously have less importance than the cells that contain numbers. The table does not include summary data, such as totals.

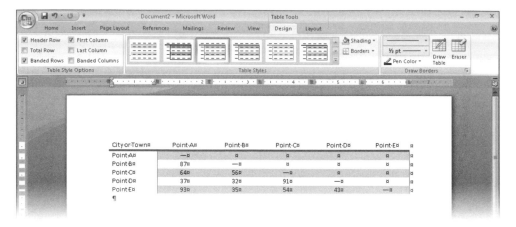

3. On the **Design** tab, in the **Table Style Options** group, clear the **Banded Rows** check box.

More

4. In the **Table Styles** group, point to each style in turn to see its live preview, and then click the **More** button.

Word displays the Table Styles gallery.

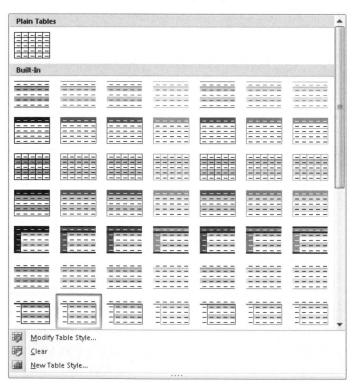

5. Explore all the styles in the gallery. When you finish exploring, click the **Medium Shading 2 – Accent 2** thumbnail.

You need to modify this style a bit, but it is a good starting point.

6. Select all the white cells by dragging through them. Then in the **Table Styles** group, click the **Borders** arrow, and in the list, click **All Borders**.

7. Select all the cells in the last row (*Point E*) by clicking to its left, and in the **Table Styles** group, in the **Borders** list, click **Borders and Shading**.

The Borders And Shading dialog box opens, displaying the borders applied to the selected cells. The thick gray borders in the Preview area indicate that different borders are applied to different cells in the selection.

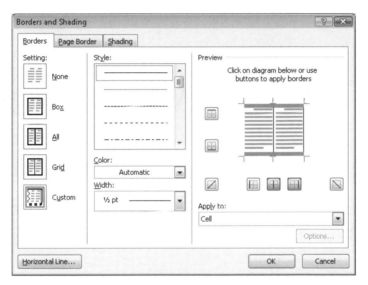

8. In the **Preview** area, click the bottom border of the diagram twice to remove all bottom borders.

9. Click the **Color** arrow, and then under **Theme Colors**, click the black box (**Black, Text 1**).

10. Click the **Width** arrow, and then in the list, click **2 1/4 pt**.

11. In the **Preview** area, click the bottom border of the diagram, and then click **OK**.

The table now has the same border at the top and bottom.

12. Select the empty cells in the *Point A* row. In the **Table Styles** group, click the **Shading** arrow, and then under **Theme Colors**, click the lightest burgundy box (**Red, Accent 2, Lighter 80%**).

13. Repeat step 12 for all the remaining blank cells in the table.

14. Select the dash in the cell at the junction of the *Point A* column and the *Point A* row, hold down the Ctrl key, and select the other four dashes.

15. On the **Mini toolbar**, click the **Font Color** arrow, and then under **Standard Colors** in the palette, click the bright **Red** box.

> **Troubleshooting** If the Mini toolbar doesn't appear, click the Font Color arrow in the Font group on the Home tab.

Show/Hide ¶

16. Click outside the table to release the selection, and then in the **Paragraph** group, click the **Show/Hide ¶** button to hide non-printing characters.

You can now judge how well the table displays its data.

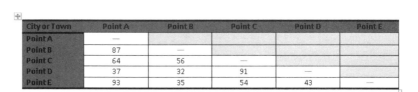

City or Town	Point A	Point B	Point C	Point D	Point E
Point A	—				
Point B	87	—			
Point C	64	56	—		
Point D	37	32	91	—	
Point E	93	35	54	43	—

 CLOSE the document without saving your changes.

Performing Calculations in a Table

When you want to perform a calculation on numbers in a Word table, you can create a *formula* that uses a built-in mathematical function. You construct a formula by using the tools in the Formula dialog box, which you can access by clicking Formula in the Data group on the Layout contextual tab. A formula consists of an equal sign (=), followed by a function name (such as SUM), followed by parentheses containing the location of the cells on which you want to perform the calculation. For example, the formula =SUM(Left) totals the cells to the left of the cell containing the formula.

To use a function other than SUM in the Formula dialog box, you click the function you want in the Paste Function list. You can use built-in functions to perform a number of calculations, including averaging (AVERAGE) a set of values, counting (COUNT) the number of values in a column or row, or finding the maximum (MAX) or minimum (MIN) value in a series of cells.

Creating Table Styles

If none of the predefined table styles meets your needs, you can create your own styles for tables in much the same way you create styles for regular text.

To create a table style:

1. On the **Design** tab, in the **Table Styles** group, click the **More** button, and then click **New Table Style**.

   The Create New Style From Formatting dialog box opens.

2. In the **Name** box, type a name for the new style.

3. Click the **Apply formatting to** arrow, and in the list, select the table element for which you are creating the new style.

4. Select the formatting options you want, until the table shown in the Preview area looks the way you want it.

5. If you want the style to be available to tables in other documents based on this template, select that option, and then click **OK**.

To apply a custom table style:

1. Select the table element to which you want to apply the new style.

2. On the **Design** tab, in the **Table Styles** group, click the **More** button, and under **Custom**, click the thumbnail for your custom style.

Although formulas commonly refer to the cells above or to the left of the active cell, you can also use the contents of specified cells or constant values in formulas. To use the contents of a cell, you type the *cell address* in the parentheses following the function name. The cell address is a combination of the column letter and the row number—for example, A1 is the cell at the intersection of the first column and the first row. A series of cells in a row can be addressed as a range consisting of the first cell and the last cell separated by a colon, such as A1:D1. For example, the formula =SUM(A1:D1) totals the values in row 1 of columns A through D. A series of cells in a column can be addressed in the same way. For example, the formula =SUM(A1:A4) totals the values in column A of rows 1 through 4.

When the built-in functions don't meet your needs, you can insert an Excel worksheet in a Word document. Part of the Microsoft Office system, Excel includes sophisticated functions for performing mathematical, accounting, and statistical calculations.

For example, you can use an Excel worksheet to calculate loan payments at various interest rates. You can insert Excel worksheet data into a Word document in the following ways:

- **By copying and pasting.** You can open Excel, enter the data and formulas, and then copy and paste the data as a table in a Word document. The data is pasted as regular text, with the formulas converted to their results.

- **By linking.** While pasting Excel worksheet data into a Word document, you can link the version in the document to the original source worksheet. You can then double-click the linked object in the document to open the source worksheet in Excel for editing. After you edit and save the worksheet, you can return to the document, right-click the linked object, and then click Update Link to display the edited version of the data.

- **By embedding.** You can create an Excel worksheet directly in a Word document by clicking the Table button in the Tables group on the Insert tab, and then clicking Excel Spreadsheet. The worksheet is created as an object with Excel row and column headers, and the Excel tabs and groups replace those of Word so that you can enter data and manipulate it using Excel.

> **Tip** If you change a value in a Word table, you must recalculate formulas manually. If you change a value in an Excel worksheet, the formulas are automatically recalculated.

In this exercise, you will perform a few calculations in a Word table. Then you'll copy and paste worksheet data, link the same data, and enter the same data in an Excel object so that you can see the three different ways of working with Excel data.

USE the *Calculations* document and the *LoanData* workbook. These practice files are located in the *Documents\Microsoft Press\2007OfficeSBS_HomeStudent\WordPresenting* folder.
OPEN the *LoanData* workbook in Excel, and then open the *Calculations* document in Word.

1. Save the practice file in the *WordPresenting* folder with the name My Calculations.

2. In the table displayed in the document, click the cell below the *Total* column heading, and on the **Layout** contextual tab, in the **Data** group, click the **Formula** button.

   The Formula dialog box opens.

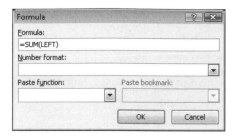

3. Select the contents of the **Formula** box, and then type =C2*B2.

4. Click the **Number format** arrow, and in the list, click **$#,##0.00;($#,##0.00)**.

5. In the **Number format** box, delete **.00** from both the positive and negative portions of the format, and then click **OK**.

You have told Word to multiply the first dollar amount under *Unit Price* by the quantity on the same row and to display the result as a whole dollar amount. Word enters the result, $60,000, in the cell containing the formula.

Memorandum

To: Nate Sun
From: Shelley Dyck
Date: October 19, 2007
Subject: Proposal for Delivery Truck Purchase

Thanks for meeting with me to discuss the possibility of purchasing delivery trucks, rather than continuing with our current lease agreement. I've gathered some information for you to review. The table below is a cost estimate for the delivery trucks I propose that we purchase. It should give you an idea of the overall cost.

Furniture	Quantity	Unit Price	Total
12 ft. truck	2	$30,000	$60,000
24 ft. truck	1	$45,000	
Van	2	$25,000	
		Total	

The best interest rate I can find for fleet sales is 5%. The payment schedule for a $155,000 loan for three years is shown on the attached Excel worksheet.

The current cost of leasing our delivery vehicles is $60,000 a year. Purchasing the

6. Repeat steps 2 through 5 for the next two cells under *Total*, adjusting the cell addresses appropriately.

7. In cell **B4**, change **2** to 3, right-click the formula in cell **D4**, and then click **Update Field**.

Word recalculates the formula and enters the new result, $75,000, in the cell.

8. Change the **Unit Price** of the **24 ft. truck** to $42,500, and then update the corresponding total.

9. Click cell **D5**, and in the **Data** group, click the **Formula** button.

10. With **=SUM(ABOVE)** in the **Formula** box, set the **Number format** to whole dollar amounts (following the method in steps 3 and 4), and then click **OK**.

You have told Word to add the amounts in the *Total* column. Word enters the result, $177,500, in the cell containing the formula.

Memorandum

To: Nate Sun
From: Shelley Dyck
Date: October 19, 2007
Subject: Proposal for Delivery Truck Purchase

Thanks for meeting with me to discuss the possibility of purchasing delivery trucks, rather than continuing with our current lease agreement. I've gathered some information for you to review. The table below is a cost estimate for the delivery trucks I propose that we purchase. It should give you an idea of the overall cost.

Furniture	Quantity	Unit Price	Total
12 ft. truck	2	$30,000	$60,000
24 ft. truck	1	$42,500	$42,500
Van	3	$25,000	$75,000
		Total	$177,500

11. Press ⌈Ctrl⌉ + ⌈End⌉ to move to the end of the document, and then on the Windows taskbar, click the **Microsoft Excel** button.

> **Troubleshooting** If you have hidden your Windows taskbar, as we have, point to the bottom of the screen to make the taskbar appear so that you can click the Microsoft Excel button.

Copy

12. On **Sheet1** of the *LoanData* workbook, select cells **A1:B8** by dragging through them. Then on the **Home** tab, in the **Clipboard** group, click the **Copy** button.

The worksheet data is copied to the Clipboard. From there it can be pasted into any Microsoft Office program.

Paste

13. Redisplay the *My Calculations* document. Then on the **Home** tab, in the **Clipboard** group, click the **Paste** button.

Word pastes a copy of the worksheet data in the document as a table.

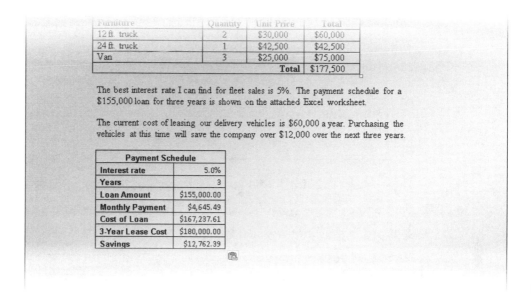

The best interest rate I can find for fleet sales is 5%. The payment schedule for a $155,000 loan for three years is shown on the attached Excel worksheet.

The current cost of leasing our delivery vehicles is $60,000 a year. Purchasing the vehicles at this time will save the company over $12,000 over the next three years.

Payment Schedule	
Interest rate	5.0%
Years	3
Loan Amount	$155,000.00
Monthly Payment	$4,645.49
Cost of Loan	$167,237.61
3-Year Lease Cost	$180,000.00
Savings	$12,762.39

14. Press Enter, and then in the **Clipboard** group, click the **Paste** arrow, and click **Paste Special**.

The Paste Special dialog box opens.

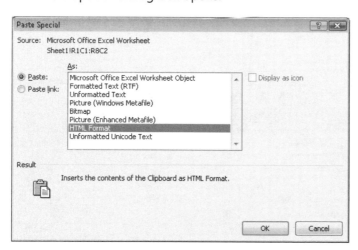

15. In the **As** list, click **Microsoft Office Excel Worksheet Object**, click **Paste link**, and then click **OK**.

Word pastes a second copy of the worksheet data as a linked table on a new page.

16. Double-click the new table.

Excel recalculates the formulas in the worksheet to reflect the new interest rate.

The linked worksheet opens in Excel.

17. Click cell **B2**, type 6, and then press ⏎ Enter ⏎.

> **Troubleshooting** If someone has already worked through this exercise using the practice files on your computer, 6.0% might already appear in cell B2. In that case, change the value to 5.0%.

Excel recalculates the formulas in the worksheet to reflect the new interest rate.

18. Save and close the workbook, and quit Excel.

19. In Word, right-click the linked table, and then click **Update Link**.

Word updates the table to reflect the change you made to the worksheet data.

20. Press Ctrl+End to move to the end of the document, press Enter twice to add some space, and then save the document.

Table

21. On the **Insert** tab, in the **Tables** group, click the **Table** button, and then click **Excel Spreadsheet**.

Word inserts an Excel object in the document.

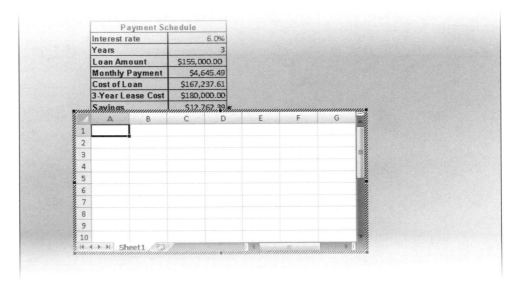

22. In row **1**, type Rate, press Tab, and then type 5%.

23. Type the following in rows **2**, **3**, and **4**:

2   Years `Tab` 3

3   Amount `Tab` $155,000

4   Payment `Tab`

24. With cell **B4** active, on the **Formulas** tab, in the **Function Library** group, click the **Financial** button, scroll the list, and then click **PMT**.

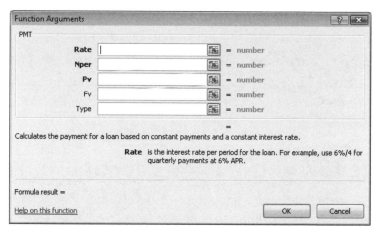

Excel enters =PMT() in cell B4 and then opens the Function Arguments dialog box so that you can enter the information needed to calculate the monthly payment on a loan of $155,000 at 5% interest for three years.

25. In the **Rate** box, type B1/12 (the annual rate per month), in the **Nper** box, type B2*12 (the number of years expressed as months), and in the **Pv** box, type B3. Then click **OK**.

Excel calculates the formula and enters the result, $4,645.49, expressed as a negative because it is money you are paying out.

> **Tip** To express the payment as a positive, you can insert a minus sign between the equal sign and PMT in the formula.

26. Drag the black handle in the lower-right corner of the Excel object up and to the left, until the frame of the object is just big enough to enclose the cells with data in them. Then click a blank area of the page to deactivate the object.

The object appears on the page as a table with barely visible borders around its cells.

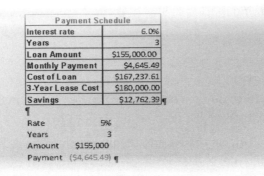

Payment Schedule	
Interest rate	6.0%
Years	3
Loan Amount	$155,000.00
Monthly Payment	$4,645.49
Cost of Loan	$167,237.61
3-Year Lease Cost	$180,000.00
Savings	$12,762.39

Rate 5%
Years 3
Amount $155,000
Payment ($4,645.49)

27. Double-click the object to activate it in Excel again, change the entry in cell **B1** to 7%, press Enter , and then click a blank area of the page.

The object's formulas have updated the monthly payment to reflect the change.

CLOSE the *My Calculations* document without saving your changes.

Using a Table to Control Page Layout

Most people are accustomed to thinking of a table as a means of displaying data in a quick, easy-to-grasp format. But tables can also serve to organize your pages in creative ways. For example, suppose you want to display two tables next to each other. The simplest way to do this is to first create a table with one tall row and two wide columns and no gridlines. You can then insert one table in the first cell and the other table in the second cell. These *nested tables* then appear to be arranged side by side.

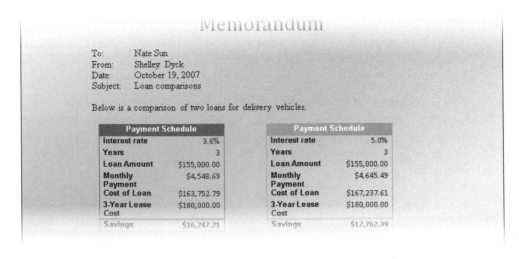

Memorandum

To: Nate Sun
From: Shelley Dyck
Date: October 19, 2007
Subject: Loan comparisons

Below is a comparison of two loans for delivery vehicles.

Payment Schedule	
Interest rate	3.6%
Years	3
Loan Amount	$155,000.00
Monthly Payment	$4,548.69
Cost of Loan	$163,752.79
3-Year Lease Cost	$180,000.00
Savings	$16,247.21

Payment Schedule	
Interest rate	5.0%
Years	3
Loan Amount	$155,000.00
Monthly Payment	$4,645.49
Cost of Loan	$167,237.61
3-Year Lease Cost	$180,000.00
Savings	$12,762.39

Deciding How to Insert Excel Data

To decide how to insert Excel data in a Word document, you need to understand how Microsoft Office system programs integrate data from outside sources. Understanding this will enable you to decide how to use information created in any other Office program, not just Excel.

If you don't need to maintain a connection with the source Excel worksheet and the data is simple enough to be edited in Word, you can copy and paste the data.

If you do need to maintain a connection with the source Excel worksheet, or if you need to be able to manipulate the data in Excel after it is incorporated into the Word document, you can use the Microsoft linking and embedding technology to insert an *object* (a file or part of a file) created in Excel into a document created in Word. The object is sometimes called the *source file*, and the document into which you are inserting the information is called the *destination file*. The difference between linking and embedding is the type of connection that is maintained between the source and destination files, as follows:

- A *linked object* is displayed in the destination file, but its data is stored in the source file. If you want to change the data, you do it in the source file. Then when you open the destination file, the linked object is updated to reflect the change.

- An *embedded object* is displayed in the destination file and its data is stored there. If you want to update the data, you do it in the destination file using the source program.

Whether an object should be linked or embedded depends on whether you need the information in the destination file to always be the same as the information in the source file. If you do, it is best to link the object so that you don't have to manually update the data in two places.

As with regular tables, you can create a nested table from scratch, by formatting existing information, or by inserting Excel data. And just like other tables, you can format a nested table either manually or using one of Word's ready-made table styles.

> **Tip** Tables can be used to organize a mixture of elements such as text, tables, charts, and diagrams. For more information, you might want to consult *Advanced Documents Inside Out* (Microsoft Press, 2007).

When creating a table to contain other elements, you might want to take advantage of the Word table-drawing feature. If you click Draw Table below the grid displayed when you click the Table button, the pointer changes to a pencil with which you can draw cells on the page. You can set up the container table visually, without having to fuss with dialog boxes and precise dimensions while you are designing the layout. Then after everything is set up the way you want it, you can use the Table Properties dialog box to fine-tune the table specifications.

In this exercise, you will draw a table to contain two other tables. You will then insert and format the nested tables.

USE the *Loan* workbook and the *Memo* and *TableAsLayout* documents. These practice files are located in the *Documents\Microsoft Press\2007OfficeSBS_HomeStudent\WordPresenting* folder.

BE SURE TO display non-printing characters before starting this exercise.

OPEN the *Loan* workbook in Excel, and then open the *Memo* document and the *TableAsLayout* document in Word.

1. Before you begin, save a copy of the *TableAsLayout* document in the *WordPresenting* folder as My Nested Tables.

> **Troubleshooting** The operations you perform in this exercise use a lot of your computer's resources. You will have better results if you save the My Nested Tables document regularly.

2. In the *My Nested Tables* document, on the **Insert** tab, in the **Tables** group, click the **Table** button, and then click **Draw Table**.

   The pointer becomes a pencil.

3. Point below the last paragraph mark in the document, and drag across and down to create a cell about 3 inches wide and 1 1/2 inches tall.

   > **Tip** The location of the pencil is marked with guides on the horizontal and vertical rulers. You can use these guides to help you draw cells of specific dimensions.

4. Point to the upper-right corner of the cell (you don't have to be precise), and drag to create another cell about the same size as the first.

   When you release the mouse button, Word joins the two cells to create the structure of a table.

5. On the **View** tab, in the **Window** group, click the **Switch Windows** button, and then click *Memo*.

6. Scroll to the bottom of the page, click anywhere in the *Payment Schedule* table, and on the **Layout** tab, in the **Table** group, click **Select**, and then click **Select Table**.

7. On the **Home** tab, in the **Clipboard** group, click the **Copy** button.

8. Switch to the *My Nested Tables* document, right-click the first cell in the table, and then click **Paste as Nested Table**.

Word inserts the table you copied into the cell and adjusts the size of the container table to fit the size of the nested table.

9. On the Windows taskbar, click the **Microsoft Excel** button to activate Sheet1 of the *Loan* workbook, select cells **A1:B8**, and then on the **Home** tab, in the **Clipboard** group, click the **Copy** button.

10. Switch back to the *My Nested Tables* document, click the second cell in the table, and then on the **Home** tab, in the **Clipboard** group, click the **Paste** button.

Word inserts the worksheet data as a nested table in the cell.

> **Troubleshooting** If the pasted table doesn't appear in the container table, minimize the document window and then maximize it.

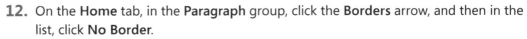

Memorandum

To: Nate Sun
From: Shelley Dyck
Date: October 19, 2007
Subject: Loan comparisons

Below is a comparison of two loans for delivery vehicles.

Payment Schedule	
Interest rate	3.6%
Years	3
Loan Amount	$155,000.00
Monthly Payment	$4,548.69
Cost of Loan	$163,752.79
3-Year Lease Cost	$180,000.00
Savings	$16,247.21

Payment Schedule	
Interest rate	5.0%
Years	3
Loan Amount	$155,000.00
Monthly Payment	$4,645.49
Cost of Loan	$167,237.61
3-Year Lease Cost	$180,000.00
Savings	$12,762.39

11. Move the pointer to the selection area adjacent to the container table, and then click to select its two cells.

Borders

12. On the **Home** tab, in the **Paragraph** group, click the **Borders** arrow, and then in the list, click **No Border**.

Word removes the borders from the container cells.

13. Click anywhere in the left table, and on the **Design** contextual tab, in the **Table Style Options** group, select the **Header Row** and **Total Row** check boxes, and clear all the other check boxes.

14. In the **Table Styles** group, display the **Table Styles** gallery, and click the thumbnail of a table style that you want to apply to the nested table.

We used Light List – Accent 4.

15. Repeat steps 13 and 14 to format the right table, perhaps using a similar table style with a different color.

We used Light List – Accent 6.

16. Turn off non-printing characters to see the results.

The nested tables now look as shown at the beginning of this topic.

CLOSE the *My Nested Tables* document, saving your changes. Then close the *Memo* document, and exit Word. Finally, close the *Loan* workbook without saving changes, and exit Excel.

Key Points

- To vary the layout of a document, you can divide text into columns.
- If your data is simple, you can create the look of a table by using tabs to set up the data as a tabular list.
- Word comes with quick tables that you can use as a starting point for creating professional, easy-to-read table formats.
- If you have already created a table, you can format it quickly by applying a table style. You can enhance the style by applying text attributes, borders, and shading.
- Formulas that perform simple calculations are easy to build in Word. For more complex calculations, you can create an Excel worksheet and then insert the worksheet data as a table in the Word document.
- Tables are great tools for organizing different types of information on the page. By using tables in creative ways, you can place information in non-linear arrangements for easy comparison or analysis.

Part II

Microsoft Office
Excel 2007

Chapter at a Glance

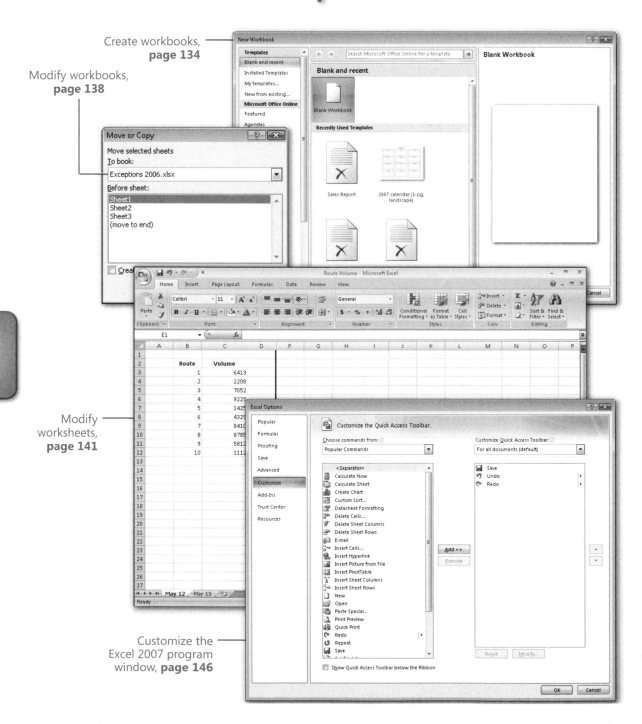

5 Setting Up a Workbook

In this chapter, you will learn how to:

✔ Create workbooks.

✔ Modify workbooks.

✔ Modify worksheets.

✔ Customize the Excel 2007 program window.

When you start Microsoft Office Excel 2007, the program presents a blank workbook that contains three worksheets. You can add or delete worksheets, hide worksheets within the workbook without deleting them, and change the order of your worksheets within the workbook. You can also copy a worksheet to another workbook or move the worksheet without leaving a copy of the worksheet in the first workbook. If you and your colleagues work with a large number of documents, you can define property values to make your workbooks easier to find when you and your colleagues attempt to locate them by using the Microsoft Windows search facility.

Another way to make Office Excel 2007 easier to use is by customizing the Excel 2007 program window to fit your work style. If you have several workbooks open at the same time, you can move between the workbook windows by using the new user interface. However, if you switch between workbooks frequently, you might find it easier to resize the workbooks so they don't take up the entire Excel 2007 window. In that case, you just need to click the title bar of the workbook you want to display.

The 2007 Microsoft Office system design team created the new user interface to reduce the number of places you have to look for commands; if you find that you use a command frequently, you can add it to the Quick Access Toolbar so it's never more than one click away.

In this chapter, you learn how to create and modify workbooks, create and modify worksheets, make your workbooks easier to find, and customize the Excel 2007 program window.

See Also Do you need only a quick refresher on the topics in this chapter? See the Quick Reference entries at the beginning of this book.

Important Before you can use the practice files in this chapter, you need to install them from the book's companion CD to their default location. See "Using the Book's CD" at the beginning of this book for more information.

Troubleshooting Graphics and operating system–related instructions in this book reflect the Windows Vista user interface. If your computer is running Windows XP and you experience trouble following the instructions as written, please refer to the "Information for Readers Running Windows XP" section at the beginning of this book.

Creating Workbooks

Every time you want to gather and store data that isn't closely related to any of your other existing data, you should create a new workbook. The default new workbook in Excel 2007 has three worksheets, although you can add more worksheets or delete existing worksheets if you want. Creating a new workbook is a straightforward process—you just click the Microsoft Office Button, click New, and identify the type of workbook you want to create.

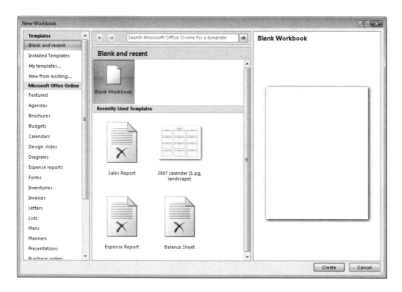

When you start Excel 2007, the program displays a new, blank workbook; you can begin to enter data in the worksheet's cells or open an existing workbook. In the exercises that follow, you'll work with some of the workbooks that have already been created for Consolidated Messenger. After you make any desired changes to a workbook, you should save the workbook to avoid losing your work.

When you save a file, you overwrite the previous copy of the file. If you have made changes that you want to save, but you want to keep a copy of the file as it was previously, you can use the Save As command to specify a name for the new file.

> **Tip** Readers frequently ask, "How often should I save my files?" It is good practice to save your changes every half hour or even every five minutes, but the best time to save a file is whenever you make a change that you would hate to have to make again.

You also can use the controls in the Save As dialog box to specify a different format for the new file and a different location in which to save the new version of the file. For example, Jenny Lysaker, the chief operating officer of Consolidated Messenger, might want to save an Office Excel file that tracks consulting expenses as an Office Excel 2003 file if she needs to share the file with a consulting firm that uses Office Excel 2003.

After you create a file, you can add additional information to make the file easier to find when you search for it using the Windows search facility. Each category of information, or *property*, stores specific information about your file. In Windows, you can search for files based on the file's author or title, or by keywords associated with the file. A file tracking the postal code destinations of all packages sent from a collection might have the keywords *postal*, *destination*, and *origin* associated with it.

To set values for your workbook's properties, click the Microsoft Office Button, point to Prepare, and click Properties to display the Document Properties panel on the user interface. The Standard version of the Document Properties panel has fields for the file's author, title, subject, keywords, category, and status, and any comments about the file. You can also create custom properties by clicking the Property Views and Options button, located just to the right of the Document Properties label, and then clicking Advanced Properties.

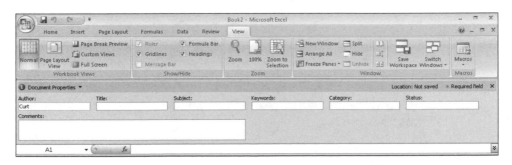

On the Custom tab of the advanced Properties dialog box, you can click one of the existing custom categories or create your own by typing a new property name in the Name field, clicking the Type arrow and selecting a data type (for example, Text, Date, Number, Yes/No), selecting or typing a value in the Value field, and then clicking Add. If you want to delete an existing custom property, move your mouse pointer down to the Properties list, click the property you want to get rid of, and click Delete. After you finish making your changes, click the OK button. To hide the Document Properties panel on the user interface, click the Close button in the upper-right corner of the panel.

In this exercise, you will create a new workbook, save the workbook under a new name, assign values to the workbook's standard properties, and create a custom property.

USE the *Exception Summary* workbook. This practice file is located in the *Documents\ Microsoft Press\2007OfficeSBS_HomeStudent\ExcelCreating* folder.
BE SURE TO start Excel 2007 before beginning these exercises.
OPEN the *Exception Summary* workbook.

Microsoft Office
Button

1. Click the **Microsoft Office Button**, and then click **Close**.

   The Exception Summary workbook closes.

2. Click the **Microsoft Office Button**, and then click **New**.

   The New Workbook dialog box opens.

3. Click **Blank Workbook**, and then click **Create**.

   A new, blank workbook appears.

4. Click the **Microsoft Office Button**, and then click **Save As**.

   The Save As dialog box opens.

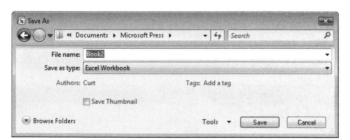

5. Use the navigation controls to display the *Documents\Microsoft Press\ 2007OfficeSBS_HomeStudent\ExcelCreating* folder. In the **File name** field, type Exceptions 2006.

6. Click the **Save** button.

Excel 2007 saves your work, and the Save As dialog box closes.

7. Click the **Microsoft Office Button**, click **Prepare**, and then click **Properties**.

The Document Properties pane appears.

8. In the **Keywords** field, type exceptions, regional, percentage.

9. In the **Category** field, type performance.

10. Click the **Property View and Options** button, and then click **Advanced Properties**.

The Exceptions 2006 Properties dialog box opens.

11. Click **Custom**.

The Custom tab appears.

12. In the **Name** field, type Performance.

13. In the **Value** field, type Exceptions.

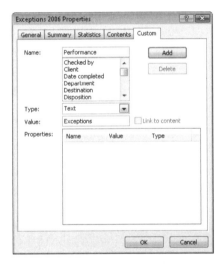

14. Click the **Add** button, and then click **OK**.

The Exceptions 2006 Properties dialog box closes.

15. On the **Quick Access Toolbar**, click the **Save** button to save your work.

Save

CLOSE the *Exceptions 2006* workbook.

Modifying Workbooks

Most of the time, you create a workbook to record information about a particular business activity, such as the number of packages that a regional distribution center handles or the average time of the last delivery on a route. Each worksheet within that workbook should thus represent a subdivision of that activity. To display a particular worksheet, just click the worksheet's tab on the tab bar (just below the grid of cells).

In the case of Consolidated Messenger, the workbook used to track daily package volumes could have a separate worksheet for each regional distribution center. New Excel 2007 workbooks contain three worksheets; because Consolidated Messenger uses nine regional distribution centers, you need to create six new ones. To create a new worksheet, click the Insert Worksheet button at the right edge of the tab bar.

When you create a worksheet, Excel 2007 assigns it a generic name such as Sheet4, Sheet5, or Sheet6. After you decide what type of data you want to store on a worksheet, you should change the default worksheet names to something more descriptive. For example, you could change the name of Sheet1 in the regional distribution center tracking workbook to Northeast. When you want to change a worksheet's name, double-click the worksheet's tab on the tab bar to highlight the worksheet name, type the new name, and press Enter.

Another way to work with more than one workbook is to copy a worksheet from another workbook to the current workbook. One circumstance in which you might consider copying worksheets to the current workbook is if you have a list of your current employees in another workbook. You can copy worksheets from another workbook by right-clicking the tab of the sheet you want to copy and, from the shortcut menu that appears, clicking Move or Copy to display the Move Or Copy dialog box.

> **Tip** Selecting the Create A Copy check box leaves the copied worksheet in its original workbook, whereas clearing the check box causes Excel 2007 to delete the worksheet from its original workbook.

After the worksheets are in the target workbook, you can change their order to make the data easier to locate within the workbook. To change a worksheet's location in the workbook, you drag its sheet tab to the desired location on the tab bar. If you want a worksheet to stand out in a workbook, you can right-click its sheet tab and use the menu that appears to change the tab's color. At the other end of the spectrum, you can hide the active worksheet by right-clicking the worksheet's tab on the tab bar and clicking Hide on the context menu that appears. When you want Excel 2007 to redisplay the worksheet, right-click any visible sheet tab and click Unhide. In the Unhide dialog box, click the sheet you want to display and click OK.

> **Note** If you copy a worksheet to another workbook, and the destination workbook has the same theme applied as the active workbook, the worksheet retains its tab color. If the destination workbook has another theme applied, the worksheet's tab color changes to reflect that theme.

If you determine that you no longer need a particular worksheet, such as one you created to store some figures temporarily, you can delete the worksheet quickly. To do so, right-click its sheet tab and then click Delete.

In this exercise, you will insert and rename a worksheet, change a worksheet's position in a workbook, hide and unhide a worksheet, copy a worksheet to another workbook, change a worksheet's tab color, and delete a worksheet.

> **USE** the *Exception Summary* workbook. This practice file is located in the *Documents\ Microsoft Press\2007OfficeSBS_HomeStudent\ExcelCreating* folder.
> **OPEN** the *Exception Summary* workbook.

Insert Worksheet

1. On the tab bar, click the **Insert Worksheet** button.

   A new worksheet appears.

2. Right-click the new worksheet's sheet tab, and then click **Rename**.

   Excel 2007 highlights the new worksheet's name.

3. Type 2007, and then press [Enter].

4. On the tab bar, right-click the **Sheet1** sheet tab, and then click **Rename**.

5. Type 2006, and then press Enter.

6. Right-click the **2006** sheet tab, point to **Tab Color**, and then, in the **Standard Colors** section of the color palette, click a green square.

    Excel 2007 changes the 2006 sheet's tab to green.

7. On the tab bar, drag the **2007** sheet tab to the left of the **Scratch Pad** sheet tab.

8. Right-click the **2007** sheet tab, and then click **Hide**.

    Excel 2007 hides the 2007 worksheet.

9. Right-click the **2006** sheet tab, and then click **Move or Copy**.

    The Move Or Copy dialog box opens.

10. Click the **To Book** arrow, and then in the list, click **New Book**.

11. Select the **Create a copy** check box.

12. Click **OK**.

     A new workbook appears, containing only the worksheet you copied into it.

Save

13. On the **Quick Access Toolbar**, click the **Save** button.

     The Save As dialog box opens.

14. In the **File name** field, type **2006 Archive**, and then press Enter.

     Excel 2007 saves the workbook, and the Save As dialog box closes.

Switch
Windows ▾

15. On the **View** tab, click the **Switch Windows** button, and then click **Exception Summary**.

     The Exception Summary workbook appears.

16. On the tab bar, right-click the **Scratch Pad** sheet tab, and then click **Delete**.

     The Scratch Pad worksheet disappears.

17. Right-click the **2006** sheet tab, and then click **Unhide**.

The Unhide dialog box opens.

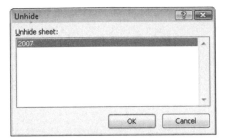

18. Click **2007**, and then click **OK**.

The Unhide dialog box closes, and the 2007 worksheet appears in the workbook.

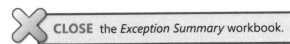

CLOSE the *Exception Summary* workbook.

Modifying Worksheets

After you put up the signposts that make your data easy to find, you can take other steps to make the data in your workbooks easier to work with. For instance, you can change the width of a column or the height of a row in a worksheet by dragging the column or row's border to the desired position. Increasing a column's width or a row's height increases the space between cell contents, making it easier to select a cell's data without inadvertently selecting data from other cells as well.

> **Tip** You can apply the same change to more than one row or column by selecting the rows or columns you want to change and then dragging the border of one of the selected rows or columns to the desired location. When you release the mouse button, all the selected rows or columns change to the new height or width.

Modifying column width and row height can make a workbook's contents easier to work with, but you can also insert a row or column between the edge of a worksheet and the cells that contain the data to accomplish this. Adding space between the edge of a worksheet and cells, or perhaps between a label and the data to which it refers, makes the workbook's contents less crowded and easier to work with. You insert rows by clicking a cell and clicking the Home tab. Then, in the Cells group, click the Insert arrow, and then in the list, click Insert Sheet Rows. Excel 2007 inserts a row above the row that contains the active cell. You insert a column in much the same way by choosing Insert Sheet Columns from the Insert button's drop-down list. When you do this, Excel 2007 inserts a column to the left of the active cell.

When you insert a row, column, or cell in a worksheet with existing formatting, the Insert Options button appears. Clicking the Insert Options button displays a list of choices you can make about how the inserted row or column should be formatted. The following table summarizes your options.

Option	Action
Format Same As Above	Applies the format of the row above the inserted row to the new row.
Format Same As Below	Applies the format of the row below the inserted row to the new row.
Format Same As Left	Applies the format of the column to the left of the inserted column to the new column.
Format Same As Right	Applies the format of the column to the right of the inserted column to the new column.
Clear Formatting	Applies the default format to the new row or column.

If you want to delete a row or column, right-click the row or column head and then, from the shortcut menu that appears, click Delete. You can temporarily hide a number of rows or columns by selecting those rows or columns and then, on the Home tab, in the Cells group, clicking the Format button, pointing to Hide & Unhide, and then clicking either Hide Rows or Hide Columns. The rows or columns you selected disappear, but they aren't gone for good, as they would be if you'd used Delete. Instead, they have just been removed from the display until you call them back. To return the hidden rows to the display, on the Home tab, in the Cells group, click the Format button, point to Hide & Unhide, and then click either Unhide Rows or Unhide Columns.

Likewise, you can insert individual cells into a worksheet. To insert a cell, click the cell that is currently in the position where you want the new cell to appear. On the Home tab, in the Cells group, click the Insert arrow, and then in the list, click Insert Cells to display the Insert dialog box. In the Insert dialog box, you can choose whether to shift the cells surrounding the inserted cell down (if your data is arranged as a column) or to the right (if your data is arranged as a row). When you click OK, the new cell appears, and the contents of affected cells shift down or to the right, as appropriate. In a similar vein, if you want to delete a block of cells, select the cells, and on the Home tab, in the Cells group, click the Delete arrow, and then in the list, click Delete Cells to display the Delete dialog box—complete with options that enable you to choose how to shift the position of the cells around the deleted cells.

> **Tip** The Insert dialog box also includes options you can click to insert a new row or column; the Delete dialog box has similar options for deleting an entire row or column.

If you want to move the data in a group of cells to another location in your worksheet, select the cells you want to move and position the mouse pointer on the selection's border. When the mouse pointer changes to a four-way arrow, you can drag the selected cells to the desired location on the worksheet. If the destination cells contain data, Excel 2007 displays a dialog box asking if you want to overwrite the destination cells' contents. If you want to replace the existing values, click the OK button. If you don't want to overwrite the existing values, click the Cancel button and insert the required number of cells to accommodate the data you want to move.

In this exercise, you will insert a column and row into a worksheet, specify insert options, hide a column, insert a cell into a worksheet, delete a cell from a worksheet, and move a group of cells within the worksheet.

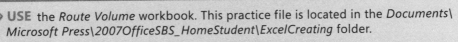

USE the *Route Volume* workbook. This practice file is located in the *Documents\
Microsoft Press\2007OfficeSBS_HomeStudent\ExcelCreating* folder.
OPEN the *Route Volume* workbook.

1. On the **May 12** worksheet, select cell A1.

2. On the **Home** tab, in the **Cells** group, click the **Insert** arrow, and then in the list, click **Insert Sheet Columns**.

   A new column A appears.

3. In the **Insert** list, click **Insert Sheet Rows**.

   A new row 1 appears.

Insert Options

4. Click the **Insert Options** button, and then click **Clear Formatting**.

   Excel 2007 removes the formatting from the new row 1.

5. Right-click the column header of column E, and click **Hide**.

   Column E disappears.

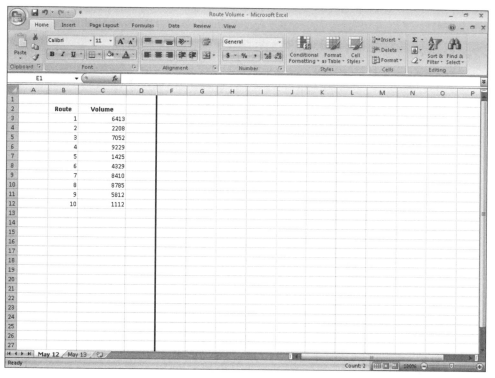

6. On the tab bar, click the **May 13** sheet tab.

   The worksheet named *May 13* appears.

7. Click cell **B6**.

8. On the **Home** tab, in the **Cells** group, click the **Delete** arrow, and then in the list, click **Delete Cells**.

   The Delete dialog box opens.

9. If necessary, click **Shift cells up**, and then click **OK**.

   The Delete dialog box closes and Excel 2007 deletes cell B6, moving the cells below it up to fill in the gap.

10. Click cell **C6**.

11. In the **Insert** list, click **Insert Cells**.

The Insert dialog box opens.

12. If necessary, click **Shift cells down,** and then click **OK**.

The Insert dialog box closes, and Excel 2007 creates a new cell C6, moving cells C6:
C11 down to accommodate the inserted cell.

13. In cell C6, type 4499, and press ⏎ Enter.

14. Select cells **E13:F13**.

15. Point to the border of the selected cells. When your mouse pointer changes to a
four-pointed arrow, drag the selected cells to cells **B13:C13**.

The dragged cells replace cells C13:D13.

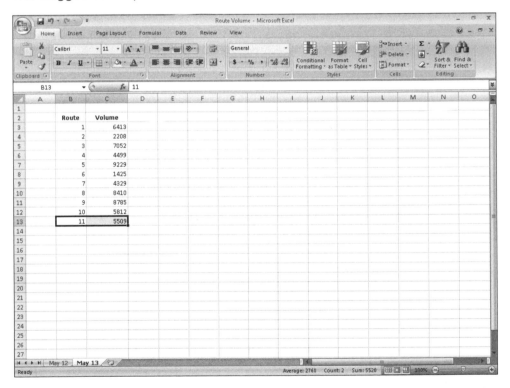

 CLOSE the *Route Volume* workbook.

Customizing the Excel 2007 Program Window

How you use Excel 2007 depends on your personal working style and the type of data collections you manage. The Excel 2007 product team interviews customers, observes how differing organizations use the program, and sets up the user interface so that you don't need to change it to work effectively. If you do find yourself wishing that you could change the Excel 2007 program window, including the user interface, you can. You can change how Excel 2007 displays your worksheets, zoom in on worksheet data, and add frequently used commands to the Quick Access Toolbar.

Zooming In on a Worksheet

One way to make Excel 2007 easier to work with is to change the program's zoom level. Just as you can "zoom in" with a camera to increase the size of an object in the camera's viewer, you can use the Excel 2007 zoom setting to change the size of objects within the Excel 2007 program window. For example, if Peter Villadsen, the Consolidated Messenger European Distribution Center Manager, displayed a worksheet that summarized his distribution center's package volume by month, he could click the View tab and then, in the Zoom group, click the Zoom button to display the Zoom dialog box. The Zoom dialog box contains controls that enable him to select a preset magnification level or to type in a custom magnification level. He could also use the Zoom control at the lower-right corner of the Excel 2007 window.

Zoom out ⌐   ⌐ Zoom in

Clicking the Zoom In control increases the size of items in the program window by 10 percent, whereas clicking the Zoom Out control decreases the size of items in the program window by 10 percent. If you want more fine-grained control of your zoom level, you can use the slider control to select a specific zoom level.

The View tab's Zoom group also contains the Zoom To Selection button, which fills the program window with the contents of any selected cells, up to the program's maximum zoom level of 400 percent.

> **Note** The mimimum zoom level in Excel 2007 is 10 percent.

Arranging Multiple Workbook Windows

As you work with Excel 2007, you will probably need to have more than one workbook open at a time. For example, you could open a workbook that contains customer contact information and copy it into another workbook to be used as the source data for a mass mailing you create in Microsoft Office Word 2007. When you have multiple workbooks open simultaneously, you can switch between them by clicking the View tab and then, in the Window group, clicking the Switch Windows button and clicking the name of the workbook you want to view.

You can arrange your workbooks within the Excel 2007 window so that most of the active workbook is shown, but the others are easily accessible by clicking the View tab and then, in the Window group, clicking the Arrange All button. Then, in the Arrange Windows dialog box, click Cascade.

Many Excel 2007 workbooks contain formulas on one worksheet that derive their value from data on another worksheet, which means you need to change between two worksheets every time you want to see how modifying your data changes the formula's result. However, you can display two copies of the same workbook, displaying the worksheet that contains the data in the original window and displaying the worksheet with the formula in the new window. When you change the data in the original copy of the workbook, Excel 2007 updates the formula result in a new window. To display two copies of the same workbook, open the desired workbook and then, on the View tab's Window group, click New Window. Excel 2007 will open a second copy of the workbook. If the original workbook's name was Exception Summary, Excel 2007 displays the name Exception Summary:1 on the original workbook's title bar and Exception Summary:2 on the second workbook's title bar.

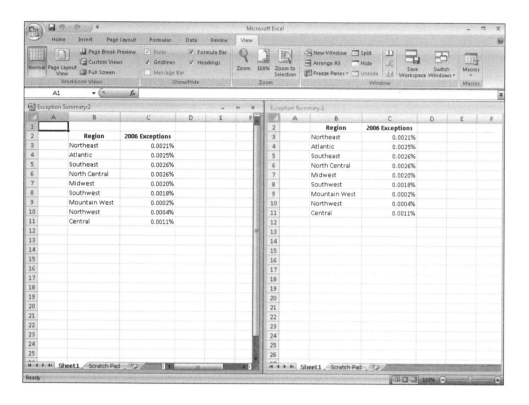

Adding Buttons to the Quick Access Toolbar

As you continue to work with Excel 2007, you might discover that you use certain commands much more frequently than others. If your workbooks draw data from external sources, you might find yourself displaying the Data tab and then, in the Connections group, clicking the Refresh All button much more often than the program's designers might have expected. You can make any button accessible with one click by adding the button to the Quick Access Toolbar, located just to the right of the Microsoft Office Button at the upper-left corner of the Excel 2007 program window.

To add a button to the Quick Access Toolbar, click the Microsoft Office Button, and click Excel Options. In the Excel Options dialog box, click the Customize name, and then in the Choose Commands From list, click the category from which you want to select the control to add. Excel 2007 displays the available commands in the list box below the Choose Commands From field. Click the control you want and then click the Add button. You can change a button's position on the Quick Access Toolbar by clicking its name in the lower-right pane and then clicking either the Move Up or Move Down button. To remove a button from the Quick Access Toolbar, click the button's name and then click the Remove button. When you're done making your changes, click the OK button.

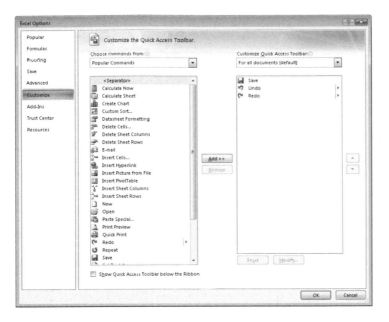

You can also choose whether your Quick Access Toolbar change affects all your workbooks or just the active workbook. To control how Excel 2007 applies your change, in the Customize Quick Access Toolbar list, click either For All Documents to apply the change to all of your workbooks or For Workbook to apply the change to the active workbook only.

In this exercise, you will change your worksheet's zoom level, zoom in to emphasize a selected cell range, switch between multiple open workbooks, cascade multiple open workbooks within the Excel 2007 program window, and add a button to the Quick Access Toolbar.

USE the *Route Volume* and *Exception Summary* workbooks. These practice files are located in the *Documents\Microsoft Press\2007OfficeSBS_HomeStudent\ExcelCreating* folder.

OPEN the *Route Volume* workbook and the *Exception Summary* workbook.

1. In the **Exception Summary** workbook, display the **2006** worksheet.

Zoom In

2. In the lower-right corner of the Excel 2007 window, click the **Zoom In** control five times.

The worksheet's zoom level changes to 150%.

3. Select cells **B2:C11**.

4. On the **View** tab, in the **Zoom** group, click the **Zoom to Selection** button.

Excel 2007 displays the selected cells so they fill the program window.

	A	B	C	D
2		**Region**	**2006 Exceptions**	
3		Northeast	0.0021%	
4		Atlantic	0.0025%	
5		Southeast	0.0026%	
6		North Central	0.0026%	
7		Midwest	0.0020%	
8		Southwest	0.0018%	
9		Mountain West	0.0002%	
10		Northwest	0.0004%	
11		Central	0.0011%	

5. On the **View** tab, in the **Zoom** group, click the **Zoom** button.

The Zoom dialog box opens.

6. Click **100%**, and then click **OK**.

The worksheet returns to its default zoom level.

7. On the **View** tab, in the **Window** group, click the **Switch Windows** button, and then click **Route Volume**.

The Route Volume workbook appears.

8. On the **View** tab, in the **Window** group, click the **Arrange All** button.

The Arrange Windows dialog box opens.

9. Click **Cascade**, and then click **OK**.

Excel 2007 cascades the open workbook windows within the Excel 2007 program window.

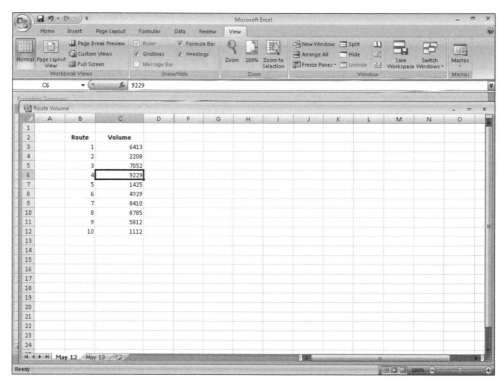

Microsoft Office Button

10. Click the **Microsoft Office Button**, and then click **Excel Options**.

The Excel Options dialog box opens.

11. Click **Customize**.

The Customize tab appears.

12. Click the **Choose commands from** arrow, and then in the list, click **Review Tab**.

The commands in the Review Tab category appear in the command list.

13. Click the **Spelling** command, and then click **Add**.

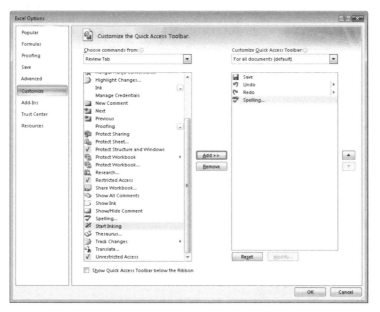

14. Click **OK**.

Excel 2007 adds the Spelling command to the Quick Access Toolbar.

CLOSE Excel if you're not continuing to the next chapter.

Key Points

- Save your work whenever you do something you'd hate to have to do again.

- Assigning values to a workbook's properties makes it easier to find your workbook using the Windows search facility.

- Be sure to give your worksheets descriptive names.

- If you want to use a worksheet's data in another workbook, you can send a copy of the worksheet to that other workbook without deleting the original worksheet.

- You can delete a worksheet you no longer need, but you can also hide a worksheet in the workbook. When you need the data on the worksheet, you can unhide it.

- You can save yourself a lot of bothersome cutting and pasting by inserting and deleting worksheet cells, columns, and rows.

- Customize your Excel 2007 program window by changing how it displays your workbooks, zooming in on data, and adding frequently used buttons to the Quick Access Toolbar.

Chapter at a Glance

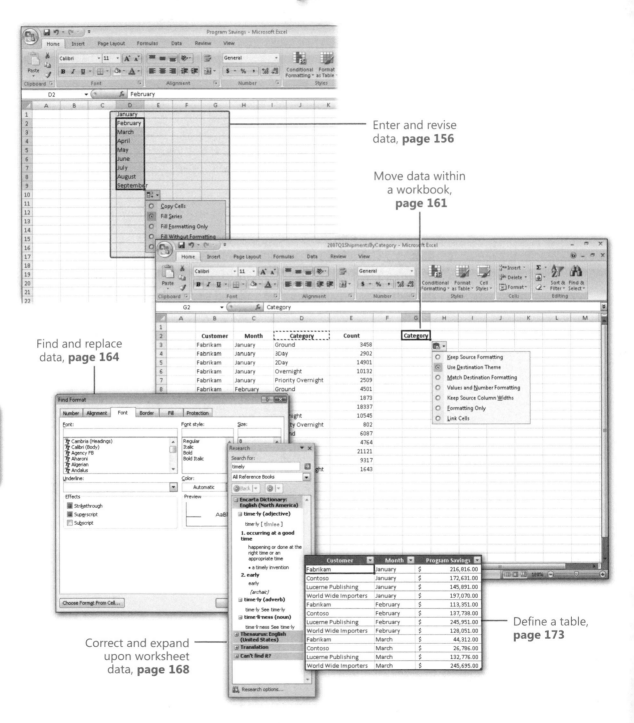

Enter and revise data, **page 156**

Move data within a workbook, **page 161**

Find and replace data, **page 164**

Correct and expand upon worksheet data, **page 168**

Define a table, **page 173**

6 Working with Data and Data Tables

In this chapter, you will learn to:

- ✔ Enter and revise data.
- ✔ Move data within a workbook.
- ✔ Find and replace data.
- ✔ Correct and expand upon worksheet data.
- ✔ Define a table.

Microsoft Office Excel 2007 enables you to visualize and present information effectively using charts, graphics, and formatting, but the data is the most important part of any workbook. By learning to enter data efficiently, you will make fewer data entry errors and give yourself more time to analyze your data so you can make decisions about your organization's performance and direction.

Office Excel 2007 provides a wide variety of tools you can use to enter and manage worksheet data effectively. For example, Excel 2007 enables you to organize your data into tables, which enables you to analyze and store your data quickly and easily. Excel 2007 also enables you to enter a data series quickly; repeat one or more values; or control how Excel 2007 formats cells, columns, and rows moved from one part of a worksheet to another. And you can do so with a minimum of effort. Excel 2007 also enables you to check the spelling of worksheet text, look up alternative words using the Thesaurus, and translate words to foreign languages.

In this chapter, you will learn how to enter and revise Excel 2007 data, move data within a workbook, find and replace existing data, use proofing and reference tools to enhance your data, and organize your data by using Excel 2007 data tables.

See Also Do you need only a quick refresher on the topics in this chapter? See the Quick Reference entries at the beginning of this book.

Important Before you can use the practice sites in this chapter, you need to install them from the book's companion CD to their default location. See "Using the Book's CD" at the beginning of this book for more information.

Troubleshooting Graphics and operating system–related instructions in this book reflect the Windows Vista user interface. If your computer is running Windows XP and you experience trouble following the instructions as written, please refer to the "Information for Readers Running Windows XP" section at the beginning of this book.

Entering and Revising Data

After you create a workbook, you can begin entering data. The simplest way to enter data is to click a cell and type a value, which is a method that works very well when you're entering a few pieces of data, but it is less than ideal when you're entering long sequences or series of values. For example, Craig Dewar, the VP of Marketing for Consolidated Messenger, might want to create a worksheet listing the monthly program savings that large customers can enjoy if they sign exclusive delivery contracts with Consolidated Messenger. To record those numbers, he would need to create a worksheet with the following layout.

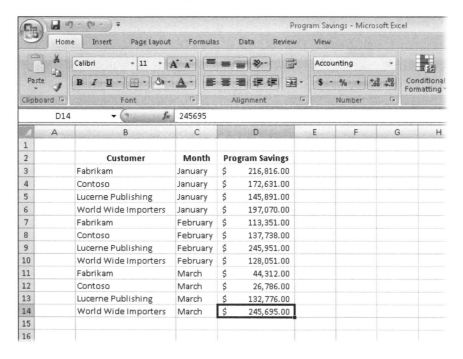

Repeatedly entering the sequence January, February, March, and so on can be handled by copying and pasting the first occurrence of the sequence, but there's an easier way to do it: use *AutoFill*. With AutoFill, you enter the first element in a recognized series, grab the *fill handle* at the lower-right corner of the cell, and drag the fill handle until the series extends far enough to accommodate your data. A similar tool, *FillSeries*, enables you to enter two values in a series and use the fill handle to extend the series in your worksheet. For example, if you want to create a series starting at 2 and increasing by 2, you can put 2 in the first cell and 4 in the second cell, select both cells, and then use the fill handle to extend the series to your desired end value.

You do have some control over how Excel 2007 extends the values in a series when you drag the fill handle. For example, if you drag the fill handle up (or to the left), Excel 2007 extends the series to include previous values. If you type *January* in a cell and then drag that cell's fill handle up (or to the left), Excel 2007 places *December* in the first cell, *November* in the second cell, and so on.

Another way to control how Excel 2007 extends a data series is by holding down the Ctrl key while you drag the fill handle. For example, if you select a cell that contains the value *January* and then drag the fill handle down, Excel 2007 extends the series by placing *February* in the next cell, *March* in the cell after that, and so on. If you hold down the Ctrl key, however, Excel 2007 repeats the value *January* in each cell you add to the series.

> **Tip** Be sure to experiment with how the fill handle extends your series and how pressing the Ctrl key changes that behavior. Using the fill handle can save you a lot of time entering data.

Other data entry techniques you'll use in this section are *AutoComplete*, which detects when a value you're entering is similar to previously entered values; *Pick From Drop-down List*, which enables you to choose a value from existing values in a column; and Ctrl+Enter, which enables you to enter a value in multiple cells simultaneously.

> **Troubleshooting** If an AutoComplete suggestion doesn't appear as you begin typing a cell value, the option might be turned off. To turn on AutoComplete, click the Microsoft Office Button, and then click Excel Options. In the Excel Options dialog box, click the Advanced category. In the Editing Options section of the dialog box, select the Enable AutoComplete For Cell Values check box, and then click OK.

The following table summarizes these data entry techniques.

Method	Action
AutoFill	Enter the first value in a recognized series and use the fill handle to extend the series.
FillSeries	Enter the first two values in a series and use the fill handle to extend the series.
AutoComplete	Type the first few letters in a cell, and if a similar value exists in the same column, Excel 2007 suggests the existing value.
Pick From Drop-down List	Right-click a cell, and from the shortcut menu that appears, choose Pick From Drop-down List. A list of existing values in the cell's column appears. Click the value you want to enter into the cell.
Ctrl+Enter	Select a range of cells to contain the same data, type the data in the active cell, and press Ctrl+Enter.

Another handy feature in the current version of Excel 2007 is the Auto Fill Options button that appears next to data you add to a worksheet using AutoFill.

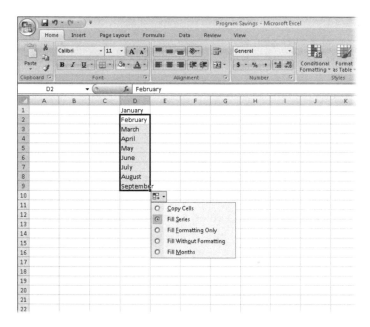

Clicking the Auto Fill Options button displays a list of actions Excel 2007 can take re-garding the cells affected by your fill operation. The options in the list are summarized in the following table.

Option	Action
Copy Cells	Copies the contents of the selected cells to the cells indicated by the Fill operation.
Fill Series	Fills the cells indicated by the Fill operation with the next items in the series.
Fill Formatting Only	Copies the format of the selected cell to the cells indicated by the Fill op-eration, but does not place any values in the target cells.
Fill Without Formatting	Fills the cells indicated by the Fill operation with the next items in the se-ries, but ignores any formatting applied to the source cells.
Fill Days, Weekdays, etc.	Changes according to the series you extend. For example, if you extend the cells *Wed*, *Thu*, and *Fri*, Excel 2007 presents two options, Fill Days and Fill Weekdays, and enables you to select which one you intended. If you do not use a recognized sequence, the option does not appear.

In this exercise, you will enter data by multiple methods, and control how Excel 2007 formats an extended data series.

USE the *Series* workbook. This practice file is located in the *Documents\Microsoft Press\2007OfficeSBS_HomeStudent\ExcelData* folder.

BE SURE TO start Excel 2007 before beginning this exercise.

OPEN the *Series* workbook.

1. On the **Monthly** worksheet, select cell **B3**, and then drag the fill handle down until it covers cells B3:B7.

   Excel 2007 repeats the value *Fabrikam* in cells B4:B7.

2. Select cell **C3**, hold down the ⌃ key, and drag the fill handle down until it covers cells C3:C7.

   Excel 2007 repeats the value *January* in cells C4:C7.

3. Select cell **B8**, and type the letter F.

   Excel 2007 displays the characters *abrikam* in reverse video.

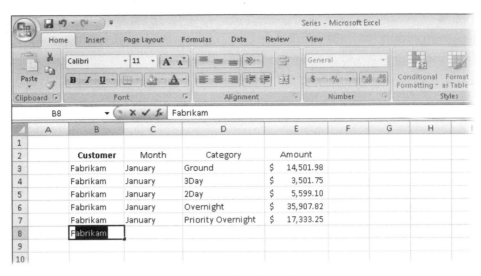

4. Press [Tab] to accept the value *Fabrikam* for the cell.

5. In cell **C8**, type February.

6. Right-click cell **D8**, and then click **Pick From Drop-down List**.

   A list of values in column D appears below cell D8.

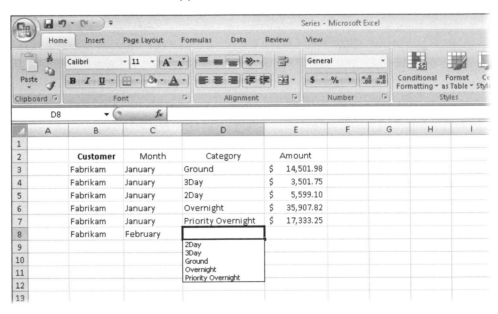

7. From the list that appeared, click **2Day**.

   The value *2Day* appears in cell D8.

8. In cell E8, type 11802.14.

   The value *$11,802.14* appears in cell E8.

9. Select cell **B2**, and then drag the fill handle so that it covers cells C2:E2.

   Excel 2007 replaces the values in cells C2:E2 with the value *Customer*.

10. Click the **Auto Fill Options** button, and then click **Fill Formatting Only**.

    Excel 2007 restores the original values in cells C2:E2 but applies the formatting of cell B2 to those cells.

 CLOSE the *Series* workbook.

Moving Data Within a Workbook

You can move to a specific cell in lots of ways, but the most direct method is to click the cell to which you want to move. The cell you click will be outlined in black, and its contents, if any, will appear in the formula bar. When a cell is outlined, it is the *active cell*, meaning that you can modify its contents. You use a similar method to select multiple cells (referred to as a *cell range*)—just click the first cell in the range and drag the mouse pointer over the remaining cells you want to select. After you select the cell or cells you want to work with, you can cut, copy, delete, or change the format of the contents of the cell or cells. For instance, Gregory Weber, the Northwestern Distribution Center Manager, might want to copy the cells that contain a set of column labels to a new page that summarizes similar data.

> **Important** If you select a group of cells, the first cell you click is designated the active cell.

You're not limited to selecting cells individually or as part of a range. For example, you might need to move a column of price data one column to the right to make room for a column of headings that indicate to which service category (ground, three-day express, two-day express, overnight, or priority overnight) a set of numbers belongs. To move an entire column (or entire columns) of data at a time, you click the column's header, located at the top of the worksheet. Clicking a column header highlights every cell in that column and enables you to copy or cut the column and paste it elsewhere in the workbook.

The Paste Options button appears next to data you copy from a cell and paste into another cell. Clicking the Paste Options button displays a list of actions that Excel 2007 can take regarding the pasted cells.

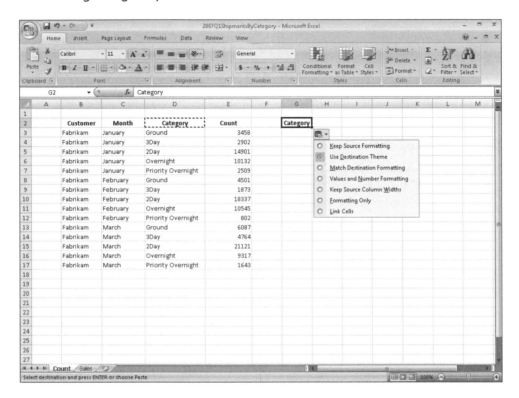

The options in the list are summarized in the following table.

Option	Action
Use Destination Theme	Pastes the contents of the Clipboard (which holds the last information selected via Cut or Copy) into the target cells and formats the data using the theme applied to the target workbook.
Match Destination Formatting	Pastes the contents of the Clipboard into the target cells and formats the data using the existing format in the target cells, regardless of the workbook's theme.
Keep Source Formatting	Pastes a column of cells into the target column; applies the format of the copied column to the new column.
Values Only	Pastes the values from the copied column into the destination column without applying any formatting.
Values And Number Formatting	Pastes the contents of the Clipboard into the target cells, keeping any numeric formats.

Option	Action
Values And Source Formatting	Pastes the contents of the Clipboard into the target cells, retaining all the source cells' formatting.
Keep Source Column Widths	Pastes the contents of the Clipboard into the target cells and resizes the columns of the target cells to match the widths of the columns of the source cells.
Formatting Only	Applies the format of the source cells to the target cells, but does not copy the contents of the source cells.

> **Troubleshooting** If the Paste Options button doesn't appear, you can turn the feature on by clicking the Microsoft Office Button and then clicking Excel Options to display the Excel Options dialog box. In the Excel Options dialog box, click the Advanced category and then, in the Cut, copy, and paste section, select the Show Paste Options buttons check box. Click OK to close the dialog box and save your setting.

In this exercise, you will copy a set of column headers to another worksheet, move a column of data within a worksheet, and select paste options for copied data.

USE the *2007Q1ShipmentsByCategory* workbook. This practice file is located in the *Documents\Microsoft Press\2007OfficeSBS_HomeStudent\ExcelData* folder.
OPEN the *2007Q1ShipmentsByCategory* workbook.

Copy

Paste

1. On the **Count** worksheet, select cells **B2:D2**.

2. On the **Home** tab, in the **Clipboard** group, click the **Copy** button.

   Excel 2007 copies the contents of cells B2:D2 to the Clipboard.

3. Create a worksheet named Sales, and display it.

4. Select cell **B2**.

5. On the **Home** tab, in the **Clipboard** group, click **Paste**.

   Excel 2007 pastes the header values into cells B2:D2.

6. Click the **Paste Options** smart tag, and then click **Keep Source Formatting**.

   Excel 2007 retains the cells' original formatting.

7. Right-click the column header of column I, and then click **Cut**.

   Excel 2007 outlines column I with a marquee.

8. Right-click the header of column E, and then click **Paste**.

Excel 2007 pastes the contents of column I into column E.

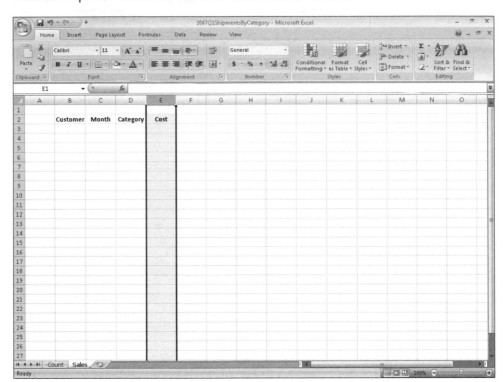

CLOSE the *2007Q1ShipmentsByCategory* workbook.

Finding and Replacing Data

Excel 2007 worksheets can contain more than one million rows of data, so it's unlikely that you would have the time to move through a worksheet a row at a time to locate the data you want to find. You can locate specific data on an Excel 2007 worksheet by using the Find And Replace dialog box, which has two tabs (one named Find; the other named Replace) that enable you to search for cells that contain particular values. Using the controls on the Find tab finds the data you specify; using the controls on the Replace tab enables you to substitute one value for another. As an example, one of Consolidated Messenger's customers might change the company name. If that's the case, you can change every instance of the old name to the new name.

When you need more control over the data that you find and replace, such as if you want to find cells in which the entire cell value matches the value you're searching for, you can click the Options button to expand the Find And Replace dialog box.

One way you can use the extra options in the Find And Replace dialog box is to identify data that requires review using a specific format. As an example, Consolidated Messenger VP of Marketing Craig Dewar could make corporate sales plans based on a projected budget for the next year. After the executive board finalizes the numbers, he could use Find Format in the Find And Replace dialog box to locate the old prices and then change them by hand.

To change a value by hand, select the cell and then either type a new value in the cell or, on the Formula Bar, select the value you want to replace and type the new value.

The following table summarizes the Find And Replace dialog box controls' functions.

Control	Function
Find What field	Contains the value you want to find or replace.
Find All button	Selects every cell that contains the value in the Find What field.
Find Next button	Selects the next cell that contains the value in the Find What field.
Replace With field	Contains the value to overwrite the value in the Find What field.
Replace All button	Replaces every instance of the value in the Find What field with the value in the Replace With field.
Replace button	Replaces the next occurrence of the value in the Find What field and highlights the next cell that contains that value.
Options button	Expands the Find And Replace dialog box to display additional capabilities.
Format button	Displays the Find Format dialog box, which you can use to specify the format of values to be found or to replace found values.
Within list box	Enables you to select whether to search the active worksheet or the entire workbook.
Search list box	Enables you to select whether to search by rows or by columns.
Look In list box	Enables you to select whether to search cell formulas or values.
Match Case check box	When checked, requires that all matches have the same capitalization as the text in the Find What field (for example, cat doesn't match Cat).
Match Entire Cell Contents check box	Requires that the cell contain exactly the same value as in the Find What field (for example, Cat doesn't match Catherine).
Close button	Closes the Find And Replace dialog box.

In this exercise, you will find a specific value in a worksheet, replace every occurrence of a company name in a worksheet, and find a cell with a particular formatting.

> **USE** the *Average Deliveries* workbook. This practice file is located in the *Documents\ Microsoft Press\2007OfficeSBS_HomeStudent\ExcelData* folder.
> **OPEN** the *Average Deliveries* workbook.

1. If necessary, click the **Time Summary** sheet tab.

   The Time Summary worksheet appears.

2. On the **Home** tab, in the **Editing** group, click **Find & Select**, and then click **Find**.

   The Find And Replace dialog box opens with the Find tab displayed.

3. In the **Find what** field, type 114.

4. Click **Find Next**.

   Excel 2007 highlights cell B16, which contains the value *114*.

5. Delete the value in the **Find What** field, and then click the **Options** button.

   The Find And Replace dialog box expands to display additional search options.

6. Click **Format**.

The Find Format dialog box opens.

7. Click the **Font** tab.

The Font tab appears.

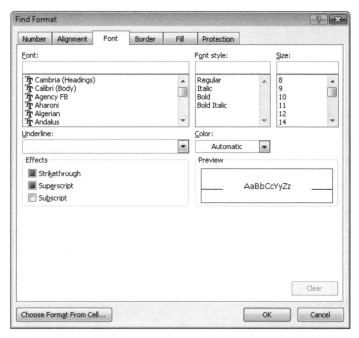

8. In the **Font Style** list, click **Italic**.

9. Click **OK**.

The Find Format dialog box closes.

10. Click **Find Next**.

Excel 2007 highlights cell D25.

11. Click **Close**.

The Find And Replace dialog box closes.

12. On the tab bar, click the **Customer Summary** sheet tab.

The Customer Summary worksheet appears.

13. On the **Home** tab, in the **Editing** group, click **Find & Select**, and then click **Replace**.

The Find And Replace dialog box opens with the Replace tab displayed.

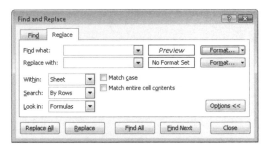

14. Click the **Format** arrow to the right of the **Find what** field, and then in the list, click **Clear Find Format**.

The format displayed next to the Find What field disappears.

15. In the **Find what** field, type Contoso.

16. In the **Replace with** field, type Northwind Traders.

17. Click **Replace All**.

18. Click **OK** to clear the message box that appears, indicating that Excel 2007 made three replacements.

19. Click **Close**.

The Find And Replace dialog box closes.

CLOSE the *Average Deliveries* workbook.

Correcting and Expanding Upon Worksheet Data

After you enter your data, you should take the time to check and correct it. You do need to verify visually that each piece of numeric data is correct, but you can make sure that the text is spelled correctly by using the Excel 2007 spelling checker. When the spelling checker encounters a word it doesn't recognize, it highlights the word and offers suggestions representing its best guess of the correct word. You can then edit the word directly, pick the proper word from the list of suggestions, or have the spelling checker ignore the misspelling. You can also use the spelling checker to add new words to a custom dictionary so that Excel 2007 will recognize them later, saving you time by not requiring you to identify the words as correct every time they occur in your worksheets. After you make a change, you can remove the change as long as you haven't closed the workbook in which you made the change. To undo a change, click the Undo button on the Quick Access Toolbar. If you decide you want to keep a change, you can use the Redo command to restore it.

If you're not sure of your word choice or if you use a word that is almost but not quite right for your meaning, you can check for alternative words by using the Thesaurus. A number of other research tools are also available, such as the Microsoft Encarta encyclopedia, which you can refer to as you create your workbook. To display those tools, on the Review tab, in the Proofing group, click Research to display the Research task pane.

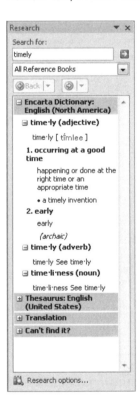

Finally, if you want to translate a word from one language to another, you can do so by selecting the cell that contains the value you want to translate, by displaying the Review tab, and then, in the Proofing group, by clicking Translate. The Research task pane appears (or changes if it's already open) and displays controls you can use to select the original and destination languages.

> **Caution**   Excel 2007 translates a sentence by using word substitutions, which means that the translation routine doesn't always pick the best word for a given context. The translated sentence might not capture your exact meaning.

In this exercise, you will check a worksheet's spelling, add two new terms to a dictionary, undo a change, search for an alternative word using the Thesaurus, and translate a word to French.

1. On the **Review** tab, in the **Proofing** group, click **Spelling**.

   The Spelling dialog box opens with the misspelled word displayed in the Not In Dictionary field.

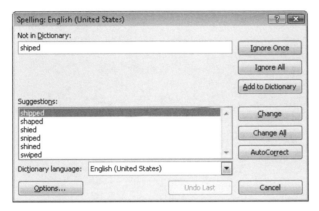

2. Verify that the word *shipped* is highlighted in the **Suggestions** pane, and then click **Change**.

   Excel 2007 corrects the word and displays the next questioned word: *withn*.

3. Click **Change**.

   Excel corrects the word and displays the next questioned word: *TwoDay*.

4. Click **Add to Dictionary**.

   Excel 2007 adds the word to the dictionary and displays the next questioned word: *ThreeDay*.

5. Click **Add to Dictionary**.

   Excel 2007 adds the word to the dictionary.

6. Click **Close**.

   The Spelling dialog box closes, and a message box appears, indicating that the spell check is complete for the selected items.

7. Click **OK** to close the message box.

8. Click cell **B6**.

9. On the **Review** tab, in the **Proofing** group, click **Thesaurus**.

   The Research task pane appears and displays a list of synonyms and antonyms for the word *overnight*.

10. On the **Review** tab, in the **Proofing** group, click **Translate**.

    The Research task pane displays the translation tools.

11. If necessary, in the **From** list, click **English (United States)**.

12. In the **To** list, click **French (France)**.

    The Research task pane displays French words that mean *overnight*.

 CLOSE the *Service Levels* workbook.

Defining a Table

Excel has always enabled you to manage lists of data effectively, enabling you to sort your worksheet data based on the values in one or more columns, limit the data displayed by using criteria (for example, show only those routes with fewer than 100 stops), and create formulas that summarize the values in visible (that is, unfiltered) cells. Customer feedback indicated that many Excel 2007 users wanted a more robust structure within Excel 2007 that enabled users to perform those operations and more. Excel 2003 included a structure called a *data list* that has evolved into the *table* in Excel 2007.

Customer	Month	Program Savings
Fabrikam	January	$ 216,816.00
Contoso	January	$ 172,631.00
Lucerne Publishing	January	$ 145,891.00
World Wide Importers	January	$ 197,070.00
Fabrikam	February	$ 113,351.00
Contoso	February	$ 137,738.00
Lucerne Publishing	February	$ 245,951.00
World Wide Importers	February	$ 128,051.00
Fabrikam	March	$ 44,312.00
Contoso	March	$ 26,786.00
Lucerne Publishing	March	$ 132,776.00
World Wide Importers	March	$ 245,695.00

To create a data table, type a series of column headers in adjacent cells and then type a row of data below the headers. Select the headers and data; on the Home tab, in the Styles group, click Format as Table; and then, from the gallery that appears, click the style you to apply to the table. When the Format as Table dialog box opens, verify that the cells in the Where is the data for your table? field reflect your current selection and that the My table has headers check box is selected, and then click OK.

Excel 2007 can also create a table from an existing data list as long as your data has a differently formatted header row, the list has no blank rows or columns within the data, and there is no extraneous data in cells immediately below or next to the list.

When you want to add data to a table, select a cell in the row immediately below the last row in the table or a cell in the column immediately to the right of the table; then type a value into the cell. After you enter the value and move out of the cell, the AutoCorrect Options smart tag appears. If you didn't mean to include the data in the table, you can click Undo Table AutoExpansion to exclude the cells from the table. If you never want Excel 2007 to include adjacent data in a table, click Stop Automatically Expanding Tables.

> **Tip** To stop Table AutoExpansion before it starts, click the Microsoft Office Button, and then click Excel Options. In the Excel Options dialog box, click Proofing, and then click the AutoCorrect Options button to display the AutoCorrect dialog box. Click the AutoFormat As You Type tab, clear the Include new rows and columns in table check box, and then click OK twice.

You can add rows and columns to a table, or remove them from a table, by dragging the resize handle at the table's lower-right corner. If your table's headers contain a recognizable series of values (such as *Region1*, *Region2*, and *Region3*), and you drag the resize handle to create a fourth column, Excel 2007 creates the column with the label *Region4*—the next value in the series.

Tables often contain data you can summarize by calculating a sum or average, or by finding the maximum or minimum value in a column. To summarize one or more columns of data, you can add a Total row to your table.

Contoso	March	$	26,786.00
Lucerne Publishing	March	$	132,776.00
World Wide Importers	March	$	245,695.00
Total		$	1,807,068.00

When you add the Total row, Excel 2007 creates a formula that calculates the sum of the values in the rightmost table column. To change that summary operation or to add a summary operation to any other cell in the Total row, click the cell, click the arrow that appears, and then click the summary operation you want to apply. Clicking the More Functions item displays the Insert Function dialog box, from which you can select any of the functions in Excel 2007.

Much as it does when you create a new worksheet, Excel 2007 gives your tables generic names such as *Table1* and *Table2*. You can change a table name to something easier to recognize by clicking any cell in the table, clicking the Design contextual tab, and then, in the Properties group, editing the value in the Table Name field. Changing a table name might not seem important, but it helps make formulas that summarize table data much easier to understand. You should make a habit of renaming your tables so you can recognize the data they contain.

See Also For more information about using the Insert Function dialog box and about referring to tables in formulas, see "Creating Formulas to Calculate Values" in Chapter 7, "Performing Calculations on Data."

If for any reason you want to convert your table back to a normal range of cells, click any cell in the table and then, on the Table Tools contextual tab, in the Tools group, click Convert to Range. When Excel 2007 displays a message box asking if you're sure you want to convert the table to a range, click OK.

In this exercise, you will create a data table from existing data, add data to a table, add a Total row, change the Total row's summary operation, and rename the table.

USE the *Driver Sort Times* workbook. This practice file is located in the *Documents\ Microsoft Press\2007OfficeSBS_HomeStudent\ExcelData* folder.

OPEN the *Driver Sort Times* workbook.

1. Select cell **B2**.

2. On the **Home** tab, in the **Styles** group, click **Format as Table**, and then select a table style.

   The Format As Table dialog box opens.

3. Verify that the range =$B$2:$C$17 appears in the **Where is the data for your table?** field and that the **My table has headers** check box is selected, and then click **OK**.

Excel 2007 creates a table from your data and displays the Design contextual tab.

4. In cell B18, type **D116**, press [Tab], type **100** in cell C18, and then press [Enter].

Excel 2007 includes the data in your table.

5. Select a cell in the table and on the **Design** contextual tab, in the **Table Style Options** group, select the **Total Row** check box.

A Total row appears in your table.

6. Select cell C19, click the arrow that appears at the right edge of the cell, and then click **Average**.

Excel 2007 changes the summary operation to Average.

Drive	Sorting Minutes
D101	102
D102	162
D103	165
D104	91
D105	103
D106	127
D107	112
D108	137
D109	102
D110	147
D111	163
D112	109
D113	91
D114	107
D115	93
D116	100
Total	**119.4375**

7. On the **Design** contextual tab, in the **Properties** group, type the value SortingSample01 in the **Table Name** field, and press [Enter].

Excel 2007 renames your table.

8. On the Quick Access Toolbar, click the **Save** button to save your work.

Save

> ✕ **CLOSE** the *Driver Sort Times* workbook. If you are not continuing directly to the next chapter, exit Excel.

Key Points

- You can enter a series of data quickly by entering one or more values in adjacent cells, selecting the cells, and then dragging the fill handle. To change how dragging the fill handle extends a data series, hold down the Ctrl key.

- Dragging a fill handle displays the Auto Fill Options button, which enables you to specify whether to copy the selected cells' values, extend a recognized series, or apply the selected cells' formatting to the new cells.

- Excel 2007 enables you to enter data by using a drop-down list, AutoComplete, and Ctrl+Enter. You should experiment with these techniques and use the one that best fits your circumstances.

- When you copy (or cut) and paste cells, columns, or rows, Excel 2007 displays the Paste Options smart tag. You can use its controls to determine which elements of the cut or copied elements Excel 2007 applies when they are pasted back into the worksheet.

- You can find and replace data within a worksheet by searching for specific values or by searching for cells that have a particular format applied.

- Excel 2007 provides a variety of powerful proofing and research tools, enabling you to check your workbook's spelling, find alternative words using the Thesaurus, and translate words between languages.

- Data tables, which are new in Excel 2007, enable you to organize and summarize your data effectively.

Chapter at a Glance

Name groups of data, **page 180**

Create formulas to calculate values, **page 184**

Summarize data that meets specific conditions, **page 191**

Find and correct errors in calculations, **page 195**

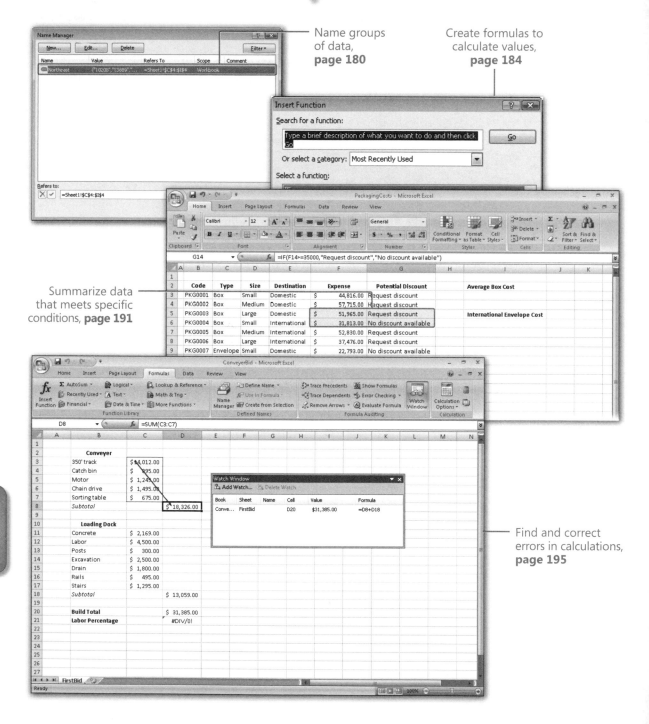

7 Performing Calculations on Data

In this chapter, you will learn to:

✔ Name groups of data.

✔ Create formulas to calculate values.

✔ Summarize data that meets specific conditions.

✔ Find and correct errors in calculations.

Microsoft Office Excel 2007 workbooks give you a handy place to store and organize your data, but you can also do a lot more with your data in Office Excel 2007. One important task you can perform is to calculate totals for the values in a series of related cells. You can also use Excel 2007 to find out other information about the data you select, such as the maximum or minimum value in a group of cells. By finding the maximum or minimum value in a group, you can identify your best salesperson, product categories you might need to pay more attention to, or suppliers that consistently give you the best deal. Regardless of your bookkeeping needs, Excel 2007 gives you the ability to find the information you want. And if you should make an error, you can find the cause and correct it quickly.

Many times, you can't access the information you want without referencing more than one cell, and it's also often true that you'll use the data in the same group of cells for more than one calculation. Excel 2007 makes it easy to reference a number of cells at once, enabling you to define your calculations quickly.

In this chapter, you'll learn how to streamline references to groups of data on your worksheets and how to create and correct formulas that summarize Consolidated Messenger's business operations.

See Also Do you need only a quick refresher on the topics in this chapter? See the Quick Reference entries at the beginning of this book.

Important Before you can use the practice files in this chapter, you need to install them from the book's companion CD to their default location. See "Using the Book's CD" at the beginning of this book for more information.

Troubleshooting Graphics and operating system–related instructions in this book reflect the Windows Vista user interface. If your computer is running Windows XP and you experience trouble following the instructions as written, please refer to the "Information for Readers Running Windows XP" section at the beginning of this book.

Naming Groups of Data

When you work with large amounts of data, it's often useful to identify groups of cells that contain related data. For example, you can create a worksheet in which cells C4:I4 hold the number of packages Consolidated Messenger's Northeast processing facility handled from 5:00 P.M. to 12:00 A.M. on the previous day.

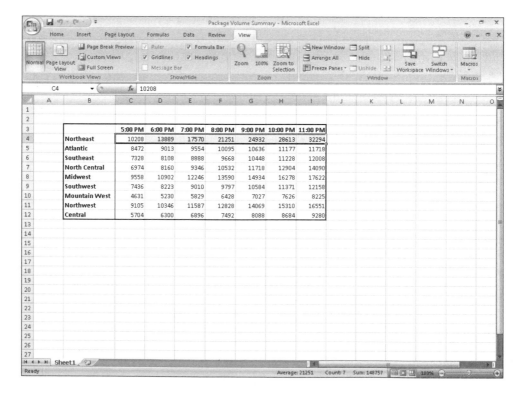

Instead of specifying the cells individually every time you want to use the data they contain, you can define those cells as a *range* (also called a *named range*). For instance, you can group the items from the preceding graphic into a range named NortheastLastDay. Whenever you want to use the contents of that range in a calculation, you can simply use the name of the range instead of specifying each cell individually.

> **Note** Yes, you could just name the range *Northeast*, but if you use the range's values in a formula in another worksheet, the more descriptive range name tells you and your colleagues exactly what data is used in the calculation.

To create a named range, select the cells you want to include in your range, click the Formulas tab, and then, in the Defined Names group, click Define Name to display the New Name dialog box. In the New Name dialog box, type a name in the Name field, verify that the cells you selected appear in the Refers To field, and then click OK. You can also add a comment about the field in the Comment field and select whether you want to make the name available for formulas in the entire workbook or just on an individual worksheet.

If the cells you want to define as a named range have a label you want to use as the range's name, you can display the Formulas tab and then, in the Defined Names group, click Create From Selection to display the Create Names From Selection dialog box. In the Create Names From Selection dialog box, select the check box that represents the label's position in relation to the data cells, and then click OK.

A final way to create a named range is to select the cells you want in the range, click in the Name box next to the formula bar, and then type the name for the range. You can display the ranges available in a workbook by clicking the Name arrow.

To manage the named ranges in a workbook, display the Formulas tab, and then, in the Defined Names group, click Name Manager to display the Name Manager dialog box.

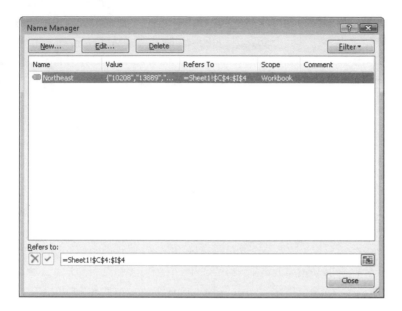

When you click a named range, Excel 2007 displays the cells it encompasses in the Refers To field. Clicking the Edit button displays the Edit Name dialog box, which is a version of the New Name dialog box, enabling you to change a named range's definition. You can also get rid of a name by clicking it, clicking the Delete button, and then clicking OK in the confirmation dialog box that opens.

> **Important** If your workbook contains a lot of named ranges, you can click the Filter button in the Name Manager dialog box and select a criterion to limit the names displayed in the Name Manager dialog box.

In this exercise, you will create named ranges to streamline references to groups of cells.

 USE the *VehicleMiles* workbook. This practice file is located in the *Documents\Microsoft Press\2007OfficeSBS_HomeStudent\ExcelFormulas* folder.
BE SURE TO start Excel 2007 before beginning this exercise.
OPEN the *VehicleMiles* workbook.

1. Select cells **C4:G4**.

2. In the **Name** box on the left of the formula bar, type **V101LastWeek**, and then press Enter .

   Excel 2007 creates a named range named *V101LastWeek*.

Name Manager

3. On the **Formulas** tab, in the **Defined Names** group, click **Name Manager**.

   The Name Manager dialog box opens.

4. Click the **V101LastWeek** name.

   The cell range to which the V101LastWeek name refers appears in the Refers To field.

5. Edit the cell range in the **Refers to** field to =LastWeekMiles!$C$4:$H$4, click **OK**, and then click the check mark button next to the **Refers to** field.

   Excel 2007 changes the named range's definition.

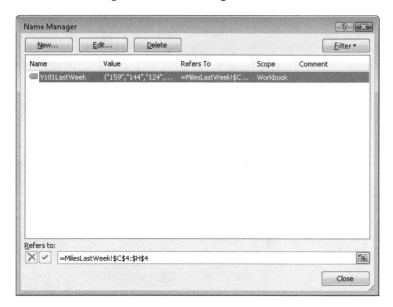

6. Click **Close**.

   The Name Manager dialog box closes.

7. Select the cell range **C5:H5**.

8. On the **Formulas** tab, in the **Defined Names** group, click **Define Name**.

    Define Name   The New Name dialog box opens.

9. In the **Name** field, type V102LastWeek.

10. Verify that the definition in the **Refers to** field is =LastWeekMiles!$C$5:$H$5.

11. Click **OK**.

    Excel 2007 creates the name and closes the New Name dialog box.

CLOSE the *VehicleMiles* workbook.

Creating Formulas to Calculate Values

After you add your data to a worksheet and define ranges to simplify data references, you can create a *formula*, or an expression that performs calculations on your data. For example, you can calculate the total cost of a customer's shipments, figure the average number of packages for all Wednesdays in the month of January, or find the highest and lowest daily package volumes for a week, month, or year.

To write an Excel 2007 formula, you begin the cell's contents with an equal (=) sign; when Excel 2007 sees it, it knows that the expression following it should be interpreted as a calculation, not text. After the equal sign, type the formula. For example, you can find the sum of the numbers in cells C2 and C3 using the formula *=C2+C3*. After you have entered a formula into a cell, you can revise it by clicking the cell and then editing the formula in the formula bar. For example, you can change the preceding formula to *=C3-C2*, which calculates the difference between the contents of cells C2 and C3.

> **Troubleshooting** If Excel 2007 treats your formula as text, make sure that you haven't accidentally put a space before the equal sign. Remember, the equal sign must be the first character!

Typing the cell references for 15 or 20 cells in a calculation would be tedious, but Excel 2007 makes it easy to handle complex calculations. To create a new calculation, click the Formulas tab, and then in the Function Library group, click Insert Function. The Insert Function dialog box opens, with a list of functions, or predefined formulas, from which you can choose.

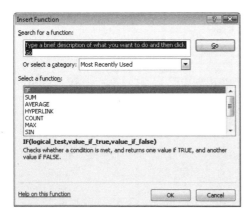

The following table describes some of the most useful functions in the list.

Function	Description
SUM	Finds the sum of the numbers in the specified cells
AVERAGE	Finds the average of the numbers in the specified cells
COUNT	Finds the number of entries in the specified cells
MAX	Finds the largest value in the specified cells
MIN	Finds the smallest value in the specified cells

Two other functions you might use are the *NOW()* and *PMT()* functions. The *NOW()* function returns the time the workbook was last opened, so the value will change every time the workbook is opened. The proper form for this function is *=NOW()*. To update the value to the current date and time, just save your work, close the workbook, and then reopen it.

The *PMT()* function is a bit more complex. It calculates payments due on a loan, assuming a constant interest rate and constant payments. To perform its calculations, the *PMT()* function requires an interest rate, the number of months of payments, and the starting balance. The elements to be entered into the function are called *arguments* and must be entered in a certain order. That order is written *PMT(rate, nper, pv, fv, type)*. The following table summarizes the arguments in the *PMT()* function.

Argument	Description
rate	The interest rate, to be divided by 12 for a loan with monthly payments
nper	The total number of payments for the loan
pv	The amount loaned (pv is short for present value, or principal)
fv	The amount to be left over at the end of the payment cycle (usually left blank, which indicates 0)
type	0 or 1, indicating whether payments are made at the beginning or at the end of the month (usually left blank, which indicates 0, or the end of the month)

If Consolidated Messenger wanted to borrow $2,000,000 at a 6 percent interest rate and pay the loan back over 24 months, you could use the *PMT()* function to figure out the monthly payments. In this case, the function would be written *=PMT(6%/12, 24, 2000000)*, which calculates a monthly payment of $88,641.22.

You can also use the names of any ranges you defined to supply values for a formula. For example, if the named range NortheastLastDay refers to cells C4:I4, you can calculate the average of cells C4:I4 with the formula =AVERAGE(NortheastLastDay). In previous versions of Excel, you had to type the name into your formula by hand. Excel 2007 enables you to add functions, named ranges, and table references to your formulas more efficiently by using the new *Formula AutoComplete* capability. Just as AutoComplete offers to fill in a cell's text value when Excel 2007 recognizes that the value you're typing matches a previous entry, Formula AutoComplete offers to fill in a function, named range, or table reference while you create a formula.

As an example, consider a worksheet that contains a two-column table named Exceptions. The first column is labeled Route; the second is labeled Count.

Route	Count
101	7
102	0
103	4
104	6
105	18
106	12
107	3
108	3
109	8
110	9
111	8
112	18
113	12
114	16
115	12
116	9
117	10
118	6
119	10
120	4

You refer to a table by typing the table name, followed by the column or row name in square brackets. For example, the table reference *Exceptions[Count]* would refer to the Exceptions table's Count column.

To create a formula that finds the total number of exceptions by using the *SUM* function, you begin by typing =SU. When you type the letter *S*, Formula AutoComplete lists functions that begin with the letter *S*; when you type the letter *U*, Excel 2007 narrows the list down to the functions that start with the letters *SU*.

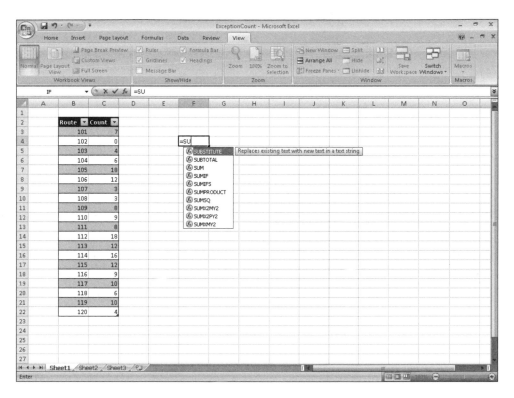

To add the *SUM* function (followed by an opening parenthesis) to the formula, click *SUM* and then press Tab. To begin adding the table column reference, type the letter *E*. Excel 2007 displays a list of available functions, tables, and named ranges that start with the letter *E*. Click Exceptions and press Tab to add the table reference to the formula. Then, because you want to summarize the values in the table's Count column, type *[Count]* to create the formula *=SUM(Exceptions[Count])*.

If you want to include a series of contiguous cells in a formula, but you haven't defined the cells as a named range, you can click the first cell in the range and drag to the last cell. If the cells aren't contiguous, hold down the Ctrl key and click the cells to be included. In both cases, when you release the mouse button, the references of the cells you selected appear in the formula.

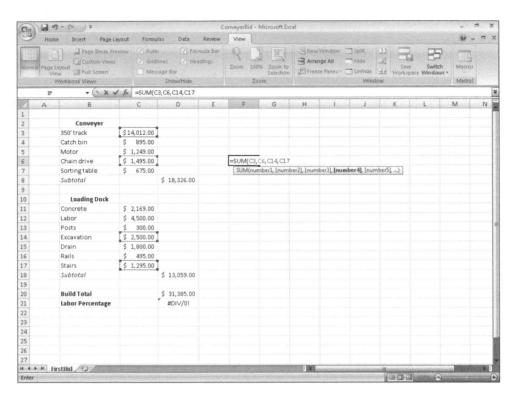

After you create a formula, you can copy it and paste it into another cell. When you do, Excel 2007 tries to change the formula so that it works in the new cells. For instance, suppose that you have a worksheet in which cell D8 contains the formula =SUM(C2:C6). Clicking cell D8, copying the cell's contents, and then pasting the result into cell D16 writes =SUM(C10:C14) into cell D16. Excel 2007 has reinterpreted the formula so that it fits the surrounding cells! Excel 2007 knows it can reinterpret the cells used in the formula because the formula uses a *relative reference*, or a reference that can change if the formula is copied to another cell. Relative references are written with just the cell row and column (for example, C14). If you want a cell reference to remain constant when the formula using it is copied to another cell, you can use an absolute reference. To write a cell reference as an absolute reference, type $ before the row name and the column number. If you want the formula in cell D16 to show the sum of values in cells C10 through C14 regardless of the cell into which it is pasted, you can write the formula as =SUM($C$10:$C$14).

Tip If you copy a formula from the formula bar, use absolute references or use only named ranges in your formula. Excel 2007 doesn't change the cell references when you copy your formula to another cell.

One quick way to change a cell reference from relative to absolute is to select the cell reference on the formula bar and then press F4. Pressing F4 cycles a cell reference through the four possible types of references:

- Relative columns and rows (for example, *C4*)
- Absolute columns and rows (for example, *$C$4*)
- Relative columns and absolute rows (for example, *C$4*)
- Absolute columns and relative rows (for example, *$C4*)

In this exercise, you will create a formula manually, revise it to include additional cells, create a formula that contains a table reference, create a formula with relative references, and change the formula so it contains absolute references.

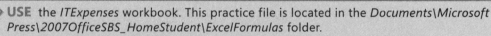

USE the *ITExpenses* workbook. This practice file is located in the *Documents\Microsoft Press\2007OfficeSBS_HomeStudent\ExcelFormulas* folder.

OPEN the *ITExpenses* workbook.

1. If necessary, display the **Summary** worksheet. Then, in cell F9, type =C4, and press ⎯Enter⎯.

   The value *$385,671.00* appears in cell F9.

2. Select cell **F9**, and then on the formula bar, erase the existing formula and type =SU.

   Formula AutoComplete displays a list of possible functions to use in the formula.

3. In the **Formula AutoComplete** list, click **SUM**, and then press ⎯Tab⎯.

   Excel 2007 changes the contents of the formula bar to *=SUM(*.

4. Select the cell range **C3:C8**, type a right parenthesis (the *)* character) to make the formula bar's contents *=SUM(C3:C8)*, and then press ⎯Enter⎯.

   The value *$2,562,966.00* appears in cell F9.

5. In cell F10, type =SUM(C4:C5), and press ⎯Enter⎯.

6. Select cell **F10**, and then on the formula bar, select the cell reference *C4* and press ⎯F4⎯.

   Excel 2007 changes the cell reference to *$C$4*.

7. On the formula bar, select the cell reference **C5**, press ⎯F4⎯, and then press ⎯Enter⎯.

   Excel 2007 changes the cell reference to *$C$5*.

8. On the tab bar, click the **JuneLabor** sheet tab.

The JuneLabor worksheet opens.

9. In cell F13, type =SUM(J.

Excel 2007 displays JuneSummary, the name of the table in the JuneLabor worksheet.

10. Press [Tab].

Excel 2007 extends the formula to read *=SUM(JuneSummary.*

11. Type [, and then in the Formula AutoComplete list, click **[Labor Expense]**, and press [Tab].

Excel 2007 extends the formula to read *=SUM(JuneSummary[Labor Expense.*

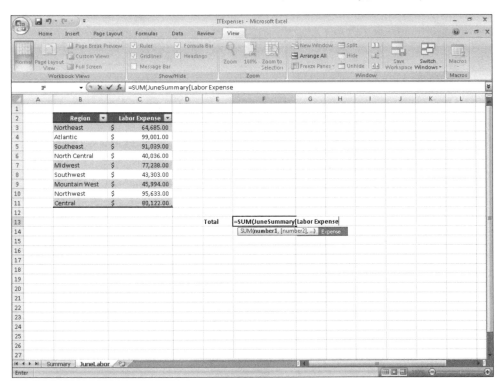

12. Type]) to complete the formula, and then press [Enter].

The value *$637,051.00* appears in cell F13.

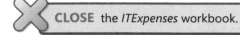

CLOSE the *ITExpenses* workbook.

Summarizing Data That Meets Specific Conditions

Another use for formulas is to display messages when certain conditions are met. For instance, Consolidated Messenger's VP of Marketing, Craig Dewar, might have agreed to examine the rates charged to corporate customers who were billed for more than $100,000 during a calendar year. This kind of formula is called a *conditional formula*, and it uses the *IF* function. To create a conditional formula, you click the cell to hold the formula and open the Insert Function dialog box. From within the dialog box, click *IF* in the list of available functions, and then click OK. The Function Arguments dialog box opens.

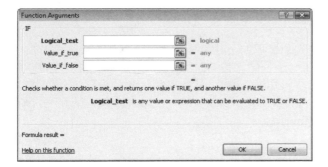

When you work with an *IF* function, the Function Arguments dialog box has three boxes: Logical_test, Value_if_true, and Value_if_false. The Logical_test box holds the condition you want to check. If the customer's year-to-date shipping bill appears in cell G8, the expression would be G8>100000.

Now you need to have Excel 2007 display messages that indicate whether Craig Dewar should evaluate the account for a possible rate adjustment. To have Excel 2007 print a message from an *IF* function, you enclose the message in quotes in the Value_if_true or Value_if_false box. In this case, you would type *"High-volume shipper—evaluate for rate decrease."* in the Value_if_true box and *"Does not qualify at this time."* in the Value_if_false box.

Excel 2007 also includes five new conditional functions with which you can summarize your data:

- *IFERROR*, which displays one value if a formula results in an error; another if it doesn't

- *AVERAGEIF*, which finds the average of values within a cell range that meet a given criterion

- *AVERAGEIFS*, which finds the average of values within a cell range that meet multiple criteria

- *SUMIFS*, which finds the sum of values in a range that meet multiple criteria

- *COUNTIFS*, which counts the number of cells in a range that meet multiple criteria

The *IFERROR* function enables you to display a custom error message instead of relying on the default Excel 2007 error messages to explain what happened. One example of an *IFERROR* formula is if you want to look up the CustomerID value from cell G8 in the Customers table by using the *VLOOKUP* function. One way to create such a formula is =IFERROR(VLOOKUP(G8,Customers,2,false),"Customer not found"). If the function finds a match for the CustomerID in cell G8, it displays the customer's name; if it doesn't find a match, it displays the text *Customer not found*.

The *AVERAGEIF* function is a variation on the existing *COUNTIF* and *SUMIF* functions. To create a formula using the *AVERAGEIF* function, you define the range to be examined, the criteria, and, if required, the range from which to draw the values. As an example, consider the following worksheet, which lists each customer's ID number, name, state, and total monthly shipping bill.

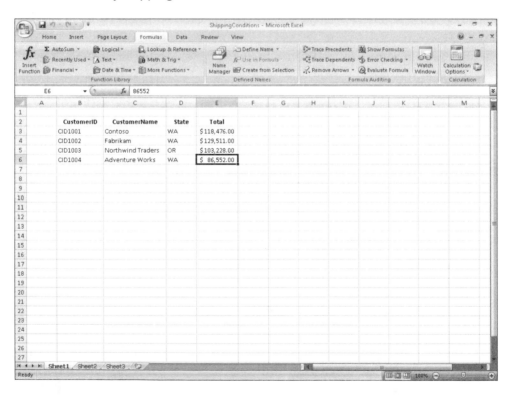

If you want to find the average order of customers from Washington State (abbreviated in the worksheet as WA), you can create the formula *=AVERAGEIF(D3:D6,"=WA", E3:E6)*.

The *AVERAGEIFS*, *SUMIFS*, and *COUNTIFS* functions extend the capabilities of the *AVERAGEIF*, *SUMIF*, and *COUNTIF* functions to allow for multiple criteria. If you want to find the sum of all orders of at least $100,000 placed by companies in Washington, you can create the formula *=SUMIFS(E3:E6, D3:D6, "=WA", E3:E6, ">=100000")*.

The *AVERAGEIFS* and *SUMIFS* functions start with a data range that contains values that the formula summarizes; you then list the data ranges and the criteria to apply to that range. In generic terms, the syntax runs *=AVERAGEIFS(data_range, criteria_range1, criteria1[,criteria_range2, criteria2...])*. The part of the syntax in square brackets is optional, so an *AVERAGEIFS* or *SUMIFS* formula that contains a single criterion works. The *COUNTIFS* function, which doesn't perform any calculations, doesn't need a data range—you just provide the criteria ranges and criteria. For example, you could find the number of customers from Washington billed at least $100,000 by using the formula *=COUNTIFS(D3:D6, "=WA", E3:E6, ">=100000")*.

In this exercise, you will create a conditional formula that displays a message if a condition is true, find the average of worksheet values that meet one criterion, and find the sum of worksheet values that meet two criteria.

> **USE** the *PackagingCosts* workbook. This practice file is located in the *Documents\Microsoft Press\2007OfficeSBS_HomeStudent\ExcelFormulas* folder.
>
> **OPEN** the *PackagingCosts* workbook.

1. In cell G3, type the formula =IF(F3>=35000,"Request discount","No discount available"), and press ⎡Enter⎤.

   Excel 2007 accepts the formula, which displays *Request discount* if the value in cell F3 is at least 35,000 and displays *No discount available* if not. The value *Request discount* appears in cell G3.

2. Click cell **G3**, and drag the fill handle down until it covers cell G14.

Excel 2007 copies the formula in cell G3 to cells G4:G14, adjusting the formula to reflect the cells' addresses. The results of the copied formulas appear in cells G4:G14.

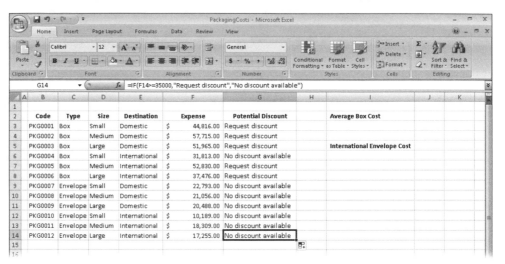

3. In cell I3, type the formula =AVERAGEIF(C3:C14, "=Box", F3:F14), and press [Enter].

   The value *$46,102.50*, which represents the average cost per category of boxes, appears in cell I3.

4. In cell I6, type =SUMIFS(F3:F14, C3:C14, "=Envelope", E3:E14, "=International").

   The value *$45,753.00*, which represents the total cost of all envelopes used for international shipments, appears in cell I6.

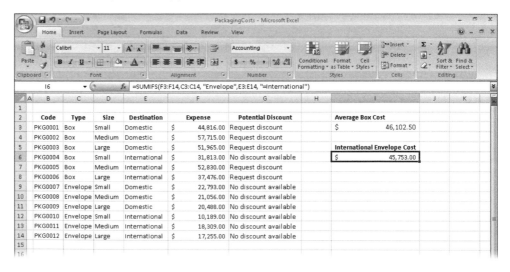

CLOSE the *PackagingCosts* workbook.

Finding and Correcting Errors in Calculations

Including calculations in a worksheet gives you valuable answers to questions about your data. As is always true, however, it is possible for errors to creep into your formulas. Excel 2007 makes it easy to find the source of errors in your formulas by identifying the cells used in a given calculation and describing any errors that have occurred. The process of examining a worksheet for errors in formulas is referred to as *auditing*.

Excel 2007 identifies errors in several ways. The first way is to fill the cell holding the formula generating the error with an *error code*. In the following graphic, cell F13 has the error code #NAME?.

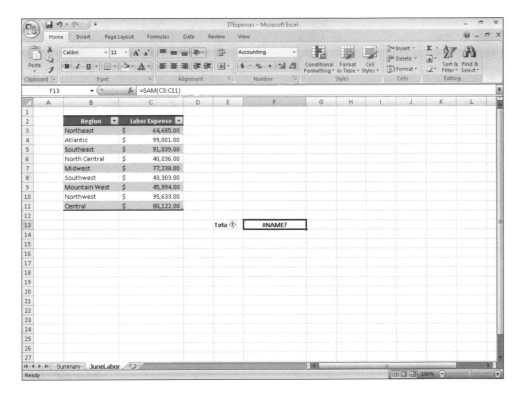

When a cell with an erroneous formula is the active cell, an Error button appears next to it. You can click the arrow to the right of the button to display a menu with options that provide information about the error and offer to help you fix it. The following table lists the most common error codes and what they mean.

Error Code	Description
#####	The column isn't wide enough to display the value.
#VALUE!	The formula has the wrong type of argument (such as text in which a *TRUE* or *FALSE* value is required).
#NAME?	The formula contains text that Excel 2007 doesn't recognize (such as an unknown named range).
#REF!	The formula refers to a cell that doesn't exist (which can happen whenever cells are deleted).
#DIV/0!	The formula attempts to divide by zero.

Another technique you can use to find the source of formula errors is to ensure that the appropriate cells are providing values for the formula. For example, you might want to calculate the total number of deliveries for a service level, but you could accidentally create a formula referring to the service levels' names instead of their quantities. You can identify what kind of error has appeared by having Excel 2007 trace a cell's *precedents*, which are the cells with values used in the active cell's formula. Excel 2007 identifies a cell's precedents by drawing a blue tracer arrow from the precedent to the active cell.

You can also audit your worksheet by identifying cells with formulas that use a value from a given cell. For example, you might use one region's daily package total in a formula that calculates the average number of packages delivered per region on a given day. Cells that use another cell's value in their calculations are known as *dependents*, meaning that they depend on the value in the other cell to derive their own value. As with tracing precedents, you can click the Formulas tab, and then in the Formula Auditing group, click Trace Dependents to have Excel 2007 draw blue arrows from the active cell to those cells that have calculations based on that value.

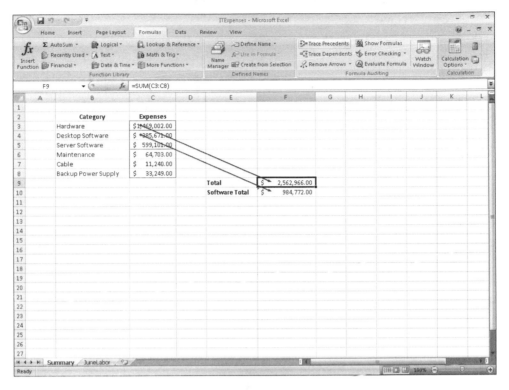

If the cells identified by the tracer arrows aren't the correct cells, you can hide the arrows and correct the formula. To hide the tracer arrows on a worksheet, display the Formulas tab, and then in the Formula Auditing group, click Remove Arrows.

If you prefer to have the elements of a formula error presented as text in a dialog box, you can use the Error Checking dialog box (which you can display by displaying the Formulas tab, and then in the Formula Auditing group, clicking the Error Checking button) to view the error and the formula in the cell in which the error occurs. You can also use the controls in the Error Checking dialog box to move through the formula one step at a time, to choose to ignore the error, or to move to the next or the previous error. If you click the Options button in the dialog box, you can also use the controls in the Excel Options dialog box to change how Excel 2007 determines what is an error and what isn't.

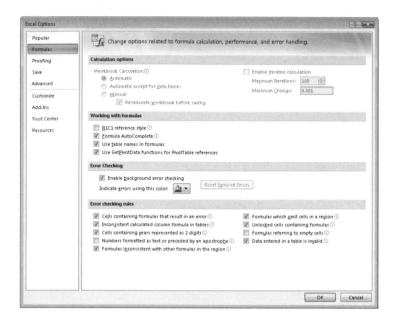

Tip You can have the Error Checking tool ignore formulas that don't use every cell in a region (such as a row or column). If you clear the Formulas that omit cells in a region check box, you can create formulas that don't add up every value in a row or column (or rectangle) without Excel 2007 marking them as an error.

For times when you just want to display the results of each step of a formula and don't need the full power of the Error Checking tool, you can use the Evaluate Formula dialog box to move through each element of the formula. To display the Evaluate Formula dialog box, you display the Formulas tab and then, in the Formula Auditing group, click the Evaluate Formula button. The Evaluate Formula dialog box is much more useful for examining formulas that don't produce an error but aren't generating the result you expect.

Finally, you can monitor the value in a cell regardless of where in your workbook you are by opening a Watch Window that displays the value in the cell. For example, if one of your formulas uses values from cells in other worksheets or even other workbooks, you can set a watch on the cell that contains the formula and then change the values in the other cells. To set a watch, click the cell you want to monitor, and then on the Formulas tab, in the Formula Auditing group, click Watch Window. Click Add Watch to have Excel 2007 monitor the selected cell.

As soon as you type in the new value, the Watch Window displays the new result of the formula. When you're done watching the formula, select the watch, click Delete Watch, and close the Watch Window.

In this exercise, you use the formula-auditing capabilities in Excel 2007 to identify and correct errors in a formula.

> **USE** the *ConveyerBid* workbook. This practice file is located in the *Documents\ Microsoft Press\2007OfficeSBS_HomeStudent\ExcelFormulas* folder.
>
> **OPEN** the *ConveyerBid* workbook.

1. Click cell **D20**.

2. On the **Formulas** tab, in the **Formula Auditing** group, click **Watch Window**.

   The Watch Window opens.

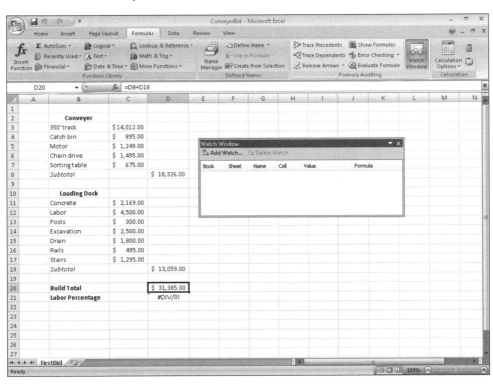

3. Click **Add Watch**, and then in the **Add Watch** dialog box, click **Add**.

Cell D20 appears in the Watch Window.

4. Click cell **D8**.

=SUM(C3:C7) appears in the formula bar.

5. On the **Formulas** tab, in the **Formula Auditing** group, click the **Trace Precedents** button.

A blue arrow appears between cell D8 and the cell range C3:C7, indicating that the cells in the range C3:C7 are precedents of the value in cell D8.

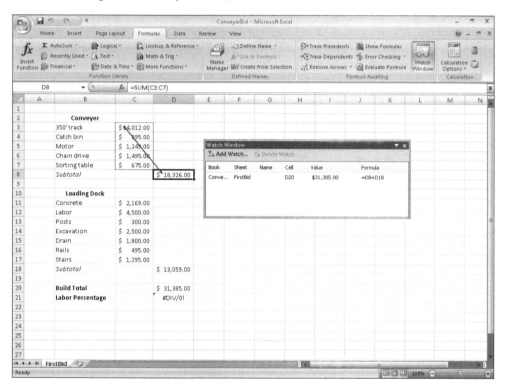

6. On the **Formulas** tab, in the **Formula Auditing** group, click the **Remove Arrows** button.

The arrow disappears.

7. Click cell **A1**.

8. On the **Formulas** tab, in the **Formula Auditing** group, click the **Error Checking** button.

   The Error Checking dialog box opens.

   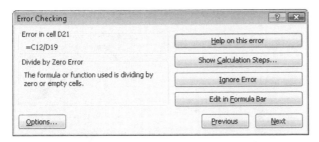

9. Click **Next**.

   Excel 2007 displays a message box indicating that there are no more errors in the worksheet.

10. Click **OK**.

    The message box and the Error Checking dialog box close.

11. On the **Formulas** tab, in the **Formula Auditing** group, click the **Error Checking** arrow, and then in the list, click **Trace Error**.

    Blue arrows appear, pointing to cell D21 from cells C12 and D19. These arrows indicate that using the values (or lack of values, in this case) in the indicated cells generates the error in cell D21.

12. On the **Formulas** tab, in the **Formula Auditing** group, click **Remove Arrows**.

    The arrows disappear.

13. In the formula bar, delete the existing formula, type =C12/D20, and press ⌷Enter⌷.

    The value *14%* appears in cell D21.

14. Click cell **D21**.

15. On the **Formulas** tab, in the **Formula Auditing** group, click the **Evaluate Formula** button.

The Evaluate Formula dialog box opens, with the formula from cell D21 displayed.

16. Click **Evaluate** three times to step through the formula's elements, and then click **Close**.

    The Evaluate Formula dialog box closes.

17. In the **Watch Window**, click the watch in the list.

18. Click **Delete Watch**.

    The watch disappears.

19. On the **Formulas** tab, in the **Formula Auditing** group, click **Watch Window**.

    The Watch Window closes.

CLOSE the *ConveyerBid* workbook. If you are not continuing directly to the next chapter, exit Excel.

Key Points

- You can add a group of cells to a formula by typing the formula, and then at the spot in the formula in which you want to name the cells, selecting the cells by using the mouse.

- Creating named ranges enables you to refer to entire blocks of cells with a single term, saving you lots of time and effort. You can use a similar technique with table data, referring to an entire table or one or more table columns.

- When you write a formula, be sure you use absolute referencing (*$A$1*) if you want the formula to remain the same when it's copied from one cell to another or use relative referencing (*A1*) if you want the formula to change to reflect its new position in the worksheet.

- Instead of typing a formula from scratch, you can use the Insert Function dialog box to help you on your way.

- You can monitor how the value in a cell changes by adding a watch to the Watch Window.

- To see which formulas refer to the values in the selected cell, use Trace Dependents; if you want to see which cells provide values for the formula in the active cell, use Trace Precedents.

- You can step through the calculations of a formula in the Evaluate Formula dialog box or go through a more rigorous error-checking procedure by using the Error Checking tool.

Chapter at a Glance

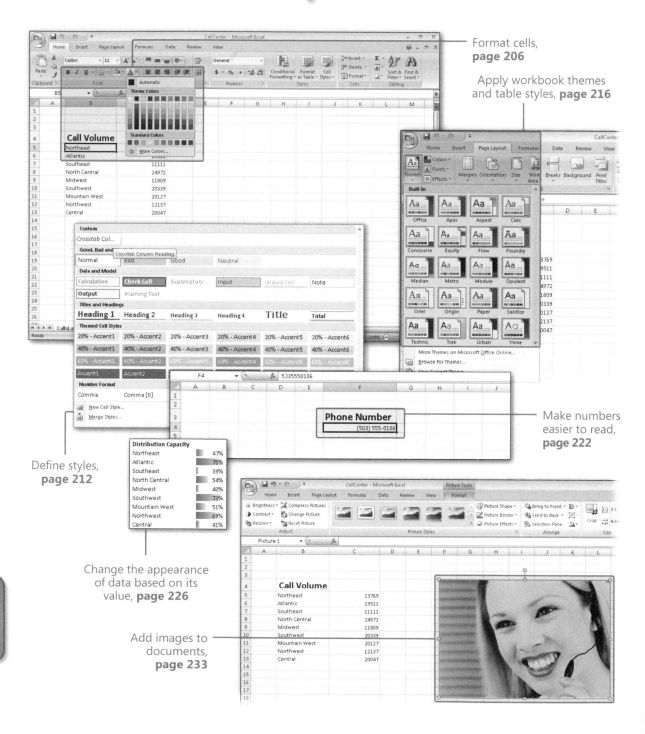

Format cells,
page 206

Apply workbook themes
and table styles, **page 216**

Make numbers
easier to read,
page 222

Define styles,
page 212

Change the appearance
of data based on its
value, **page 226**

Add images to
documents,
page 233

8 Changing Workbook Appearance

In this chapter, you will learn to:

- ✔ Format cells.
- ✔ Define styles.
- ✔ Apply workbook themes and table styles.
- ✔ Make numbers easier to read.
- ✔ Change the appearance of data based on its value.
- ✔ Add images to documents.

Entering data into a workbook efficiently saves you time, but you must also ensure that your data is easy to read. Microsoft Office Excel 2007 gives you a wide variety of ways to make your data easier to understand; for example, you can change the font, character size, or color used to present a cell's contents. Changing how data appears on a worksheet helps set the contents of a cell apart from the contents of surrounding cells. The simplest example of that concept is a data label. If a column on your worksheet has a list of days, you can set a label (for example, Day) apart easily by presenting it in bold type that's noticeably larger than the type used to present the data to which it refers. To save time, you can define a number of custom formats and then apply them quickly to the desired cells.

You might also want to specially format a cell's contents to reflect the value in that cell. For instance, Jenny Lysaker, the chief operating officer of Consolidated Messenger, might want to create a worksheet that displays the percentage of improperly delivered packages from each regional distribution center. If that percentage exceeds a threshold, she could have Office Excel 2007 display a red traffic light icon, indicating that the center's performance is out of tolerance and requires attention.

In addition to changing how data appears in the cells of your worksheet, you can also use headers and footers to add page numbers, current data, or graphics to the top and bottom of every printed page.

In this chapter, you'll learn how to change the appearance of data, apply existing formats to data, make numbers easier to read, change data's appearance based on its value, make printouts easier to follow, and position your data on the printed page.

See Also Do you need only a quick refresher on the topics in this chapter? See the Quick Reference entries at the beginning of this book.

Important Before you can use the practice files in this chapter, you need to install them from the book's companion CD to their default location. See "Using the Book's CD" at the beginning of this book for more information.

Troubleshooting Graphics and operating system–related instructions in this book reflect the Windows Vista user interface. If your computer is running Windows XP and you experience trouble following the instructions as written, please refer to the "Information for Readers Running Windows XP" section at the beginning of this book.

Formatting Cells

Excel 2007 spreadsheets can hold and process lots of data, but when you manage numerous spreadsheets it can be hard to remember from a worksheet's title exactly what data is kept in that worksheet. Data labels give you and your colleagues information about data in a worksheet, but it's important to format the labels so that they stand out visually. To make your data labels or any other data stand out, you can change the format of the cells in which the data is stored.

	A	B	C	D	E
1					
2					
3					
4		Call Volume			
5		Northeast	13769		
6		Atlantic	19511		
7		Southeast	11111		
8		North Central	24972		
9		Midwest	11809		
10		Southwest	20339		
11		Mountain West	20127		
12		Northwest	12137		
13		Central	20047		

Most of the tools you need to change a cell's format can be found on the Home tab. You can apply the formatting represented on a button by selecting the cells you want to apply the style to and then clicking the appropriate button. If you want to set your data labels apart by making them appear bold, click the Bold button. If you have already made a cell's contents bold, selecting the cell and clicking the Bold button will remove the formatting.

> **Tip** Deleting a cell's contents doesn't delete the cell's formatting. To delete a cell's format-ting, select the cell and then, on the Home tab, in the Editing group, click the Clear button and then click Clear Formats.

Buttons in the Home tab's Font group that give you choices, such as the Font Color control, have an arrow at the right edge of the button. Clicking the arrow displays a list of options accessible for that control, such as the fonts available on your system or the colors you can assign to a cell.

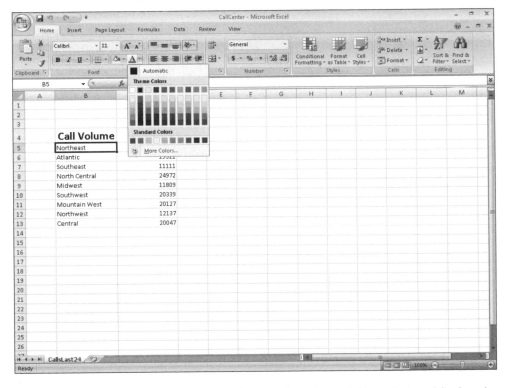

Another way you can make a cell stand apart from its neighbors is to add a border around the cell. To place a border around one or more cells, select the cells and then choose the border type you want by selecting the type of border to apply from the Border list in the Font group. Excel 2007 does provide more options—to display the full range of border types and styles, in the Border list, click More Borders. The Border tab of the Format Cells dialog box contains the full range of tools you can use to define your cells' borders.

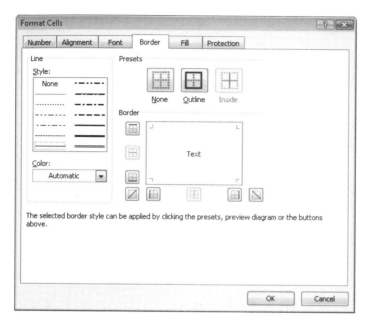

Another way you can make a group of cells stand apart from its neighbors is to change its shading, or the color that fills the cells. On a worksheet that tracks total package volume for the past month, Jenny Lysaker could change the fill color of the cells holding her data labels to make the labels stand out even more than by changing the formatting of the text used to display the labels.

> **Tip** You can display the most commonly used formatting controls by right-clicking a selected range. When you do, a Mini toolbar containing a subset of the Home tab formatting tools appears at the top of the shortcut menu.

If you want to change the attributes of every cell in a row or column, you can click the header of the row or column you want to format and then select your desired format.

One task you can't perform using the tools on the Home tab is to change the standard font for a workbook, which is used in the Name box and on the formula bar. The standard font when you install Excel 2007 is Calibri, a simple font that is easy to read on a computer screen and on the printed page. If you want to choose another font, click the Microsoft Office Button, and then click Excel Options. On the Popular page of the Excel Options dialog box, set the values in the Use This Font and Font Size list boxes to pick your new display font.

> **Important** The new standard font doesn't take effect until you exit Excel 2007 and restart the program.

In this exercise, you emphasize a worksheet's title by changing the format of cell data, adding a border to a cell range, and then changing a cell range's fill color. After those tasks are complete, you change the default font for the workbook.

USE the *VehicleMileSummary* workbook. This practice file is located in the *Documents\ Microsoft Press\2007OfficeSBS_HomeStudent\ExcelAppearance* folder.

BE SURE TO start Excel 2007 before beginning this exercise.

OPEN the *VehicleMileSummary* workbook.

1. Click cell **D2**.

Bold

2. On the **Home** tab, in the **Font** group, click the **Bold** button.

   Excel 2007 displays the cell's contents in bold type.

Font Size

3. In the **Font** group, click the **Font Size** arrow, and then in the list, click **18**.

   Excel 2007 increases the size of the text in cell D2.

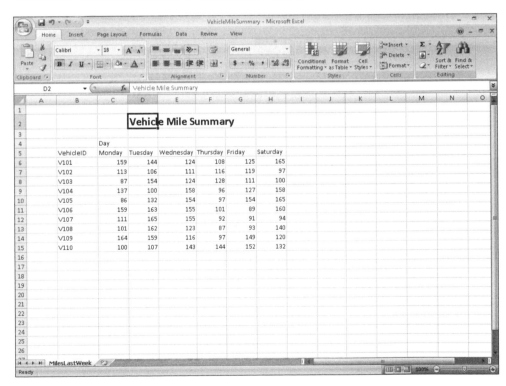

4. Select cells **B5** and **C4**.

5. On the **Home** tab, in the **Font** group, click the **Bold** button.

Excel 2007 displays the cells' contents in bold type.

6. Select the cell ranges **B6:B15** and **C5:H5**.

7. In the **Font** group, click the **Italic** button.

Italic

Excel 2007 displays the cells' contents in italic type.

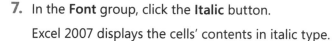

	A	B	C	D	E	F	G	H	I
1									
2				Vehicle Mile Summary					
3									
4			Day						
5		VehicleID	Monday	Tuesday	Wednesday	Thursday	Friday	Saturday	
6		V101	159	144	124	108	125	165	
7		V102	113	106	111	116	119	97	
8		V103	87	154	124	128	111	100	
9		V104	137	100	158	96	127	158	
10		V105	86	132	154	97	154	165	
11		V106	159	163	155	101	89	160	
12		V107	111	165	155	92	91	94	
13		V108	101	162	123	87	93	140	
14		V109	164	159	116	97	149	120	
15		V110	100	107	143	144	152	132	
16									

8. Select the cell range **C6:H15**.

9. In the **Font** group, click the **Border** arrow, and then in the list, click **Outside Borders**.

Border

Excel 2007 places a border around the outside edge of the selected cells.

10. Select the cell range **B4:H15**.

11. In the **Border** list, click **Thick Box Border**.

Excel 2007 places a thick border around the outside edge of the selected cells.

12. Select the cell ranges **B4:B15** and **C4:H5**.

13. In the **Font** group, click the **Fill Color** arrow and then, in the **Standard Colors** section of the color palette, click the yellow button.

Fill Color

Excel 2007 changes the selected cells' background color to yellow.

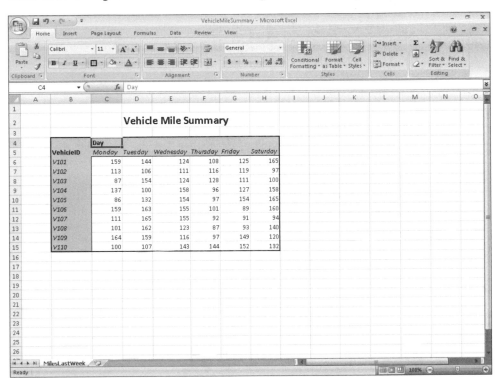

Microsoft Office
Button

14. Click the **Microsoft Office Button**, and then click **Excel Options**.

The Excel Options dialog box opens.

15. If necessary, click **Popular** to display the **Popular** tab.

16. In the **When creating new workbooks** section, in the **Use this font** list, click **Verdana**.

Verdana appears in the Use This Font field.

17. Click **Cancel**.

The Excel Options dialog box closes without saving your change.

 CLOSE the *VehicleMileSummary* workbook.

Defining Styles

As you work with Excel 2007, you will probably develop preferred formats for data labels, titles, and other worksheet elements. Instead of adding the format's characteristics one element at a time to the target cells, you can have Excel 2007 store the format and re-call it as needed. You can find the predefined formats available to you by displaying the Home tab, and then in the Styles group, clicking Cell Styles.

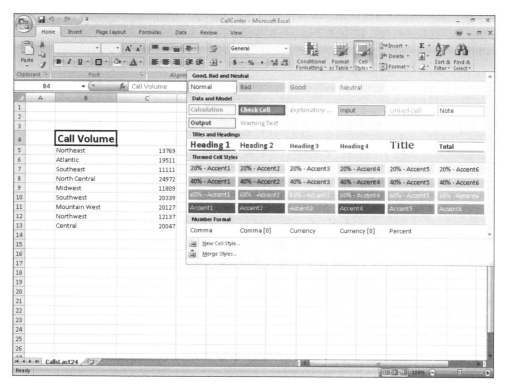

Clicking a style from the Cell Styles gallery applies the style to the selected cells, but Excel 2007 goes a step beyond previous versions of the program by displaying a live preview of a format when you hover your mouse pointer on it. If none of the existing styles is what you want, you can create your own style by displaying the Cell Styles gallery and, at the bottom of the gallery, clicking New Cell Style to display the Style dialog box. In the Style dialog box, type the name of your new style in the Style Name field, and then click Format. The Format Cells dialog box opens.

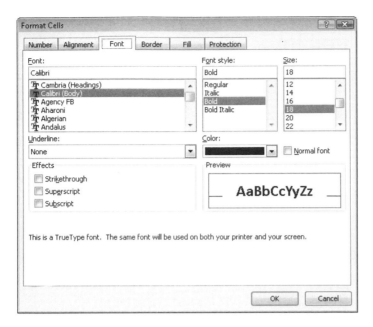

After you set the characteristics of your new style, click OK to make your style available in the Cell Styles gallery. If you ever want to delete a style, display the Cell Styles gallery, right-click the style, and then click Delete.

The Style dialog box is quite versatile, but it's overkill if all you want to do is apply formatting changes you made to a cell to the contents of another cell. To do so, use the Format Painter button, found in the Home tab's Clipboard group. Just click the cell that has the format you want to copy, click the Format Painter button, and select the target cells to have Excel 2007 apply the copied format to the target range.

In this exercise, you will create a style, apply the new style to a data label, and then use the Format Painter to apply the style to the contents of another cell.

 USE the *HourlyExceptions* workbook. This practice file is located in the *Documents\ Microsoft Press\2007OfficeSBS_HomeStudent\ExcelAppearance* folder.
OPEN the *HourlyExceptions* workbook.

1. On the **Home** tab, in the **Styles** group, click **Cell Styles**, and then **New Cell Style**.

The Style dialog box opens.

2. In the **Style name** field, type Crosstab Column Heading.

3. Click the **Format** button.

   The Format Cells dialog box opens.

4. Click the **Alignment** tab.

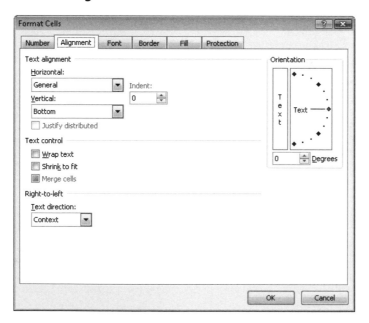

5. In the **Horizontal** list, click **Center**.

Center appears in the Horizontal field.

6. Click the **Font** tab.

7. In the **Font style** list, click **Italic**.

The text in the Preview pane appears in italicized text.

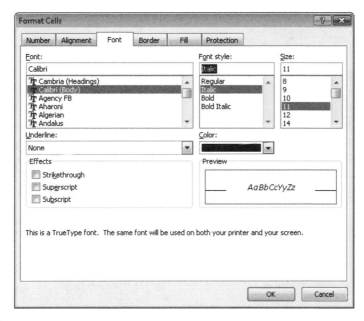

8. Click the **Number** tab.

The Number tab of the Format Cells dialog box is displayed.

9. In the **Category** list, click **Time**.

The available time formats appear.

10. In the **Type** pane, click **1:30 PM**.

11. Click **OK** to accept the default time format.

The Format Cells dialog box closes, and your new style's definition appears in the Style dialog box.

12. Click **OK**.

The Style dialog box closes.

13. Select cells **C4:N4**.

14. On the **Home** tab, in the **Styles** group, click **Cell Styles**.

Your new style appears at the top of the gallery, in the Custom group.

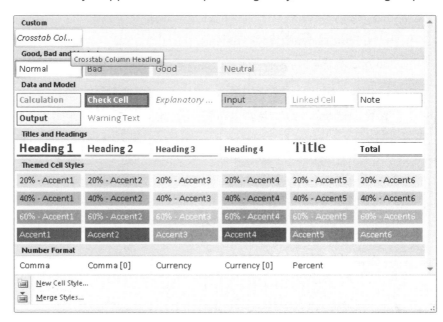

15. Click the **Crosstab Column Heading** style.

Excel 2007 applies your new style to the selected cells.

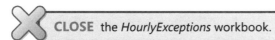

CLOSE the *HourlyExceptions* workbook.

Applying Workbook Themes and Table Styles

The 2007 Microsoft Office system includes powerful new design tools that enable you to create attractive, professional documents quickly. The Excel 2007 product team implemented the new design capabilities by defining workbook themes and table styles. A *theme* is a way to specify the fonts, colors, and graphic effects that appear in a workbook. Excel 2007 comes with many themes installed.

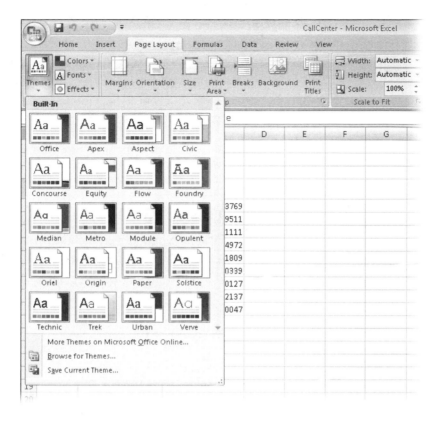

To apply an existing workbook theme, display the Page Layout tab. Then, in the Themes group, click Themes, and then click the theme you want to apply to your workbook. By default, Excel 2007 applies the Office theme to your workbooks.

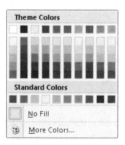

The theme colors appear in the top segment of the color palette—the standard colors and the More Colors link, which displays the Colors dialog box, appear at the bottom of the palette. If you format workbook elements using colors from the theme colors portion of the color palette, applying a different theme changes that object's colors.

You can change a theme's colors, fonts, and graphic effects by displaying the Page Layout tab, and then in the Themes group, selecting new values from the Colors, Fonts, and Effects lists. To save your changes as a new theme, display the Page Layout tab, and then in the Themes group, click Themes, and then click Save Current Theme. Use the controls in the dialog box that opens to record your theme for later use. Later, when you click the Themes button, your custom theme will appear at the top of the gallery.

> **Note** When you save a theme, you save it as an Office Theme file. You can apply the theme to Microsoft Office Word 2007 and Microsoft Office PowerPoint 2007 files as well.

Just as you can define themes and apply them to entire workbooks, you can apply and define table styles. You select a table's initial style when you create it; to create a new table style, display the Home tab, and then in the Styles group, click Format as Table. In the Format as Table gallery, click New Table Style to display the New Table Quick Style dialog box.

Type a name for the new style, select the first table element you want to format, and then click Format to display the Format Cells dialog box. Define the element's formatting, and then click OK. When the New Table Quick Style dialog box reopens, its Preview pane displays the overall table style and the Element Formatting section displays the selected element's appearance. Also, in the Table Element list, Excel 2007 displays the element's name in bold to indicate it has been changed.

If you want to make your new style the default for any new tables created in the current workbook, select the Set As Default Table Quick Style For This Document check box. When you click OK, Excel 2007 saves your custom table style.

See Also For more information about creating Excel tables, see "Defining a Table" in Chapter 6, "Working with Data and Data Tables."

In this exercise, you will create a new workbook theme, change a workbook's theme, create a new table style, and apply the new style to a table.

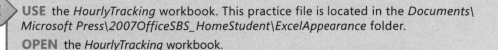

USE the *HourlyTracking* workbook. This practice file is located in the *Documents\ Microsoft Press\2007OfficeSBS_HomeStudent\ExcelAppearance* folder.
OPEN the *HourlyTracking* workbook.

1. If necessary, click any cell in the table.

2. On the **Home** tab, in the **Styles** group, click **Format as Table**, and then click the style at the upper-left corner of the **Table Styles** gallery.

   Excel 2007 applies the style to the table.

3. On the **Home** tab, in the **Styles** group, click **Format as Table**, and then click **New Table Style**.

   The New Table Quick Style dialog box opens.

4. In the **Name** field, type Exception Default.

5. In the **Table Element** list, click **Header Row**.

6. Click **Format**.

   The Format Cells dialog box opens.

7. Click the **Fill** tab.

   The Fill tab appears.

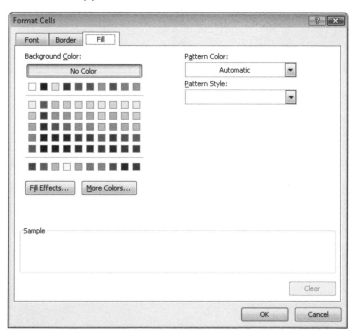

8. In the first row of color squares, just below the **No Color** button, click the third square from the left.

   The new background color appears in the Sample pane of the dialog box.

9. Click **OK**.

   The Format Cells dialog box closes. When the New Table Quick Style dialog box reopens, the Header Row table element appears in bold, and the Preview pane's header row is shaded.

10. In the **Table Element** list, click **Second Row Stripe**, and then click **Format**.

    The Format Cells dialog box opens.

11. Click the **No Color** button, and click the third square from the left again.

    The new background color appears in the Sample pane of the dialog box.

12. Click **OK**.

    The Format Cells dialog box closes. When the New Table Quick Style dialog box reopens, the Second Row Stripe table element appears in bold, and every second row is shaded in the Preview pane.

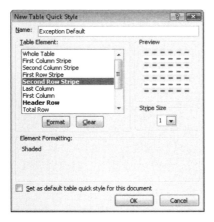

13. Click **OK**.

    The New Table Quick Style dialog box closes.

14. On the **Home** tab, in the **Styles** group, click **Format as Table**. In the gallery that appears, in the **Custom** section, click the new format.

    Excel 2007 applies the new format.

15. On the **Page Layout** tab, in the **Themes** group, click the **Fonts** arrow, and then in the list, click **Verdana**.

Excel 2007 changes the theme's font to Verdana.

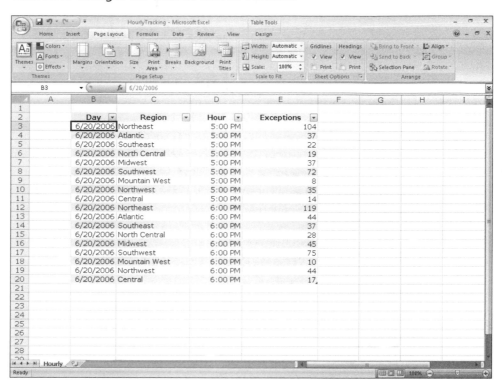

16. In the **Themes** group, click the **Themes** button, and then click **Save Current Theme**.

The Save Current Theme dialog box opens.

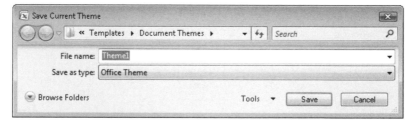

17. In the **File name** field, type **Verdana Office**, and then click **Save**.

Excel 2007 saves your theme.

18. In the **Themes** group, click the **Themes** button, and then click **Origin**.

Excel 2007 applies the new theme to your workbook.

 CLOSE the *HourlyTracking* workbook.

Making Numbers Easier to Read

Changing the format of the cells in your worksheet can make your data much easier to read, both by setting data labels apart from the actual data and by adding borders to define the boundaries between labels and data even more clearly. Of course, using formatting options to change the font and appearance of a cell's contents doesn't help with idiosyncratic data types such as dates, phone numbers, or currency.

For example, consider U.S. phone numbers. These numbers are 10 digits long and have a 3-digit area code, a 3-digit exchange, and a 4-digit line number written in the form (###) ###-####. Although it's certainly possible to type a phone number with the expected formatting in a cell, it's much simpler to type a sequence of 10 digits and have Excel 2007 change the data's appearance.

You can tell Excel 2007 to expect a phone number in a cell by opening the Format Cells dialog box to the Number tab and displaying the formats under the Special category.

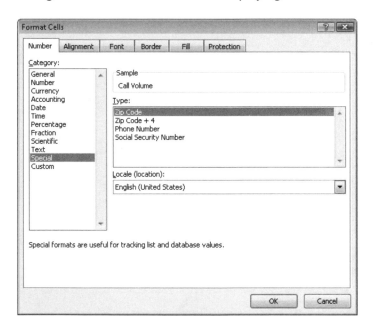

Clicking Phone Number from the Type list tells Excel 2007 to format 10-digit numbers in the standard phone number format. As you can see by comparing the contents of the active cell and the contents of the formula bar in the next graphic, the underlying data isn't changed, just its appearance in the cell.

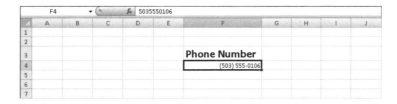

> **Troubleshooting** If you type a nine-digit number in a field that expects a phone number, you won't see an error message; instead, you'll see a two-digit area code. For example, the number 425555012 would be displayed as (42) 555-5012. An 11-digit number would be displayed with a 4-digit area code.

Just as you can instruct Excel 2007 to expect a phone number in a cell, you can also have it expect a date or a currency amount. You can make those changes from the Format Cells dialog box by choosing either the Date category or the Currency category. The Date category enables you to pick the format for the date (and determine whether the date's appearance changes due to the Locale setting of the operating system on the computer viewing the workbook). In a similar vein, selecting the Currency category displays controls to set the number of places after the decimal point, the currency symbol to use, and the way in which Excel 2007 should display negative numbers.

> **Tip** The new Excel 2007 user interface enables you to set the most common format changes by using the controls in the Home tab's Number group.

You can also create a custom numeric format to add a word or phrase to a number in a cell. For example, you can add the phrase per month to a cell with a formula that calculates average monthly sales for a year to ensure that you and your colleagues will recognize the figure as a monthly average. To create a custom number format, click the Home tab, and then click the Number Dialog Box Launcher to display the Format Cells dialog box. Then, if necessary, click the Number tab.

In the Category list, click Custom to display the available custom number formats in the Type list. You can then click the base format you want and modify it in the Type box. For example, clicking the 0.00 format causes Excel 2007 to format any number in a cell with two digits to the right of the decimal point.

> **Tip** The zeros in the format indicate that the position in the format can accept any number as a valid value.

To customize the format, click in the Type box and add any symbols or text you want to the format. For example, typing a dollar ($) sign to the left of the existing format and then typing *"per month"* to the right of the existing format causes the number 1500 to be displayed as *$1500.00 per month*.

> **Important** You need to enclose any text in quotes so that Excel 2007 recognizes the text as a string to be displayed in the cell.

In this exercise, you assign date, phone number, and currency formats to ranges of cells in your worksheet. After assigning the formats, you test them by entering customer data.

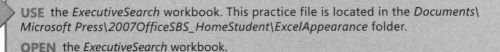

> **USE** the *ExecutiveSearch* workbook. This practice file is located in the *Documents\ Microsoft Press\2007OfficeSBS_HomeStudent\ExcelAppearance* folder.
>
> **OPEN** the *ExecutiveSearch* workbook.

1. Click cell **A3**.

Dialog Box
Launcher

2. On the **Home** tab, click the **Font** Dialog Box Launcher.

   The Format Cells dialog box opens.

3. If necessary, click the **Number** tab.

4. In the **Category** list, click **Date**.

   The Type list appears with a list of date formats.

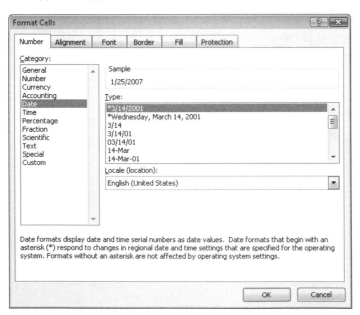

5. In the **Type** list, click **3/14/01**.

> **Caution** Be sure to click the format without the asterisk (*) in front of the sample date.

6. Click **OK** to assign the chosen format to the cell.

7. Click cell **G3**.

8. On the **Home** tab, click the **Font** Dialog Box Launcher.

9. If necessary, click the **Number** tab in the **Format Cells** dialog box.

10. In the **Category** list, click **Special**.

    The Type list appears with a list of special formats.

11. In the **Type** list, click **Phone Number**, and then click **OK**.

    The contents of the cell change to (425) 555-0102, matching the format you chose earlier, and the Format Cells dialog box closes.

12. Click cell **H3**.

13. Click the **Font** Dialog Box Launcher.

14. If necessary, click the **Number** tab in the **Format Cells** dialog box.

15. In the **Category** list, click **Custom**.

    The contents of the Type list are updated to reflect your choice.

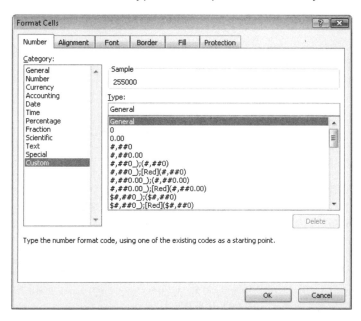

16. In the **Type** list, click the **#,##0** item.

#,##0 appears in the Type box.

17. In the **Type** box, click to the left of the existing format, and type $. Then click to the right of the format, and type "before bonuses".

18. Click **OK** to close the dialog box.

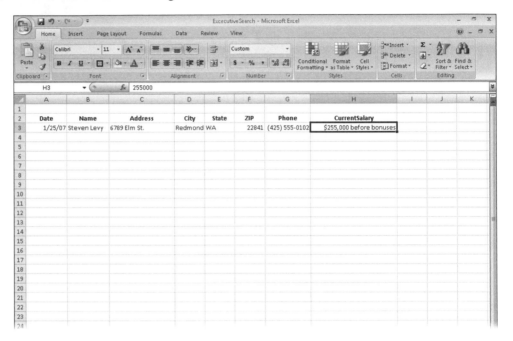

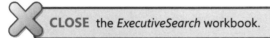

CLOSE the *ExecutiveSearch* workbook.

Changing the Appearance of Data Based on Its Value

Recording package volumes, vehicle miles, and other business data in a worksheet enables you to make important decisions about your operations. And as you saw earlier in this chapter, you can change the appearance of data labels and the worksheet itself to make interpreting your data easier.

Another way you can make your data easier to interpret is to have Excel 2007 change the appearance of your data based on its value. These formats are called *conditional formats* because the data must meet certain conditions to have a format applied to it.

For instance, if chief operating officer Jenny Lysaker wanted to highlight any Thursdays with higher-than-average weekday package volumes, she could define a conditional format that tests the value in the cell recording total sales, and that will change the format of the cell's contents when the condition is met.

In previous versions of Excel, you could have a maximum of three conditional formats. There's no such limit in Excel 2007; you may have as many conditional formats as you like. The other major limitation of conditional formats in Excel 2003 and earlier versions was that Excel stopped evaluating conditional formats as soon as it found one that applied to a cell. In other words, you couldn't have multiple conditions be true for the same cell! In Excel 2007, you can control whether Excel 2007 stops or continues after it discovers that a specific condition applies to a cell.

To create a conditional format, you select the cells to which you want to apply the format, display the Home tab, and then in the Styles group, click Conditional Formatting to display a menu of possible conditional formats. Excel 2007 enables you to create all the conditional formats available in previous versions of the program and offers many more conditional formats than were previously available. Prior to Excel 2007, you could create conditional formats to highlight cells that contained values meeting a certain condition. For example, you could highlight all cells that contain a value over 100, contain a date before 1/28/2007, or contain an order amount between $100 and $500. In Excel 2007, you can define conditional formats that change how the program displays data in cells that contain values above or below the average values of the related cells, that contain values near the top or bottom of the value range, or that contain values duplicated elsewhere in the selected range.

When you select which kind of condition to create, Excel 2007 displays a dialog box that contains fields and controls you can use to define your rule. To display all your rules, display the Home tab, and then in the Styles group, click Conditional Formatting. From the menu that appears, click Manage Rules to display the Conditional Formatting Rules Manager.

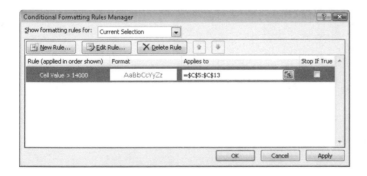

The Conditional Formatting Rules Manager, which is new in Excel 2007, enables you to control your conditional formats in the following ways:

- Creates a new rule by clicking the New Rule button
- Changes a rule by clicking the rule and then clicking the Edit Rule button
- Removes a rule by clicking the rule and then clicking the Delete Rule button
- Moves a rule up or down in the order by clicking the Move Up or Move Down button
- Controls whether Excel 2007 continues evaluating conditional formats after it finds a rule to apply by selecting or clearing a rule's Stop If True check box
- Saves any new rules and closes the Conditional Formatting Rules Manager by clicking OK
- Saves any new rules without closing the Conditional Formatting Rules Manager by clicking Apply
- Discards any unsaved changes by clicking Cancel

> **Note** Clicking the New Rule button in the Conditional Formatting Rules Manager opens the New Formatting Rule dialog box. The commands in the New Formatting Rule dialog box duplicate the options displayed when you click the Home tab's Conditional Formatting button.

After you create a rule, you can change the format applied if the rule is true by clicking the rule and then clicking the Edit Rule button to display the Edit Formatting Rule dialog box. In that dialog box, click the Format button to display the Format Cells dialog box. After you define your format, click OK.

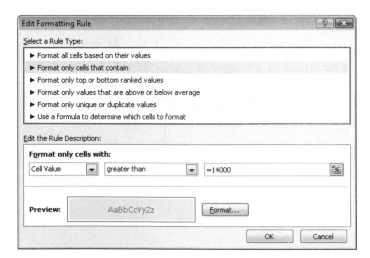

> **Important** Excel 2007 doesn't check to make sure that your conditions are logically consistent, so you need to be sure that you enter your conditions correctly.

Excel 2007 also enables you to create three new types of conditional formats: data bars, color scales, and icon sets. Data bars summarize the relative magnitude of values in a cell range by extending a band of color across the cell.

Distribution Capacity		
Northeast		47%
Atlantic		75%
Southeast		39%
North Central		54%
Midwest		40%
Southwest		73%
Mountain West		51%
Northwest		69%
Central		41%

Color scales compare the relative magnitude of values in a cell range by applying colors from a two-color or three-color set to your cells. The intensity of a cell's color reflects the value's tendency toward the top or bottom of the values in the range.

Distribution Capacity	
Northeast	47%
Atlantic	75%
Southeast	39%
North Central	54%
Midwest	40%
Southwest	73%
Mountain West	51%
Northwest	69%
Central	41%

Icon sets are collections of three, four, or five images that Excel 2007 displays when certain rules are met.

Distribution Capacity	
Northeast	
Atlantic	
Southeast	
North Central	
Midwest	
Southwest	
Mountain West	
Northwest	
Central	

When you click a color scale or icon set in the Conditional Formatting Rule Manager and then click the Edit Rule button, you can control when Excel 2007 applies a color or icon to your data.

> **Caution** Be sure to not include cells that contain summary formulas in your conditionally formatted ranges. The values, which could be much higher or lower than your regular cell data, could throw off your formatting comparisons.

In this exercise, you create a series of conditional formats to change the appearance of data in worksheet cells displaying the package volume and delivery exception rates of a regional distribution center.

USE the *Dashboard* workbook. This practice file is located in the *Documents\Microsoft Press\2007OfficeSBS_HomeStudent\ExcelAppearance* folder.

OPEN the *Dashboard* workbook.

1. Select cells **C4:C12**.

2. On the **Home** tab, in the **Styles** group, click **Conditional Formatting**. From the menu that appears, point to **Color Scales**, and then in the top row of the palette that appears, click the second pattern from the left.

   Excel 2007 formats the selected range.

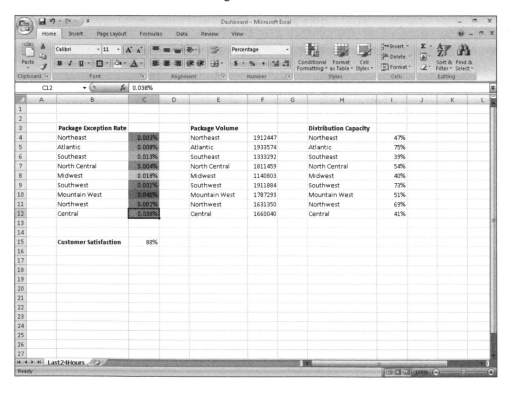

3. Select cells **F4:F12**.

4. On the **Home** tab, in the **Styles** group, click **Conditional Formatting**. From the menu that appears, point to **Data Bars**, and then click the light blue data bar format.

Excel 2007 formats the selected range.

5. Select cells **I4:I12**.

6. On the **Home** tab, in the **Styles** group, click **Conditional Formatting**. From the menu that appears, point to **Icon Sets**, and then in the left-hand column of the list of formats that appears, click the three traffic lights.

Excel 2007 formats the selected cells.

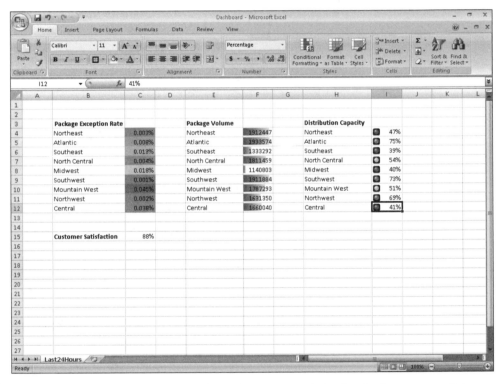

7. With the range I4:I12 still selected, on the **Home** tab, in the **Styles** group, click **Conditional Formatting**, and then click **Manage Rules**.

The Conditional Formatting Rules Manager opens.

8. Click the icon set rule, and then click **Edit Rule**.

The Edit Formatting Rule dialog box opens.

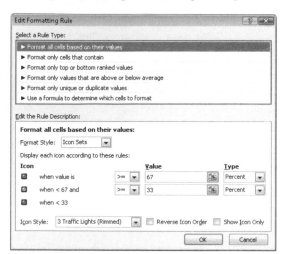

9. Select the **Reverse Icon Order** check box.

   Excel 2007 reconfigures the rules so the red light icon is at the top and the green light icon is at the bottom.

10. In the red light icon's row, in the **Type** list, click **Percent**.

11. In the red light icon's **Value** field, type 80.

12. In the yellow light icon's row, in the **Type** list, click **Percent**.

13. In the yellow light icon **Value** field, type 67.

14. Click **OK** twice to clear the **Edit Formatting Rule** dialog box and the **Conditional Formatting Rules Manager**.

    Excel 2007 formats the selected cell range.

15. Click cell **C15**.

16. On the **Home** tab, in the **Styles** group, click **Conditional Formatting**. From the menu that appears, point to **Highlight Cells Rules**, and then click **Less Than**.

    The Less Than dialog box opens.

17. In the left field, type 96%.

18. In the **With** list, click **Red text**.

19. Click **OK**.

    The Less Than dialog box closes, and Excel 2007 displays the text in cell C15 in red.

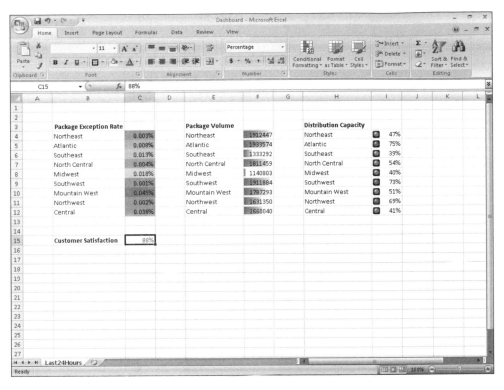

CLOSE the *Dashboard* workbook.

Adding Images to Documents

Establishing a strong corporate identity helps customers remember your organization and the products and services you offer. Setting aside the obvious need for sound management, two important physical attributes of a strong retail business are a well-conceived shop space and an eye-catching, easy-to-remember logo. After you or your graphic artist has created a logo, you should add the logo to all your documents, especially any that might be seen by your customers. Not only does the logo mark the documents as coming from your company but it also serves as an advertisement, encouraging anyone who sees your worksheets to call or visit your company.

One way to add a picture to a worksheet is to display the Insert tab, and then in the Illustrations group, click Picture. Clicking Picture displays the Insert Picture dialog box, which enables you to locate the picture you want to add from your hard disk. When you insert a picture, the Picture Tools contextual tab appears with the Format contextual tab right below it. You can use the tools on the Format contextual tab to change the picture's contrast, brightness, and so on. The controls in the Picture Styles group enable you to place a border around the picture, change the picture's shape, or change a picture's effects (such as shadow, reflection, or rotation in three dimensions). Other tools, found in the Arrange and Size groups, enable you to rotate, reposition, and resize the picture.

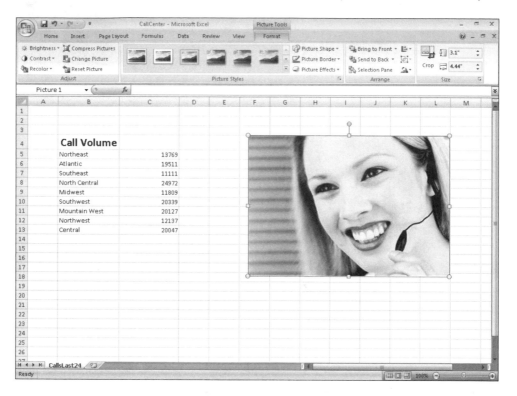

You can also resize a picture by clicking it and then dragging one of the handles that appear on the graphic. If you accidentally resize a graphic by dragging a handle, just click the Undo button to remove your change. If you want to generate a repeating image in the background of a worksheet, forming a tiled pattern behind your worksheet's data, you can display the Page Layout tab, and then in the Page Setup group, click Background. In the Sheet Background dialog box, click the image that you want to serve as the background pattern for your worksheet and click OK.

> **Tip** To remove a background image from a worksheet, display the Page Layout tab, and then in the Page Setup group, click Delete Background.

In this exercise, you add an image to an existing worksheet, change the graphic's location on the worksheet, reduce the size of the graphic, change the image's brightness and contrast, rotate and crop the image, delete the image, and then set the image as a repeating background for the worksheet.

USE the *CallCenter* workbook and the *callcenter* and *acbluprt* images. These practice files are located in the *Documents\Microsoft Press\2007OfficeSBS_HomeStudent\ExcelAppearance* folder.

OPEN the *CallCenter* workbook.

Picture

1. On the **Insert** tab, click **Picture**.

   The Insert Picture dialog box opens.

2. Browse to the *Documents\Microsoft Press\2007OfficeSBS_HomeStudent\ExcelAppearance* folder, and then double-click *callcenter.jpg*.

   The image appears on your worksheet.

3. Move the image to the upper-left corner of the worksheet, grab the handle at the lower-right corner of the image, and drag it up and to the left until it no longer obscures the Call Volume label.

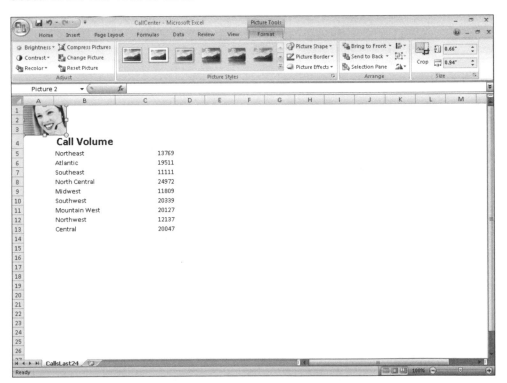

Background

4. On the **Page Layout** tab, in the **Page Setup** group, click **Background**.

   The Sheet Background dialog box opens.

5. Browse to the *Documents\Microsoft Press\2007OfficeSBS_HomeStudent\ExcelAppearance* folder, and then double-click *acbluprt.jpg*.

   Excel 2007 repeats the image to form a background pattern.

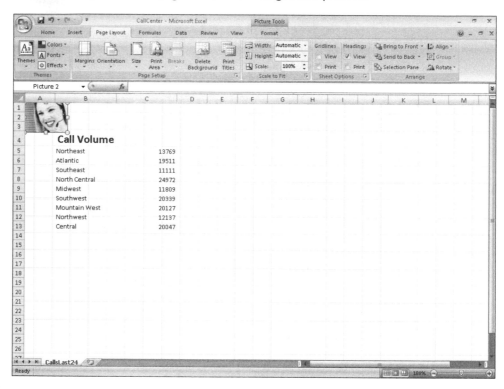

Delete Background

6. On the **Page Layout** tab, in the **Page Setup** group, click **Delete Background**.

   Excel 2007 removes the background image.

    CLOSE the *CallCenter* workbook, and then exit Excel.

Key Points

- If you don't like the default font in which Excel 2007 displays your data, you can change it.

- You can use cell formatting, including borders, alignment, and fill colors, to emphasize certain cells in your worksheets. This emphasis is particularly useful for making column and row labels stand out from the data.

- Excel 2007 comes with a number of existing styles that enable you to change the appearance of individual cells. You can also create new styles to make formatting your workbooks easier.

- If you want to apply the formatting from one cell to another cell, use the Format Painter to copy the format quickly.

- There are quite a few built-in document themes and table formats you can apply to groups of cells. If you see one you like, use it and save yourself lots of formatting time.

- Conditional formats enable you to set rules so that Excel 2007 changes the appearance of a cell's contents based on its value.

- Adding images can make your worksheets more visually appealing and make your data easier to understand.

Part III

Microsoft Office
PowerPoint 2007

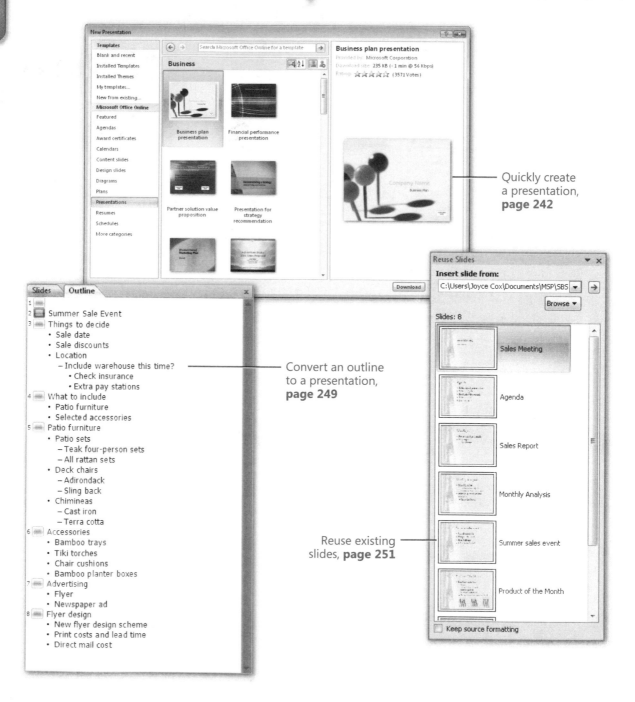

Quickly create a presentation, **page 242**

Convert an outline to a presentation, **page 249**

Reuse existing slides, **page 251**

9 Starting a New Presentation

In this chapter, you will learn to:

✔ Quickly create a presentation.

✔ Create a presentation based on a ready-made design.

✔ Convert an outline to a presentation.

✔ Reuse existing slides.

To work efficiently with Microsoft Office PowerPoint 2007, you must be able to decide the best way to start a presentation. The New Presentation window provides several options for creating a new presentation:

● If you need help with both the presentation's content and its look, you can download a complete presentation from Microsoft Office Online and then customize it to meet your needs.

● If you have already created a presentation that is close enough in content and design to be a good starting point, you can use that presentation as the basis for the new one.

● If you have content ready but need help with the look of the presentation, you can base your presentation on one of the design templates that comes with PowerPoint. These templates include graphics, colors, fonts, and styles. You can also base your presentations on your own custom templates.

● If you have created an outline of a presentation in Microsoft Office Word, you can import the outline into PowerPoint to create an instant slide show.

● If you know what your content and design will be and you want to build the presentation from scratch, you can start with a blank presentation.

This chapter will help you become familiar with these methods so that you can decide the best approach for each new presentation you create.

In this chapter, you will create several new presentations: one based on an example from Office Online, one based on a practice file stored on your hard disk, one based on a design template, and one based on a Word outline. You will also add slides to a presentation and insert slides from one presentation into another.

See Also Do you need only a quick refresher on the topics in this chapter? See the Quick Reference entries at the beginning of this book.

> **Important** Before you can use the practice files in this chapter, you need to install them from the book's companion CD to their default location. See "Using the Book's CD" at the beginning of this book for more information.

> **Troubleshooting** Graphics and operating system–related instructions in this book reflect the Windows Vista user interface. If your computer is running Windows XP and you experience trouble following the instructions as written, please refer to the "Information for Readers Running Windows XP" section at the beginning of this book.

Quickly Creating a Presentation

When you first start PowerPoint, a blank presentation is displayed in the presentation window, ready for you to enter text and design elements. If you want to create a presentation from scratch, this is the place to start.

> **Tip** If you are already working in PowerPoint, you can open a new blank presentation by clicking the Microsoft Office Button, clicking New, and then in the New Presentation window, double-clicking Blank Presentation.

However, creating presentations from scratch is time-consuming and requires quite a bit of skill and knowledge about PowerPoint. Even people with intermediate and advanced PowerPoint skills can save time by capitalizing on the work someone else has already done. In the New Presentation window, you can preview and download presentations that are available from Office Online and then customize these *templates* to meet your needs. You can also use any presentation that you have already created and saved on your hard disk as the basis for the new presentation.

When you create a new presentation based on a template, you are not opening the template; instead you are creating a new file that has all the characteristics of the template. The new file is temporary until you save it.

In this exercise, you will create two new presentations: one based on an example from Office Online, and the other based on a practice file stored on your hard disk.

> **Troubleshooting** Be sure your computer is connected to the Internet before starting this exercise. If it is not, you can read through the steps below but you won't be able to access the presentations available on Office Online.

USE the *Creating* presentation. This practice file is located in the *Documents\Microsoft Press\2007OfficeSBS_HomeStudent\PptStarting* folder.
BE SURE TO start PowerPoint before beginning this exercise.

Microsoft Office
Button

1. Click the **Microsoft Office Button**, and then click **New**.

   The New Presentation window opens.

2. In the left pane, under **Microsoft Office Online**, click **Presentations**.

   The center pane now lists categories of presentations that are available from Office Online.

3. In the center pane, click **Business**.

   The center pane now displays images of all the ready-made business presentations that are available from Office Online. The selected presentation is indicated by an orange frame, and information about that presentation appears in the right pane.

> **Troubleshooting** Don't be alarmed if your list of presentations is different than ours. New presentations are continually being added. In fact, it is worth checking Office Online frequently, just to see what's new.

4. Scroll the center pane, noticing the wide variety of presentations available.

5. About half way down the pane, click the **Company meeting presentation** image, and then in the lower-right corner of the window, click **Download**.

   A message box tells you that you can download templates from Office Online only if you are running a genuine version of PowerPoint.

6. Click **Continue**.

> **Tip** If you don't want this message box to appear every time you download a template, select the Do Not Show This Message Again check box before you click Continue.

After your version of PowerPoint is validated, a presentation based on the selected template opens on your screen in Normal view. The Slides tab shows thumbnails of the slides, and the title slide appears in the Slide pane.

Next Slide

7. Below the scroll bar on the right side of the screen, click the **Next Slide** button repeatedly to display each slide of the presentation in turn.

The slides contain generic instructions about the sort of information that you might want to include in a presentation for a company meeting. You can replace these instructions with your own text.

Save

8. On the **Quick Access Toolbar**, click the **Save** button.

PowerPoint suggests the title of the first slide as the name of the file.

9. Navigate to your *Documents\Microsoft Press\2007OfficeSBS_HomeStudent\ PptStarting* folder, and save the presentation with the name My Company Meeting.

The title bar now displays *My Company Meeting* as the name of the open presentation.

10. Display the **New Presentation** window again, and then in the left pane, under **Templates**, click **New from existing**.

The New From Existing Presentation dialog box opens.

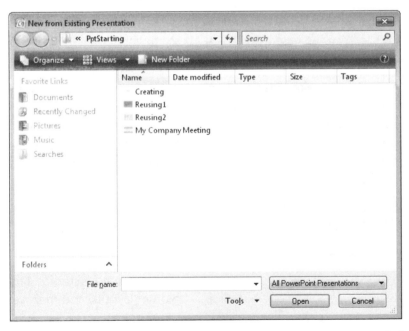

11. With the contents of the *PptStarting* folder displayed, double-click the *Creating* file.

A quick glance at the title bar tells you that instead of opening the *Creating* presentation, PowerPoint has opened a new presentation based on *Creating*.

12. On the **Quick Access Toolbar**, click the **Save** button.

Because this presentation is a new file, PowerPoint displays the Save As dialog box so that you can name the presentation.

13. Save the file in the *PptStarting* folder with the name My Sales Meeting.

The title bar now displays *My Sales Meeting* as the name of the active presentation.

 CLOSE the *My Sales Meeting* and *My Company Meeting* presentations.

Creating a Presentation Based on a Ready-Made Design

When you don't need help with the content of a presentation but you do need help with its design, you can start a new presentation based on a *design template*. A design template is a blank presentation with formatting, a color scheme, and sometimes graphics already applied to it. You can base a presentation on a design template from Office Online, or you can design your own presentation and save it as a template.

When you create a presentation based on a design template, PowerPoint supplies a *title slide* and leaves it to you to add the other slides you need. You add a slide by clicking the Add Slide button in the Slides group on the Home tab. This technique adds a new slide with the default layout immediately after the current slide. If you want to add a slide with a different layout, you can select the layout you want from the Add Slide list.

> **Tip** You can also add new slides by pressing keyboard shortcuts while you are entering text on the Outline tab. For more information, see "Entering Text" in Chapter 10, "Working with Slide Text."

In this exercise, you will start a new presentation based on a design template, add a new slide with the default layout, add slides with other layouts, and then delete a slide. There are no practice files for this exercise.

BE SURE TO start PowerPoint and close any open presentations before beginning this exercise.

Microsoft Office
Button

1. Click the **Microsoft Office Button**, and then click **New**.

2. In the left pane of the **New Presentation** window, under **Microsoft Office Online**, click **Design slides**.

    The center pane now displays categories of ready-made designs.

Back

3. In the center pane, click each category in turn, scroll through the thumbnails of the various design collections, and click the **Back** button at the top of the center pane to return to the list of categories.

4. In the center pane, click the **Business** category.

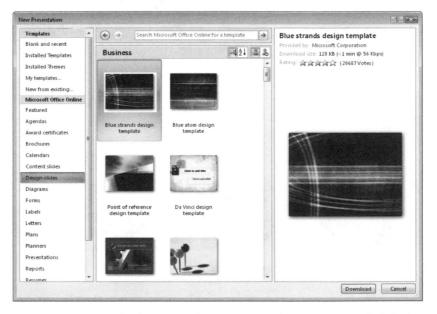

5. Scroll about a third of the way down the list of templates, and click the **Trust design template**. Then in the lower-right corner of the window, click **Download**, and if the **Microsoft Office Genuine Advantage** message box appears, click **Continue**.

    A new presentation with a single title slide opens on your screen in Normal view. The Slides tab shows a thumbnail of the slide, and the slide itself appears in the Slide pane.

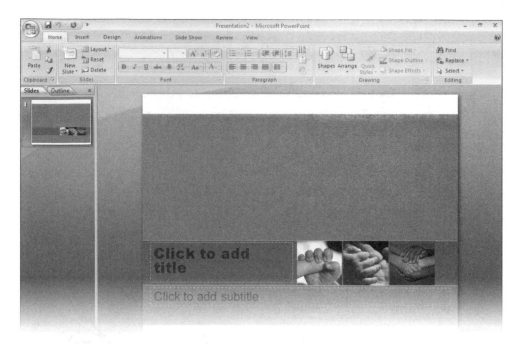

6. On the **Home** tab, in the **Slides** group, click the **New Slide** button (not its arrow).

PowerPoint adds Slide 2 to the presentation with the default Title And Content layout. This layout is designed to accommodate a title and either text or graphic content—a table, chart, diagram, picture, clip art image, or movie clip.

7. In the **Slides** group, click the **New Slide** arrow, and then in the list, click **Two Content**.

8. In the **Slides** group, click the **New Slide** button.

PowerPoint adds another slide with the Two Content layout. For all but the title slide, simply clicking the New Slide button adds a slide with the layout of the active slide.

9. Continue adding slides, selecting a different layout each time so that you can see what each one looks like.

10. At the top of the **Overview** pane, on the **Slides** tab, click **Slide 2**. Then in the **Slides** group, click the **Delete** button.

PowerPoint removes the slide from the presentation and renumbers all the sub-sequent slides.

 CLOSE the presentation without saving your changes.

Converting an Outline to a Presentation

You can insert an outline created in another program into a PowerPoint presentation. The text can be a Word document (*.doc* or *.docx*) or a *Rich Text Format (RTF)* file (*.rtf*). PowerPoint uses the heading styles in the inserted document to create slide titles and bullet points.

In this exercise, you will convert a Word outline into a presentation.

USE the *Converting* document. This practice file is located in the *Documents\Microsoft Press\2007OfficeSBS_HomeStudent\PptStarting* folder.

OPEN a new blank presentation.

New
Slide▾

1. On the **Home** tab, in the **Slides** group, click the **New Slide** arrow, and then below the slide thumbnails, click **Slides from Outline**.

    The Insert Outline dialog box opens.

2. Navigate to your *Documents\Microsoft Press\2007OfficeSBS_HomeStudent\PptStarting* folder, and then double-click the *Converting* file.

3. After the outline is converted, in the **Overview** pane, click the **Outline** tab to get an idea of the content of the presentation.

    PowerPoint has converted each level-1 heading into a slide title, each level-2 heading into a bullet point, and each level-3 heading into a subpoint.

4. On the **Outline** tab, right-click the empty title of **Slide 1**, which is blank, and then click **Delete Slide**.

CLOSE the presentation without saving your changes.

Tip You can start a new presentation from a Word outline by using the Open command. Click the Microsoft Office Button, and then click Open. In the Open dialog box, click the All PowerPoint Presentations setting, and in the list of file types, click All Files. Then locate and double-click the outline document you want to use.

Exporting a Presentation as an Outline

When you want to use the text from a presentation in another program, you can save the presentation outline as an RTF file. Many programs, including the Microsoft Windows and Macintosh versions of Word and older versions of PowerPoint, can import outlines saved in RTF with their formatting intact.

To save a presentation as an RTF file, follow these steps:

1. Click the **Microsoft Office Button**, and then click **Save As**.

   The Save As dialog box opens.

2. In the **File name** box, specify the name of the file.

3. Click the **Save as type** arrow, and then in the list, click **Outline/RTF**.

4. Navigate to the folder where you want to store the outline, and click **Save**.

   PowerPoint saves the presentation's outline in RTF format with the designated name in the designated folder.

Reusing Existing Slides

If your presentations often include one or more slides that provide the same basic information, you don't have to recreate the slides for each presentation. For example, if you create a slide that shows your company's product development cycle for one new product presentation, you might want to use variations of that same slide in all new product presentations. You can easily tell PowerPoint to copy a slide and insert in a specific location in a different presentation. The slide will assume the formatting of its new presentation.

In this exercise, you will insert slides from a presentation stored on your hard disk into the active presentation.

USE the *Reusing1* and *Reusing2* presentations. These practice files are located in the *Documents\Microsoft Press\2007OfficeSBS_HomeStudent\PptStarting* folder.

OPEN the *Reusing1* presentation.

1. On the **Slides** tab of the **Overview** pane, click **Slide 3**.

2. On the **Home** tab, in the **Slides** group, click the **New Slide** arrow, and then in the list, click **Reuse Slides**.

    The Reuse Slides task pane opens.

3. In the **Reuse Slides** task pane, click the **Open a PowerPoint File** link.

    PowerPoint displays the Browse dialog box with the contents of your *Documents* folder displayed.

4. Navigate to your *Documents\Microsoft Press\2007OfficeSBS_HomeStudent\ PptStarting* folder, and then double-click the *Reusing2* presentation.

    Thumbnails of all the slides in the presentation appear in the Reuse Slides task pane.

5. Scroll the task pane, and click the seventh thumbnail, titled *Bamboo Product Line*.

PowerPoint inserts the selected slide from the *Reusing2* presentation as Slide 4 in the *Reusing1* presentation. The slide takes on the design of the presentation in which it is inserted.

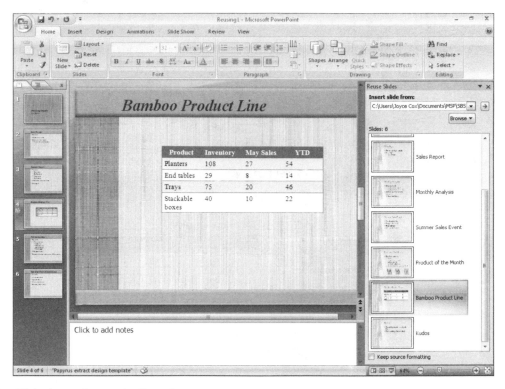

Close

6. Click the task pane's **Close** button.

CLOSE the *Reusing1* presentation without saving your changes.

Working with a Slide Library

If your organization is running Microsoft Office SharePoint Server 2007 and has enabled *slide libraries*, you and your colleagues can store slides or even entire presentations in the library so that they are available for use in any presentation. You can then repurpose the slides instead of having to create them from scratch.

For example, suppose a graphically gifted person has developed a slide with a sophisticated chart showing the percentage of income derived from the sale of different categories of merchandise. He or she can store the slide in a slide library so that other people can use it in their presentations without having to take the time to develop a similar chart. Larger organizations might even have people on staff with responsibility for creating this type of slide, so that they can ensure that all slide shows convey the same information in the same professional way.

To store slides in a slide library:

1. Click the **Microsoft Office Button**, point to **Publish**, and then click **Publish Slides**. The Publish Slides dialog box opens.

2. In the **Publish Slides** dialog box, select the check box for the slide you want to store in the library.

   You can also right-click a slide that you want to publish and then click Publish Slides to display the dialog box with that slide already selected.

3. If the URL of your SharePoint slide library does not appear in the **Publish To** box, click the box, and type the URL.

4. Click **Publish** to store the slide in the slide library.

To insert a slide from a slide library:

1. Click the slide after which you want the new slide to appear.

2. On the **Home** tab, in the **Slides** group, click the **New Slide** arrow, and then in the list, click **Reuse Slides**.

3. In the **Reuse Slides** task pane, in the **Insert slide from** box, type the URL of your SharePoint slide library, and then click the **Go** arrow.

4. Double-click the thumbnail of the slide you want to insert in the active presentation.

Key Points

- How you create a new presentation depends on whether you need help developing the content or the design.

- Office Online provides many presentation templates that you can customize to meet your needs.

- If you are required to use a particular design for a presentation, such as one with corporate colors and branding, it is often simpler to start with the design and then add your own content.

- Repurposing an existing presentation to fit the needs of a different audience is a useful technique that saves development time.

- Repurposing materials developed in other programs, such as Word, capitalizes on the compatibility of the 2007 Office system.

- Repurposing existing slides is another way to save time and ensure consistency.

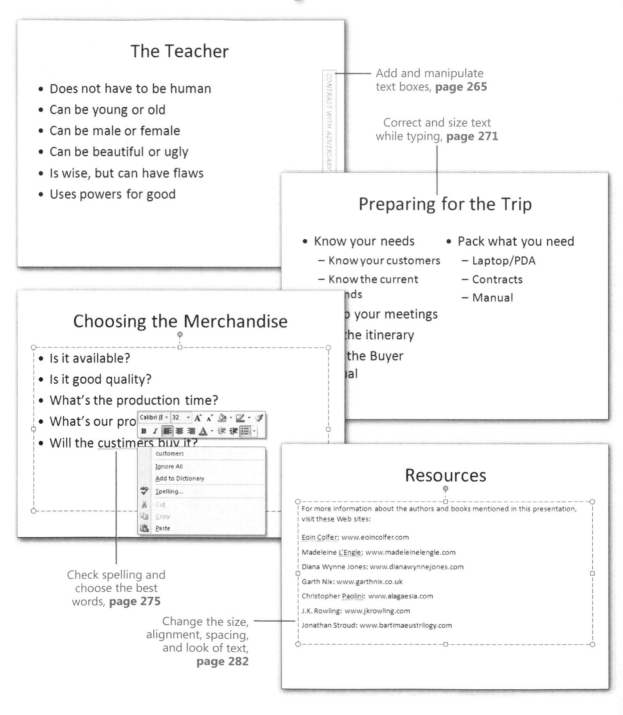

The Teacher

- Does not have to be human
- Can be young or old
- Can be male or female
- Can be beautiful or ugly
- Is wise, but can have flaws
- Uses powers for good

Add and manipulate text boxes, **page 265**

Correct and size text while typing, **page 271**

Preparing for the Trip

- Know your needs
  - Know your customers
  - Know the current [tre]nds
  - [Ma]p your meetings
  - [Finalize] the itinerary
  - [Contact] the Buyer
  - [Manu]al
- Pack what you need
  - Laptop/PDA
  - Contracts
  - Manual

Choosing the Merchandise

- Is it available?
- Is it good quality?
- What's the production time?
- What's our pro[fit?]
- Will the custimers buy it?

Calibri (E ▾ 32 ▾ A˄ A˅ 🖌 ▾ ✐ ▾ ✐
B I ≣ ≣ ≣ A ▾ ≔ ≔ ≣ ▾

- customers
- Ignore All
- Add to Dictionary
- 🔖 Spelling...
- ✂ Cut
- 📋 Copy
- 📋 Paste

Check spelling and choose the best words, **page 275**

Resources

For more information about the authors and books mentioned in this presentation, visit these Web sites:

Eoin Colfer: www.eoincolfer.com

Madeleine L'Engle: www.madeleinelengle.com

Diana Wynne Jones: www.dianawynnejones.com

Garth Nix: www.garthnix.co.uk

Christopher Paolini: www.alagaesia.com

J.K. Rowling: www.jkrowling.com

Jonathan Stroud: www.bartimaeustrilogy.com

Change the size, alignment, spacing, and look of text, **page 282**

10 Working with Slide Text

In this chapter, you will learn to:

- ✔ Enter text.
- ✔ Edit text.
- ✔ Add and manipulate text boxes.
- ✔ Correct and size text while typing.
- ✔ Check spelling and choose the best words.
- ✔ Find and replace text and fonts.
- ✔ Change the size, alignment, spacing, and look of text.

In later chapters of this book, we show you ways to add fancy effects to electronic slide shows to really grab the attention of your audience. But no amount of animation, jazzy colors, and supporting pictures will convey your message if the words on the slides are inadequate to the task. For most of your presentations, text is the foundation on which you build everything else, so this chapter shows you various ways to work with text to ensure that the words on your slides are accurate, consistent, and appropriately formatted.

In this chapter, you will learn how to enter and edit text on slides, on the Outline tab, and in text boxes. You will see how the AutoCorrect feature can help you avoid typographical errors, and how the spell-checking feature can help you correct misspellings after the fact. For those times when a word or phrase is correct but you want to substitute a different word or phrase, you will learn how to replace one word with another throughout a presentation by using the Find And Replace feature, which you also use to ensure the consistent use of fonts. Finally, you will vary the size, alignment, spacing, and look of words and phrases on individual slides.

See Also Do you need only a quick refresher on the topics in this chapter? See the Quick Reference entries at the beginning of this book.

Important Before you can use the practice files in this chapter, you need to install them from the book's companion CD to their default location. See "Using the Book's CD" at the beginning of this book for more information.

Troubleshooting Graphics and operating system–related instructions in this book reflect the Windows Vista user interface. If your computer is running Windows XP and you experience trouble following the instructions as written, please refer to the "Information for Readers Running Windows XP" section at the beginning of this book.

Entering Text

When you add a new slide to a presentation, the layout you select indicates the type and position of the objects on the slide with *placeholders*. For example, a Title And Content slide has placeholders for a *title* and either a bulleted list with one or more levels of *bullet points* (and subordinate levels called *subpoints*) or an illustration such as a table, chart, graphic, or movie clip. You can enter text directly into a placeholder on a slide in the Slide pane, or you can enter text on the Outline tab of the Overview pane, where the entire presentation is displayed in outline form.

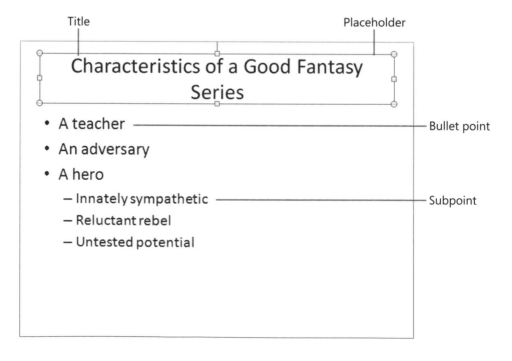

> **Tip** If you want to add text to a slide that has no text placeholder—for example, if you want to add an annotation to a graphic—you can create an independent text box and enter the text there. For information about creating text boxes, see "Adding and Manipulating Text Boxes" later in this chapter.

When you point to a placeholder on a slide or to text on the Outline tab, the pointer changes to an I-beam. When you click the placeholder or text, a blinking insertion point appears where you clicked to indicate where characters will appear when you type. As you type, the text appears both on the slide and on the Outline tab.

In this exercise, you will enter slide titles, bullet points, and subpoints, both directly in slides and on the Outline tab. There are no practice files for this exercise.

> **BE SURE TO** start PowerPoint before beginning this exercise.
> **OPEN** a new, blank presentation.

1. In the **Slide** pane, click the slide's **Click to add title** placeholder.

   A selection box surrounds the placeholder, and a blinking insertion point appears in the center of the box, indicating that the text you type will be centered in the placeholder.

2. Type **The Taguien Cycle**.

   Do not type the period. By tradition, slide titles have no periods. PowerPoint's spell-checking feature indicates with a red wavy underline that *Taguien* is a possible spelling error. This word is a proper name and is correct.

   > **Tip** If you make a typing error while working through this exercise, press Backspace to delete the mistake, and then type the correct text. For information about checking and correcting spelling, see "Checking Spelling and Choosing the Best Words" later in this chapter.

3. In the **Overview** pane, click the **Outline** tab, and notice that the text you typed also appears there.

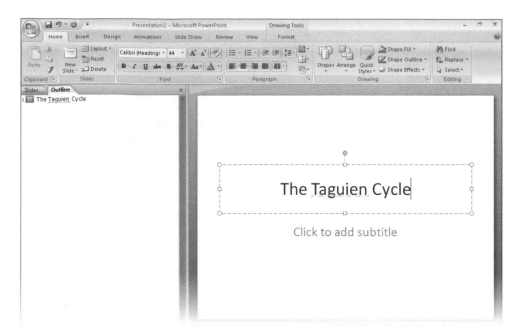

4. In the **Slide** pane, click the **Click to add subtitle** placeholder.

   The title placeholder is deselected, and the subtitle placeholder is selected.

5. Type A New Series for Young Adults, and then press Enter to move the insertion point to a new line in the same placeholder.

6. Type Judy Lew, Project Editor.

   As you enter titles and bullet points throughout the exercises, don't type any ending punctuation marks.

Save

7. On the **Quick Access Toolbar**, click the **Save** button, and save the presentation in the *PptWorking* subfolder with the name My Proposal.

   We won't tell you to save your work again in this exercise. Suffice it to say that you should save often.

8. Add a new slide with the **Title and Content** layout.

   See Also For information about adding slides, see "Creating a Presentation Based on a Ready-Made Design" in Chapter 9, "Starting a New Presentation."

   PowerPoint creates a new slide with placeholders for a title and a bulleted list. The Outline tab now displays an icon for a second slide, and the status bar displays *Slide 2 of 2*.

9. Without clicking anywhere, type Rationale.

If you start typing on an empty slide without first selecting a placeholder, PowerPoint enters the text into the title placeholder. The title appears on both the slide and the Outline tab.

10. On the **Outline** tab, click to the right of *Rationale*, and then press ⌷Enter⌷.

PowerPoint adds a new slide to the presentation, and an icon for Slide 3 appears in the Outline pane.

11. Press the ⌷Tab⌷ key.

The Slide 3 icon changes to a bullet on Slide 2. The bullet is gray until you enter text for the bullet point.

12. Type Lucerne currently has no offering for young adults, and then press ⌷Enter⌷.

PowerPoint adds a new bullet at the same level.

13. Type Fantasy series have been hits in this hard-to-please market, and then press ⌷Enter⌷.

14. Type Customers are turning to other publishers to meet demand, and then press ⌷Enter⌷.

15. Press ⌷Shift⌷ + ⌷Tab⌷.

On the Outline tab, the bullet changes into an icon for Slide 3. The new slide is displayed in the Slide pane.

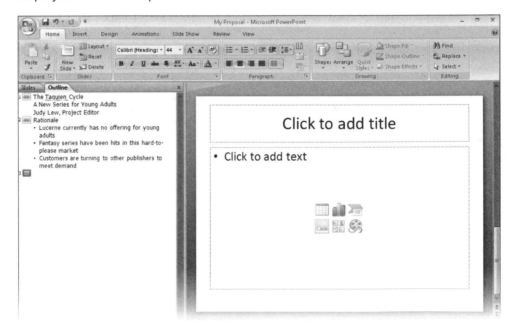

16. Type Characteristics of a Good Fantasy Series, press ⌷Enter⌷, and then press ⌷Tab⌷.

This slide title is too long to fit in the title placeholder at its default font size, so PowerPoint decreases the size to make it fit.

See Also For more information about the AutoFit feature, see "Correcting Text While Typing" later in this chapter.

17. Type A teacher, press ⌷Enter⌷, type An adversary, press ⌷Enter⌷, type A hero, and then press ⌷Enter⌷.

Increase List Level

18. On the **Home** tab, in the **Paragraph** group, click the **Increase List Level** button.

PowerPoint creates a subpoint.

> **Tip** You can use the Increase List Level button to change slide titles to bullet points and bullet points to subpoints both on the slide and on the Outline tab. You can also use the Decrease List Level button to change subpoints to bullet points and bullet points to slide titles in both places. However, when you are entering text on the Outline tab, it is quicker to use keys—Tab and Shift+Tab—to perform these functions than it is to take your hands off the keyboard to use your mouse.

19. Type Innately sympathetic, press ⌷Enter⌷, type Reluctant rebel, press ⌷Enter⌷, and then type Untested potential.

20. Press ⌷Ctrl⌷+⌷Enter⌷.

Instead of creating another bullet, PowerPoint creates a new slide.

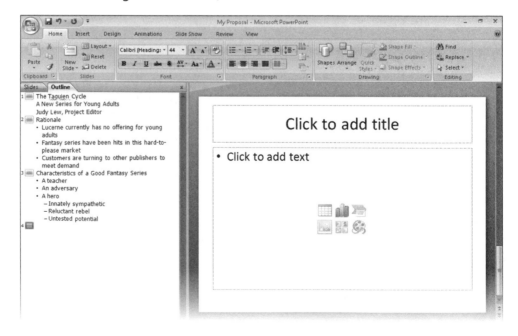

21. Save your work.

 CLOSE the My Proposal presentation.

Editing Text

After you enter text, you can change it at any time. You can insert new text by clicking where you want to make the insertion and simply typing. Before you can change existing text, you have to *select* it by using the following techniques:

- Select an individual word by double-clicking it. The word and the space following it are selected. Punctuation following a word is not selected.

- Select adjacent words, lines, or paragraphs by dragging through them.

- Alternatively, position the insertion point at the beginning of the text you want to select, hold down the Shift key, and either press an arrow key to select characters one at a time or click at the end of the text you want to select.

- Select an entire slide title by clicking its slide icon on the Outline tab.

- Select an entire bullet point or subpoint by clicking its bullet on either the Outline tab or the slide.

- Select all the text in a placeholder by clicking inside the placeholder and then clicking Select and then Select All in the Editing group on the Home tab.

    See Also For more information about the Select feature, see "Finding and Replacing Text and Fonts" later in this chapter.

Selected text appears highlighted in the location where you made the selection—that is, on either the slide or the Outline tab. To replace a selection, you type the new text. To delete the selection, you press either the Delete key or the Backspace key.

To move a selection to a new location, you can simply drag it. You can also move and copy text by using the Cut or Copy and Paste buttons in the Clipboard group on the Home tab. You can work on the slide itself when moving or copying text within a slide, but it is more efficient to work on the Outline tab when moving or copying text between slides.

If you change your mind about a change you have made, you can reverse it by clicking the Undo button on the Quick Access Toolbar. If you undo an action in error, you can click the Redo button on the Quick Access Toolbar to reverse the change.

To undo multiple actions at the same time, you can click the earliest action you want to undo in the Undo list. You can undo actions only in the order in which you performed them—that is, you cannot reverse your fourth previous action without first reversing the three actions that followed it.

> **Tip** The number of actions you can undo is set to 20, but you can change that number by clicking the Microsoft Office Button, clicking PowerPoint Options, clicking Advanced, and then under Editing Options, changing the Maximum Number Of Undos setting.

In this exercise, you will delete and replace words, as well as move bullet points and subpoints around on slides and on the Outline tab.

> **USE** the *Editing* presentation. This practice file is located in the *Documents\Microsoft Press\ 2007OfficeSBS\PptWorking* folder.
> **OPEN** the *Editing* presentation.

1. On the **Outline** tab, in the **Slide 1** subtitle, double click the word **New**.

   When you select text on either the Outline tab or the slide, a small toolbar (called the *Mini toolbar*) containing options for formatting the text appears. If you ignore the Mini toolbar, it fades from view.

   See Also For information about using the Mini toolbar, see "Changing the Size, Alignment, Spacing, and Look of Text" later in this chapter.

2. Press the Del key.

3. In the **Slide 3** title, double-click **Good**, and then type Hit followed by a space.

   What you type replaces the selection. Notice that the text also changes in the Slide pane.

4. Press End, and then press Backspace seven times to delete the word *Series*.

5. On the slide, click the bullet to the left of *Reluctant rebel*.

   The entire subpoint is selected, including the invisible paragraph mark at the end.

> **Troubleshooting** When you want to work with a bullet point or subpoint as a whole, you need to ensure that the invisible paragraph mark at its end is included in the selection. If you drag across the text, you might miss the paragraph mark. As a precaution, hold down the Shift key and press End to be sure that the paragraph mark is part of the selection.

Cut

Paste

6. On the **Home** tab, in the **Clipboard** group, click the **Cut** button.

7. Click to the left of the word *Innately*, and then click the **Paste** button.

   The first two subpoints have effectively switched places.

8. On the **Outline** tab, click the bullet point to the left of *A hero* to select the bullet point and its subpoints.

9. Drag the selection up and to the left of *A teacher*.

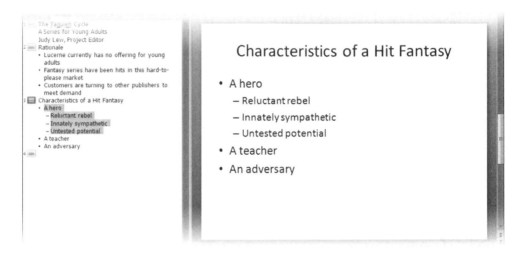

Undo

10. On the **Quick Access Toolbar**, click the **Undo** button to reverse your last editing action.

    The Redo button appears on the Quick Access Toolbar, to the right of Undo. When you point to the Undo or Redo button, the name in the ScreenTip reflects your last editing action—for example, Redo Drag And Drop.

Redo

11. On the **Quick Access Toolbar**, click the **Redo** button to restore the editing action.

CLOSE the *Editing* presentation without saving your changes.

Adding and Manipulating Text Boxes

The size and position of the placeholders on a slide are dictated by the slide's design. Every slide you create with a particular design has the same placeholders in the same locations, and the text you type in them has the same format.

When you want additional text to appear on the slide, such as annotations or minor points that do not belong in a bulleted list, you can create a *text box* by using the Text Box button in the Text group on the Insert tab. You can create a text box in two ways:

● You can click the Text Box button, click the slide where you want the text to appear, and then type. The text box grows to fit what you type on a single line, even expanding beyond the border of the slide if necessary.

● You can click the Text Box button, drag a box where you want the text to appear on the slide, and then type. When the text reaches the right boundary of the box, the height of the box expands by one line so that the text can wrap. As you continue typing, the width of the box stays the same, but the height grows as necessary to accommodate all the text.

When you click in a text box, an insertion point appears, and the box is surrounded by a dashed border. You can then edit the text—for example, you can add, delete, or correct words and punctuation. Clicking the dashed border changes it to a solid border. You can then manipulate the text box as a unit—for example, you can size, move, or copy it as a whole.

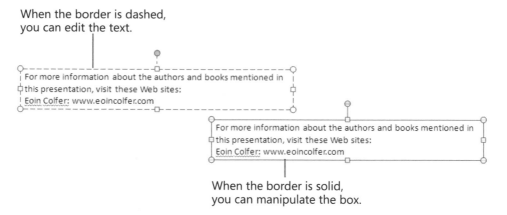

You can drag the *handles* around the border of the box to change its size and shape. By default, PowerPoint adjusts the box to fit the text within it. If you want to create a text box of a specific size or shape, you can right-click the box's border, click Format Shape, click Text Box in the Format Shape dialog box, and then change the settings. In this dialog box, you can also specify whether PowerPoint should shrink the text to fit the box if it won't all fit at the default size (18 points), and whether the text should wrap within the box.

> **Tip** If you want to change the size, shape, or behavior of a placeholder on an individual slide, you can use the same techniques as those you use with text boxes. If you want to make changes to the same placeholder on every slide, you should make the adjustments on the presentation's master slide."

Sometimes you will want the text in a text box to be oriented differently than the rest of the text on the slide. When a text box is selected, a green rotating handle is attached to its upper-middle handle. You can drag this handle to change the angle of the text.

> **Tip** You can also change the direction of text on the Text Box page of the Format Shape dialog box. In the Text Direction list, click one of the Rotate options. Or you can click Stacked to keep the individual characters horizontal but make them run from top to bottom in the box instead of from left to right.

When a text box is surrounded by a solid border, you can move or copy the text box anywhere on the slide. Dragging its border is the most efficient way to move a text box within a single slide, and you can copy it just as easily by holding down the Ctrl key while you drag it.

To deselect the text box, you click a blank area of the slide. The border then disappears. If you want a text box to have a border when it is not selected, you can display the Format Shape dialog box, and on the Line Color page, select either Solid Line or Gradient Line. You can then fine-tune the border's color or gradient to achieve the effect you want.

In this exercise, you will select and deselect a placeholder to see the effect on its border. You will create one text box whose height stays constant while its width increases and another whose width stays constant while its height increases. You will manipulate these text boxes by rotating and moving one of them and sizing the other. You will also make a text box border a solid line that is visible when the text box is not selected.

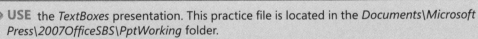

USE the *TextBoxes* presentation. This practice file is located in the *Documents\Microsoft Press\2007OfficeSBS\PptWorking* folder.
OPEN the *TextBoxes* presentation.

1. Move to **Slide 2**, and then on the slide, click the slide title.

    The placeholder is selected for editing, as indicated by the blinking insertion point and the dashed border.

2. Point to the border of the placeholder, and when the pointer changes to a four-headed arrow, click the mouse button once.

The placeholder is selected as a unit, as indicated by the solid border. Although you won't usually want to change the size or location of a text placeholder, while the placeholder has a solid border, you can size and move it just like any other text box. Your changes will affect only the placeholder on the current slide, not corresponding placeholders on other slides.

3. To deselect the placeholder, click outside it in a blank area of the slide.

4. Move to **Slide 5**, and then click the bulleted list placeholder.

5. On the **Insert** tab, in the **Text** group, click the **Text Box** button, and then point immediately below the lower-left handle of the placeholder for the bulleted list.

The pointer changes shape to an upside-down T.

6. Click the slide to create a text box.

A small, empty text box appears with a blinking insertion point inside it.

- Can be beautiful or ugly
- Is wise, but can have flaws
- Uses powers for good

7. Type **Contrast with Adversary on Slide 6**.

The width of the text box increases to accommodate the text as you type it.

- Can be beautiful or ugly
- Is wise, but can have flaws
- Uses powers for good

Contrast with Adversary on Slide 6

8. To rotate the text so that it reads vertically instead of horizontally, drag the green rotating handle that is attached to the upper-middle handle 90 degrees clockwise.

9. Point to the border of the box (not to a handle), and then drag the box to the right edge of the slide.

10. Right-click the border of the box, and then click **Format Shape**.

11. In the **Format Shape** dialog box, click **Line Color**.

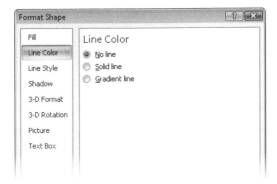

12. Click **Solid line**, click the **Color** arrow, and in the top row of the **Theme Colors** palette, click the orange box (**Orange, Accent 6**). Then click **Close**.

13. Click a blank area of the slide to deselect the text box, and then move to **Slide 2**.

14. On the **Insert** tab, in the **Text** group, click the **Text Box** button, point to the center of the area below the bulleted list, and drag approximately 2 inches to the right and ½ inch down.

    No matter what height you make the box, it snaps to a standard height when you release the mouse button.

15. Type Need to decide whether to offer the series to one author or to multiple writers.

    The width of the box does not change, but the box's height increases to accommodate the complete entry.

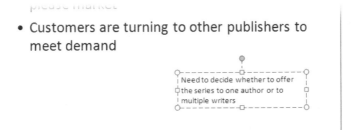

16. Click the border of the text box to select it as a unit, point to the solid border, and drag the box to the lower-left corner of the slide, so that its left border aligns with the text of the bullet points.

17. Point to the handle in the lower-right corner of the box, and drag up and to the right until the box is two lines high and the same width as the bullet points.

18. Click a blank area of the slide to deselect the text box.

• Customers are turning to other publishers to meet demand

Need to decide whether to offer the series to one author or to multiple writers

CLOSE the *TextBoxes* presentation without saving your changes.

Changing the Default Font for Text Boxes

When you create a text box, PowerPoint applies default settings such as the font, size, and style—regular, bold, and italic—as well as other effects—underline, small capitals, embossing, and so on. To save yourself some formatting steps, you can change the default settings for the presentation you are working on. Here's how:

1. In a new, blank presentation, create a text box and enter some text in it.

2. Select the text, and then on the **Home** tab, click the **Font** Dialog Box Launcher.

3. Select the font, font style, size, color, underline style, and effects you want to apply to all the text boxes you create from now on in this presentation, and then click **OK**.

   You can also add other effects, such as a fill color, outline formatting, or a special effect.

4. Select the text box itself, right-click its border, and then click **Set as Default Text Box**.

5. Create another text box on the same slide, and then enter text in it.

   The text appears with the new default settings.

Correcting and Sizing Text While Typing

We all make mistakes while typing test in a presentation. To help you ensure that these mistakes don't go uncorrected, PowerPoint uses the *AutoCorrect* feature to catch and automatically correct common capitalization and spelling errors. For example, if you type *teh* instead of *the* or *WHen* instead of *When*, AutoCorrect corrects the entry.

You can customize AutoCorrect to recognize misspellings you routinely type or to ignore text you do not want AutoCorrect to change. You can also create your own AutoCorrect entries to automate the typing of frequently used text. For example, you might customize AutoCorrect to enter the name of your organization when you type only an abbreviation.

In addition to using AutoCorrect to correct misspellings as you type, PowerPoint uses the AutoFit feature to size text to fit its placeholder. For example, if you type more text than will fit in a title placeholder, AutoFit shrinks the font size so that it all fits. The first time AutoFit changes the font size, it displays the AutoFit Options button to the left of the placeholder. Clicking this button displays a menu that gives you control over automatic sizing. For example, you can stop sizing text for the current placeholder while retaining your global AutoFit settings. You can also display the AutoCorrect dialog box, where you can change the AutoFit settings.

In this exercise, you will add an AutoCorrect entry and use AutoCorrect to fix a misspelled word. Then you will use AutoFit to size text so that it fits within its placeholder and to make a long bulleted list fit on one slide by converting its placeholder to a two-column layout.

USE the *Correcting* presentation. This practice file is located in the *Documents\Microsoft Press\2007OfficeSBS_HomeStudent\PptWorking* folder.

OPEN the *Correcting* presentation.

Microsoft Office Button

1. Click the **Microsoft Office Button**, click **PowerPoint Options**, and then in the left pane of the **PowerPoint Options** window, click **Proofing**.

2. Under **AutoCorrect options**, click **AutoCorrect Options**.

   The AutoCorrect dialog box opens.

> **Troubleshooting** If the AutoCorrect tab is not active, click it to display its options.

3. In the lower part of the dialog box, scroll through the huge table of misspellings.

When you type one of the entries in the first column, PowerPoint automatically substitutes the correct spelling from the second column.

4. In the **Replace** box above the table, type travil, and then press Tab.

5. In the **With** box, type travel, and then click **Add**.

Now if you type *travil* in any presentation, PowerPoint will replace it with *travel*.

6. Click **OK** to close the **AutoCorrect** dialog box, and then click **OK** again to close the **PowerPoint Options** window.

7. Move to **Slide 4**, click to the left of the word *advisories*, type travil, and then press [Space].

PowerPoint corrects the word *travil* to *travel*.

8. Move to **Slide 3**, click to the right of the word *need* in the last bullet point, and then press [Enter].

9. Press [Tab] to convert the new bullet point to a subpoint, type Laptop/PDA, and then press [Enter].

10. Add Contracts and Manual as two additional subpoints, pressing [Enter] after each one.

PowerPoint makes the text of the bulleted list smaller so that all the bullet points and subpoints fit in the placeholder. The AutoFit Options button appears in the lower-left corner of the slide.

11. Click the **AutoFit Options** button to display a list of options.

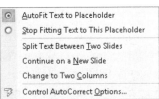

AutoFit Options

○ AutoFit Text to Placeholder
○ Stop Fitting Text to This Placeholder

Split Text Between Two Slides
Continue on a New Slide
Change to Two Columns

⌇ Control AutoCorrect Options...

12. Click **Change to Two Columns**.

The placeholder is instantly formatted to accommodate a two-column bulleted list, with the last bullet point and its subpoints at the top of the second column. All the bullet points in both columns increase in size.

13. Click a blank area of the slide to deselect the placeholder.

Preparing for the Trip

- Know your needs
  - Know your customers
  - Know the current trends
- Set up your meetings
- Plan the itinerary
- Read the Buyer manual

- Pack what you need
  - Laptop/PDA
  - Contracts
  - Manual

CLOSE the *Correcting* presentation without saving your changes.

Smart Tags

If you frequently use certain types of information, such as the date and time, names, street addresses, or telephone numbers, you can take advantage of the *Smart Tags* feature, which enables PowerPoint to recognize the information. When Smart Tags are turned on, PowerPoint displays a dotted line under the text to indicate that it has been flagged with a smart tag. Pointing to the underlined text displays the Smart Tag Actions button. You can click this button to display a menu of actions associated with that type of information.

You can check which types of information will be flagged with a smart tag by following these steps:

1. Click the **Microsoft Office Button**, click **PowerPoint Options**, click **Proofing**, and then click **AutoCorrect Options**.

2. In the **AutoCorrect** dialog box, click the **Smart Tags** tab.

To see what other Smart Tags are available, you can click More Smart Tags and explore a Web site that features smart tags developed by Microsoft and other companies.

Checking Spelling and Choosing the Best Words

The AutoCorrect feature is very useful if you frequently type the same misspelling. However, most misspellings are the result of erratic finger-positioning errors or memory lapses. You can use two different methods to ensure that the words in your presentations are spelled correctly in spite of these random occurrences:

- By default, PowerPoint's spelling checker checks the spelling of the entire presentation—all slides, outlines, notes pages, and handout pages—against its built-in dictionary. To draw attention to words that are not in its dictionary and that might be misspelled, PowerPoint underlines them with a red wavy underline. You can right-click a word with a red wavy underline to display a menu with a list of possible spellings. You can choose the correct spelling from the menu or tell PowerPoint to ignore the word. To turn off this feature, you can click the Microsoft Office Button, click PowerPoint Options, click Proofing, and then clear the Check Spelling As You Type check box.

- Instead of dealing with potential misspellings while you are creating a presentation, you can check the entire presentation in a single session by clicking the Spelling button in the Proofing group on the Review tab. PowerPoint then works its way through the presentation, and if it encounters a word that is not in its dictionary, it displays the Spelling dialog box. After you indicate how PowerPoint should deal with the word, it moves on and displays the next word that is not in its dictionary, and so on.

The English-language version of the 2007 Office release includes English, French, and Spanish dictionaries. If you use a word or phrase from a different language, you can mark it so that PowerPoint doesn't flag it as a misspelling.

You cannot make changes to PowerPoint's main dictionary, but you can add correctly spelled words that are flagged as misspellings to PowerPoint's supplemental dictionary (called CUSTOM.DIC). You can also create and use custom dictionaries and use dictionaries from other Microsoft programs.

PowerPoint can check your spelling, but it can't alert you if you are not using the best word. Language is often contextual—the language you use in a presentation to club members is different from the language you use in a business presentation. To make sure you are using words that best convey your meaning in any given context, you can use the *Thesaurus* to look up alternative words, or *synonyms*, for a selected word.

In this exercise, you will correct a misspelled word, mark a non-English word, and check the spelling of an entire presentation. You will then use the Thesaurus to replace a word on a slide with a more appropriate one.

USE the *Spelling* presentation. This practice file is located in the *Documents\Microsoft Press\2007OfficeSBS_HomeStudent\PptWorking* folder.

OPEN the *Spelling* presentation.

1. Move to **Slide 6**, add a fifth bullet point, and then type Will the custimers buy it?

   PowerPoint flags the word *custimers* as a possible error with a red wavy underline.

2. Right-click **custimers**.

   PowerPoint doesn't know whether you want to format the word or correct its spelling, so it displays both a Mini toolbar and a menu.

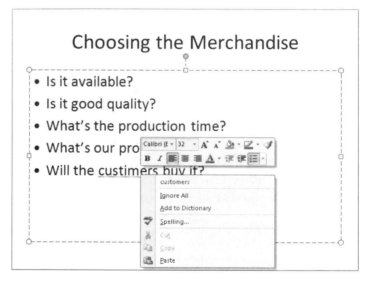

3. On the menu, click **customers** to replace the misspelled word.

4. Move to **Slide 5**.

   The Filipino word *Kumusta* has been flagged as a possible error.

5. Right-click **Kumusta**.

   The spelling checker suggests *Kumquats* as the correct spelling.

6. Press Esc to close the menu without making a selection.

7. With the insertion point still in **Kumusta**, on the **Review** tab, in the **Proofing** group, click the **Language** button.

   The Language dialog box opens.

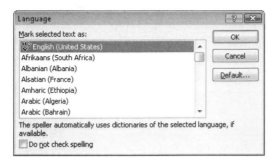

8. Scroll down the list of languages, click **Filipino**, and then click **OK**.

   Behind the scenes, PowerPoint marks *Kumusta* as a Filipino word, and the word no longer has a red wavy underline.

9. Move to **Slide 1**, and then on the **Review** tab, in the **Proofing** group, click the **Spelling** button.

   PowerPoint begins checking the spelling in the presentation. The spelling checker stops on the word *itinarary* and displays the Spelling dialog box.

10. In the **Spelling** dialog box, click **Change**.

    PowerPoint replaces *itinaray* with the suggested *itinerary* and then stops on the word *advizories*, suggesting *advisories* as the correct spelling.

> **Tip** You can click the AutoCorrect button in the Spelling dialog box to add the misspelling and the first suggested spelling of a word to the AutoCorrect substitution table.

11. Click **Change**.

    Next the spelling checker stops on *Dyck*. This term does not appear in the dictionary, but you know that it is a proper name that is spelled correctly.

12. Click **Add**.

    The term *Dyck* is added to the CUSTOM.DIC dictionary. A message box tells you that PowerPoint has finished the spelling check.

> **Tip** If you do not want to change a word or add it to the supplemental dictionary, you can click Ignore or Ignore All. The spelling checker then ignores that word or all instances of the word in the presentation in subsequent spell checking sessions.

13. Click **OK**.

14. On **Slide 5**, select the word **proper** (but not the space following the word).

15. On the **Review** tab, in the **Proofing** group, click the **Thesaurus** button.

Thesaurus

The Research task pane opens, displaying a list of synonyms with equivalent meanings.

> **Tip** If you want to translate the selected word into a different language instead of find a synonym for it, you can click Translate in the Proofing group on the Review tab to display the Research task pane with a Translation area.

16. In the **Research** task pane, click the minus sign to the left of *polite* to bring more of the synonym list into view.

17. Under **good**, decide which word you want to substitute for the selection, point to the word until an arrow appears, click the arrow, and then click **Insert**.

If you don't see an obvious substitute for the selected word, you can click a word that is close in the Thesaurus list and synonyms for that word will be displayed.

18. Close the **Research** task pane.

 CLOSE the *Spelling* presentation without saving your changes.

> **Tip** For many words, there is a quicker way to find a suitable synonym. Right-click the word, and point to Synonyms. You can then either click one of the suggested words or click Thesaurus to display the Research task pane.

Finding and Replacing Text and Fonts

You can locate and change specific text in a presentation by using the buttons in the Editing group on the Home tab to do the following:

- Click Find to locate each occurrence of a word, part of a word, or a phrase. In the Find dialog box, you enter the text, and then click Find Next. You can specify whether PowerPoint should locate matches with the exact capitalization or *case*— that is, if you specify *person*, PowerPoint will not locate *Person*—and whether it should locate matches for the entire text—that is, if you specify *person*, PowerPoint will not locate *personal*.

- Click Replace to locate each occurrence of a word, part of a word, or a phrase and replace it with something else. In the Replace dialog box, you enter the text you want to find and what you want to replace it with, click Find Next, and then click Replace to replace the found occurrence or Replace All to replace all occurrences. Again, you can specify whether to match capitalization and whole words.

  In the Replace list, click Replace Fonts to find and replace a font in a presentation. In the Replace Font dialog box, you specify the font you want to change and the font you want PowerPoint to replace it with.

- Click a text placeholder on a slide, click Select in the Editing group, and then click Select All to select all the text in that placeholder. If you select the placeholder itself, clicking Select and then Select All adds all the other objects on that slide to the selection. You can then work with all the objects as a unit. Clicking Select and then Selection Pane displays the Selection And Visibility task pane, where you can specify whether particular objects should be displayed or hidden.

> **Tip** You might want to hide an object if you are using the slide in similar presentations for two different audiences, one of which needs more detail than the other.

In this exercise, you will use the Replace feature to find and replace a word, and then you'll use Replace Fonts to find and replace a font. You will also display the Selection And Visibility task pane and hide an object on a slide.

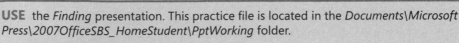

USE the *Finding* presentation. This practice file is located in the *Documents\Microsoft Press\2007OfficeSBS_HomeStudent\PptWorking* folder.

OPEN the *Finding* presentation.

1. On the **Home** tab, in the **Editing** group, click the **Replace** button.

The Replace dialog box opens.

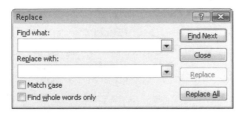

> **Tip** You can move a dialog box on the screen so that it does not hide the text you are working with by dragging its title bar.

2. In the **Find what** box, type verdigris and press Tab.

3. In the **Replace with** box, type Verdigris.

4. Select the **Match case** check box to locate text that exactly matches the capitalization you specified and replace it with the capitalization you specified.

5. Click **Find Next**.

PowerPoint finds and selects the word *verdigris* on Slide 3.

6. Click **Replace**.

PowerPoint replaces *verdigris* with *Verdigris*, and then locates the next match.

7. Click **Replace All**.

An alert box tells you that PowerPoint has finished searching the presentation and that the Replace All operation changed two occurrences of the text.

8. Click **OK**, and then in the **Replace** dialog box, click **Close**.

9. Click a blank area of the current slide to release the selection.

10. In the **Editing** group, click the **Replace** arrow, and then in the list, click **Replace Fonts**.

The Replace Font dialog box opens.

11. With **Arial** selected in the **Replace** list, click the **With** arrow, and then in the list, click **Calibri**.

12. Click **Replace**.

    All the Arial text in the presentation changes to Calibri.

13. Click **Close** to close the **Replace Font** dialog box.

14. Move to **Slide 6**, and in the **Editing** group, click the **Select** button, and then click **Selection Pane**.

    The Selection And Visibility task pane opens.

    The task pane indicates that there are four objects on this slide, but a quick count reveals that only three of them are visible.

15. Under **Shapes on this Slide** in the task pane, click the box to the right of **Rectangle 4**.

    An eye appears in the box to the right of Rectangle 4, and that object—a text box—is now displayed at the bottom of the slide.

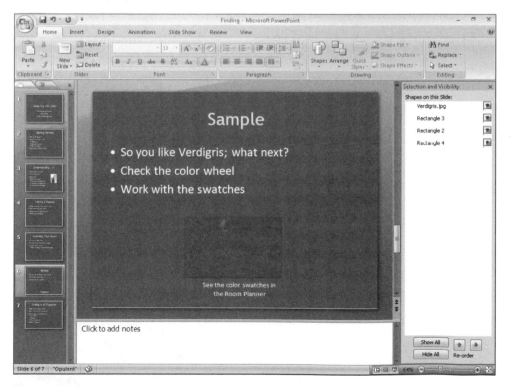

16. In the task pane, click the box to the right of **Rectangle 4** again.

The eye disappears, and the text box is now hidden again.

17. Close the **Selection and Visibility** task pane.

 CLOSE the *Finding* presentation without saving your changes.

Changing the Size, Alignment, Spacing, and Look of Text

Earlier in this chapter we discussed the AutoFit feature, which shrinks the size of text that overflows a placeholder so that it fits in the allocated space. If you want to keep the size of the text in a presentation consistent, you can turn off this automatic text shrinking. You then have two ways to adjust the size of placeholders to fit their text:

- By manually dragging the handles around a selected placeholder.
- By clicking Resize Shape To Fit Text on the Text Box page of the Format Shape dialog box.

See Also   For more information about AutoFit, see "Correcting and Sizing Text While Typing" earlier in this chapter.

Of course, you can also manually control the size of text by using options in the Font group on the Home tab. You can either click the Increase Font Size or Decrease Font Size button or set a precise size in the Font Size box.

To control the way text is aligned within a placeholder, you can click the text and then click one of the following alignment buttons in the Paragraph group on the Home tab:

- The Align Text Left button aligns text against the placeholder's left edge. It is the usual choice for paragraphs.
- The Center button aligns text in the middle of the placeholder. It is often used for titles and headings.
- The Align Text Right button aligns text against the placeholder's right edge. It is not used much for titles and paragraphs, but you might want to use it in text boxes.
- The Justify button aligns text against both the left and right edges, adding space between words to fill the line.

You can adjust the vertical spacing between all the lines of text in the placeholder by clicking the Line Spacing button in the Paragraph group and making a selection. If you want to adjust the space before or after a paragraph, you need to display the Paragraph dialog box, either by clicking the Line Spacing button and then clicking More at the bottom of the menu or by clicking the Paragraph Dialog Box Launcher. You can then adjust the Before and After settings for the paragraph as a unit.

In addition to changing the look of paragraphs, you can also manipulate the look of individual words. After selecting the characters you want to format, you can make changes by using buttons in the Font group on the Home tab, as follows:

● You can change the font.

● You can apply attributes, including bold, italic, underlining, and shadow and strikethrough effects.

● You can increase or decrease the space between the letters in a selection.

● You can change the capitalization of the words—for example, you can change small letters to capital letters.

● You can change the color of the characters.

In this exercise, you will change the size of the text in a placeholder and then adjust the size of the placeholder both automatically and manually. You will experiment with text alignment, decrease line spacing, and increase paragraph spacing. Then you will use buttons in the Font group to format words so that they stand out and look attractive.

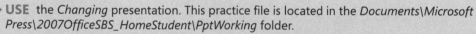

USE the *Changing* presentation. This practice file is located in the *Documents\Microsoft Press\2007OfficeSBS_HomeStudent\PptWorking* folder.
OPEN the *Changing* presentation.

1. Move to **Slide 2**, and in the **Slide** pane, click anywhere in the bulleted list.

2. On the **Home** tab, in the **Editing** group, click the **Select** button, and then click **Select All**.

The note at the bottom of the slide is not selected because it was entered in a separate text box, not in the placeholder.

Decrease
Font Size

3. On the **Home** tab, in the **Font** group, click the **Decrease Font Size** button twice.

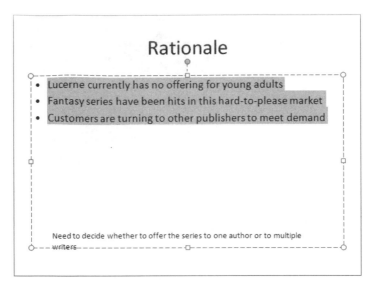

Font Size

4. Experiment with the size by clicking the **Font Size** arrow, and then pointing to various sizes in the list to get a live preview of the effect.

5. Finish by clicking **24** in the list.

   Now suppose you want to make room for a graphic to the right of the bulleted list.

6. Point to the placeholder's right-middle handle, and when the pointer changes to a two-headed arrow, drag to the left until the right border of the placeholder is aligned with the right end of the slide title.

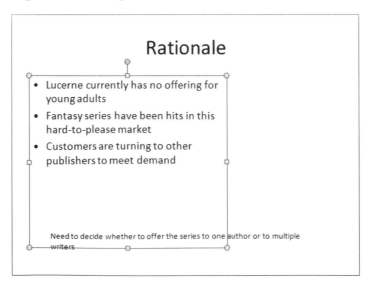

7. Right-click the placeholder's border, and then click **Format Shape**.

Troubleshooting This command is available only if you right-click the placeholder's border while the pointer is a four-headed arrow. If you don't see the command, click away from the menu, and try again.

The Format Shape dialog box opens.

8. Click **Text Box**, click **Resize shape to fit text**, and then click **Close**.

The placeholder shrinks in size so that it is just big enough to hold its text.

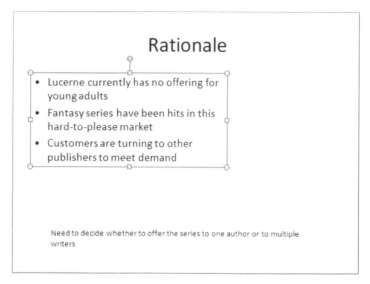

9. Move to **Slide 7**, and then click the text box containing the Web addresses.

If this text box contained only one paragraph, you could simply click the text box and then click a button in the Paragraph group to apply the paragraph formatting you want. However, the text box contains multiple paragraphs, and you first need to select them all.

10. On the **Home** tab, in the **Editing** group, click the **Select** button, and then click **Select All**.

11. In the **Paragraph** group, click the **Align Text Left** button.

The text is now left-aligned and easier to read.

Align Text Left

Tip You want your slides to be as easy to read as possible, especially if you will be delivering your presentation to a large audience, some of whom might be sitting some distance away from the screen. Constantly evaluate whether the effects you apply to your slides enhance readability and understanding.

12. Select the seven Web site lines (not the first paragraph).

Line Spacing

13. In the **Paragraph** group, click the **Line Spacing** button, and then click **1.5**.

14. Click the first paragraph, and then click the **Paragraph** Dialog Box Launcher.

    The Paragraph dialog box opens.

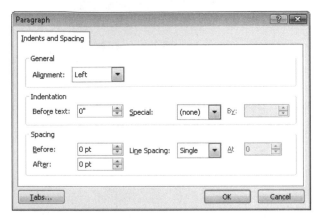

15. Under **Spacing**, change the **After** setting to **12**, and then click **OK**.

    The line spacing and paragraph spacing have both increased.

16. Move to **Slide 5**, and then select all the text in the text box at the right side of the slide.

17. In the **Font** group, click the **Change Case** arrow, and then in the list, click **UPPERCASE**.

The terms *lowercase* and *uppercase* come from the old days of typesetting, when individual letters were manually assembled into words, sentences, and paragraphs for printing. The small versions of the letters were kept in alphabetical order in the lower case, where they were easier for the typesetter to reach, and the capital versions were kept in the upper case.

Italic

18. With the text still selected, in the **Font** group, click the **Italic** button.

Font Color

19. Click the **Font Color** arrow, and then in the palette, point to each of the colors in the top **Theme Colors** row in turn.

As you point, the selected text changes color to give you a live preview of the effect.

20. At the right end of the top **Theme Colors** row, click the orange box (**Orange, Accent 6**).

21. Click a blank area of the slide to see the effect of your changes.

CLOSE the *Changing* presentation without saving your changes, and if you are not continuing on to the next chapter, exit PowerPoint.

Key Points

- You can enter and edit text both on the Outline tab or directly on a slide, depending on which is most efficient at any particular time.

- Text in placeholders provides consistency across an entire presentation. But you are not limited to using placeholders. You can place text wherever you want it on a slide by using text boxes.

- PowerPoint provides assistance by correcting common spelling errors and adjusting the size of text so that it fits optimally on a slide.

- You can take advantage of the Find and Replace features to ensure consistent use of terms and fonts throughout a presentation.

- Although PowerPoint provides the structure for a presentation so that you can focus on your message, you can manually change the formatting, location, and size of text at any time.

Chapter at a Glance

Characteristics of a Hit Fantasy

- A hero
- An ally
- A teacher
- An adversary
- An innocent

- A problem
- A journey
- A skill or power
- A battle
- A twist

Change the layout
of a slide, **page 290**

Apply a theme,
page 295

SALES MEETING
May Results

Agenda

Review of key objectives
How did we do?
Organizational overview
Top issues facing the company
Review of our progress
Key spending areas
Headcount
Goals for the coming year

Switch to a different
color scheme, **page 297**

Add shading and
texture to the background
of a slide, **page 302**

The Taguien Cycle

A Series for Young Adults
Judy Lew, Project Editor

11 Adjusting the Layout, Order, and Look of Slides

In this chapter, you will learn to:

✔ Change the layout of a slide.

✔ Rearrange slides in a presentation.

✔ Apply a theme.

✔ Switch to a different color scheme.

✔ Use colors that are not part of the scheme.

✔ Add shading and texture to the background of a slide.

In Chapter 10, "Working with Slide Text," you looked at ways to work with the text on your slides. In this chapter, you will step back and focus on big-picture issues that can affect the success of a Microsoft Office PowerPoint 2007 presentation.

For each slide to accomplish its purpose, it needs to present its content in the most effective way. The layout of individual slides and the order of slides in the presentation contribute significantly to the logical development of your message. And an overall consistent look, punctuated by variations that add weight exactly where it is needed, can enhance the likelihood that your message will be well received and absorbed by your intended audience.

In this chapter, you will change the layout of a slide, rearrange slides in a presentation, and apply a theme to a presentation. You will also switch to a different color scheme and use colors that are not part of the scheme. Finally, you will add shading and texture to the background of a slide.

See Also Do you need only a quick refresher on the topics in this chapter? See the Quick Reference entries at the beginning of this book.

Important Before you can use the practice files in this chapter, you need to install them from the book's companion CD to their default location. See "Using the Book's CD" at the beginning of this book for more information.

Troubleshooting Graphics and operating system–related instructions in this book reflect the Windows Vista user interface. If your computer is running Windows XP and you experience trouble following the instructions as written, please refer to the "Information for Readers Running Windows XP" section at the beginning of this book.

Changing the Layout of a Slide

When you add a new slide to a presentation, you can specify which of several predefined layouts you want to use, or you can add a blank slide and create a custom layout. If you decide after you create a slide that you want it to have a different predefined layout, you can change the layout by displaying the slide, clicking the Layout button in the Slides group on the Home tab, and then making a selection.

See Also For information about adding slides, see "Creating a Presentation Based on a Ready-Made Design" in Chapter 9, "Starting a New Presentation."

If the slide already contains content, you can add the elements of a different layout to the existing layout without disturbing the existing content. For example, if you decide to add a chart to a slide that already contains a title and a bulleted list, clicking the Layout button and then clicking the Two Content layout adds a content placeholder to the right of the bulleted list placeholder.

If you make changes to the layout of a slide—for example, by sizing or moving a placeholder—but then decide you want to revert to the original layout, you can reapply the layout (without losing text you have already entered) by clicking the Reset button in the Slides group on the Home tab.

In this exercise, you will change the layout of a slide, change the size of the layout's placeholders, and then restore the layout.

1. Display **Slide 3**, and then on the **Home** tab, in the **Slides** group, click the **Layout** button.

   The Layout gallery includes the same layouts that are available for new slides.

2. Click the **Two Content** layout.

   PowerPoint adds a placeholder to the right of the bulleted list.

3. Click the bullet in the placeholder on the right side of the slide, and then type the following bullet points, pressing ⎡Enter⎤ after each one except the last:

   A problem

   A journey

   A skill or power

   A battle

   On the Outline tab, the bullet points are grouped to indicate that they appear in different placeholders.

4. Drag the bottom middle handle of the right placeholder upward until the placeholder is big enough only for its bullet points.

5. Repeat step 4 for the left placeholder.

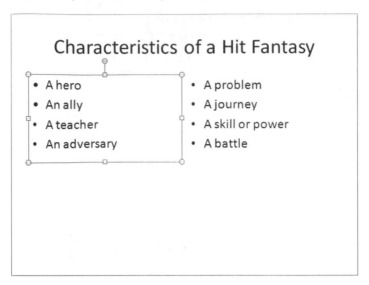

Now suppose you want to add more bullet points to each placeholder. You could manually enlarge the placeholders, but here's a quicker way.

6. On the **Home** tab, in the **Slides** group, click the **Reset** button.

The placeholders expand to their original size.

7. Click to the right of *adversary* in the left placeholder, press Enter , and then type An innocent.

8. Click to the right of *battle* in the right placeholder, press Enter , and then type A twist.

CLOSE the *Layout* presentation without saving your changes.

Rearranging Slides in a Presentation

After you have created several slides, whether by adding them and entering text or by importing them from another presentation, you might want to rearrange the order of the slides so that they effectively communicate your message. You can rearrange a presentation in two ways:

● On the Slides tab, you can drag slides up and down to change their order.

● To see more of the presentation at the same time, you can switch to Slide Sorter view. You can then drag slide thumbnails into the correct order.

In this exercise, you will use the Slides tab and Slide Sorter view to logically arrange the slides in a presentation, and add a slide to a presentation.

 USE the *Rearranging* presentation. This practice file is located in the *Documents\Microsoft Press\2007OfficeSBS_HomeStudent\PptAdjusting* folder.
OPEN the *Rearranging* presentation.

1. On the **Outline** tab, move to **Slide 3**, and notice the order of the bullet points.

   This summary slide lists all the main players in the series on the left, and the main plot requirements on the right.

2. On the **Outline** tab of the **Overview** pane, scroll through the presentation, noticing that the slide order is different than that of the bullet points on Slide 3.

   > **Tip** On the Outline tab, you can collapse bullet points under slide titles so that you can see more of the presentation at one time. Double-click the icon of the slide whose bullet points you want to hide. Double-click again to redisplay the bullet points. To expand or collapse the entire outline at once, right-click the title of a slide, point to Expand or Collapse, and then click Expand All or Collapse All.

3. In the **Overview** pane, click the **Slides** tab, and then scroll so that you can see both Slide 5 and Slide 8.

4. Drag the thumbnail for **Slide 8** (*The Teacher*) upward to the space above the thumbnail for **Slide 6** (*The Problem*), but don't release the mouse button yet.

   The thumbnail itself remains in place, but a bar indicates where the slide will move to when you release the mouse button.

5. Release the mouse button.

PowerPoint moves the slide to its new location and renumbers the subsequent slides.

Slide Sorter

6. At the right end of the status bar, on the **View** toolbar, click the **Slide Sorter** button.

PowerPoint displays the presentation as a set of thumbnails. Because you have only 13 slides in this presentation, there is room to make the thumbnails bigger so that they are easier to read.

Zoom In

7. On the slider at the right end of the status bar, click the **Zoom In** button twice to change the Zoom percentage to 80%.

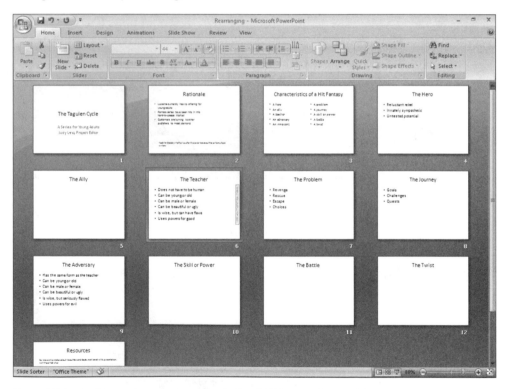

8. Drag **Slide 9** (*The Adversary*) to the left of **Slide 7** (*The Problem*).

Slide 9 moves to its new location, and again PowerPoint repositions and renumbers the subsequent slides in the presentation.

> **Tip** You can move slides from one open presentation to another in Slide Sorter view. Display both presentations in Slide Sorter view, and then on the View tab, in the Window group, click the Arrange All button. You can then drag slides from one presentation window to another.

If you check the results against Slide 3, you will see that the slide for *The Innocent* is missing. You can add a slide in Slide Sorter view, but you cannot enter or edit text in this view.

9. With **Slide 7** (*The Adversary*) still selected, add a **Title and Content** slide to the presentation.

PowerPoint inserts the new slide after the selected slide.

10. Double-click **Slide 8**.

PowerPoint returns to the previous view—in this case, Normal view—with Slide 8 active.

11. On the slide, click the title placeholder, and then type The Innocent.

 CLOSE the *Rearranging* presentation without saving your changes.

Applying a Theme

When you create a presentation based on a template or a ready-made design, the presentation includes a theme—a combination of colors, fonts, formatting, graphics, and other elements that gives the presentation a coherent look. Even a presentation developed from scratch has a theme, albeit one that consists of only a white background and a very basic set of font styles and sizes.

If you want to change the theme applied to a presentation, you can choose a new one from the Themes group on the Design tab. With the live preview feature, you can easily try different effects until you find the one you want.

In this exercise, you will change the theme applied to a presentation that was created from a template. You will also apply a theme to a presentation that was created from scratch.

 USE the *Theme1* and *Theme2* presentations. These practice files are located in the *Documents\Microsoft Press\2007OfficeSBS_HomeStudent\PptAdjusting* folder.
OPEN the *Theme1* and *Theme2* presentations.

More

1. With *Theme1* active, on the **Design** tab, in the **Themes** group, click the **More** button to the right of the thumbnails.

The Themes gallery opens, displaying all the available themes.

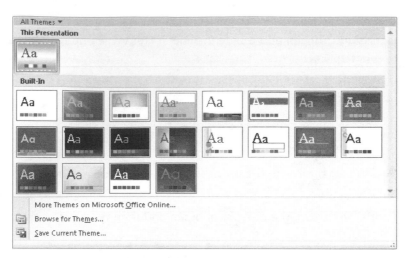

2. Point to each theme thumbnail in turn to see a live preview of what the presentation will look like with that theme applied.

3. Click the **Technic** thumbnail to apply that theme to the entire presentation.

   Instead of a blue background with text in the Times New Roman font, the presentation now has a tan striped background with text in the Franklin Gothic font.

4. Switch to the *Theme2* presentation, display the **Themes** gallery, and then click the **Apex** thumbnail.

   Instead of a white background with text in the Calibri font, the presentation now has a gray watermarked background with text in the Lucida and Book Antiqua fonts.

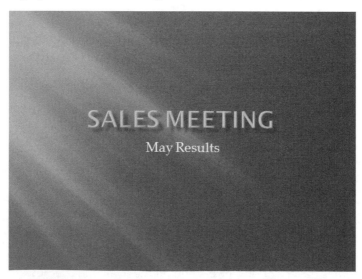

CLOSE the *Theme1* and *Theme2* presentations without saving your changes.

Switching to a Different Color Scheme

Every presentation you create with PowerPoint 2007, even a blank one, has a set of colors associated with it. This *color scheme* consists of 12 complementary colors designed to be used for the following elements of a slide:

- Use the four Text/Background colors for dark or light text on a dark or light background.
- Use Accent 1 through Accent 6 for the colors of objects other than text.
- Use Hyperlink to draw attention to hyperlinks.
- Use Followed Hyperlink to indicate visited hyperlinks.

In the palette displayed in color galleries such as the Font Color gallery in the Font group on the Home tab, 10 of the 12 colors appear with light to dark gradients. (The two background colors are not represented in these palettes.)

Understanding color schemes can help you create professional-looking presentations that use an appropriate balance of color. You are not limited to using the colors in a presentation's color scheme, but because they have been selected by professional designers based on good design principles, using them ensures that your slides will be pleasing to the eye.

To view the color schemes you can apply to a presentation, you click the Colors button in the Themes group on the Design tab to display a Colors gallery with live preview capabilities. When you find the color scheme you want, click it to change the color scheme of the presentation.

If none of the color schemes is exactly what you are looking for, you can create your own by clicking Create New Theme Colors at the bottom of the Colors gallery and assembling colors in the Create New Theme Colors dialog box. After you save the scheme, you can apply it to one or all of the slides in a presentation.

In this exercise, you will examine the color scheme of a presentation, apply a different color scheme to an entire presentation, create your own scheme, and change the color scheme of only one slide.

USE the *ColorScheme* presentation. This practice file is located in the *Documents\Microsoft Press\2007OfficeSBS_HomeStudent\PptAdjusting* folder.

OPEN the *ColorScheme* presentation.

1. On the **Design** tab, in the **Themes** group, click the **Colors** button.

   The Colors gallery opens.

   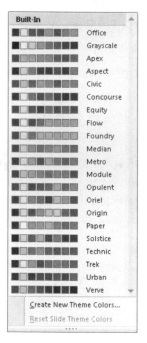

2. In the gallery, point to a few color schemes and watch the live preview effect on the active slide.

3. Click **Verve** to switch the color scheme of the theme applied to the presentation.

   Notice that the theme retains all its other characteristics, such as the font and background graphic; only the colors change. This color scheme is a good starting point.

4. In the **Themes** group on the **Design** tab, click the **Colors** button.

5. At the bottom of the **Colors** gallery, click **Create New Theme Colors**.

   The Create New Theme Colors dialog box opens, displaying the Verve theme colors.

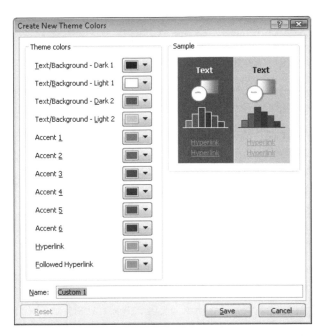

6. In the **Theme colors** area, click the **Text/Background – Dark 2** button.

    A gallery of colors related to the Verve theme colors opens.

7. In the **Theme Colors** palette, click the box in the third row of the range below the dark blue box.

    When you are pointing to the correct box, a ScreenTip labeled *Dark Blue, Accent 6, Lighter 40%* appears.

8. At the bottom of the dialog box, click **Save**.

    The dialog box closes and PowerPoint applies the new color scheme to the presentation, changing the background color of all the slides to bright blue.

9. Display **Slide 2**, and in the **Themes** group, click the **Colors** button.

    Notice that your new custom color scheme appears in the Custom area at the top of the Colors gallery.

10. Right-click the **Opulent** color scheme, and then click **Apply to Selected Slides**.

    PowerPoint applies the Opulent color scheme to only the selected slide, changing its background color to purple.

 CLOSE the *ColorScheme* presentation without saving your changes.

Changing a Theme's Fonts and Effects

In addition to changing a theme's color scheme, you can also change its fonts and effects by following these steps:

1. On the **Design** tab, in the **Themes** group, click the **Fonts** button.

    The Fonts gallery lists the combination of fonts that is used by each of the themes, in alphabetical order by theme. The top font in each combination is used for titles, and the bottom font is used for other slide text.

2. Click the font combination you want to use in the current presentation.

    > **Tip** You can create a custom font combination by clicking Create New Theme Fonts at the bottom of the gallery and then specifying the font combination you want in the Create New Theme Fonts dialog box.

3. On the **Design** tab, in the **Themes** group, click the **Effects** button.

    Like the Fonts gallery, the Effects gallery displays the combination of effects that is applied to shapes by each of the themes.

4. Click the effect combination you want to use in the current presentation.

    Your changes are stored with the presentation and do not affect the default theme.

Using Colors That Are Not Part of the Scheme

Although working with the 12 colors of a harmonious color scheme enables you to create presentations with a pleasing design impact, you might want to use a wider palette. You can add colors that are not part of the color scheme by selecting the element whose color you want to change and then choosing a standard color from the Colors palette or from the almost infinite spectrum of colors available in the Colors dialog box.

After you add a color, it becomes available on all the palettes that appear when you click a button that applies color—for example, the Font Color button in the Font group on the Home tab. The color remains on the palettes even if you change the theme applied to the presentation.

In this exercise, you will change the color of a slide title and will then apply the same color to other elements of the presentation.

USE the *OtherColors* presentation. This practice file is located in the *Documents\Microsoft Press\2007OfficeSBS_HomeStudent\PptAdjusting* folder.

OPEN the *OtherColors* presentation.

Font Color

1. On **Slide 1**, select the title of the presentation, and then on the **Home** tab, in the **Font** group, click the **Font Color** arrow.

   A color palette appears.

   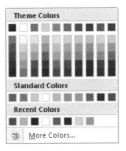

2. At the bottom of the color palette, click **More Colors**.

   The Colors dialog box opens.

3. In the **Colors** spectrum, click in the brightest green shade.

   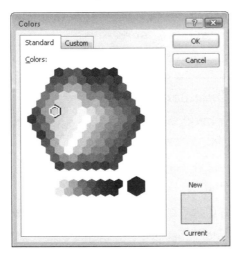

4. Click **OK**.

   The title changes to the selected shade of green, outlined in red.

5. Display **Slide 5**, select the text following the third bullet point, and then click the **Font Color** arrow.

   The color that you just applied appears at the left end of the Recent Colors palette and is now available for use throughout the presentation.

6. Under **Recent Colors**, click the **Green** box.

More

7. On the **Design** tab, in the **Themes** group, click the **More** button to display the **Themes** gallery, and then click **Median**.

    The third bullet point retains the color you just applied even though you have switched themes.

CLOSE the *OtherColors* presentation without saving your changes.

Adding Shading and Texture to the Background of a Slide

In PowerPoint, you can customize the *background* of a slide by adding a solid color, a color gradient, a texture, or even a picture.

A color gradient is a visual effect in which a solid color gradually changes from light to dark or dark to light. PowerPoint offers several gradient patterns, each with several variations. You can also choose a preset arrangement of colors from professionally designed backgrounds in which the different colors gradually merge.

If you want something fancier than a gradient, you can give the slide background a texture, or you can use a picture. PowerPoint comes with several preset textures that you can easily apply to the background of slides.

Adding a Picture to the Slide Background

You can add a picture to a slide's background, either as a single object or as a tiled image that fills the entire slide. Here's how:

1. On the **Design** tab, in the **Background** group, click the **Background Styles** button, and then click **Format Background**.

2. In the **Format Background** dialog box, click **Picture or texture fill**.

3. Click **File**, navigate to the folder that contains the picture you want to use, and then double-click the file name.

4. To make the picture fill the entire slide, select the **Tile picture as texture** check box.

5. To use the picture in the background of the current slide, click **Close**, or to use it in the background of all slides, click **Apply to All**.

In this exercise, you will add a shade to a slide background and then change the background from shaded to textured.

1. On the **Design** tab, in the **Background** group, click the **Background Styles** button.

2. In the **Background** gallery, point to each style in turn to see a live preview of its effects.

3. Click the last thumbnail in the second row (**Style 8**).

4. Click the **Background Styles** button again, and then click **Format Background** at the bottom of the gallery.

   The Format Background dialog box opens.

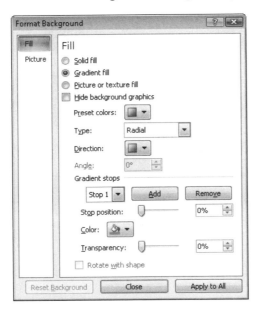

   Tip Clicking the Preset Colors button displays a gallery of professionally designed color gradients, which range from a single color to sets of several colors.

5. Click the **Type** arrow, and then in the list, click **Rectangular**.

6. Click the **Direction** button, and at the right end of the gallery, click the **From Corner** effect.

7. Under **Gradient stops**, drag the **Stop position** slider to the right until the adjacent setting is **80%**.

8. Click the **Color** button, and then in the **Theme Colors** palette, click the green color in the top row.

9. Click **Close**.

   PowerPoint applies the shaded background only to the current slide.

10. Click the **Background Styles** button again, and then click **Format Background**.

11. In the **Format Background** dialog box, click **Picture or texture fill**.

12. Click the **Texture** button, and then in the gallery, click **Denim**.

13. Click the **Apply to All** button, and then click **Close**.

    PowerPoint applies the textured background to the current slide and all the other slides in the presentation.

The Taguien Cycle

A Series for Young Adults
Judy Lew, Project Editor

CLOSE the *Background* presentation without saving your changes. If you are not continuing directly to the next chapter, exit PowerPoint.

Key Points

- After you create a slide, you can easily modify its layout.
- If you manually change the layout of a slide, you can restore the default layout.
- You can change the order of slides by rearranging them on the Slides tab or in Slide Sorter view.
- You can easily change the look and feel of a presentation by switching from one predefined theme to another. If you like all the elements of a theme except its colors, you can apply a different color scheme.
- You can apply a color scheme to one or all the slides in a presentation.
- You can create your own color schemes, and you can add colors that aren't part of the current scheme to selected parts of a slide.
- To dress up the background of one slide or of all the slides in a presentation, you can apply a solid color, a color gradient, a texture, or a picture.

Chapter at a Glance

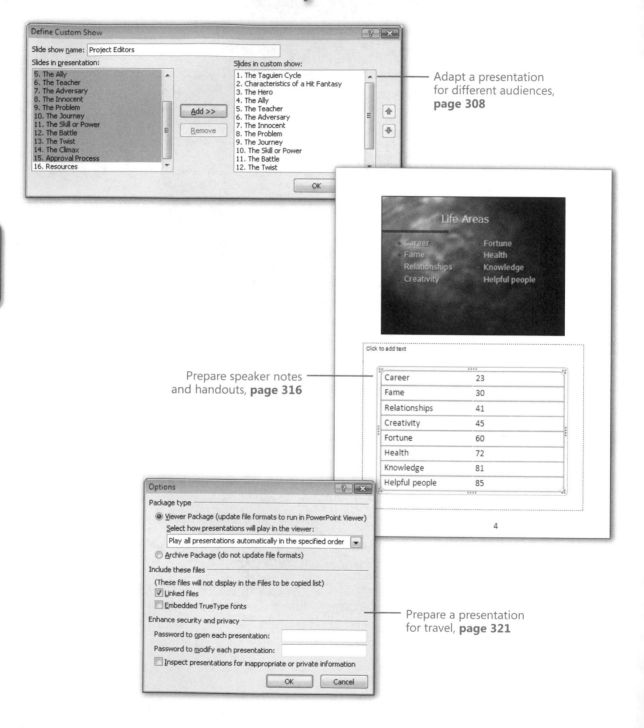

Adapt a presentation for different audiences, **page 308**

Prepare speaker notes and handouts, **page 316**

Prepare a presentation for travel, **page 321**

12 Delivering a Presentation Electronically

In this chapter, you will learn to:

✔ Adapt a presentation for different audiences.

✔ Rehearse a presentation.

✔ Prepare speaker notes and handouts.

✔ Prepare a presentation for travel.

✔ Show a presentation.

The goal of all the effort involved in creating a presentation is to be able to effectively deliver it to a specific audience. With Microsoft Office PowerPoint 2007, you can easily deliver a presentation from your computer as an electronic slide show. In Slide Show view, instead of the slide appearing in a presentation window within the PowerPoint program window, the slide occupies the entire screen.

Before you can deliver a presentation, you need to perform several tasks to ensure its success. You can hide individual slides to adapt the presentation for a specific audience, or if you know that you will be giving variations of the same presentation to different audiences, you can save a set of slides as a separate presentation that you will show only if appropriate. You can tailor the speed at which slides appear, to appropriately fit your presentation to the allotted time. To support your delivery of the presentation, you can prepare speaker notes, and to help your audience retain your message, you can prepare handouts. Finally, if you are delivering the presentation at a remote location, you will want to use the Package For CD feature to ensure that you take all the necessary files with you.

When you deliver a slide show from your computer, you navigate through slides by clicking the mouse button or by pressing the arrow keys. You can move forward and backward one slide at a time, and you can jump to specific slides as the needs of your audience dictate. During the slide show, you can mark up slides with an on-screen pen or highlighter to emphasize a point.

In this chapter, you will adapt a presentation for two audiences, first by creating a custom slide show, and then by hiding a slide. You will apply slide timings to a presentation, rehearse it, and have PowerPoint set the timings for you. You will enter speaker notes in both the Notes pane and in Notes Page view, customize the Notes master, and print speaker notes and handouts. Then you will save a presentation package on a CD and run it from the CD by using the presentation viewer that comes with PowerPoint. Finally, you will deliver a presentation and mark up slides while showing them.

See Also Do you need only a quick refresher on the topics in this chapter? See the Quick Reference entries at the beginning of this book.

Important Before you can use the practice files in this chapter, you need to install them from the book's companion CD to their default location. See "Using the Book's CD" at the beginning of this book for more information.

Troubleshooting Graphics and operating system–related instructions in this book reflect the Windows Vista user interface. If your computer is running Windows XP and you experience trouble following the instructions as written, please refer to the "Information for Readers Running Windows XP" section at the beginning of this book.

Adapting a Presentation for Different Audiences

If you plan to deliver variations of the same presentation to different audiences, you should prepare a single presentation containing all the slides you are likely to need for all the audiences. Then you can select slides from the presentation that are appropriate for a particular audience and group them as a *custom slide show*. When you need to deliver the presentation for that audience, you open the main presentation and show the subset of slides by choosing the custom slide show from a list.

For example, suppose you need to pitch an idea for a new product or service to both a team of project managers and a company's executive team. Many of the slides would be the same for both groups, but the presentation to the executive team would include more in-depth competitive and financial analysis. You would develop the executive team's presentation first and then create a custom slide show for the project managers by using a subset of the slides in the executive presentation.

Sometimes you might want to be able to make an on-the-spot decision during a presentation about whether to display a particular slide. You can give yourself this flexibility by hiding the slide so that you can skip over it if its information doesn't seem useful to a particular audience. If you decide to include the slide's information in the presentation, you can display it by pressing the letter H or by using the Go To Slide command.

In this exercise, you will select slides from an existing presentation to create a custom slide show for a different audience. You will also hide a slide and then see how to display it when necessary.

USE the *Adapting* presentation. This practice file is located in the *Documents\Microsoft Press\2007OfficeSBS_HomeStudent\PptDelivering* folder.
BE SURE TO start PowerPoint before beginning this exercise.
OPEN the *Adapting* presentation.

Custom
Slide Show ▾

1. On the **Slide Show** tab, in the **Start Slide Show** group, click the **Custom Slide Show** button, and then click **Custom Shows**.

The Custom Shows dialog box opens.

2. Click **New**.

The Define Custom Show dialog box opens. The default custom show name is selected in the Slide Show Name box.

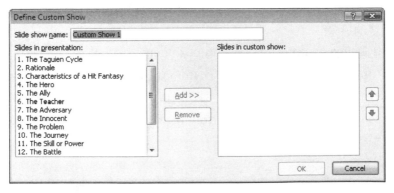

3. In the **Slide show name** box, type Project Editors.

4. In the **Slides in presentation** list, click **1. The Taguien Cycle**, and then click **Add**.

Slide 1 appears as Slide 1 in the Slides In Custom Show box on the right.

5. In the **Slides in presentation** list, click **3. Characteristics of a Hit Fantasy**, scroll the list, hold down the ⎣Shift⎦ key, and click **15. Approval Process**. Then click **Add**.

The slides appear in sequential order in the Slides In Custom Show box on the right.

6. Click **OK**.

7. In the **Custom Shows** dialog box, click **Show** to start the custom slide show.

8. Click the mouse button to advance through all the slides, including the blank one at the end of the show.

9. In Normal view, on the **Slide Show** tab, in the **Start Slide Show** group, click the **Custom Slide Show** button.

   Project Editors has been added to the list. Clicking this option will run the custom slide show.

10. In the list, click **Custom Shows**.

11. In the **Custom Shows** dialog box, verify that **Project Editors** is selected, and then click **Edit**.

    The Define Custom Show dialog box opens.

12. At the bottom of the **Slides in custom show** box, click **14. Approval Process**, and then click **Remove**.

    PowerPoint removes the slide from the custom slide show, but not from the main presentation.

> **Tip** To change the order of the list, select a slide and click the Up arrow or the Down arrow to the right of the Slides In Custom Show box.

13. Click **OK** to close the **Define Custom Show** dialog box, and then click **Close** to close the **Custom Shows** dialog box.

14. In the **Overview** pane, scroll to the bottom of the **Slides** tab, right-click **Slide 12**, and then click **Hide Slide**.

On the Slides tab, PowerPoint puts a box with a diagonal line around the number 12, and dims the slide contents to indicate that it is hidden.

> **Tip** In Slide Sorter view, you can select a slide and then on the Slide Show tab, in the Set Up group, click the Hide Slide button.

Slide Show

15. Display **Slide 11**, and on the **View** toolbar, click the **Slide Show** button. Then press `Space` to move to the next slide.

Because Slide 12 is hidden, PowerPoint skips from Slide 11 to Slide 13.

16. Press the ⬅ key to move back to Slide 11.

17. Right-click anywhere on the screen, point to **Go to Slide**, and then click **(12) The Battle**.

The number is in parentheses because the slide is hidden. When you click it, the hidden slide appears in Slide Show view.

18. Press `Esc` to end the slide show.

 CLOSE the *Adapting* presentation without saving your changes.

Rehearsing a Presentation

When delivering a slide show, you can move from slide to slide in the following ways:

- **Manually.** You control when you move by clicking the mouse button, pressing keys, or clicking commands.
- **Automatically.** PowerPoint displays each slide for a predefined length of time and then displays the next slide.

The length of time a slide appears on the screen is controlled by its *slide timing*. By default, slide timings are divided equally among the animations for each slide. So if a slide has a title and four bullet points that are all animated and you assign a timing of 1 minute to the slide, the five elements will appear at 12-second intervals.

To apply a timing to a single slide, to a group of slides, or to an entire presentation, you first select the slides, and then under Advance Slide in the Transition To This Slide group on the Animations tab, select the Automatically After check box and enter the number of minutes and/or seconds you want each slide to remain on the screen.

> **Tip** If you are delivering the presentation in Slide Show view and want to prevent PowerPoint from advancing to the slide according to a slide timing, press the letter S on your keyboard, or right-click the current slide and click Pause. To continue the presentation, press the letter S again, or right-click the slide and click Resume.

If you don't know how much time to allow for the slide timings of a presentation, you can rehearse the slide show while PowerPoint automatically tracks and sets the timings for you, reflecting the amount of time you spend on each slide during the rehearsal. During the slide show, PowerPoint displays each slide for the length of time you indicated during the rehearsal. In this way, you can synchronize an automatic slide show with a live narration or demonstration.

In this exercise, you will set the timing for one slide and then apply it to an entire presentation. Then you will rehearse the presentation and have PowerPoint set slide timings according to the amount of time you display each slide during the rehearsal.

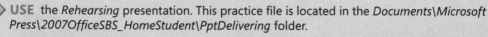

USE the *Rehearsing* presentation. This practice file is located in the *Documents\Microsoft Press\2007OfficeSBS_HomeStudent\PptDelivering* folder.
OPEN the *Rehearsing* presentation.

1. On the **Animations** tab, in the **Transition to This Slide** group, under **Advance Slide**, select the **Automatically After** check box, and then type or select **00:03**.

   Because both check boxes under Advance Slide are selected, the slide will advance either after three seconds or when you click the mouse button.

Slide Show

2. On the **View** toolbar, click the **Slide Show** button.

   Slide 1 is displayed for three seconds, and then PowerPoint moves to Slide 2.

Slide Sorter

3. Press [Esc] to end the show, and then on the **View** toolbar, click the **Slide Sorter** button.

   Below the lower-left corner of Slide 1 is the slide timing you just applied.

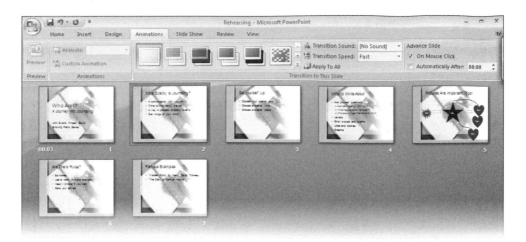

4. Click **Slide 1**, and then on the **Animations** tab, in the **Transition to This Slide** group, click the **Apply To All** button.

   The slide timing you applied to Slide 1 is now applied to all the slides.

   > **Important** When you click Apply To All, all the transition effects applied to the current slide are transferred to the other slides. If you have applied different transitions to different slides, those individually specified transitions are overwritten. So it's a good idea to apply all the effects that you want the slides to have in common first. Then you can select individual slides and customize their effects.

5. Switch to Slide Show view, watch as the slides advance, and then click the mouse button when the black screen is displayed.

6. Under **Advance Slide** in the **Transition to This Slide** group, clear the **Automatically After** check box, and then click **Apply To All**.

   The slide timings disappear from below the slides.

7. With Slide 1 selected, on the **Slide Show** tab, in the **Set Up** group, click the

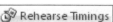 **Rehearse Timings** button.

   The screen switches to Slide Show view, starts the show, and displays the Rehearsal toolbar in the upper-left corner of the screen. A Slide Time counter is timing the length of time Slide 1 remains on the screen.

Next

8. Wait about 10 seconds, and then on the **Rehearsal** toolbar, click the **Next** button.

9. Work your way slowly through the slide show, clicking **Next** to move to the next slide.

Repeat

10. If you want to repeat the rehearsal for a particular slide, on the **Rehearsal** toolbar, click the **Repeat** button to reset the Slide Time for that slide to 0:00:00.

> **Tip** If you want to start the entire rehearsal over again, click the Rehearsal toolbar's Close button, and when a message asks whether you want to keep the existing timings, click No.

When you reach the end of the slide show, a message box displays the elapsed time for the presentation and asks whether you want to apply the recorded slide timings.

11. Click **Yes**.

The screen switches back to Slide Sorter view, where the recorded timings have been added below each slide.

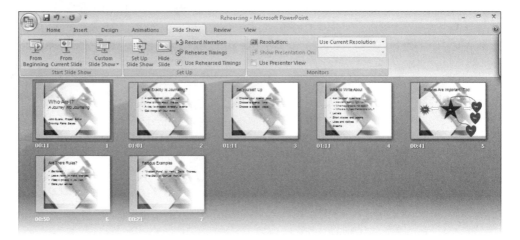

12. Click the **Animations** tab.

The timing for the active slide, Slide 1, appears in the Automatically After box under Advance Slide in the Transition To This Slide group.

13. If the **Automatically After** setting is not a whole second, click the Up arrow to adjust the time up to the next whole second.

You can manually adjust the timing of any slide by selecting it and changing the setting in this box.

14. On the **View** toolbar, click the **Slide Show** button.

The slides advance according to the recorded timings.

15. Press Esc at any time to stop the slide show.

 CLOSE the *Rehearsing* presentation without saving your changes.

Creating a Self-Running Presentation

When slide timings have been applied to a PowerPoint presentation, the presentation can be set up to run automatically, either once or continuously. For example, you might want to set up a self-running presentation for a product demonstration in a store.

To set up a self-running presentation:

1. Open the presentation, and then on the **Slide Show** tab, in the **Set Up** group, click the **Set Up Slide Show** button.

   The Set Up Show dialog box opens.

2. In the **Show type** area, click **Browsed at a kiosk (full screen)**.

   When you click this option, the Loop Continuously Until 'Esc' check box in the Show Options area becomes unavailable so that you cannot clear it. Any narration or animation attached to the presentation will play with the presentation unless you select the Show Without Narration or Show Without Animation check box.

3. Click **OK**.

4. To test the show, display **Slide 1**, and on the **View** toolbar, click the **Slide Show** button.

   The presentation runs continuously, using its transitions, animations, and slide timings.

5. Press Esc to stop the slide show, and then save the presentation with a different name.

When you are ready to run the presentation, you can navigate to the folder where it is stored, and double-click it. The slide show opens in the view in which it was saved. Switch to Slide Show view to start the presentation. You can press Esc to stop the slide show at any time.

Preparing Speaker Notes and Handouts

If you will be delivering your presentation before a live audience, you will probably need some speaker notes to guide you. Each slide in a PowerPoint presentation has a corresponding notes page. As you create each slide, you can enter notes that relate to the slide's content by simply clicking the Notes pane and typing. If you want to include something other than text in your speaker notes, you must switch to Notes Page view by clicking the Notes Page button in the Presentation Views group on the View tab. When your notes are complete, you can print them so that they are readily available to guide the presentation.

As a courtesy for your audience, you might want to supply handouts showing the presentation's slides so that people can take notes. You don't need to do anything special to create handouts. Printing them requires a few simple decisions, such as how many slides you want to appear on each page.

Notes and handouts have their own masters, and you can customize them by using the same techniques you use to customize slide masters. Usually, you will find that the default masters are more than adequate, but if you want to make changes, you click Notes Master or Handout Master in the Presentation Views group on the View tab to display the respective masters.

In this exercise, you will enter speaker notes for a couple of slides in the Notes pane. You will then switch to Notes Page view, insert a graphic in one note and a table in another, customize the Notes master, and then print speaker notes and handouts.

> **USE** the *NotesHandouts* presentation and the *YinYang* graphic. These practice files are located in the *Documents\Microsoft Press\2007OfficeSBS_HomeStudent\PptDelivering* folder.
>
> **OPEN** the *NotesHandouts* presentation.

1. With Slide 1 selected, in the **Notes** pane, click the **Click to add notes** placeholder, type Welcome and introductions, and then press [Enter].

2. Type Logistics, press [Enter], and then type Establish knowledge level.

3. Display **Slide 2**, and in the **Notes** pane, type Talk about the main concepts.

4. Display **Slide 3**, and in the **Notes** pane, type Complementary energies, and then press [Enter] twice.

5. On the **View** tab, in the **Presentation Views** group, click the **Notes Page** button.

   Slide 3 is displayed in Notes Page view, with the view percentage set so that the entire page will fit in the window.

Notes Page

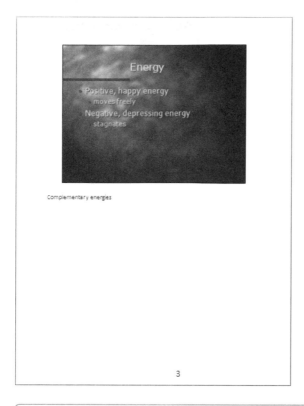

3

> **Tip** If you have trouble seeing the notes at this view percentage, click the Zoom button in the Zoom group on the View tab. Then when the Zoom dialog box opens, select or type a larger percentage, and click OK.

6. On the **Insert** tab, in the **Illustrations** group, click the **Picture** button.

7. In the **Insert Picture** dialog box, navigate to your *Documents\Microsoft Press\ 2007OfficeSBS_HomeStudent\PptDelivering* folder, and then double-click the *YinYang* graphic.

8. Drag the image down below the note you typed in step 4.

   The picture is visible in Notes Page view.

Next Slide

9. At the bottom of the scroll bar, click the **Next Slide** button to move to Slide 4.

Table

10. On the **Insert** tab, in the **Tables** group, click the **Table** button, and then drag to create a table that is two columns wide and eight rows high.

11. Drag the table by its border down into the notes placeholder, and then on the **Design** contextual tab in the **Table Style Options** group, clear the **Header Row** and **Banded Rows** check boxes.

12. Enter the following information, pressing Tab to move from cell to cell and from row to row:

Career 23
Fame 30
Relationships 41
Creativity 45
Fortune 60
Health 72
Knowledge 81
Helpful people 85

The speaker notes now include the page numbers in a reference work where you can find additional information if required during the presentation.

13. On the **View** tab, in the **Presentation Views** group, click the **Normal** button, and then drag the splitter bar above the Notes pane up to expand it.

The table is not visible in Normal view.

Notes
Master

14. Drag the splitter bar down again. Then on the **View** tab, in the **Presentation Views** group, click the **Notes Master** button.

The Notes Master appears, and the Notes Master tab is added to the Ribbon.

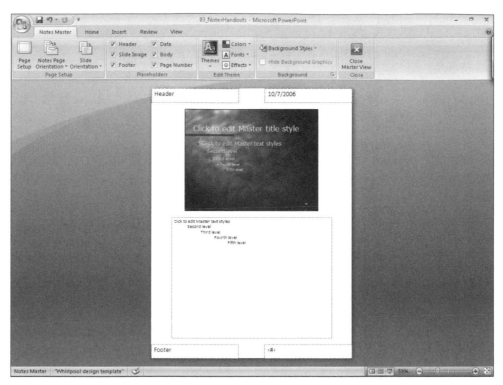

15. In the upper-left corner of the page, click the header placeholder, and then type Feng Shui.

16. In the lower-left corner of the page, click the footer placeholder, and then type Beginners' Class.

Normal

17. On the **View** toolbar, click the **Normal** button to return to Normal view.

18. Click the **Microsoft Office Button**, and then click **Print**.

The Print dialog box opens.

Microsoft Office
Button

19. Click the **Print what** arrow, click **Notes Pages** in the list, and then click **OK**.

You now have a copy of the speaker notes to refer to during the presentation.

20. Display the **Print** dialog box again, and then change the **Print what** setting to **Handouts**.

You can print audience handouts in six formats: one, two, three, four, six, or nine slides per page. The default, six, is set on the Handout master, but you can change it in the Print dialog box.

21. Under **Handouts**, click the **Slides per page** arrow, and in the list, click **3**.

When you print three slides per page, PowerPoint adds lines for notes to the right of each slide, as shown in the diagram on the right side of the dialog box.

22. In the lower-left corner of the dialog box, click **Preview**.

The first page of the handouts appears in Print Preview.

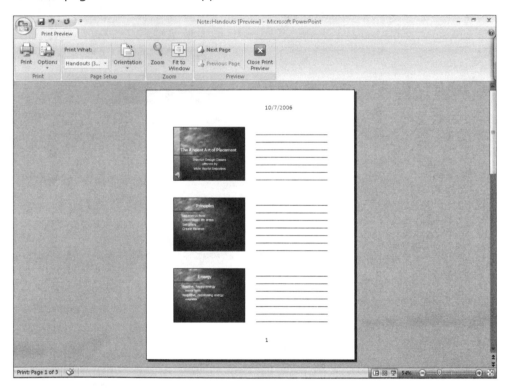

23. On the **Print Preview** tab, in the **Print** group, click the **Print** button, and then click **OK**.

Print

24. Return to Normal view.

   CLOSE the *NotesHandouts* presentation without saving your changes.

Preparing a Presentation for Travel

When you develop a presentation on the computer from which you will be delivering it, you will have all the fonts, linked objects, and other components of the presentation available when the lights go down and you launch your first slide. However, if you will deliver your presentation from a different computer, you need to make sure the fonts, linked objects, and any other necessary items are available.

With PowerPoint 2007, you can use the *Package for CD* feature to help you gather all the presentation components and save them to a CD or other type of removable media so that they can be transported to a different computer. Linked files are included in the presentation package by default. TrueType fonts are stored with the presentation if you click Embedded TrueType Fonts while creating the package. (When you include embedded fonts, the file size increases significantly.)

> **Tip** You can embed fonts when you package a presentation, or you can do it when you first save the presentation. In the Save As dialog box, click Tools, click Save Options, and on the Save page, select the Embed Fonts In The File check box. Then click Embed Only The Characters Used In The Presentation to embed only the characters in the font set that are actually used, or click Embed All Characters to embed the entire font set.

When you use Package For CD, by default the presentation will be set up to run automatically in the *Microsoft Office PowerPoint Viewer*. You can then send the CD containing the presentation package to people who do not have PowerPoint installed on their computers, and they will be able to view the presentation in the PowerPoint Viewer.

In this exercise, you will use Package For CD to create a presentation package on a CD. You will then run the presentation using the PowerPoint Viewer.

> **USE** the *Travel* presentation. This practice file is located in the *Documents\Microsoft Press\ 2007OfficeSBS_HomeStudent\PptDelivering* folder.
>
> **BE SURE TO** have a blank CD available. If your computer does not have a CD burner, you can follow along with the exercise but you will not be able to complete steps 8 through 16.
>
> **OPEN** the *Travel* presentation.

MIcrosoft Office Button

1. Click the **Microsoft Office Button**, click **Save As**, and then save the current presentation in the *PptDelivering* folder, with the name My Organization 101.

2. Click the **Microsoft Office Button**, point to **Publish**, and then click **Package for CD**.

   A message box tells you that your file will be converted to the PowerPoint 97-2003 format so that it is compatible with the PowerPoint Viewer.

3. Click **OK**.

   The Package For CD dialog box opens.

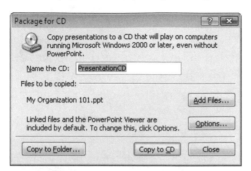

4. In the **Name the CD** box, type Organization.

   The open presentation, its linked files, and the PowerPoint Viewer will be included in the presentation package by default, but you need to specifically include embedded fonts.

5. Click **Options**.

   The Options dialog box opens.

6. Under **Package type**, leave **Viewer Package** selected, but click the **Select how presentations will play in the viewer** arrow, and then in the list, click **Let the user select which presentation to view**.

Clicking Viewer Package includes the PowerPoint Viewer. If you click Archive Package, the package contains only the presentation.

7. Under **Include these files**, select the **Embedded TrueType fonts** check box, and then click **OK**.

> **Important** Be sure to select the Embedded TrueType Fonts check box if a presentation includes fonts that don't come with the version of Microsoft Windows running on the presentation computer or the 2007 Microsoft Office system programs. Then the presentation will look the same on a computer on which the fonts aren't installed as it does on your computer.

8. Insert a blank CD in your CD burner, and then click **Copy to CD**.

   If your computer does not have a CD burner, click Copy To Folder instead, and then select the folder in which you want to store the package.

> **Tip** PowerPoint 2007 does not support the direct burning of content to a DVD. If you prefer to burn to a DVD rather than a CD, first copy your presentation to a folder on your computer, and then use DVD-burning software to create the DVD.

9. When PowerPoint asks you to verify that you want to include linked content, click **Yes**.

10. When you see a message that the copy operation was successful, click **No** to indicate that you don't want to copy the same package to another CD.

11. Click **Close** to close the **Package for CD** dialog box.

Close

12. At the right end of the title bar, click the **Close** button to close the presentation and quit PowerPoint.

13. Remove the CD from your CD burner, and then re-insert it.

> **Troubleshooting** If you are running the package from your computer, navigate to the folder where the package is stored, and double-click the *Organization* folder (the name you assigned in step 4). Then double-click PPTVIEW to start the Presentation Viewer.

After a few seconds, the PowerPoint Viewer starts. The first time you run this program, you need to click Accept to accept the terms of the program's license agreement. Then a dialog box opens in which you can select the presentation you want to run.

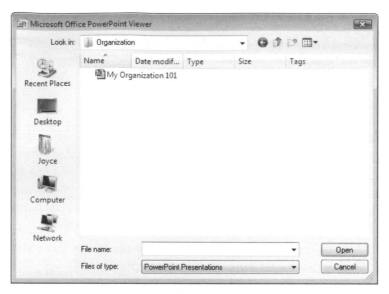

14. In the list of file and folder names, double-click **My Organization 101**.

    The PowerPoint Viewer displays the presentation's title slide.

15. Click the mouse button to advance through the slides in the PowerPoint Viewer, and then press the [Esc] key to end the presentation.

    The PowerPoint Viewer closes.

16. Close the **Microsoft Office PowerPoint Viewer** dialog box.

Showing a Presentation

To start a slide show from Normal or Slide Sorter view, you click the Slide Show button to display the current slide full screen. Then the simplest way to move linearly from one slide to the next is to click the mouse button without moving the mouse. But you can also move around by using the keyboard in the following ways:

● To move to the next slide, press the Spacebar, the Down Arrow key, or the Right Arrow key.

● To move to the previous slide, press the Page Up key or the Left Arrow key.

● To end the presentation, press the Esc key.

If you need to move to a slide other than the next one or the previous one, you can move the mouse pointer to display an inconspicuous toolbar in the lower-left corner of the slide. You can use this toolbar in the following ways:

- To move to the next slide, click the Next button.
- To move to the previous slide, click the Previous button.
- To jump to a slide out of sequence (even if it is hidden), click the Navigation button, click Go To Slide, and then click the slide.
- To display the slides in a custom slide show, click the Navigation button, click Custom Show, and then click the show.
- To display a list of keyboard shortcuts for carrying out slide show tasks click the Navigation button, and then click Help . For example, you can press the H key to show the next hidden slide, press the E key to erase pen annotations, or press the A key to show the pointer arrow.
- To end the presentation, click the Navigation button, and then click End Show.

> **Tip** You can also display the Navigation button's menu by right-clicking the slide.

During a presentation, you can reinforce your message by drawing on the slides with an electronic "pen" or changing the background behind text with a highlighter. You simply click the Pen button on the toolbar that appears when you move the mouse, click the tool you want, and then begin drawing or highlighting. You can change the pen or highlighter color to make it stand out on the slide by clicking the Pen button, clicking Ink Color, and then selecting the color you want.

In this exercise, you will move around in various ways while delivering a presentation. You'll also use a pen tool to mark up one slide, change the color, and mark up another.

USE the *Showing* presentation. This practice file is located in the *Documents\Microsoft Press\2007OfficeSBS_HomeStudent\PptDelivering* folder.
OPEN the *Showing* presentation.

Slide Show

1. With Slide 1 selected in Normal view, on the **View** toolbar, click the **Slide Show** button.

   The background of the first slide is displayed.

2. Click anywhere on the screen, and then click again.

   First the title moves onto the slide from the top, and then the subtitle moves onto the slide from the bottom.

3. Click the mouse button to advance to Slide 2.

   The slide contents move in from the right.

4. Press the ◀ key to display the previous slide, and then press the ▶ key to display the next slide.

5. Move the mouse.

The pointer appears on the screen, and the shadow toolbar appears in the lower-left corner.

> **Troubleshooting** If the pop-up toolbar doesn't appear, press the Esc key to end the slide show. Then click the Microsoft Office Button, click PowerPoint Options, click Advanced, and in the Slide Show section, select the Show Popup Toolbar check box, and click OK.

Next

6. On the toolbar, click the **Next** button (the button at the right end of the shadow toolbar) to display Slide 3.

7. Right-click anywhere on the screen, and then click **Previous** to redisplay Slide 2.

8. Right-click anywhere on the screen, point to **Go to Slide**, and then in the list of slide names, click **7 Pulling It All Together**.

Navigation

9. Display the toolbar, click the **Navigation** button, and then click **Next** to display Slide 8.

10. Use various navigation methods to move around the slide show until you are comfortable moving around.

11. Right-click anywhere on the screen, and then click **End Show**.

Slide 8 appears in Normal view.

> **Tip** If you click all the way through to the end of the presentation, PowerPoint displays a black screen to indicate that the next click will return you to the previous view. If you do not want the black screen to appear at the end of a presentation, click the Microsoft Office Button, click PowerPoint Options, and click Advanced. Then in the Slide Show area, clear the End With Black Slide check box, and click OK. Then clicking while the last slide is displayed will return you to the previous view.

12. Display **Slide 5**, and switch to Slide Show view.

13. Right-click anywhere on the screen, point to **Pointer Options**, and click **Felt Tip Pen**.

The pointer changes to resemble the tip of a felt tip pen.

> **Important** When the pen tool is active in Slide Show view, clicking the mouse does not advance the slide show to the next slide. You need to switch back to the regular pointer to use the mouse to advance the slide.

14. Draw a line under the word *Colorizing* in the title.

<u>Colorizing</u> Your Room
- Where to add color
- Furniture and accessory changes
- How to match colors
  – Does Verdigris work with Realgar?

15. Right-click the screen, point to **Pointer Options**, and then click **Erase All Ink on Slide**.

The line is erased.

16. Press [Space] to move to the next slide.

Pen

17. Display the toolbar, click the **Pen** button, point to **Ink Color**, and then in the palette, click a light purple color.

18. Draw circles around *color wheel* and *swatches*.

Sample
- So you like Verdigris; what next?
- Check the (color wheel)
- Work with the (swatches)

19. Right-click anywhere on the screen, point to **Pointer Options**, and then click **Arrow**.

    The pen tool changes back to the regular pointer, and you can now click the mouse button to advance to the next slide.

20. Press ⎋Esc to stop the slide show.

    A message asks whether you want to keep your ink annotations.

21. Click **Discard**.

    Slide 6 appears in Normal view.

CLOSE the *Showing* presentation without saving your changes, and if you are not continuing directly on to the next chapter, exit PowerPoint.

Using Two Monitors

If your computer can support two monitors, or if you will be presenting a slide show from your computer through an overhead projector, you might want to check out Presenter view. In this view, you can control the slide show on one monitor while the audience sees the presentation in Slide Show view on the other monitor or the projector screen.

To deliver a slide show on one monitor and use Presenter view on another:

1. Open the PowerPoint presentation you want to set up.

2. On the **Slide Show** tab, in the **Set Up** group, click **Set Up Slide Show**.

   The Set Up Show dialog box opens.

3. Under **Multiple monitors**, click the **Display slide show on** arrow, and then in the list, click the name of the monitor you want to use to deliver the presentation.

   The slide show will run full-screen on the specified monitor.

4. Under **Multiple monitors**, select the **Show Presenter View** check box, and then click **OK**.

5. Switch to Slide Show view to start the slide show on the specified monitor.

6. On the other monitor, use the Presenter view navigation tools to control the presentation.

   You can see details about what slide or bullet point is coming next, see your speaker notes, jump directly to any slide, black out the screen during a pause in the presentation, and keep track of the time.

Key Points

- When you don't want to include all the slides in a presentation for a particular audience, you can use a subset of the slides to create a custom slide show. You can also hide slides and then display them only if appropriate.

- You can assign timings to slides manually, or you can rehearse the presentation and record the slide timings from the rehearsal. The presentation automatically advances from one slide to the next have the specified time has elapsed.

- You can easily create speaker notes to ensure a smooth delivery or print handouts to ensure that your audience can easily follow along with your presentation.

- To run the presentation on a computer other than the one you developed the presentation on, you can create a presentation package. Including the PowerPoint Viewer in the package enables the presentation can run on a computer on which PowerPoint is not installed.

- Knowing how to use all the toolbar buttons, commands, and keyboard shortcuts to navigate in Slide Show view will ensure a smoother presentation delivery.

- To emphasize a point, you can mark up slides during a slide show by using different pen tools and different colors. You can save or discard these annotations.

Part IV

Microsoft Office One Note 2007

Chapter at a Glance

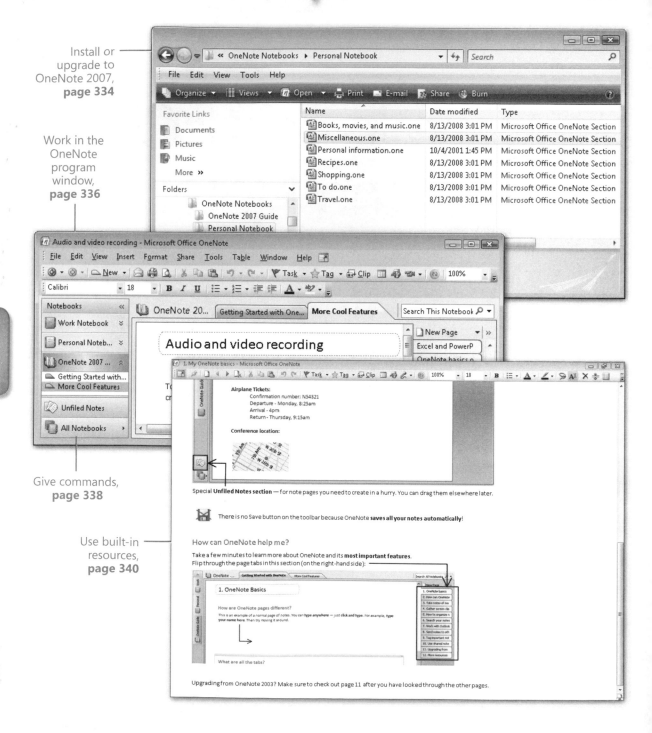

13 Getting Started with OneNote

In this chapter, you will learn to:

✔ Install or upgrade to OneNote 2007.

✔ Work in the OneNote program window.

✔ Give commands.

✔ Use built-in resources.

✔ Customize OneNote.

Microsoft Office OneNote 2007 is a handy program that makes it possible to electronically collect and store bits and pieces of information. You can use OneNote to:

● Collect, save, and safeguard information in one place.

● Take notes in a class or meeting.

● Organize information in ways that are logical to you.

● Search for information when you need it.

After you spend a short time using OneNote, you will undoubtedly find many uses for it. (For example, before writing this chapter, I stored all my research notes in OneNote.)

As with all organizational systems, OneNote is most effective if you use it on a regular basis. By developing consistent data collection and storage practices, you will be able to most efficiently locate stored information whenever you need it. Eventually, you might even wonder how you ever survived without it!

In this chapter, you will learn about OneNote installation considerations, explore the OneNote working environment and storage structure, and learn how to move around and work in OneNote. You will also investigate resources within OneNote that you can refer to for more information.

See Also Do you need only a quick refresher on the topics in this chapter? See the Quick Reference entries at the beginning of this book.

> **Important** There are no practice files for this chapter other than those provided with OneNote. For more information about practice files, see "Using the Book's CD" at the beginning of this book.

> **Troubleshooting** Graphics and operating system–related instructions in this book reflect the Windows Vista user interface. If your computer is running Windows XP and you experience trouble following the instructions as written, please refer to the "Information for Readers Running Windows XP" section at the beginning of this book.

Installing or Upgrading to OneNote 2007

OneNote 2007 is available with three editions of the 2007 Microsoft Office system: Home and Student (the subject of this book), Ultimate (the premium edition for home use), and Enterprise (the premium edition for business use, available only to volume licensing customers). It is also available as a stand-alone retail product, so you can add the program to any other edition of the Office system or use OneNote independently.

If you have been using OneNote 2003, you should be aware of the following before installing OneNote 2007:

- If you *install* OneNote 2007 rather than *upgrade* from OneNote 2003 to OneNote 2007, both versions of the application will be available from the Start menu on your computer.

- The first time you start OneNote 2007, it copies any existing OneNote 2003 notebooks from the *Documents\My Notebook* folder (the default OneNote 2003 notebook location) to the *Documents\OneNote Notebooks* folder (the default OneNote 2007 notebook location) and upgrades the copies to the OneNote 2007 file format. This process can be time consuming. The original notes might be split into multiple notebooks if necessary to conform to the OneNote 2007 file-storage model.

- You can open a OneNote 2003 notebook in OneNote 2007 and view the notes it contains. If you try to edit the notes, OneNote 2007 offers the option of upgrading the active notebook section.

- You cannot open a OneNote 2007 notebook in OneNote 2003. (A file converter might become available in the future, but none is available at this time.)

Tip For information about available converters and add-ins for OneNote and other Office system programs, visit the Downloads area of the Office Online Web site at

office.microsoft.com/downloads/

You can browse downloads on the site by selecting a program in the left pane, or you can search for a specific download by entering keywords in the Search box at the top of the page.

If you are considering upgrading to OneNote 2007 but haven't yet done so, here are some of the new features that you might find useful:

- **Support for multiple notebooks, computers, and users.** You can maintain separate notebooks for different purposes, merge multiple notebooks into one notebook, access a notebook from another computer, or invite other people to collaborate simultaneously in adding notes to a notebook.

- **Support for Microsoft Office Outlook.** You can send information between Outlook 2007 or Outlook 2003 and OneNote 2007, and synchronize task lists between the two programs.

- **Web page references.** You can send Web content from Windows Internet Explorer to OneNote. When you do so, OneNote also collects and stores information about the source of the Web content, so you can easily reference or return to the source.

- **Hyperlinks.** You can link to specific notes and pages to move around a notebook's content in logical ways.

- **Document references.** You can insert a file as an attachment into a notebook page, or insert the file's contents.

- **Really cool search capability.** You can very quickly locate information in text, images, and audio files.

- **OneNote Mobile.** You can capture information on a Windows Mobile device and synchronize it with a OneNote notebook.

Tip Do you want to try before you buy? You can find more information about OneNote 2007, including a free, fully featured trial version and a free online test drive (take it!) at

office.microsoft.com/OneNote/

At the end of the trial period, the functionality of the trial version will be limited. You can still view and print existing notes, but you can't update them or create new notes. You can restore full functionality (without losing your notes) by installing a genuine licensed copy of OneNote.

Working in the OneNote Program Window

In the same way that the Windows storage structure reflects that of a physical office (with a desktop, folders, and files), the OneNote storage structure reflects a three-ring binder. Each *notebook* is divided into *sections*, and each section is divided into *pages*. If you want to extend the analogy, you can format the page background to resemble various types of ruled paper.

See Also For information about changing the background of a notebook page, see "Creating Pages and Sections," in Chapter 14, "Creating and Configuring Notebooks."

In Windows Explorer, each notebook is represented by a folder in your *Documents\ OneNote Notebooks* folder. Each section of a notebook is stored as an *.one file* within the notebook folder. (And if you're wondering—yes, you can move a section between notebooks by moving the *.one* file between folders.)

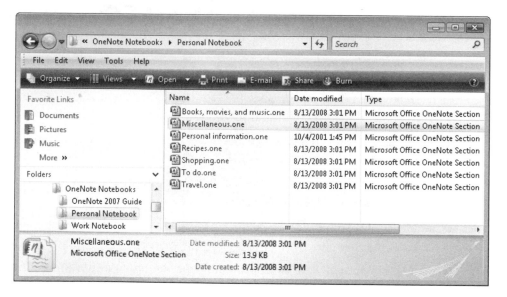

When you start OneNote for the first time, the program opens a ready-made notebook. Thereafter, starting the program opens the notebook you worked with in the previous OneNote session.

Information about the active notebook content is available in three areas of the OneNote program window.

Notebook header

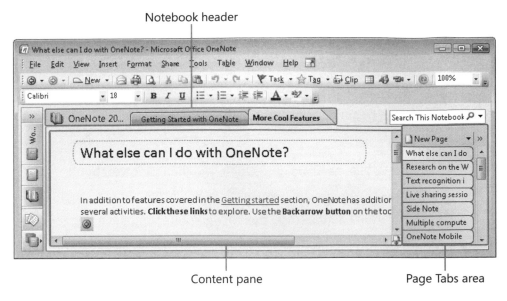

Content pane   Page Tabs area

- The *content pane* in the center of the program window displays the active notebook page.

- The *notebook header* above the content pane displays the name of the active notebook and section tabs that you can click to move between sections of the active notebook.

  The area at the left end of the notebook header that displays the notebook name has space for only 11 characters. If the notebook name is longer than 11 characters, OneNote displays the first 10 characters of the name followed by an ellipsis (...) to indicate that the entire name does not fit.

- The *Page Tabs area* to the right of the content pane displays page tabs you can click to move between pages of the active section. You can shrink the Page Tabs area by clicking the Collapse Page Tabs button in the upper-right corner.

  By default, the Page Tabs area displays a tab for each page in the current section. You can filter the tabs to make it easier to locate specific content.

»

Collapse
Page Tab

Working with Multiple Notebooks

You can have multiple notebooks open at one time, and you can easily switch between two notebooks without specifically saving the content you've been working with. If you don't need to access an open notebook any more, you can close it. Closed notebooks do not appear on the Navigation Bar.

To open a notebook:

1. On the **File** menu, point to **Open**, and then click **Notebook**.
2. Browse to the *Documents\OneNote Notebooks* folder.
3. Click (don't double-click) the folder representing the notebook you want to open, and then click **Open**.

To close a notebook:

→ On the **Navigation Bar**, right-click the notebook button, and then click **Close this Notebook**.

   Or

→ On the **File** menu, click **Close this Notebook** to close the active notebook.

Giving Commands

OneNote 2007 does not have the *Microsoft Office Fluent user interface* (most easily identified by the task-based command groupings arranged on the tabs of the Office Fluent Ribbon) adopted by the other programs in the Home and Student edition of the 2007 Microsoft Office system. Commands for working with OneNote and notebook content are available in three areas of the OneNote program window.

Tip In this book, we display the Standard and Formatting toolbars on separate rows so you can see all their commands at one time. Your toolbar arrangement might look different.

To display or hide a toolbar, right-click anywhere in the toolbar area and then click the toolbar you want to toggle on or off. To move a toolbar, drag it by its move handle (the vertical line of four dots at the left end of the toolbar). You can *float* a toolbar anywhere on the screen by dragging it over the content pane. To dock a floating toolbar at the top or right edge of the program window, simply double-click its title bar.

Menu bar   Toolbar area

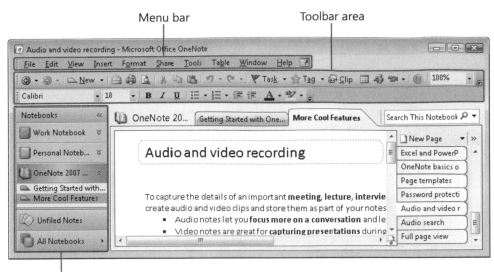

Navigation Bar

- The *menu bar* contains commands organized on drop-down menus.

Full Page View

Clicking the Full Page View button at the right end of the menu bar maximizes the content area by hiding the menu bar, the Navigation Bar, and the Page Tabs area, and replacing the currently displayed toolbars with the Full Page View toolbar.

Clicking the active Full Page View button at the left end of the toolbar returns the window to its previous state.

- The *toolbar area* displays the active command toolbars. Available toolbars include Standard, Formatting, Audio And Video Recording, Drawing Tools, My Pens, Outlining, Outlook Tasks, Tags, and Writing Tools.

- The Navigation Bar displays links to open notebooks and notebook sections, and to the Unfiled Notes section. Depending on the size of the program window, your screen resolution, the number of open notebooks, and other factors, the Navigation Bar might not be large enough to display all of the available information. Clicking All Notebooks at the bottom of the Navigation Bar displays the All Notebooks List window, which contains links to each section of each open notebook.

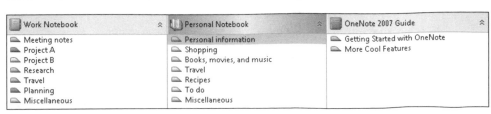

Collapse
Navigation Bar

You can minimize the Navigation Bar to a vertical button bar by clicking the Collapse Navigation Bar button in its upper-right corner.

See Also For information about opening more than one notebook, see the sidebar "Working with Multiple Notebooks" earlier in this chapter.

Giving some commands in OneNote causes a *task pane* containing specialized commands to appear on the right side of the program window. You can display the task pane at any time by clicking Task Pane on the View menu or by right-clicking the toolbar area and clicking Task Pane on the *context menu*. Clicking the Other Task Panes button displays a list of the available task panes.

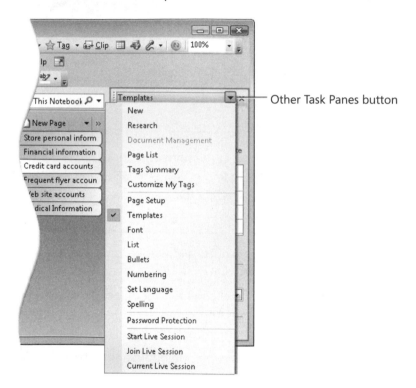

Other Task Panes button

Using Built-In Resources

The default OneNote 2007 installation includes the OneNote 2007 Guide notebook. This reference provides examples of the types of information you can collect in OneNote and ways that you can work with it, organized in two sections:

● The *Getting Started with OneNote* section is a 12-page manual containing basic information about how and why to use OneNote.

● The *More Cool Features* section includes 23 pages of ideas, examples, and instructions.

In this exercise, you will take a quick tour of the OneNote 2007 Guide notebook while learning to move among sections and pages, rename sections and pages, display different views of a page, and display more information about notebook elements. We encourage you to investigate other pages of the Guide that interest you, to see examples of the techniques you will learn in this book.

BE SURE TO install OneNote 2007 before beginning this exercise.

1. On the **Start** menu, point to **All Programs**, click **Microsoft Office**, and then click **Microsoft Office OneNote 2007**.

OneNote starts, displaying the first page of the OneNote 2007 Guide notebook or, if you've used OneNote before, the page that was open when you exited. A Work Notebook and Personal Notebook are also open. The active notebook name appears at the left end of the content header, followed by tabs representing the notebook sections. Depending on your previous use of OneNote, other open notebooks might also appear on the Navigation Bar.

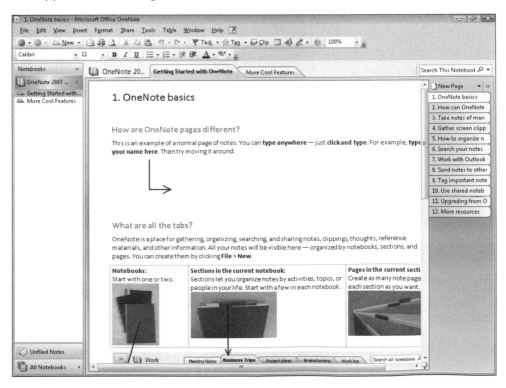

> **Troubleshooting** If you have previously used OneNote on this computer, or if your computer administrator has stipulated an alternative default notebook, the OneNote 2007 Guide notebook might not be open. Don't worry; following step 2 will take care of this problem.

2. Do the following to make your program window look like ours:

Expand
Navigation Bar

- If the **Navigation Bar** is minimized, click the **Expand Navigation Bar** button.
- If the **OneNote 2007 Guide** button does not appear on the Navigation Bar, open that notebook by following the steps in the sidebar "Working with Multiple Notebooks" earlier in this chapter.

> **Troubleshooting** If your school or organization has a specialized OneNote environment, the OneNote 2007 Guide notebook might not be available. You can follow along with this exercise by substituting any available notebook.

Expand
Page Tabs

- If the **Page Tabs** area is minimized, click the **Expand Page Tabs** button.
- If the OneNote 2007 Guide is not the active notebook, click the **OneNote 2007 Guide** button on the Navigation Bar.
- If the OneNote Basics page is not the active page, click the **Getting Started with OneNote** section tab, and then click the **1. OneNote basics** page tab.
- Right-click anywhere in the toolbar area. On the context menu that appears, select only **Standard** and **Formatting**, and clear the selection of any other visible toolbars.
- Arrange the Standard and Formatting toolbars above each other in the toolbar area, below the menu bar, so that all their commands are visible.

3. On the **Navigation Bar**, right-click the **Work Notebook** button, and then click **Close this Notebook**. Then use the same method to close the Personal Notebook.

See Also For information about the various types of notebook templates that are available, see "Creating a Notebook for Use on One Computer" in Chapter 14, "Creating and Configuring Notebooks."

4. At the top of the content pane, in the page title box containing the text *1. OneNote basics*, click to place the insertion point before *OneNote*.

Notice that the number is part of the page title.

5. Type My, and then press ⎡Space⎤.

As you type, the title shown on the page tab to the right changes to reflect your edits.

6. In the notebook header, point to the partially hidden notebook title, which appears to the right of the notebook icon.

A ScreenTip appears, displaying the full notebook title.

7. In the notebook header, point to the **More Cool Features** tab.

A ScreenTip displays the complete path to the section file (the .one file). Notice that the file name matches the section name.

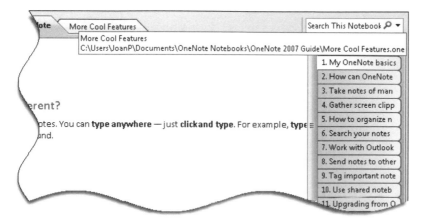

8. Click the **More Cool Features** tab.

The selected section opens, displaying the first page in the section or, if you have previously viewed this section, the last page you accessed. In the Page Tabs area, notice that the pages in this notebook are not numbered like the pages of the Getting Started section.

9. In the **Page Tabs** area, point to a page tab whose title appears to be cut off.

A ScreenTip displays the entire page title and the date the page was created.

10. Click a page tab displaying a title that interests you.

OneNote displays the selected page.

11. On the **Navigation Bar**, point to the **More Cool Features** button.

A ScreenTip displays the complete path to the section file (the .one file). A section tab icon indicates that this button represents a section. Notice that the section tab icon color matches that of the corresponding section tab.

See Also For information about section colors, see the sidebar "Formatting Notes, Pages, and Sections" in Chapter 15, "Collecting Information in a Notebook."

12. Right-click the **More Cool Features** button, and then click **Rename**.

The button name is selected for editing.

13. Double-click the word *More*.

Only the word *More* is selected for editing.

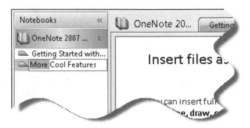

14. Type Really, and then press ⏎ Enter.

The names on the button and on the section tab change to reflect your edit. You can rename a section by using this technique with the Navigation Bar button or the section tab.

15. Point to the **Really Cool Features** button on the **Navigation Bar**, and then to the **Really Cool Features** section tab in the notebook header.

The ScreenTip indicates that OneNote has changed the .one file name to match the new section name.

16. On the **Navigation Bar**, click the **Getting Started with OneNote** button to return to that section.

Full Page View

17. At the right end of the menu bar, click the **Full Page View** button.

OneNote displays the selected page with only the Full Page View toolbar and scroll bar visible.

18. Scroll the page to view its contents.

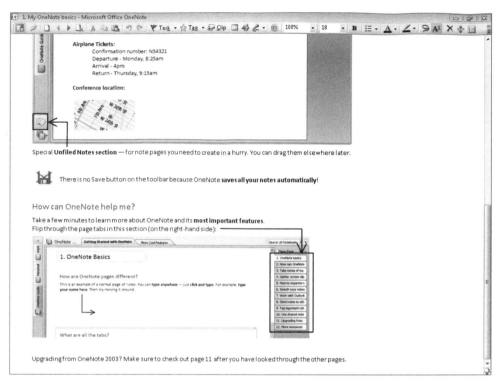

19. Point to the buttons on the Full Page View toolbar to familiarize yourself with these commands, which are considered to be among the most commonly used. Then click the **Toolbar Options** button at the right end of the Full Page View toolbar to display the additional commands available from this toolbar.

Toolbar Options button

The OneNote 2007 user interface features interactive toolbars that adjust to suit the way you work. OneNote remembers the commands you use, and displays those you use most often on the visible portion of the toolbar. Other commands are available from the Toolbar Options menu. When you use a command from the Toolbar Options menu, its button moves to the visible toolbar, displacing the button of a less frequently used command.

20. On the **Toolbar Options** menu, point to **Add or Remove Buttons**, and then point to **Full Page View**.

OneNote displays a menu listing all the available Full Page View toolbar commands. You can select and clear selections on this menu to specify the commands you want to be available from the toolbar. This particular toolbar contains an unusually large number of commands, because it is the only toolbar you can display in Full Page View. You can scroll the list by pointing to the arrow at the bottom of the list (or at the top, after you've scrolled to the bottom).

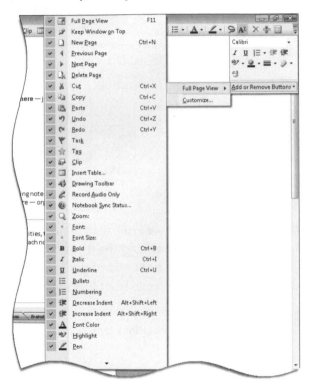

Clearing a selection on this menu entirely removes the associated command from the toolbar and the Toolbar Options menu. You can restore a removed command by redisplaying this menu and selecting the command.

> **Note** To restore a toolbar to its original state, display the associated toolbar menu, and then click Reset Toolbar at the bottom of the command list.

Close

21. With the page displayed in Full Page View, click the **Close** button in the upper-right corner of the OneNote program window.

Without prompting you to save changes, OneNote closes.

22. Restart OneNote by repeating step 1 or by clicking **Microsoft Office OneNote 2007** in the **Recently Used Programs** list on the **Start** menu.

OneNote reopens in the standard view (not Full Page View), displaying the page that was active when you closed it. The changes you made to the notebook structure—the section name and page name—are intact.

23. On the **File** menu, click **Close this Notebook**.

The OneNote 2007 Guide notebook closes. The OneNote program window remains open, displaying the Unfiled Notes section.

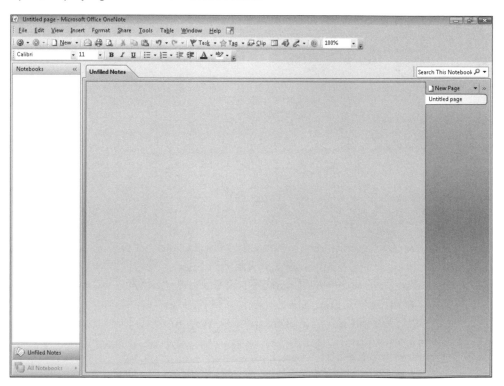

See Also For information about the Unfiled Notes section, see "Sending Content to OneNote" in Chapter 15, "Collecting Information in a Notebook."

 CLOSE the OneNote program window if you are not continuing directly to the next chapter.

Customizing OneNote

In this book, we discuss the default behavior of OneNote—the way the program works if you don't change any of its settings. As with all Office programs, there are a number of adjustments—major and minor—that you can make to modify the program to suit your needs. The majority of these are available from the Options window, which you can open by clicking Options on the Tools menu.

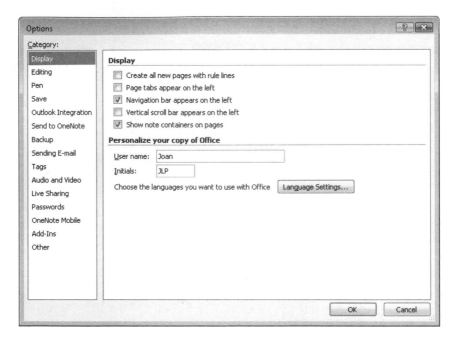

Like the Options windows in other 2007 Microsoft Office system programs, the OneNote Options window presents a wide variety of settings divided into category-specific pages. You can control the appearance of the program window; change your user information; set the default font, file location, and backup frequency; change the way OneNote handles text and paragraph commands, Web notes, and printouts; control security settings; and much more. Investigate this window at your own convenience.

Key Points

- OneNote simplifies the process of collecting and storing electronic information.

- OneNote 2007 supports multiple notebooks, computers, and users, and has many useful new features.

- You can upgrade notebooks created in OneNote 2003 to be compatible with OneNote 2007.

- OneNote 2007 does not use the Microsoft Office Fluent user interface; commands are available from menus and toolbars.

- OneNote 2007 stores information in the *Documents\OneNote Notebooks* folder. Each "notebook" consists of a folder containing a .one file corresponding to each section within the notebook.

- The default OneNote 2007 installation includes the OneNote 2007 Guide, a notebook containing examples and ideas for using OneNote in your home, school, or business environment.

- You can customize many aspects of the appearance and behavior of OneNote to fit your needs.

Chapter at a Glance

Create a notebook for use on one computer, **page 352**

Create a notebook for use on multiple computers, **page 356**

Create pages and sections, **page 361**

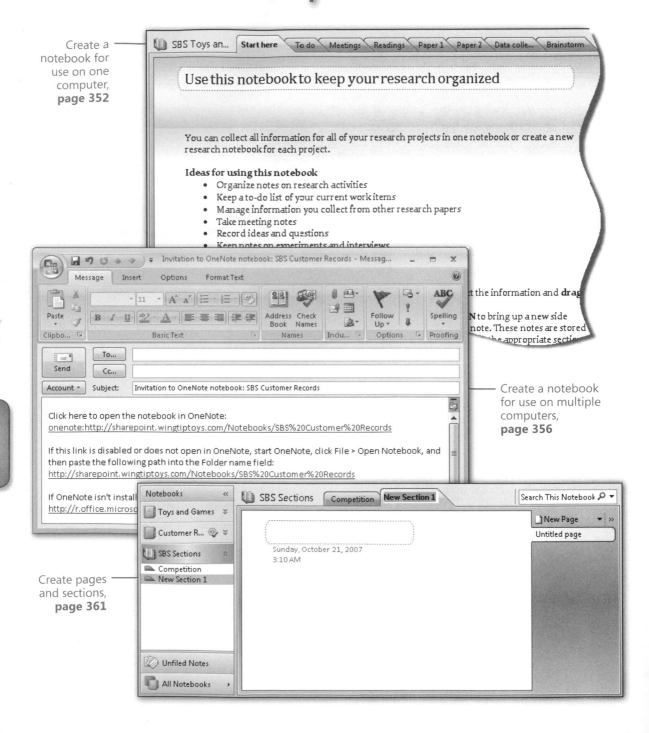

14 Creating and Configuring Notebooks

In this chapter, you will learn to:

✔ Create a notebook for use on one computer.

✔ Create a notebook for use on multiple computers.

✔ Create pages and sections.

In Chapter 13, "Getting Started with OneNote," we discussed the basic Microsoft Office OneNote 2007 data storage structure (notebooks, sections, and pages) and took a tour of a sample notebook that comes with OneNote. The sample notebook contains two sections and a total of 35 pages—quite a lot of information. This organizational structure might be useful for the type of information you want to collect and save, but as you'll see in this chapter, there are many ways of structuring a notebook. The important thing is to create a structure that is easy for you to move around in, so that you can easily find the information you want when you want it.

OneNote 2003 offered only a single-user, single-computer notebook model. OneNote 2007 no longer has these limitations—you can access your notebook from multiple computers, or multiple people can access a shared notebook. The ability to contribute and edit content in a shared notebook simultaneously with other people opens up many new possibilities for collaboration.

In this chapter, you will create a OneNote notebook on your computer and learn how to create a notebook that you can access from more than one computer. Then you will add pages and sections to your notebook so that you are ready to start storing information.

See Also Do you need only a quick refresher on the topics in this chapter? See the Quick Reference entries at the beginning of this book.

Important Before you can use the practice file in this chapter, you need to install it from the book's companion CD to its default location. See "Using the Book's CD" at the beginning of this book for more information.

Troubleshooting Graphics and operating system–related instructions in this book reflect the Windows Vista user interface. If your computer is running Windows XP and you experience trouble following the instructions as written, please refer to the "Information for Readers Running Windows XP" section at the beginning of this book.

Creating a Notebook for Use on One Computer

The simplest OneNote notebook structure, created by the *blank notebook* template, consists of one section containing one page—an .one file contained in a folder. You can add content to a blank notebook (also known as *populating* the notebook) and then organize it into pages and sections, or you can create an organizational structure and then populate it. The best method will vary depending on the way you plan to use the notebook—whether you are working on a highly structured project or collecting a wide variety of information.

When you want to start by creating the organizational structure, you might find it convenient to base a new notebook on one of the eight specialized notebook templates that come with OneNote 2007:

- **Clients Notebook.** This notebook template includes three Client sections and an Open Issues section.

- **Personal Notebook.** This notebook template includes Personal Information; Shopping; Books, Movies, And Music; Travel; Recipes; To Do; and Miscellaneous sections.

- **Professional Services Notebook.** This notebook template includes Proposals, Meeting And Call Notes, Research And Analysis, Report And Client Deliverables, and Business Administration sections.

- **Research Notebook.** This notebook template includes two Paper sections and To Do, Meetings, Readings, Data Collection, and Brainstorm sections.

● **Shared Notebook – Group Project.** This notebook template includes Meeting Notes, Goals And Schedule, Drafts, Tasks And Issues, Research, and Team Information sections.

● **Shared Notebook – Reference Materials.** This notebook template includes three Topic sections and Team Information, Tools, and Links sections.

● **Student Semester Notebook.** This notebook template includes three Class sections, two Project sections, and To Do and Student Club sections.

● **Work Notebook.** This notebook template includes two Project sections and Meeting Notes, Research, Travel, Planning, and Miscellaneous sections.

The sections and pages created by these templates contain tips and ideas intended to help you use the notebook effectively. Additional notebook templates available from Microsoft Office Online are designed to help facilitate a variety of situations, such as planning a landscape project or a wedding, house hunting or moving, and various legal situations.

In this exercise, you will create a research notebook for use on only one computer. We encourage you to repeat this exercise with other notebook templates, to gain more insight into the options provided by OneNote.

> **BE SURE TO** start OneNote before beginning this exercise.

1. On the **File** menu, point to **New**, and then click **Notebook**.

   The New Notebook Wizard starts.

2. Scroll the list of available notebooks, and then click **Research Notebook**.

3. In the **Name** box, enter SBS Toys and Games.

   > **Important** The name of this notebook begins with *SBS* so that you can easily differentiate it from your own notebooks.

4. Click the **Color** arrow, and then click the **Apple** square in the lower-left corner of the **Color** palette.

   > **Tip** If you don't select a color, OneNote will assign one for you. You can change the notebook color at any time.

The selected color appears on the Color button.

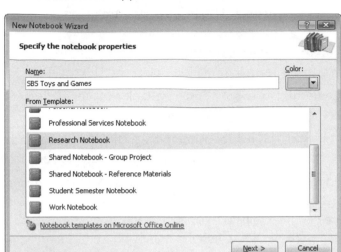

5. In the **New Notebook Wizard**, click **Next**.

The Who Will Use This Notebook page opens.

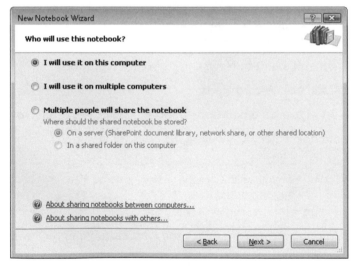

6. With **I will use it on this computer** selected, click **Next**.

See Also For information about notebooks that will be used on more than one computer, see "Creating a Notebook for Use on Multiple Computers" later in this chapter.

See Also For information about creating a notebook that will be shared with other people, click the About Sharing Notebooks With Others link at the bottom of the Who Will Use This Notebook page.

The Confirm Notebook Location page opens.

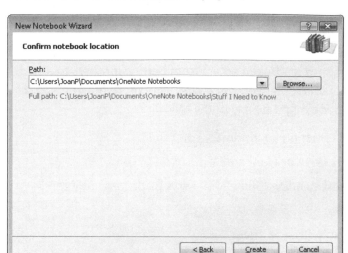

7. Confirm that the **Path** box specifies your *Documents\OneNote Notebooks* folder as the location of the new notebook. Then click **Create**.

OneNote creates the notebook and displays its Start Here section.

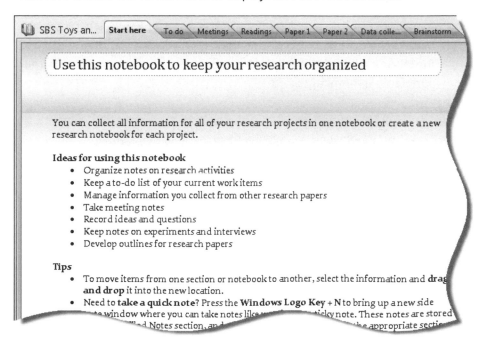

Notice that the Start Here section tab and the active page background are the apple green color you selected in step 4.

Creating a Notebook for Use on Multiple Computers

If you work on more than one computer (such as a desktop computer and a mobile computer) and have read/write access from both computers to a shared location, you can create a notebook that you can access from more than one computer. An appropriate shared location might be any of the following:

- A shared folder on your primary computer
- A network drive or file share
- A Microsoft Windows SharePoint Services document library
- A Web site
- A removable storage drive

If you store the notebook in a shared folder on your primary computer, you can open it from any other computer for which you have the same *login credentials*. Choose a storage location that will be available when you need it; for example, if you turn off your desktop computer while traveling with your mobile computer, a notebook stored on the desktop computer might not be accessible when you need it.

OneNote creates an offline copy of the notebook on each secondary computer you access the notebook from. OneNote synchronizes the offline copy with the original notebook when the secondary computer is connected to the shared location and OneNote is running.

Sharing an Existing Notebook

If you create a notebook for use on only one computer and later decide you want to access the notebook from multiple computers, you can easily do so.

- If your primary computer can be accessed through a network or workgroup, you can share the notebook from its original location.

- If your primary computer cannot be accessed through a network or workgroup, or if you do not log in to your primary and secondary computers with the same credentials, you can move the notebook to a shared location.

To share a notebook from its original location (on a computer running Windows Vista):

1. Close the notebook. Then in Windows Explorer, open the folder that contains the notebook folder (by default, your *Documents\OneNote Notebooks* folder).

2. Click the notebook folder, and then on the toolbar, click **Share**.

3. In the **File Sharing** window, click the user list arrow, click **Everyone**, and then click **Add**.

4. In the **Everyone** row of the user list, click the **Permission Level** arrow, and then click **Contributor**.

5. In the **File Sharing** window, click **Share**.

To move a notebook to a shared location:

1. Close the notebook. Then in Windows Explorer, open the folder that contains the notebook folder (by default, your *Documents\OneNote Notebooks* folder).

2. In a second instance of Windows Explorer, navigate to the shared location.

3. Point to the notebook folder, hold down the right mouse button, and drag the folder from its original location to the shared location. When you release the mouse button, click **Move**.

After making the notebook accessible from a shared location, follow these steps to generate an e-mail message containing the connection information:

1. In OneNote, on the **File** menu, point to **Open**, and then click **Notebook**.

2. In the **Open Notebook** dialog box, browse to the shared location, click the notebook folder, and then click **Open**.

3. On the **Share** menu, click **Send Shared Notebook Link to Others**.

In this exercise, you will create a notebook that you can access from multiple computers.

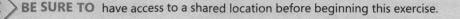

> **BE SURE TO** have access to a shared location before beginning this exercise.

1. On the **File** menu, point to **New**, and then click **Notebook**.

   The New Notebook Wizard starts.

2. In the **Name** box, enter SBS Customer Records.

3. In the **From Template** list, click **Clients Notebook**.

4. In the top row of the **Color** palette, click the **Yellow** box. Then click **Next**.

5. On the **Who will use this notebook** page, click **I will use it on multiple computers**, and then click **Next**.

6. On the **Confirm notebook location** page, enter the shared location in the **Path** box; or click the **Browse** button, navigate to the shared location where you want to store the notebook, and then click **Select**.

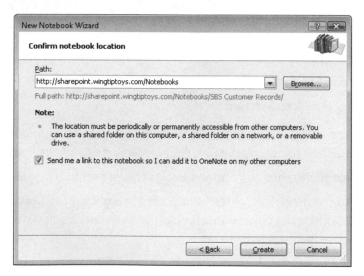

7. If Microsoft Office Outlook or another e-mail program is installed and configured on your computer, leave the **Send me a link** check box selected; otherwise, clear the check box. Then click **Create**.

If you need to enter credentials to access the shared location, you will be prompted to do so.

OneNote creates the notebook and, if the Send Me A Link check box was selected, creates an e-mail message containing information you can use to access the notebook from another computer. (If Outlook isn't already running, OneNote will start it for you.)

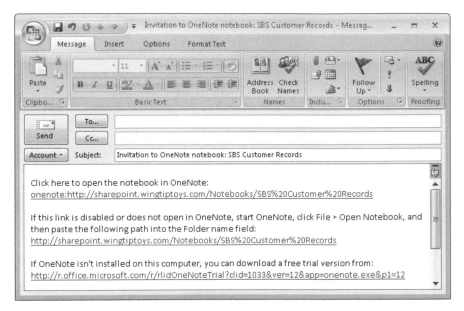

8. Address the e-mail message to yourself and send it.

> **Tip** You can open the notebook from another computer by clicking the link in the e-mail message or by browsing to the shared location from within OneNote.

9. Now take a look at the SBS Customer Records notebook.

ActiveSync icon

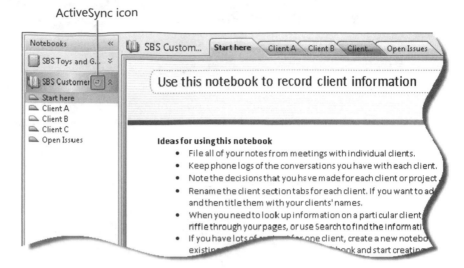

On the Navigation Bar, the ActiveSync icon to the right of the notebook name indicates synchronization status of the shared notebook. When OneNote is not actively synchronizing the primary notebook with the copies on other computers, one of the following indicators appears on the icon:

- A green check mark indicates a successful synchronization.
- A yellow caution triangle indicates a synchronization error.
- A red slashed circle indicates that the local copy of the notebook is offline.

You can view the synchronization status and settings by clicking the ActiveSync icon.

Stop Sharing a Notebook

If you no longer want to use a notebook on multiple computers, you can make it inaccessible by changing the sharing permissions. From OneNote, open the shared notebook. Then on the Share menu, click Stop Sharing Notebook, and click Yes in the confirmation dialog box that appears. Or from Windows, open the folder containing the notebook folder, click the notebook folder, and then on the toolbar, click Share. In the File Sharing window, click Stop sharing.

Creating Pages and Sections

As we discussed briefly in the previous topic, you can create content and then move it into an organizational structure, or you can create an organizational structure and then create content within it. In this topic, we discuss creating storage structures within OneNote.

See Also For information about rearranging content within a notebook structure, refer to "Moving and Removing Information" in Chapter 16, "Organizing and Locating Information."

A new notebook contains whatever sections and pages are specified by the selected notebook template. The most basic notebook, a blank notebook, contains one section and one page. Regardless of the notebook template you choose, you can easily create new pages on which to collect information and subdivide pages into *subpages*. You can also create new sections in which to organize the pages. You can further organize information by grouping sections together in *section groups*.

So how do you know when to create a page, subpage, section, or section group? The answer is dictated by the following:

- The nature of the information you are collecting. In a Customer Records notebook, you will obviously want to include a section for each client, and in a Project Records notebook, you will want one section per project.

- The volume of information. There is no point in collecting information unless you can quickly and easily retrieve it when you need it. On an ideal page, all the information is visible at a glance, without too much scrolling. If you have to scroll, maybe some of the information should be organized on subpages. Similarly, in an ideal section, all the pages and subpages are visible at a glance in the Page Tabs area. If there are too many page tabs, maybe some of the pages should be organized in new sections. And if not all the sections are visible in the notebook header at a glance, maybe it is time to organize the sections in section groups.

The important thing to remember is that the organizational structure of a notebook should be dynamic—in other words, it should change as the information in the notebook changes.

Creating Pages and Subpages

When first created, each section contains one blank, untitled page. You can add plain blank pages, blank pages of a special size or with a special background, or specialized pages containing content guides.

Blank page options include the following:

- Specific sizes, including Statement, Letter, Tabloid, Legal, A3-A6, B4-B6, Postcard, Index Card, and Billfold
- Simple backgrounds, including College Ruled, Small Grid, or 16 solid colors
- Nearly 70 decorative backgrounds displaying various illustrated or photographic elements in the title bar, corner, margin, or background of an otherwise blank page

Specialized page options are based on content templates, which are divided into the following categories:

- Academic templates, including Simple and Detailed Lecture Notes, Lecture Notes And Study Questions, Math/Science Class Notes, and History Class Notes
- Business templates, including Project Overview and six types of Meeting Notes
- Planners templates, including three types of To Do List

You can quickly create a new page or subpage in the current section by selecting an option from the New Page menu at the top of the Page Tabs area.

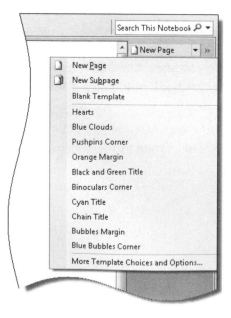

Clicking More Template Choices And Options displays the Templates task pane. You can preview any page template by clicking it in the list. The first time you click a template in the task pane, OneNote creates a page based on that template; subsequent clicks apply the selected template to the created page.

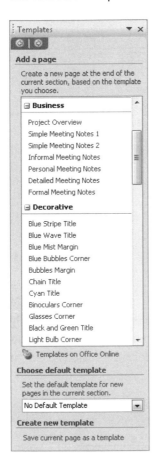

Tip You can't apply a template from the Templates task pane to an existing page, but from the Page Setup task pane, you can apply a background color or create your own page template. For more information, see the sidebar "Formatting Notes, Pages, and Sections" in Chapter 15, "Collecting Information in a Notebook."

Naming Pages

To assign a page title, you enter text in the title box located in the upper-left corner of the page.

You can enter as much text as you want in the title box; after the first eight characters, the box expands to fit the text. When the text exceeds the maximum for the page width, it wraps to the next line. You could enter thousands of characters in the title box, but I recommend that you keep page titles short. Because OneNote processes the title text each time it displays the page, long titles slow down the program response time, and you can't use the program while it is processing the text.

At the default Page Tabs area width, the first 20 characters of the page title appear on the page tab at the right side of the OneNote program window. You can easily change the width of the Page Tabs area by pointing to the border between the active page and the tab area, and then when the insertion point changes to a double-headed arrow, dragging the border to the left or right.

> **Tip** The Page Tabs area is part of the program window, so when you switch between pages, sections, or notebooks, its width doesn't change. The configuration of common elements such as the Navigation Bar, toolbars, and Page Tabs area remains constant, and changing them for one page changes them for all the pages.

Creating Sections and Section Groups

You have fewer options to consider when creating sections, because there is only one type of section. Unlike pages, sections don't have special templates. You can change a section color to differentiate it from other sections, perhaps as a visual reminder to yourself, and you can safeguard a section by assigning an access password to it.

When a notebook contains a lot of information, you might want to consider creating a section group. This useful organizational tool is an entirely separate set of sections and pages within a notebook. You can move sections to and among section groups.

In this exercise, you will add pages and subpages to a section, and then add a section and a section group to a notebook.

USE the *SBS Sections* notebook. This practice file is located in the *Documents\Microsoft Press\2007OfficeSBS_HomeStudent\OneCreating* folder.

BE SURE TO start OneNote before beginning this exercise.

1. On the **File** menu, point to **Open**, and then click **Notebook**.

   The Open Notebook dialog box displays the contents of your OneNote Notebooks folder.

2. In the **Favorite Links** list, click **Documents**. Then in the file list, double-click the *Microsoft Press* folder, double-click the *2007OfficeSBS_HomeStudent* folder, and double-click the *OneCreating* folder.

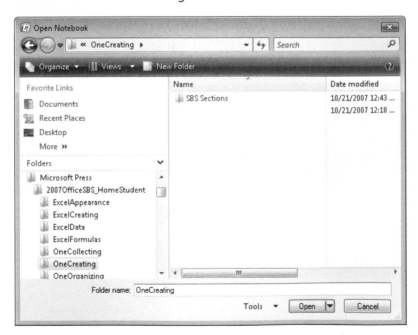

   The *SBS Sections* folder within the *OneCreating* folder is actually a OneNote notebook.

3. Click the *SBS Sections* folder, and then click **Open**.

The SBS Sections notebook opens. This typical example of a blank notebook contains one section named *Competition*, and one page, which is currently blank.

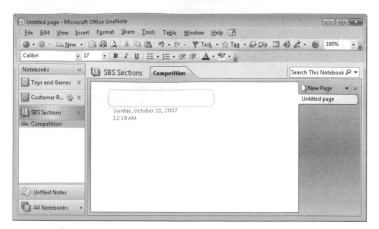

4. On the Standard toolbar, click the **New** arrow, and then in the list, click **Page**.

   OneNote creates a second untitled page in the Competition section.

5. In the **Page Tabs** area, click the **New Page** button.

   OneNote creates a third untitled page. The title box of each page is blank, and the page tab identifies each as Untitled Page.

6. In the **Page Tabs** area, click the **New Page** arrow, and then in the list, click **Pushpins Corner**.

   > **Troubleshooting** The templates available in the New Page list change to reflect your recent choices. If Pushpins Corner is not available, click More Template Choices And Options, and then in the Templates task pane, expand the Decorative category, and click Pushpins Corner.

   The new page changes to reflect the Pushpins Corner decorative template.

7. In the page title box, type Sharp Ideas.

   As you type, the title appears on the page tab.

8. In the **New Page** list, click **New Subpage**.

OneNote creates a page that is subordinate to the Sharp Ideas page. Notice that the subpage has the same template as its parent page.

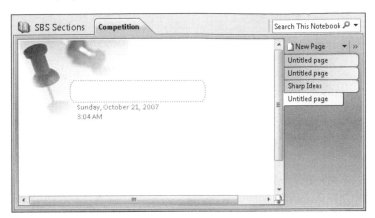

New Section

9. On the Standard toolbar, click the **New Section** button.

OneNote creates a section containing one blank untitled page. The section name is selected for editing.

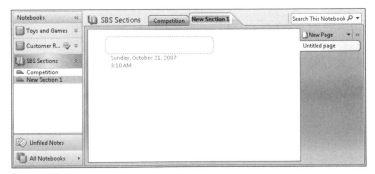

10. Type Ideas, and then press [Enter].

11. On the Standard toolbar, click the **New** arrow, and then in the list, click **Section Group**.

OneNote creates a section group and selects the section name for editing.

12. Type Analysis, and then press [Enter].

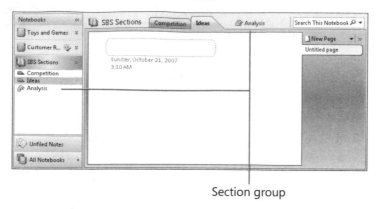

Section group

13. In the notebook header or on the **Navigation Bar**, click the **Analysis** section group button.

The section group contains no sections or pages.

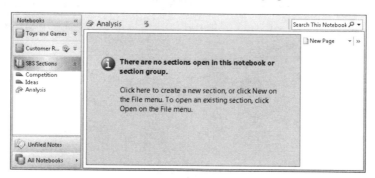

14. On the **Navigation Bar**, drag the **Competition** section to the **Analysis** section group.

The selected section and its pages move to the section group.

CLOSE the *SBS Toys and Games*, *SBS Customer Records*, and *SBS Sections* notebooks. If you're not continuing directly to the next chapter, exit OneNote.

Key Points

- You can create a notebook for your own personal use on one computer or on multiple computers.

- When planning your information-storage system, you can start with a blank notebook or with one of the ready-made notebook templates that come with OneNote 2007.

- The organizational structure of a notebook is dynamic and changes to reflect the information you collect.

- You collect information on pages. When you have a lot of information on one page, individual items of information might be easier to find if you organize them on subpages.

- Pages are contained within sections. You can create additional sections to organize different types of information.

- When you have a lot of sections, you can organize them in section groups.

Chapter at a Glance

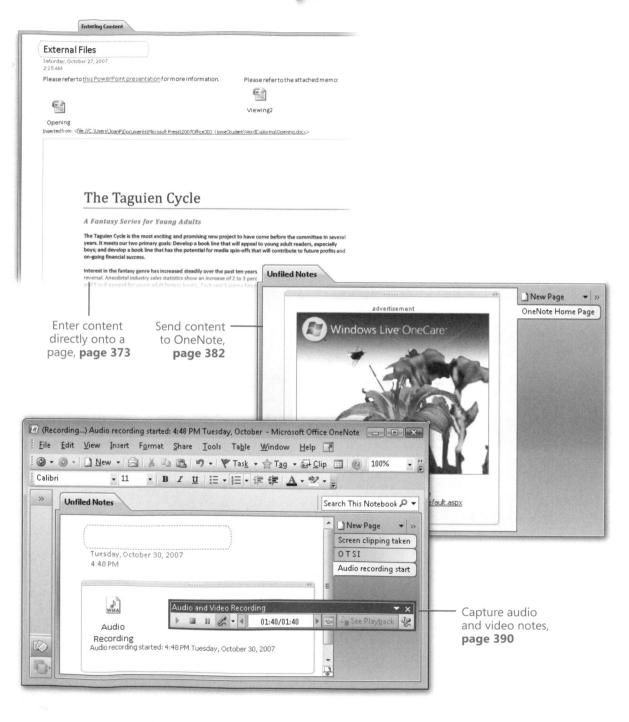

Enter content directly onto a page, **page 373**

Send content to OneNote, **page 382**

Capture audio and video notes, **page 390**

15 Collecting Information in a Notebook

In this chapter, you will learn to:

✔ Understand note containers.

✔ Enter content directly onto a page.

✔ Send content to OneNote.

✔ Capture audio and video notes.

✔ Quickly capture notes.

In Chapter 14, "Creating and Configuring Notebooks," we discussed creating a Microsoft Office OneNote notebook, sections, and pages within which to store electronic information. In this chapter, we move on to the task of collecting and storing the information.

OneNote 2007 provides two primary information collection interfaces: the OneNote program window and the OneNote Side Note utility. In addition, you might find convenient links in other programs—such as the Send To OneNote command on the Windows Internet Explorer Tools menu, and the Send To OneNote 2007 print location available in the Print dialog box of any Windows program—which make it easy to collect information without starting or switching to OneNote. If you have a mobile phone or other device running Windows Mobile, you can capture information by using OneNote Mobile (which comes free with the full version of OneNote 2007), and you can synchronize data with a local or network notebook by using Microsoft ActiveSync.

You can store pretty much any type of electronic information in a OneNote notebook, including text, graphics, photos, Web clippings and pages, hyperlinks, audio clips, and video clips. You can store as much or as little information as you want on each individual page.

In this chapter, you will first learn about the way that notes are stored in OneNote. Then you will collect text, graphics, handwritten notes, screen clippings, Web notes, and media clips by using various methods.

See Also Do you need only a quick refresher on the topics in this chapter? See the Quick Reference entries at the beginning of this book.

Important Before you can use the practice files in this chapter, you need to install them from the book's companion CD to their default location. See "Using the Book's CD" at the beginning of this book for more information.

Troubleshooting Graphics and operating system–related instructions in this book reflect the Windows Vista user interface. If your computer is running Windows XP and you experience trouble following the instructions as written, please refer to the "Information for Readers Running Windows XP" section at the beginning of this book.

Understanding Note Containers

Each unit of content on a notebook page exists within a *note container*. Similar to a text box in Microsoft Office Word or Microsoft Office PowerPoint, a note container consists of a frame that has a *move handle* and a *sizing handle*. Each object (such as a text block, image, or URL) within the note container has an *object selector*.

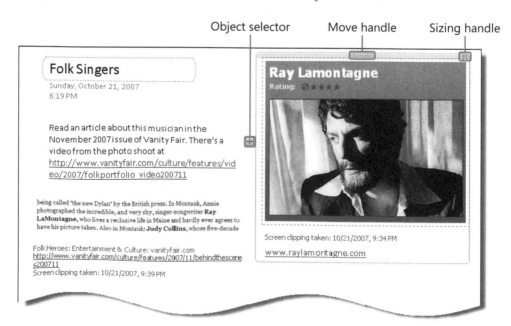

Unlike a text box in other programs, you don't have to insert a note container on the page before entering content into it—simply click anywhere on the page and type or paste content, or insert it from another source, to create the container. A note container may contain any sort of content, such as text, images, handwritten notes, screen clippings, or Web notes.

You can manipulate a note container on the page in the same way that you would manipulate a text box or other type of content frame in a word-processing or graphics program. You can change its size, relocate it on the page, and cut, copy, or delete it. You can merge the contents of multiple note containers, which is simpler than cutting content from one and pasting it into another.

The contents of an entire page may occupy one note container or many. While you work in OneNote, the frame of the active note container is visible, but the frames of the other note containers are not. Pointing to the content displays the note container's frame, and pointing to an object within the active container displays the object selector. You can manipulate individual objects within the container by dragging, clicking, or right-clicking the associated object selector.

Entering Content Directly onto a Page

The simplest type of information you will store in your OneNote notebook, and probably the most common, is text. You can enter text by typing directly on the notebook page or by pasting it from another source. But you aren't limited to simple text entry. You can insert attachments, formatted file contents, images, multimedia objects, and handwritten notes, all with a minimum amount of effort.

> **Tip** When deciding how much information to include on a notebook page, consider whether you want to scroll the page. If you want to see all the information at a glance, limit the content to about 30 lines of standard text.

Referencing External Files

When conducting research, you might identify an entire file of information—such as a document, image, or video clip—that you want to include in your notebook. You can store this information in the following three ways:

- Link to the external file on a local drive, network drive, or Web site.
- Insert the file as an attachment.
- Insert the file's contents.

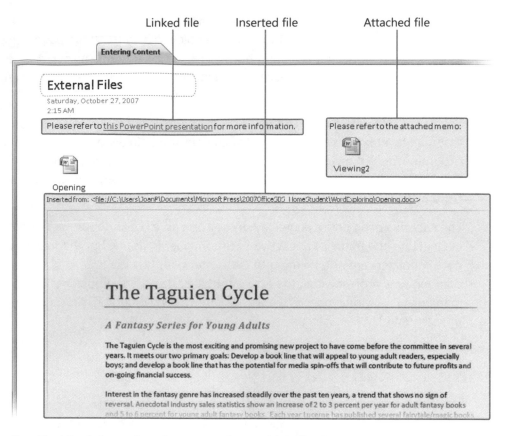

See Also For information about capturing multimedia clips directly in OneNote, see "Capturing Audio and Video Notes" later in this chapter.

Tip OneNote automatically inserts the date and time when you send content from another source to OneNote. (See "Sending Content to OneNote," later in this chapter.) To add this information to notes that you enter directly, click Date And Time on the Insert menu.

Creating Handwritten Notes

On any computer that has a mouse, you can enter "handwritten" notes by using a pen tool that you control with the mouse. On a Tablet PC, you can enter handwritten notes by using the *tablet pen*, just as you would in other handwriting-enabled programs.

Tip OneNote automatically saves all your changes, so you don't need to. For this reason, you will never be prompted to choose whether to save a notebook when you close it.

Inserting Images

You can easily insert one or more photos or other image files onto a OneNote page by pointing to Pictures on the Insert menu and then clicking From Files. In the Insert Picture dialog box, you can select as many image files as you want to insert on the page.

Keep in mind that images will come in at their original size, which might be considerably larger than you want to view them on the page. To resize an inserted image:

1. Point to the edge of the image so that a dashed outline appears. When the pointer changes to a four-headed arrow, click the image outline.

   Sizing handles appear in the corners and at the center of each side of the image.

2. Drag a sizing handle to resize the image.

   - Drag a corner sizing handle to maintain the image's *aspect ratio*.
   - Drag an edge handle to resize the image in one direction only.

The OneNote 2007 Guide states that you can also insert clip art (graphics, photos, sounds, and movies) into your notes. It's true that you can, but not in the way you might be accustomed to—there is no Insert Clip Art command in OneNote as there is in practically every other Office system program. To insert clip art, you must first access the clip art data source from another program or from the Microsoft Clip Organizer.

To insert clip art from another program:

1. In Word (or another program that supports clip art), click the **Clip Art** button in the **Illustrations** group on the **Insert** menu.

2. In the **Clip Art** task pane, locate the clip art you want.

3. Point to the clip art, click the arrow that appears, and then click **Copy**.

4. Switch to OneNote, and paste the clip art from the Clipboard onto the page.

To insert clip art from the Clip Organizer:

1. On the **Start** menu, click **All Programs**, click **Microsoft Office**, click **Microsoft Office Tools**, and then click **Microsoft Clip Organizer**.

2. In the **Clip Organizer**, locate the clip art you want.

3. Point to the clip art, click the arrow that appears, and then click **Copy**.

4. Switch to OneNote, and paste the clip art from the Clipboard onto the page.

Formatting Notes, Pages, and Sections

You can change the appearance of text in notes, in much the same way that you do in other Microsoft Office system programs.

OneNote supports character-level formatting such as font face, size, and color, but doesn't support styles. So, for example, you can indicate a heading within text by formatting the characters as bold or in a larger font, but you can't format it or assign it an outline level by applying a style. You can, however, assign outline levels (1 through 5) to paragraphs by indenting the paragraph. OneNote allows you to choose to hide levels, which gives you the equivalent of an outline view.

To change the paragraph indentation for the purpose of assigning a level:

1. Click to place the insertion point at the beginning of the paragraph.
2. Press the [Tab] key to increase the level, or press the [Backspace] key or [Shift]+[Tab] to decrease the level.

To hide one or more levels of text within a note:

→ Right-click the note container header, point to Hide Levels Below, and then click the lowest level you want visible.

OneNote does not support as many paragraph formatting options as you might be accustomed to using within a typical word-processing program such as Word. You can change the width of all the paragraphs in a note by dragging the right edge of the note container. However, you can't do any of the following:

● Change the width of an individual paragraph (except by inserting carriage returns).
● Change the paragraph alignment to right-align, center, or justify its content.
● Outline a paragraph.

By default, OneNote displays notebook pages with a blank white background. You can modify the appearance of the page in several ways. For example, you can:

● Change the page size, orientation, or margins.
● Change the page background to a picture, or to any of 16 pre-selected background colors. The available colors are reasonably muted so they don't obscure the page content.
● Display any of four horizontal rule patterns (Narrow, College, Standard, and Wide) or four grid rule patterns (Small, Medium, Large, and Very Large).
● Hide or change the color of the rule lines.

These and other options are available from the Page Setup task pane, which you can display by right-clicking a page tab and then clicking Page Setup.

> **Tip** Changing the size, orientation, background, or other attribute of a page does not affect other pages of the notebook.

You can change the color of a section tab and the pages within the section by clicking the page tab, pointing to Section Color, and clicking the color you want.

In this exercise, you will enter text; insert, attach, and manipulate images; and create a handwritten note by using the OneNote writing tools.

> **USE** the *SBS Collecting* notebook, the *Organization101* presentation, and the *Arizona01*, *Arizona02*, *Arizona03*, and *Logo_ADatum* images. These practice files are located in the *Documents\Microsoft Press\2007OfficeSBS_HomeStudent\OneCollecting* folder.
>
> **BE SURE TO** start OneNote before beginning this exercise.
>
> **OPEN** the *SBS Collecting* notebook, and display the Entering Content section.

1. On the Text Notes page, click to position the insertion point on the page, and then type Collecting information in OneNote is easy!

    OneNote creates a visible note container when you type the first character, and then expands the note container to fit the remaining text.

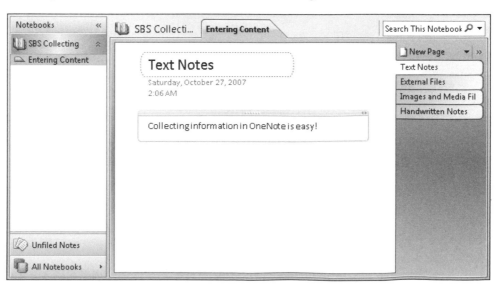

2. On the **Insert** menu, click **Files as Printouts**.

   The Choose Document To Insert dialog box opens.

3. Browse to the *Documents\Microsoft Press\2007OfficeSBS_HomeStudent\OneCollecting* folder. Click the *Organization101* presentation, and then click **Insert**.

   OneNote inserts the presentation file as an attachment, the Inserted From reference, and then each slide of the presentation. Each slide is an individually sizable object.

4. In the **Page Tabs** area, click the **Images and Media Files** page tab.

5. On the **Insert** menu, point to **Pictures**, and then click **From Files**.

   The Insert Picture dialog box opens.

6. If necessary, browse to the *Documents\Microsoft Press\2007OfficeSBS_HomeStudent\ OneCollecting* folder. Click the *Logo_ADatum* image, and then click **Insert**.

   The inserted image appears on the page.

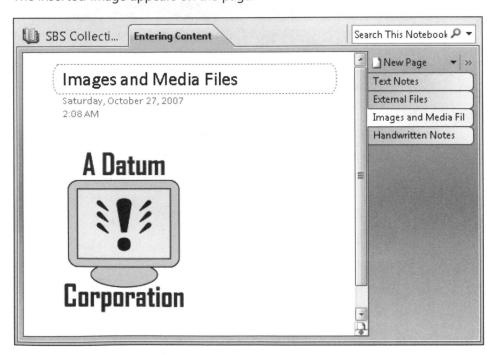

7. Point to the inserted image.

   Instead of a note container, a dotted outline appears, to indicate that the image can be sized on the notebook page.

8. Click the image.

   Sizing handles appear on each side and corner of the inserted image.

9. Drag the handles to change the height and width of the image, making it smaller and roughly square.

10. Right-click the image to view the additional options.

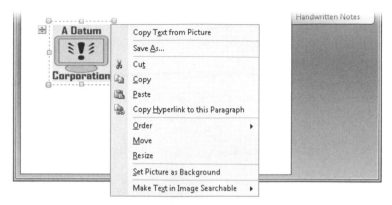

11. Click to place the insertion point to the right of the logo. Then on the **Insert** menu, click **Files**.

The Choose A File Or Set Of Files To Insert dialog box opens.

12. If necessary, browse to the *Documents\Microsoft Press\2007OfficeSBS_HomeStudent\ OneCollecting* folder. Click the *Arizona01* image, hold down the [shift] key, and then click the *Arizona03* image.

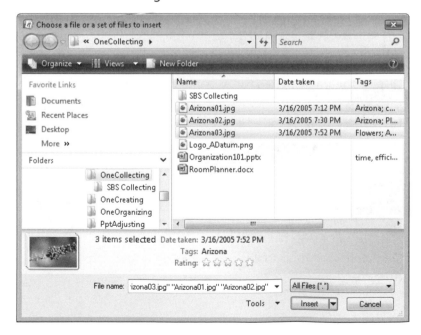

13. In the **Choose a file** dialog box, click **Insert**.

The icons and filenames representing the inserted images appear on the page.

> **Troubleshooting** The displayed icons represent the program that is set up on your computer as the default program for this file type (the program the file opens in when you double-click it). The icons shown on your notebook page might not match the icons shown here.

14. Point to the *Arizona01* image to display a ScreenTip containing file information.

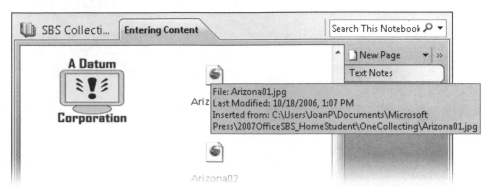

15. Double-click the *Arizona01* image. If a warning message appears, select the **Don't show this again** check box, and then click **OK**.

The image opens in the default program.

16. Close the image to return to OneNote.

17. Display the Handwritten Notes page. Right-click in the toolbar area, and then click **Writing Tools** to display the Writing Tools toolbar. Arrange the toolbars so all the writing tools are visible.

Writing Tools toolbar

Pen

18. On the Writing Tools toolbar, click the **Pen** arrow, and then in the list, click **Blue (thin)**.

19 Point to the notebook page.

The pointer resembles a blue dot.

20. By dragging the pen on the notebook page, draw a picture depicting a possible business logo.

Type Text or
Select Object

21. On the Writing Tools toolbar, click the **Type Text or Select Object** button. Then point to your drawing.

A note container appears around the drawing.

22. Click to place the insertion point on the page to the right of the note containing the logo, and then type Logo idea.

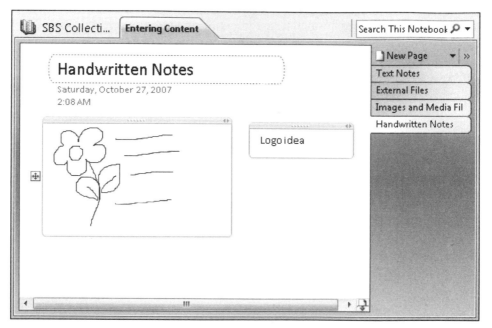

23. Experiment on your own with additional pens, colors, and commands from the Writing Tools toolbar.

CLOSE the Writing Tools toolbar and the *SBS Collecting* notebook.

Sending Content to OneNote

Collecting on-screen information in a OneNote notebook falls under the "easiest thing since sliced bread" classification. You can send content from any screen to OneNote as a *screen clipping*, or send an entire Web page as a Web note. When viewing a Web page, you can send the entire page to your notebook without leaving Windows Internet Explorer.

When you clip or send content to OneNote, OneNote stores it temporarily in the *Unfiled Notes section*. Unfiled Notes is not part of any notebook; it is a separate file stored in your *Documents\OneNote Notebooks* folder. Screen clippings and Web notes remain in the Unfiled Notes section until you move them elsewhere. When it is convenient to display the OneNote program window, you can move either the screen clipping's note container or the entire page to any notebook.

See Also For more information about moving notebook content, see "Moving and Removing Information" in Chapter 16, "Organizing and Locating Information."

> **Tip** You can create pages directly in the Unfiled Notes section.

Collecting Screen Clippings

The screen clipping feature first became available as an add-in to OneNote 2003 and is fully incorporated into OneNote 2007. You can use the OneNote Screen Clipper to capture an image of anything that is visible on your computer screen. After you display the content you want to send to OneNote, you can start the Screen Clipper in several ways, including the following:

- If your keyboard has a *Windows logo key*, press Windows logo key+S.
- Right-click the OneNote icon in the notification area of the taskbar, and then click Create Screen Clipping.
- In the OneNote program window, click the Clip button on the Standard toolbar, or click Screen Clipping on the Insert menu.

When the Screen Clipper is active, a transparent white overlay appears on the screen, and instructions in a notification explain how to capture the screen clipping. Drag with your mouse or pen to define the area you want to "clip." (As you drag, the white overlay becomes clear in the area you define.) When you release the mouse button or lift the pen, the clipping appears on a new, untitled page of the Unfiled Notes section, along with the date and time you created the clipping. If you clipped content from a Web page, the Web page name and URL are also stored in the note container, and the notebook page title is set to the Web page name.

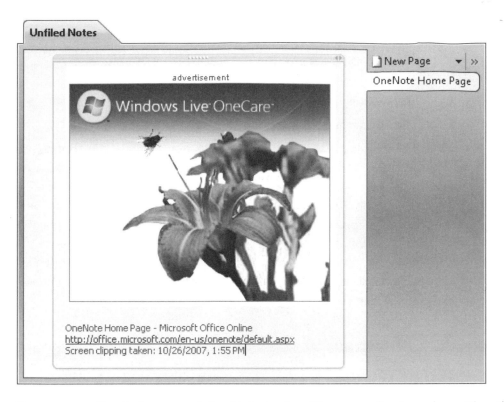

You can specify what you want OneNote to do with screen clippings, by setting the default action. The options are:

- **Copy To Clipboard Only.** OneNote copies the screen clipping to the *Clipboard*. You can paste it into OneNote or another application by pressing Ctrl+V or by using the Paste command in the application.

- **Copy To Clipboard And Unfiled Notes (Show Image).** This is the default setting. OneNote copies the screen clipping to the Clipboard, pastes it into your Unfiled Notes section, and displays the OneNote window so that you can verify that the content was clipped, add notes to it, or move it to another section.

- **Copy To Clipboard And Unfiled Notes (Don't Show Image).** This setting allows you to continue working uninterrupted. OneNote copies the screen clipping to the Clipboard and pastes it into your Unfiled Notes section, but does not display the OneNote window.

To change the default action, right-click the OneNote icon in the notification area of the taskbar, point to Options, point to Screen Clipping Defaults, and then click the setting you want.

Collecting Web Notes

From Internet Explorer, you can send an entire Web page to OneNote. To capture a Web note:

1. Display the Web page you want to send to OneNote.

2. On the **Tools** menu, click **Send to OneNote**.

OneNote processes the Web note in the background while you continue working in Internet Explorer, and stores the Web note in the Unfiled Notes section. As was the case with the screen clipping taken from a Web site, the Web page title appears as the note page title. The Web page content—including text, images, hyperlinks, and similar content—appears on the note page. Depending on the complexity of the content, you might notice that the page layout in OneNote doesn't precisely reflect the on-screen layout. If the page formatting depends on styles stored in an external style sheet, the fonts, sizes, and other elements controlled by the style sheet will not be displayed as intended.

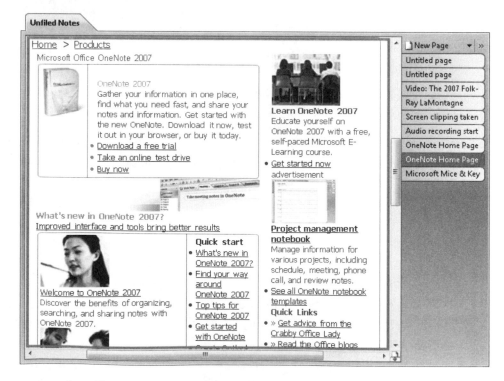

You can specify where you want OneNote to save the information you send to OneNote from Internet Explorer or through the Send To Microsoft OneNote print driver. Use one of the options on the following page.

- **New Page In Section.** This is the default setting. OneNote creates a new page for each note in the Unfiled Notes section or another section that you specify.
- **New Page In The Current Section.** OneNote creates a page in whatever section is currently active.
- **On The Current Page.** OneNote adds the Web page content to the active page.

To change the default location, click Options on the Tools menu, display the Send To OneNote page, select the Web note and printout locations you want, and then click OK.

In this exercise, you will create a screen clipping, a Web page screen clipping, and a Web note. Then you will delete all the captured notes. There is no practice file for this exercise.

> **BE SURE TO** close or minimize any open windows. Then start OneNote and close any open notebooks before beginning this exercise.

Unfiled Notes

1. At the bottom of the **Navigation Bar**, click the **Unfiled Notes** button.

   > **Tip** When the Navigation Bar is expanded, the button name appears next to its icon.

   OneNote displays either the empty section or an untitled page; or, if you already have unfiled notes, the most recently viewed or collected page.

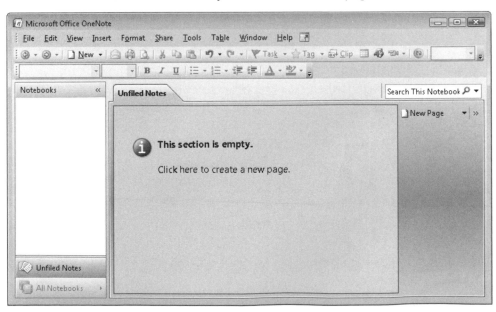

> **Tip** If no page is active, many toolbar and menu commands are unavailable.

Minimize

2. On the OneNote title bar, click the **Minimize** button to display your Windows desktop.

A Windows taskbar button represents the minimized program window.

OneNote icon

3. In the notification area at the right end of the taskbar, right-click the **OneNote** icon, and then click **Create Screen Clipping**.

See Also The ScreenTip that appears for this notification area icon changes depending on the default action associated with it. For more information about the functionality of this notification area icon, see "Quickly Capturing Notes" later in this chapter.

A translucent white screen covers the desktop.

> **Tip** If you change your mind about taking the screen clipping, press the Esc key to remove the white screen.

4. Drag to select an area of your desktop (preferably an area displaying something interesting).

As you drag, the screen covering the selected area becomes clear, so you can see the content you are selecting. When you release the mouse button, a second OneNote window opens, displaying the Unfiled Notes section and a new page containing your screen clipping. (The second taskbar button indicates that this is a second window.) The note container might be active or inactive, depending on the position of your pointer.

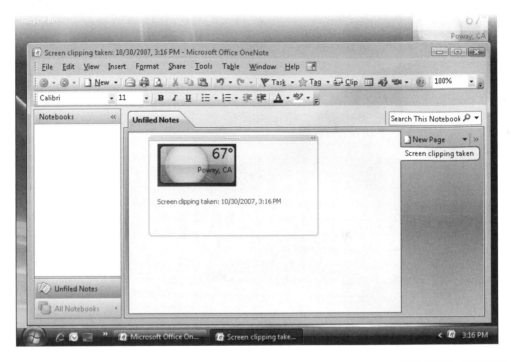

> **Troubleshooting** If the OneNote window doesn't open, your default Screen Clipping action might be set to only copy the image to the Clipboard or to not display the image. For more information, see the "Collecting Screen Clippings" section of this topic.

The OneNote title bar and associated taskbar button, the page tab, and the screen clipping note container all identify the date and time the screen clipping was taken.

5. Click to place the insertion point under the collected screen clipping.

6. Start Internet Explorer, and display a Web site of your choice.

For the purposes of this exercise, we are using our company Web site at *www.otsi.com*.

7. Press 🖽+⟨S⟩ (hold down the 🖽 key and then press the ⟨S⟩ key).

> **Troubleshooting** If your keyboard does not have a Windows logo key, switch to the OneNote screen clipping window. Then on the Insert menu, click Screen Clipping.

A translucent white screen covers the displayed Web page. Any active animation on the page is frozen.

8. Drag to select an area of the Web page.

When you release the mouse button, OneNote adds the screen clipping to the Unfiled Notes section, where you placed the insertion point. Notice that the program window title bar still reflects the date and time of the original screen clipping.

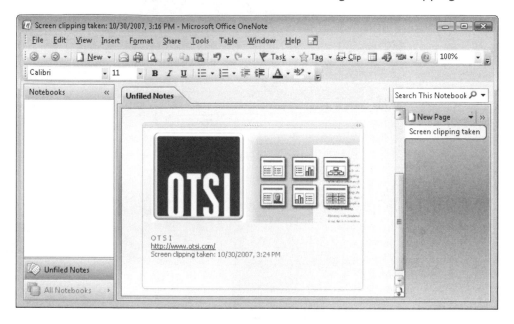

> **Tip** If you take a screen clipping without placing the insertion point on the page, OneNote places the clipped content on a new page.

Close

9. On the title bar of the active OneNote window, click the **Close** button.

10. Click the taskbar button of the original OneNote program window.

Notice that the screen clipping page is immediately visible in this window.

11. Right-click the taskbar button of the active OneNote window, and then click **Close**, leaving only the Internet Explorer window open.

12. On the **Tools** menu, click **Send to OneNote**.

A window displaying a progress bar appears briefly in the lower-right corner of the screen, and a corresponding taskbar button appears on the taskbar.

When the progress bar reaches the end, the Web note has been successfully stored on a new page in the Unfiled Notes section.

13. If necessary, switch to OneNote to view the collected Web page.

The previous screen clipping page tab is also visible.

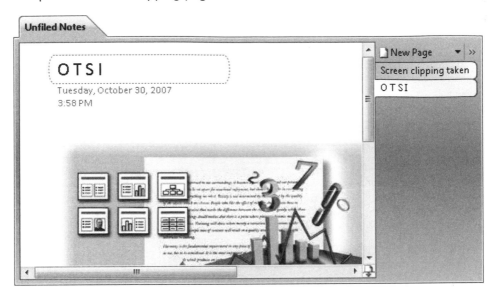

> **Troubleshooting** If the Web note is inserted on the same page as the screen clippings, or in a section other than Unfiled Notes, your Web Notes collection location might be set to something other than the default. For more information, see the "Collecting Web Notes" section immediately preceding this exercise.

14. Compare the captured Web note to the original page content. At the bottom of the page, note the Inserted From link back to the original page.

15. In the **Page Tabs** area, click the active page tab, and press [Ctrl]+[A] to select all the pages in the Unfiled Notes section. Then press [Del] to remove them from OneNote.

> **Troubleshooting** OneNote does not prompt you to confirm the deletion of the selected pages. If you accidentally delete content that you want to restore, click Undo Delete on the Edit menu (or press Ctrl+Z).

 CLOSE the OneNote program window and the Internet Explorer window.

Capturing Audio and Video Notes

If your computer system includes a microphone, such as a built-in microphone or (preferably) a freestanding or headset peripheral microphone, you can record audio directly into OneNote. Similarly, if your system includes a video camera, such as a Web cam, you can record video directly into OneNote.

If you haven't already configured your audio and video input and output devices by using the wizards available through Windows, you can do so in OneNote by using the Tuning Wizard, which is accessible from the Audio And Video page of the Options window.

> **Tip** To display the Options window, click Options on the Tools menu.

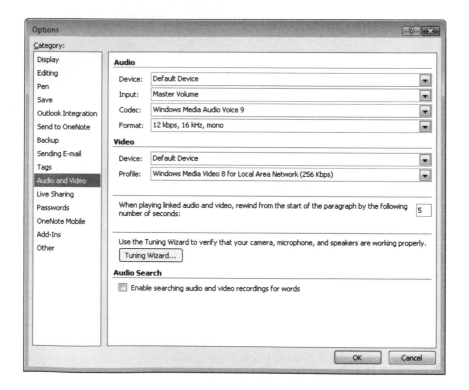

> **Troubleshooting** If you don't have a microphone or camera installed on your system, the lists in the corresponding area will be empty.

See Also For information about searching audio and video recordings, see "Searching for Information" in Chapter 16, "Organizing and Locating Information."

Recording Audio

To create an audio recording in OneNote:

1. Ensure that your computer system includes a microphone. If necessary, run the Tuning Wizard to configure the microphone input levels.

    See Also For information about setting up a microphone or other peripheral device, refer to the ***Windows Step by Step*** book specific to your version of Windows.

2. Display the page on which you want to insert the audio or video clip.

3. On the **Insert** menu, click **Audio Recording**.

    OneNote inserts an Audio Clip icon indicating the audio file type (based on your choice on the Audio And Video page of the Options window) and the recording start time, and displays the floating Audio And Video Recording toolbar.

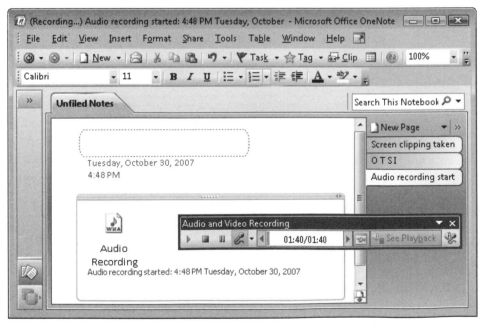

Stop

4. Speak, sing, or otherwise deliver the audio content you want to record. When you finish, click the **Stop** button on the Audio And Video Recording toolbar.

If you haven't previously made an Audio Search selection, the Did You Know About Audio Search window opens.

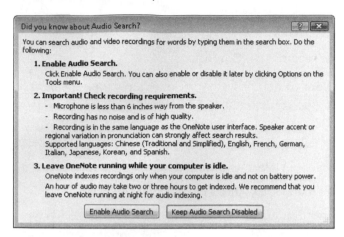

If you want to make a selection at this time, click the Enable Audio Search or Keep Audio Search Disabled button. Otherwise, you can click the Close button on the window title bar.

See Also For information about searching audio and video recordings, see "Searching for Information" in Chapter 16, "Organizing and Locating Information."

Recording Video

The process for creating a video recording is similar to creating an audio recording. Ensure that your computer system includes a video camera, and display the page where you want the recording to appear. Then click Video Recording on the Insert menu, or click the Record arrow on the Audio And Video Recording toolbar and then click Record Video.

OneNote inserts an icon indicating the video file type (based on your choice on the Audio And Video page of the Options window) and the recording start time, and displays the floating Audio And Video Recording toolbar, if it isn't already displayed. A video window opens, displaying the video input from your camera.

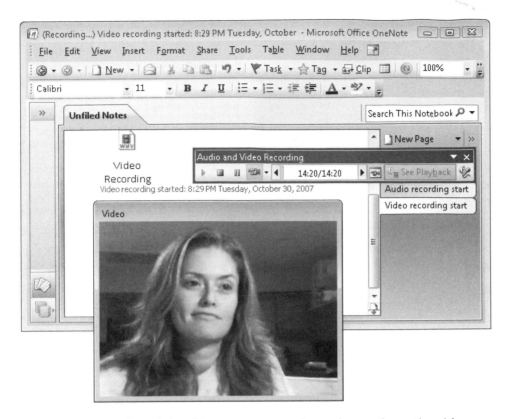

Naturally, the quality of the video you capture depends greatly on the video camera, lighting, setting, and other factors not specific to OneNote.

Hide Video
Window

The video window is a "stay on top" window. You can move it around the screen (independently of the program window) by dragging its title bar, and change its size by dragging the outer borders. If you don't want to display the video window while you capture the video clip, click the Hide Video Window button on the Audio And Video Recording toolbar.

Playing Back a Recording

You can pause, stop, and start recording by clicking the buttons on the Audio And Video Recording toolbar; but, as implied by its name, you can't play back the recordings. To play back an audio or video recording, double-click the Audio Clips or Video Clips icon on the notebook page.

Collecting Information by Using a Mobile Device

Mobile phones have become increasingly common around the world, and have become far more than the audio communication devices they originally represented. Smartphones and Pocket PCs running Windows Mobile provide a portable link to your computer, network, business contacts, friends, and family. In addition to placing and receiving calls, many mobile devices can display documents, spreadsheets, and other files; run e-mail and instant messaging programs; and record audio, video, and still photographs.

If you have a mobile device running Windows Mobile that you synchronize with your computer by using ActiveSync, you can collect information in the OneNote Mobile program, which comes with OneNote. After installing OneNote, you might be prompted to install OneNote Mobile on your mobile device the next time you synchronize data. If the installation doesn't occur automatically, or if you dismiss the automatic installation, you can manually install OneNote Mobile by following these steps:

1. Start OneNote, and connect your mobile device to the computer.
2. On the **Tools** menu, click **Options**.
3. In the **Category** list, click **OneNote Mobile**.
4. Click the **Install OneNote Mobile** button, and follow the instructions in the setup program.

See Also For more information about using OneNote Mobile, refer to the OneNote Help file.

Where Is the OneNote Icon?

If the OneNote icon does not appear in the notification area when the program is running, follow these steps to verify that the feature is turned on:

1. In OneNote, click **Options** on the **Tools** menu.

2. In the **Options** window, in the **Category** list, click **Other**.

3. Select the **Place OneNote icon in the notification area of the taskbar** check box, and then click **OK**.

If the check box is selected and the icon still doesn't appear, follow these steps to verify that the icon is not hidden:

1. Right-click a blank area of the taskbar or notification area, or of the Windows **Start** button, and then click **Properties**.

2. In the **Taskbar and Start Menu Properties** dialog box, display the **Notification Area** tab.

3. In the **Icons** area, click **Customize**.

4. In the **Icon** list, locate the **One Note** icon (the label will vary depending on the action assigned to it). Click the corresponding behavior, and then in the list, click **Show**.

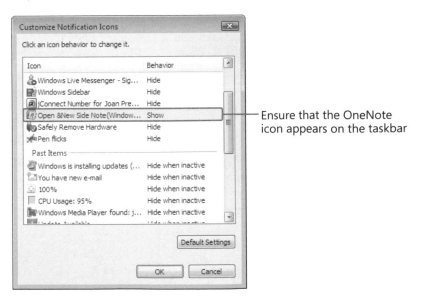

Ensure that the OneNote icon appears on the taskbar

5. Click **OK** twice to close the dialog boxes and save your changes.

Quickly Capturing Notes

It is not necessary to start OneNote each time you want to take notes or otherwise store information. You can quickly activate an input interface by clicking the OneNote icon that appears in the notification area of the Windows taskbar. Clicking the icon opens a Side Note into which you can immediately type or paste information.

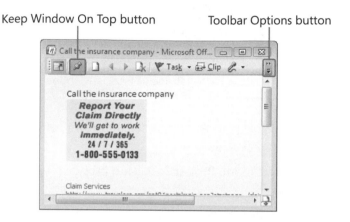

You can also open a Side Note from within the OneNote program window by clicking New Side Note Window on the Window menu, or by pressing Ctrl+Shift+M.

The toolbar at the top of the Side Note window is the same toolbar that appears when you display a page in Full Page view in the OneNote program window. You work with content in a Side Note in the same way you work with it in the OneNote program window—because, in fact, that is precisely what you are doing. If you click the Full Page View button in the Side Note window (and then enlarge the window to provide perspective), you will find yourself working in a page in the Unfiled Notes section.

The purpose of the Side Note window is to provide a small and easily accessible interface to OneNote. Because of the small size of the Side Note window, only a few commands are accessible at a time. You can choose a command that is not visible by clicking the Toolbar Options button and then clicking the button you want.

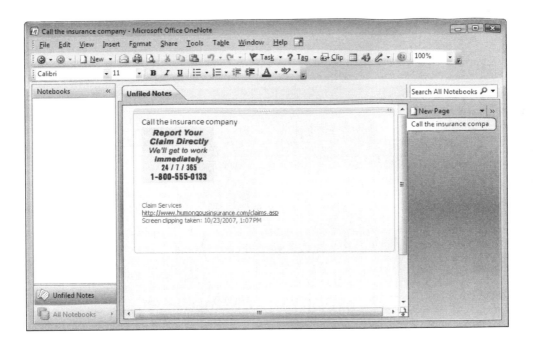

> **Troubleshooting** The Full Page View toolbar changes to display the commands you use most often. The commands shown on your toolbar will not necessarily match those shown in this book.

See Also For more information about the Full Page View toolbar, see "Giving Commands" and "Using Built-In Resources" in Chapter 13, "Getting Started with OneNote."

When the Keep Window On Top button is active, you can position the Side Note in a convenient location on your screen, changing its size as necessary, and enter information as you want to. When the Side Note window is on top, it can get in the way of other windows, information, or commands that you might want to access, so you will want to choose a location that doesn't interfere with your work. You can change the height or width of the window by dragging any side or corner of it.

Right-clicking the OneNote icon displays a list of options for collecting information.

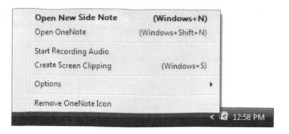

You can change the action that occurs when you click the OneNote icon to suit your needs. For example, if you frequently record audio, you might make that the default action. The available actions are Open New Side Note (the default), Open OneNote, Start Recording Audio, and Create Screen Clipping.

To change what happens when you click the OneNote icon:

→ Right-click the **OneNote** icon, point to **Options**, point to **OneNote Icon Defaults**, and then click the action you want.

CLOSE any open notebooks. If you are not continuing directly to the next chapter, exit OneNote.

Key Points

- Notes are stored on a page in note containers. Each object within a note container can be manipulated separately.
- You can resize images inserted on a page and open file attachments directly from a page.
- You can use the OneNote writing tools to create handwritten notes and drawings.
- You can collect and store selected images of anything displayed on your screen by using the Screen Clipper.
- You can collect and store an entire Web page by using the Send To OneNote command on the Internet Explorer Tools menu.
- You can jot down a quick note by clicking the Open New Side Note icon in the notification area of the taskbar, or by pressing Windows+N to open a Side Note.
- You can choose the action that occurs when you click the OneNote icon.

Chapter at a Glance

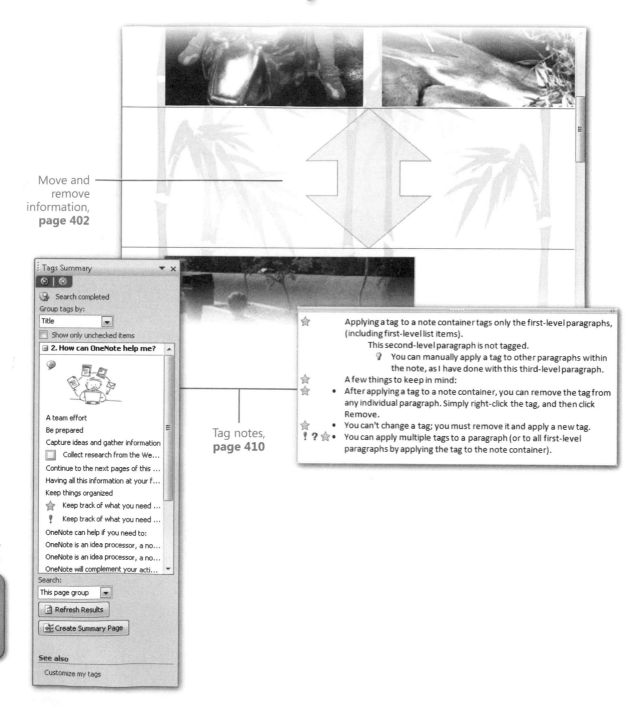

Move and remove information,
page 402

Tag notes,
page 410

Tags Summary

Search completed

Group tags by:

Title

☐ Show only unchecked items

2. How can OneNote help me?

A team effort

Be prepared

Capture ideas and gather information

☐ Collect research from the We...

Continue to the next pages of this ...

Having all this information at your f...

Keep things organized

☆ Keep track of what you need ...

❗ Keep track of what you need ...

OneNote can help if you need to:

OneNote is an idea processor, a no...

OneNote is an idea processor, a no...

OneNote will complement your acti... ▾

Search:

This page group ▾

⟳ Refresh Results

✦ Create Summary Page

See also

Customize my tags

☆ Applying a tag to a note container tags only the first-level paragraphs, (including first-level list items).

This second-level paragraph is not tagged.

💡 You can manually apply a tag to other paragraphs within the note, as I have done with this third-level paragraph.

☆ A few things to keep in mind:

☆ • After applying a tag to a note container, you can remove the tag from any individual paragraph. Simply right-click the tag, and then click Remove.

☆ • You can't change a tag; you must remove it and apply a new tag.

❗ ❓ ☆ • You can apply multiple tags to a paragraph (or to all first-level paragraphs by applying the tag to the note container).

16 Organizing and Locating Information

In this chapter, you will learn to:

✔ Move and remove information.

✔ Tag notes.

✔ Search for information.

In previous chapters, we discussed working in Microsoft Office OneNote 2007, creating a notebook, and collecting and storing information of many types from many sources. If you use OneNote on a regular basis, you will soon have a large collection of information. And chances are, even if you start out with a logically organized notebook, you will need to restructure content from time to time.

OneNote provides several means by which you can call attention to a note for a specific purpose or make it easier to retrieve one note or related notes stored on different pages and in different sections. One method, using OneNote tags, enables you to assign notes to different categories and then generate a report containing the categorized notes. With OneNote, you can also search across many more types of information than you are accustomed to, making it easy to find stored information.

In this chapter, you will learn how to move information on a page, between pages, between sections, and between notebooks. You will learn how to restructure a page after deleting content, tag notes for organizational purposes, and flag notes for follow-up. Finally, you will learn how to search for content within a OneNote notebook.

See Also Do you need only a quick refresher on the topics in this chapter? See the Quick Reference entries at the beginning of this book.

Important Before you can use the practice files in this chapter, you need to install them from the book's companion CD to their default location. See "Using the Book's CD" at the beginning of this book for more information.

Troubleshooting Graphics and operating system–related instructions in this book reflect the Windows Vista user interface. If your computer is running Windows XP and you experience trouble following the instructions as written, please refer to the "Information for Readers Running Windows XP" section at the beginning of this book.

Moving and Removing Information

The techniques you use to move and delete content within a note container are largely the same as those you use in other 2007 Microsoft Office system programs, so we won't use up valuable space discussing those editing techniques here. However, to organize content within a notebook, you also need to know how to manipulate the note container itself, as well as pages, sections, and entire notebooks.

Manipulating Objects on a Page

You can move a note, file, image, or other object on a page in several ways. For example, you can:

- Drag the note by its header.
- Select the note, and then drag it by any part. (The pointer changes to a four-headed arrow to indicate that you can drag.)
- Right-click the note, click Move, and then press the arrow keys (or hold down the Ctrl key and press the arrow keys to move in smaller increments).
- Right-click the note header, click Cut, right-click the new note location, and then click Paste.

The final method, cutting and pasting, is the only way to move an object to another page or section.

Tip To merge the contents of two note containers, hold down the Shift key while dragging one note container by its move handle over the other note container. The merged contents appear in separate paragraphs. You can break one note container into two containers by dragging the object selector of any paragraph or object away from the note container to a different location on the page.

When you delete content from a note container, any following content moves to fill the empty space, and the note container shrinks accordingly. When you move, resize, or delete an entire note container, other content on the page does not move to fill the empty space. You can close up empty space between notes on a page by using the Insert Or Remove Extra Writing Space tool available from the Insert menu or the Writing Tools toolbar. (On the Insert menu, this command name is shortened to Extra Writing Space.)

> **Tip** You can split one note into two by using the Insert Or Remove Extra Writing Space tool. With the tool active, point to the place in the note container where you want to separate the information. The pointer changes to a downward-pointing arrow accompanied by a heavy blue horizontal line. Drag downward to separate the note content into two containers.

Moving Pages, Sections, and Notebooks

Moving larger chunks of content is simple. The following table lists some ways you can manipulate pages and sections.

To move this...	Do this...
A page or subpage within a section	Drag the page tab up or down in the page tab list.
A page to another section	Drag the page tab to the target section tab in the notebook header or in the Navigation Pane.
A page to another notebook	Drag the page tab to the target notebook section in the Navigation Pane.
A section within a notebook	Drag the section tab left or right in the notebook header. Drag the section tab to the new location in the Navigation Pane. Right-click the section tab, and then click Move. In the Move Section To dialog box, click the location where you want to move the section, and then click Move Before or Move After.
A section to another notebook	Drag the section tab to the new location in the Navigation Pane. Right-click the section tab, and then click Move. In the Move Section To dialog box, click the notebook where you want to move the section, and then click Move Into.
A notebook on the Navigation Pane	Drag the notebook title up or down in the Notebooks list.

Note that the target notebook must be open to move content to it by using any of the methods listed in the preceding table.

Accessing Information from Multiple Locations

Sometimes you might find that information you have collected belongs in more than one location within your notebook. For example, you might want to access information about a project both from a page that is specific to that project and from a page or section that is specific to the group working on the project. You could copy the information from one location to the other. If you update the stored information, though, you will need to update it in both places. An alternative that resolves this problem is to keep the information in one place and link to it from another. OneNote provides a simple method of copying a link to the Clipboard from any note or page. When you insert the copied link, it helpfully contains the first 20 or so characters of the text from the target location. You can add more information to the link as necessary.

Simulating a Table of Contents

OneNote doesn't support the use of heading styles, so you can't display a *Document Map*–type hierarchical view of a notebook's content or insert an automatically created table of contents, as you can in Microsoft Office Word. For this reason, Word is still a superior choice for the collection and organization of large amounts of text.

If you want to create a table of contents for a notebook or section, you can manually insert hyperlinks on one page to provide a means of jumping to other pages or to specific notes on other pages. When you create a hyperlink to a page or note, the hyperlink address refers to that target even if you move the page or note.

In this exercise, you will move a page between sections and move a note between pages. You will also create a hyperlink to a note. Then after deleting an object from a page, you will adjust the remaining space.

>   **USE** the *SBS Moving* notebook. This practice file is located in the *Documents\Microsoft Press\2007OfficeSBS_HomeStudent\OneOrganizing* folder.
>
> **OPEN** the *SBS Moving* notebook, and collapse the Navigation Bar.

1. In the notebook header, click the **Pictures** section. Then click each page in turn.

   This section contains a few pages of photographs and a page of company logos.

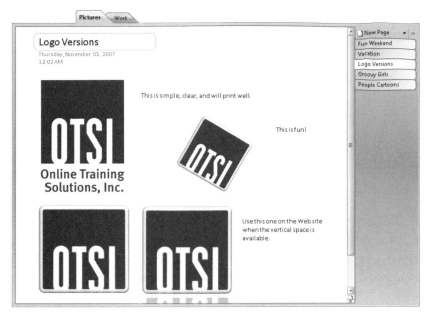

2. In the notebook header, click the **Work** section. Then click each page in turn.

   This section contains information about work-related projects, contacts, and a to-do list.

   The page displaying the company logos belongs in the Work section rather than the Pictures section.

3. Return to the **Pictures** section, click the **Logo Versions** page tab, and then point to the tab.

   The page tab turns gold, and a ScreenTip displays information about the page—the position of the page within the section and the date the page was created.

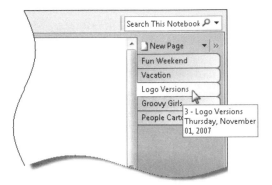

4. Drag the **Logo Versions** page tab to the **Work** section tab, releasing it as soon as the pointer changes to an arrow with a dotted box under it.

The Logo Versions page disappears, and the next page in the section (Groovy Girls) is visible. The Pictures section remains active.

> **Troubleshooting** If you pointed to the Work section tab until the first page of that section was displayed, simply click the Pictures section tab to reactivate it so that you can see that the page is no longer present.

5. In the notebook header, click the **Work** section tab.

   The Logo Versions page tab is at the bottom of the Page Tabs area.

6. Return to the **Pictures** section.

   The Groovy Girls page also belongs in the Work section, because the photos depict the company owners.

7. Drag the **Groovy Girls** page tab to the **Work** section tab, but do not release the mouse button.

   After a short pause, the Work section becomes active.

8. Continue dragging the **Groovy Girls** page to the **Page Tabs** area. Release the mouse button when the page position indicator is located between the **To Do List** and **OTSI** page tabs.

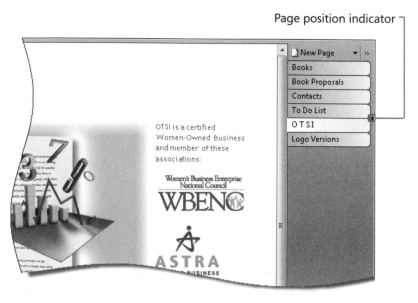

The Groovy Girls page appears in the selected position, but isn't displayed. The active page of the Work section remains active.

9. In the **Work** section, display the **Books** page.

   The note at the bottom of the page belongs on the To Do List page.

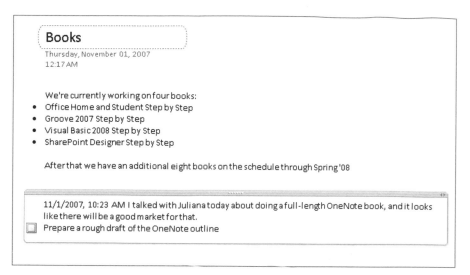

10. Right-click the note container header, and click **Cut**. Then right-click the **To Do List** page tab, and click **Paste**.

    OneNote moves the selected note to the bottom of the destination page.

    Suppose you would like to be able to jump directly to this note from the original Books page.

11. Right-click any part of the note container, and then click **Copy Hyperlink to this Paragraph**. Return to the **Books** page, right-click near the original note location, and then click **Paste**.

    A hyperlink identified by the first 20 or so characters of the link text appears.

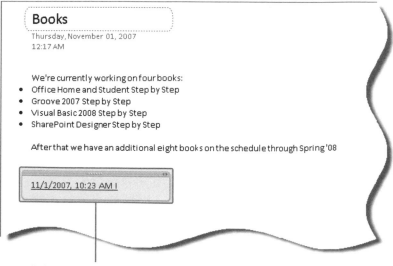

Hyperlink to a note on another page

12. Switch to the **Pictures** section, and then display the **Fun Weekend** page.

The page contains several photos of friends enjoying a weekend in San Diego. A few photos of San Diego Zoo residents are mixed in.

13. Scroll the page until you see the photo of two hippos underwater. If possible, position the page so you can also see the photos above and below it.

14. Point to the photo, and then select it by clicking the dashed line that appears. Then press the ⌈Del⌋ key.

The photo disappears from the page, leaving an empty space. You could fill the space by moving each of the photos below in turn, but OneNote provides a more efficient solution.

15. On the **Insert** menu, click **Extra Writing Space**. (Or, if you have the Writing Tools toolbar displayed, click the **Insert or Remove Extra Writing Space** button.) Then point to the page.

The pointer changes to a double-headed arrow, and a thick blue line appears across the page at the location of the pointer. The line moves vertically with the pointer.

16. Point near the bottom of the empty space, and drag upward.

As you drag, a blue arrow appears in the empty space to indicate the space between the pointer and the next object on the page.

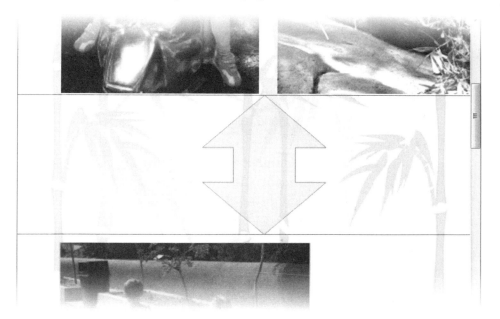

17. Release the mouse button when the vertical distance between the upper and lower pictures is what you want.

CLOSE the *SBS Moving* notebook.

> ## Working with Multiple Instances of a Notebook
>
> From time to time, you might need to see more than one page in the same notebook so that you can work with them at the same time. For example, you might want to work on a page in Full Page view while displaying another instance of the same notebook with the section tabs and page tabs visible, so that you can easily move around the notebook to locate references.
>
> OneNote 2007 supports multiple concurrent sessions of a notebook. That's a fancy way of saying that you can open a second instance of the same notebook in a second OneNote program window; configure each window as you want it; and add, remove, or edit content in either window. The changes you make in one program window are reflected in the other after a short pause, or as soon as you activate the other window.
>
> To open multiple concurrent sessions of a notebook:
>
> → On the **Window** menu, click **New Window**.
>
> The new window opens on top of the original window. You can use this technique to display two, three, or more instances of the same notebook. You can switch among the program windows by clicking the corresponding Windows taskbar buttons or by selecting the window you want from the Window menu. You can close the program windows in any order.
>
> You can manually arrange the notebook windows on your screen, but unlike Microsoft Office Word, Microsoft Office Excel, and Microsoft Office PowerPoint, OneNote does not include a command to automatically arrange the open windows.

Tagging Notes

You can insert comments or other annotations about the content you collect in a notebook in several ways. For example, you can:

- Tag a note or paragraph with a built-in or custom tag.
- Insert note text on top of an image.
- Handwrite notes by using a Tablet PC pen.
- Handwrite notes by using the OneNote pen.
- Add a note to your Microsoft Office Outlook task list.

In this topic, we discuss tagging notes. OneNote tags are a convenient (and fun) feature that make it simple to assign information to a category, bring it to your attention, or mark it for later follow-up. OneNote includes 29 built-in tags, including the 9 in the following list, which have been selected by Microsoft as the most common and assigned keyboard shortcuts (Ctrl+1 through Ctrl+9):

- To Do
- Important
- Question
- Remember For Later
- Definition
- Highlight
- Contact
- Address
- Phone Number

Other built-in tags you might want to use include Web Site To Visit, Idea, Password, Movie To See, Book To Read, Music To Listen To, Remember For Blog, Discuss With, Send In E-mail, and Call Back. Most tags are associated with a unique symbol that appears to the left of the tagged text. Some tags apply character formatting, paragraph formatting, or highlighting to the tagged paragraph, in addition to or instead of inserting a symbol.

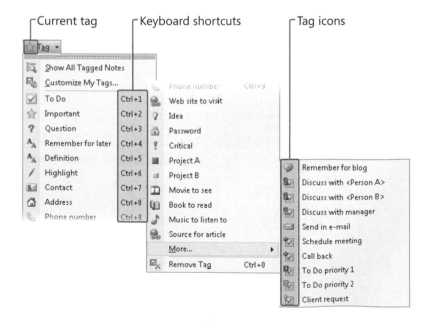

Before applying a tag, you indicate how you want it applied in one of two ways:

- To tag a specific paragraph within a note, place the insertion point anywhere in the paragraph (or select it). The tag appears immediately to the left of the paragraph.

- To tag all the first-level (non-indented) paragraphs in a note, select the note container. OneNote considers bulleted items to be first-level paragraphs unless you specifically indent them. The tag appears in the left margin of the note container.

  See Also For information about paragraph levels, see the sidebar "Formatting Notes, Pages, and Sections" in Chapter 15, "Collecting Information in a Notebook."

Bulleted list items are considered first-level paragraphs unless you indent them.

The tag area expands to accommodate multiple tags.

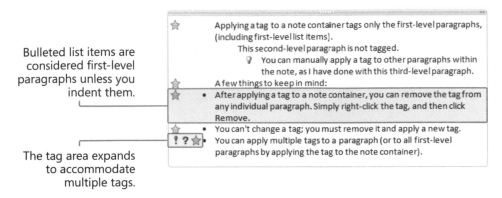

Applying a tag to a note container tags only the first-level paragraphs, (including first-level list items).
This second-level paragraph is not tagged.
You can manually apply a tag to other paragraphs within the note, as I have done with this third-level paragraph.
A few things to keep in mind:
- After applying a tag to a note container, you can remove the tag from any individual paragraph. Simply right-click the tag, and then click Remove.
- You can't change a tag; you must remove it and apply a new tag.
- You can apply multiple tags to a paragraph (or to all first-level paragraphs by applying the tag to the note container).

> **Tip** You can tag text at the paragraph level only; you cannot tag specific words.

After indicating the paragraph you want to tag, you can apply the tag in several ways:

- On the Standard toolbar, click the Tag button to apply the currently selected tag (the tag used most recently).

- In the Tag list, click the tag you want to apply.

- Press one of the nine key combinations to apply the tag assigned to that combination.

You can use options in the Customize My Tags task pane to modify or delete existing tags, create your own tags, and change the order of tags on the menu. To display this task pane, click Customize My Tags on the Tag menu.

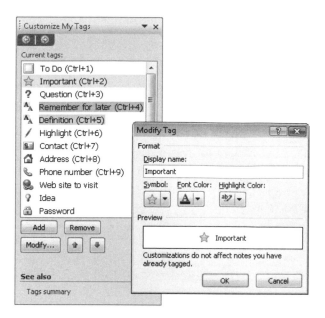

When creating or modifying a tag, you can choose from 138 symbols, 40 font colors, 15 highlight colors, or any combination of symbol, font color, and highlighting.

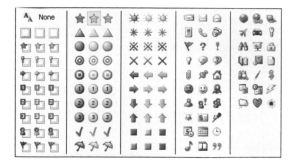

So far, tagging probably sounds fun and cool. Tags are a nice tool for bringing items on a page to your attention, keeping checklists, or other uses. But here's the real value of note tags: You can display a collated view of your notes in the Tags Summary task pane, and generate note pages containing lists of tagged notes. The first characters of the note text are visible in the list. (The number of characters depends on the width of the task pane.) You can group the notes by the type of tag, by section title, by page title, or by date, or you can list them in alphabetical order by the note text. Instead of displaying all notes from all notebooks, you can limit the results to the notes in a specific location (active page group, active section, active section group, or active notebook) or to notes modified during a certain date range (today, yesterday, this week, last week, or older). You can't, however, limit the results to a combination of notes in a specific location and notes modified during a date range.

Synchronizing Notes with Outlook Tasks

OneNote 2007 is particularly convenient for Microsoft Office Outlook users, because it integrates tightly with Outlook tasks and messaging. Flagging a note as a task in OneNote automatically adds the task to your Outlook task list. Updating the status of a task in either place immediately and seamlessly updates it in both.

You can jump from Outlook to the notebook page associated with a flagged task. You can flag a task on any page of a notebook and return directly to that page from Outlook by clicking the Link To Task In OneNote attachment created in the task item window.

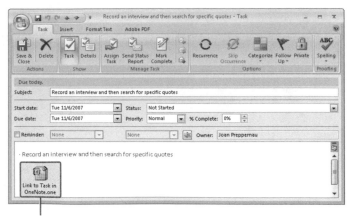

Link to the
associated
notebook page

When you open a notebook from the Outlook task, you can choose whether to open the entire notebook or only the relevant section.

See Also Outlook 2007 is not part of the Home and Student Edition of the 2007 Microsoft Office system, but is available as part of the Basic, Standard, Professional Plus, and Enterprise editions, or as a stand-alone application. For helpful information about Outlook 2007, refer to *Microsoft Office Outlook 2007 Step by Step*, by Joan Preppernau and Joyce Cox (Microsoft Press, 2007).

In this exercise, you will tag notes and view your tagged notes. You will also generate a page that summarizes tagged notes.

> **USE** the *OneNote 2007 Guide* notebook provided with OneNote 2007. This practice file is located in the *Documents\OneNote Notebooks* folder.
>
> **OPEN** the *OneNote 2007 Guide* notebook.

Collapse
Navigation Bar

1. If the **Navigation Bar** is expanded, click the **Collapse Navigation Bar** button to maximize the size of the content pane.

2. In the **Getting Started with OneNote** section, display the page titled 2. **How can OneNote help me?**

3. Point to the note text to display the note container.

All the text is stored in one note container. Applying a tag to the container will tag all the first-level paragraphs on the page.

See Also For information about splitting note containers, see "Moving and Removing Information," earlier in this chapter.

4. In turn, point to each of the graphics on the right side of the page.

Each of the three graphics is a separate object on the page within a frame, not a note container.

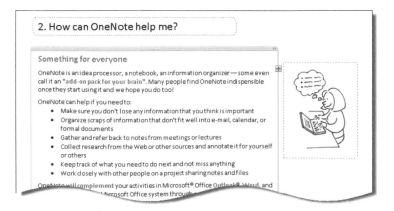

5. Click the note container header to select the note content. On the Standard toolbar, click the **Tag** arrow, and then in the list, click **Remember for later**.

6. Click away from the note container to see the results.

Each first-level paragraph is highlighted in yellow. The Remember For Later tag applies highlighting but does not insert a tag symbol.

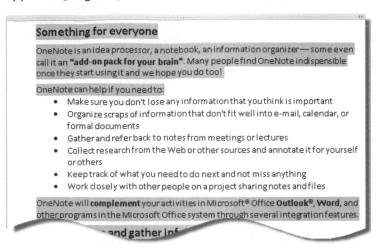

7. Click to place the insertion point anywhere in the first paragraph under the second heading (the paragraph beginning with *You can quickly capture*). Then in the **Tag** list, click **Idea**.

   A light bulb symbol appears to the left of the first line of the paragraph.

8. In the same paragraph, select the words *gather clippings from the Web*. Then in the **Tag** list, click **To Do**.

   Although the selected text occurs halfway through the paragraph, the tag symbol appears to the left of the first line of the paragraph. OneNote cannot tag specific text within a paragraph.

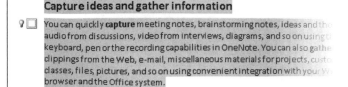

The To Do tag symbol in the Tag list is a check box containing a red check mark. The inserted To Do tag symbol is an empty check box. When you complete the task you have set for yourself, you can insert the check mark to indicate completion.

9. Click the **To Do** symbol.

   A red check mark appears in the check box. You can toggle check marks on and off in any of the 27 check box–based tag symbols.

10. To the right of the tagged paragraph, point to the graphic depicting a man creating documents, pictures, and message on his computer, and then click the dotted frame of the object.

> **Tip** If you click the graphic rather than its frame before applying a tag, OneNote inserts the tag symbol in a new note container in the location you clicked. You can enter text in the new note container, and the text rather than the graphic will appear in the Tags Summary task pane.

11. In the **Tag** list, point to **More**, and then click **Remember for blog**.

   The Remember For Blog symbol, a conversation balloon, appears to the left of the midpoint sizing handle of the graphic.

12. Use any of the methods described earlier in this topic to insert an additional five tags of your choice, anywhere on this page.

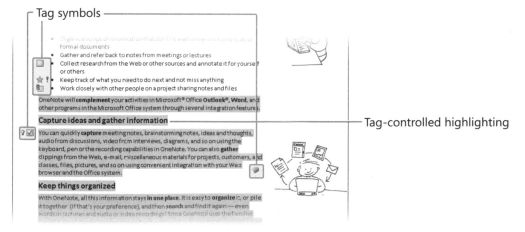

13. In the **Tag** list, click **Show All Tagged Notes**.

   The Tags Summary task pane opens, displaying the first characters of the tagged content in all the open notebooks, grouped by tag name. Tagged graphics appear in their entirety.

14. In the **Group tags by** list, click **Title** to sort the list by page title, and in the **Search** list, click **This page group**. If **2. How can OneNote help me?** does not appear at the top of the list, scroll the list to display it.

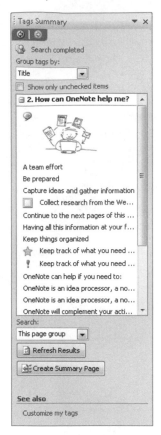

> **Troubleshooting** Your list will vary depending on what tags you inserted.

Notice that some items in the list are preceded by tag symbols, and others are not. Those without symbols are tagged with highlighting or font color.

15. Click items in the list to jump to the corresponding notes. Then experiment on your own with different ways of grouping the tags.

16. At the bottom of the **Tags Summary** task pane, click the **Create Summary Page** button.

A new page appears in the active section, containing the full text of the tagged content in the order that it currently appears in the Tags Summary task pane.

CLOSE the Tags Summary task pane, and delete the summary page from the section.

Searching for Information

If you use OneNote as it is meant to be used, you will eventually find yourself with a large collection of information. Organizing the information by using the tools and techniques discussed in this chapter makes it easier to know where to look to retrieve stored information. However, if you know specific details about the information you're looking for, you can quickly locate it by using one of the available search and filter functions.

In the previous topic, we discussed locating tagged notes from the Tags Summary task pane. You can use the following tools to locate content that isn't tagged:

- The *Search box* is where you type text you know is contained in the note you are looking for. Click the Search button to generate a results list.

- The *Search menu* at the right end of the Search box enables you to search for written or spoken text in content within the active section, a group of sections, the active notebooks, or all notebooks. OneNote will locate the search text in handwritten, typed, or scanned content, or in an audio or video file.

- The Page List task pane displays a list of notebook pages containing the search results. These results are ordered by the date on which you last changed any information on the page, by section, or by page title. You can limit the results to pages in a specific location (active section, active section group, active notebook) or search all notebooks.

When you are looking for information you have stored in your notebook, you can search not only the text of the notes, but also the text of images. For example, if you store scanned business card images in OneNote, a search for a name, company name, address, or other information on the business card will locate the scanned image. OneNote 2007 supports image text search in English, French, and Spanish. You can change the search text language of an individual image by right-clicking the image, pointing to Make Text In Image Searchable, and then clicking the text search language. You can also disable text search for a specific language from this menu.

Here's a fun experiment to try:

1. Using your digital camera or mobile phone, take a photo of a business card (or other printed item).

2. Transfer the photo to your computer, by copying it or sending it in an e-mail message.

3. Insert the photo into OneNote.

4. Enter text displayed in the photo into the **Search** box, and then click the **Search** button.

Search

OneNote 2007 includes an Audio Search feature that you can use to search for spoken text in good-quality audio and video recordings. Audio Search is not available by default; you must specifically enable it.

To enable Audio Search:

1. On the **Tools** menu, click **Options**.

2. In the **Options** window, display the **Audio and Video** page.

3. Under **Audio Search**, select the **Enable searching audio and video recordings for words** check box.

   The Did You Know About Audio Search window opens.

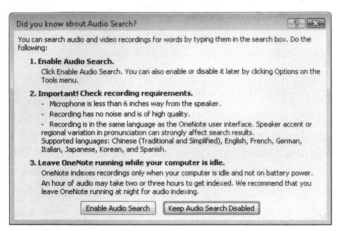

4. Click the **Enable Audio Search** button, and then in the **Options** window, click **OK**.

   OneNote indexes the audio and video recordings while you're not using your computer; the indexing process is somewhat slow, so you won't be able to search for spoken words immediately.

See Also For more information about searching for content in spoken text, see the Audio Search page in the More Cool Features section of the OneNote 2007 Guide notebook.

Tip Microsoft recommends a 2 gigahertz (GHz) or higher processor and 1 gigabyte (GB) or higher of RAM for the OneNote Audio Search feature.

The OneNote 2007 Guide notebook that comes with OneNote 2007 includes many different types of content that you can search. To practice, open the OneNote 2007 Guide notebook, display the page titled "6. Search your notes" in the Getting Started With OneNote section, and follow the Try It Now steps.

 CLOSE the OneNote program window after completing this chapter.

Key Points

- You can move notes on a page, pages within and between sections, and sections between notebooks.

- When you delete a note from a page, the content that follows the note on the page does not move up to fill the empty space.

- You can use the Insert Or Remove Extra Writing Space tool to decrease or increase the space between notes, or to split one note into two.

- OneNote will generate a hyperlink to a note, page, section, or notebook, that you can paste onto a page. The hyperlink displays the first 20 or so characters of the target notebook or section name, page title, or note text.

- You can open a second instance of a notebook in a separate OneNote program window, configure each window as you want it, and edit content in either window.

- You can assign one or more tags to any paragraph or object on a page. In the Tags Summary task pane, you can display a collated list of tags by location or date, and generate a summary page of selected tags.

- OneNote 2007 integrates with Outlook 2007. Flagging a note in OneNote creates an Outlook task that is editable from either program.

- You can search text, images, and audio recordings for specific text and display a list of search results ordered by section, title, or date.

Glossary

active cell In Excel, the cell that is currently selected and open for editing.

arguments In Excel, the specific data a function requires to calculate a value.

arithmetic operator An operator that is used with numerals: + (addition), - (subtraction), * (multiplication), or / (division). See also *operator*.

aspect ratio In computer displays and graphics, the ratio of the width of an image or image area to its height. The aspect ratio is an important factor in maintaining correct proportions when an image is printed, rescaled, or incorporated into another document.

attribute An individual item of character formatting, such as style or color, that determines how text looks.

auditing In Excel, the process of examining a worksheet for errors.

AutoComplete A feature that provides the ability to complete data entry for a cell based on similar values in other cells in the same column.

AutoCorrect A feature that corrects common capitalization and spelling errors (such as changing *teh* to *the*) as you type them.

AutoFill In Excel, the ability to extend a series of values based on the contents of one cell.

background In PowerPoint, the underlying scheme, including colors, shading, texture, and graphics, that appears behind the text and objects on a slide.

blank notebook In OneNote, the default notebook template; a notebook containing one section and one untitled page.

building block In Word, frequently used text saved in a gallery, from which it can be inserted quickly into a document.

bullet point An item in a list in which each list entry is preceded by a symbol, rather than by a number.

case The capitalization (uppercase or lowercase) of a word or phrase. In title case, the first letter of all important words is capitalized. In sentence case, only the first letter of the first word is capitalized.

cell A box at the intersection of a column and row in a table or worksheet.

cell address In Excel, the location of a cell, expressed as its column letter and row number, as in A1.

cell range In Excel, a reference to a connected group of cells.

character formatting The collection of attributes applied to text.

character spacing The space between characters, which can be expanded or contracted so that characters are pushed apart or pulled together.

character style A variation of a font, such as bold or italic.

Click and Type A feature that allows you to double-click a blank area of a document to position the insertion point in that location, with the appropriate paragraph alignment already in place.

Clipboard A storage area shared by all Office programs where cut or copied items are stored.

color scheme In PowerPoint, a set of 12 complementary colors used for different elements of a slide. A color scheme consists of a background color, a color for lines and text, and additional colors balanced to provide a professional look.

column In a chart, a vertical representation of plotted data from a table or worksheet. In page layout, the area between margins where text is allowed to flow. (Pages can have one column or multiple columns.)

column break A break inserted in the text of a column to force the text below it to move to the next column.

conditional format A format that is applied only when cell contents meet certain criteria.

conditional formula A formula that calculates a value using one of two different expressions, depending on whether a third expression is true or false.

constant A value that does not change based on other factors; a non-variable value.

content pane The pane of a program window in which the active document appears.

context menu Also referred to as a shortcut menu, a menu of commands or options specific to a selected element, that appears when you right-click a user-interface or content element.

custom slide show A set of slides extracted from a presentation to create a slide show for an audience that doesn't need to see the entire presentation.

demote In an outline, the process of changing a heading to a lower-level heading or body text.

dependents The cells with formulas that use the value from a particular cell.

deselect Clicking away from selected data or controls to release the selection.

design template A presentation file containing only design elements that can be used as a basis for creating new presentations.

desktop publishing A process that creates pages by combining text and objects such as tables and graphics in a visually appealing way.

destination file A file into which you insert an object created in another program.

Dialog Box Launcher In the Microsoft Office Fluent user interface, a button in the lower-right corner of a command group, labeled with an arrow, that opens a related dialog box or task pane.

digital signature A security mechanism used on the Internet that relies on two keys, one public and one private, that are used to encrypt messages before transmission and to decrypt them on receipt.

Document Map In Word, a pane that displays a linked outline of a document's headings and allows you to jump to a heading in the document by clicking it in the Document Map.

document window The window that provides a workspace for an open document.

Draft view A view that displays the content of a document with a simplified layout.

drag-and-drop editing A way of moving or copying selected text by dragging it with the mouse pointer.

dragging A way of moving objects by pointing to them, holding down the mouse button, moving the mouse pointer to the desired location, and then releasing the button.

embedded object An object that is created in a different program but that is incorporated into a document.

error code In Excel, a brief message that appears in a worksheet cell, describing a problem with a formula or a function.

field A placeholder that tells Word to supply the specified information in the specified way. Also, the set of information of a specific type in a data source, such as all the last names in a contacts list.

fill handle The square at the lower-right corner of a cell that you drag to indicate other cells that should hold values in the series defined by the active cell.

fill series The ability to extend a series of values based on the contents of two cells, where the first cell has the starting value for the series and the second cell indicates the increment.

flow The way text continues from the bottom of one column to the top of the next column.

Fluent See *Microsoft Office Fluent user interface*.

font A set of characters of the same typeface (such as Arial), style (such as italic), and weight (such as bold). A font consists of all the characters available in a specific style and weight for a specific design; a typeface consists of the design itself. Fonts are used by computers for on-screen display and by printers for hard-copy output. In both cases, the fonts are stored either as bitmaps (patterns of dots) or as outlines (defined by a set of mathematical formulas). Even if the computer cannot simulate a font on the screen, programs may be able to send information about the font to a printer, which can then reproduce the font if a description is available.

font color One of a range of colors that can be applied to text.

font effect An attribute, such as superscript, small capital letters, or shadow, that can be applied to a font.

font size The size of the characters in a font, in points.

font style An attribute that changes the look of text. The most common font styles are regular (or plain), italic, bold, and bold italic.

footer A region at the bottom of a page whose text can be applied to some or all of the pages in a printed document.

formula An expression used to calculate a value.

Formula AutoComplete In Excel, the feature that makes it possible to enter a formula quickly by selecting functions, named ranges, and table references that appear when you begin to type the formula into a cell.

Full Screen Reading view In Word, a view that displays as much of the content of the document as will fit in the screen at a size that is comfortable for reading.

gallery A grouping of thumbnails that display options visually.

global formatting A theme or style applied to an entire document.

gridlines Lines that visually clarify the information in a chart.

group In the Microsoft Office Fluent user interface, a category of buttons on a tab.

handle See *sizing handle*.

header A region at the top of a page whose text can be repeated on all or some of the pages of a printed document.

Help button A button with a question mark (?) at the right end of the Ribbon that can be clicked to open the program Help window.

hover To point to an object, such as a menu name or button, for a second or two to display more information, such as a submenu or ScreenTip.

indent marker A marker on the horizontal ruler that controls the indentation of text from the left or right side of a document.

justify To make all lines of text in a paragraph or column fit the width of the document or column, with even margins on each side.

key combination A combination of two or more keys that perform an action when pressed at the same time. Also called a *keyboard shortcut*.

landscape The orientation of a horizontal page whose width is larger that its height.

line break A manual break that forces the text that follows it to the next line. Also called a *text wrapping break*.

linked object An object that exists in a source file and that is inserted in a document with a link to that source file.

live preview A feature of the Microsoft Office Fluent user interface that displays the effects of applying a formatting option to the currently selected content.

login credentials The user name and password that identify and authenticate you when accessing a computer, system, or site.

manual page break A page break inserted to force subsequent information to appear on the next page.

margin Blank space around a column in which text can flow on the page.

menu bar In the traditional Office user interface (without the Ribbon), a rectangular bar displayed at the top of the a program window, from which menus can be opened by the user. Names of available menus are displayed on the menu bar; clicking one causes the list of commands or options on that menu to be displayed.

Microsoft Office Button A button that provides access to a menu with commands that manage Office documents as a whole (rather than document content).

Microsoft Office Fluent user interface The Office program interface introduced with core programs in the 2007 Office system. The key features of the Office Fluent user interface are the Ribbon, the Microsoft Office Button, the Quick Access Toolbar, contextual tabs, galleries, and live preview.

Microsoft Office PowerPoint Viewer A viewer with which you can display presentations on a computer that does not have PowerPoint installed.

Mini toolbar A toolbar of formatting commands that appears when you select text. Specific to programs that feature the Microsoft Office Fluent user interface.

move handle The handle by which you can drag a docked toolbar. The move handle is represented by a row of four dots at the left end of the toolbar.

named range A group of related cells defined by one name.

nested table A table that is positioned inside another table.

note container In OneNote, the smallest data storage unit. Notes on a page are stored within note containers; each note container can be individually manipulated.

notebook The folder containing OneNote data files. See also *.one file*.

notebook header In OneNote, the area above the content pane that displays the notebook name, section tabs, and section groups.

object An item, such as a graphic, video clip, sound file, or worksheet, that can be inserted in a document and then selected and modified.

object selector In OneNote, the handle that appears to the left of a text paragraph, graphic, table, or other individually selectable item within a note container or on a page.

Office menu The menu that appears when you click the Microsoft Office Button. This menu contains commands related to managing documents (such as creating, saving, and printing).

.one file The OneNote data file format. Each .one file contains the content of one section. The .one file name is the same as the section name in the program window; changing one changes the other.

orientation The direction—horizontal or vertical—in which a page is laid out.

orphan At the bottom of a page, a single line of a paragraph that continues on the next page.

Outline view In Word, a view that shows headings and body text and can be used to evaluate and reorganize the structure of a document.

Package for CD In PowerPoint, a feature to help you gather all the components of a presentation and store them to a CD or another type of removable media so that they can be transported to a different computer.

page In OneNote, a titled data storage unit within a section.

Page Tabs area In OneNote, the area to the right of the content pane from which you can select and manipulate pages within the active section.

paragraph In word processing, a block of text of any length that ends when you press the Enter key.

paragraph formatting Collectively, the settings used to vary the look of paragraphs.

paragraph style A set of formatting that can be applied to the paragraph containing the insertion point by selecting the style from a list.

parent folder A folder containing another folder (the child folder).

Pick From List In Excel, the feature that makes it possible to enter a value into a cell by choosing a value from the set of values already entered in cells in the same column.

placeholder An area on a slide into which you should enter a specific type of content.

point The unit of measure for expressing the size of characters in a font, where 72 points equals 1 inch.

portrait The orientation of a vertical page whose width is smaller than its height.

Print Layout view A view that shows how a document will look when printed.

promote In an outline, to change body text to a heading, or to change a heading to a higher-level heading.

Quick Access Toolbar In the Microsoft Office Fluent user interface, a toolbar that displays the Save, Undo, and Repeat buttons by default, but can be customized to show other commands.

Quick Styles A feature of programs that use the Microsoft Office Fluent user interface; predefined sets of formatting options that you can apply to document elements.

quick table A preformatted table of sample data that you can edit for your own purposes.

range In Excel, a group of related cells.

read-only Available for viewing but protected from alterations.

relative reference In Excel, a cell reference in a formula, such as =B3, that refers to a cell that is a specific distance away from the cell that contains the formula. For example, if the formula =B3 were in cell C3, copying the formula to cell C4 would cause the formula to change to =B4.

Ribbon In the Microsoft Office Fluent user interface, an area at the top of the program window in which commands are organized by task. See also *Microsoft Office Fluent user interface*.

Rich Text Format (RTF) A text format that can be opened by many programs and that is used in PowerPoint to export presentation content as an outline.

screen clipping In OneNote, a captured image of content shown on the screen. OneNote provides a tool for defining, capturing, and importing screen clippings directly into the program window.

ScreenTip Information displayed in a small window when you rest the pointer over a button or window element.

Search box The text box into which you enter words or phrases you want to search for.

Search menu The menu from which you specify the scope of a search operation.

section In OneNote, an organizational unit containing a group of pages that you can view separately from other notebook content. See also *.one file*.

section break A break inserted so that subsequent information can have different page formatting (such as different orientation) than preceding information.

section group In OneNote, a subdivision of a notebook containing a group of sections that you can view separately from other notebook sections. A section group is contained within a subfolder of the *OneNote Notebooks* folder.

select To make an object, graphic, or text active, usually by clicking it with the mouse, so that it can be moved or modified.

selection area An area in a document's left margin in which you can click and drag to select blocks of text.

sizing handle A handle at the side or in the corner of a selected object, which you can drag to make the object larger or smaller.

slide library In PowerPoint, a place on a SharePoint site where co-workers store slides that other people can use.

slide timing In PowerPoint, the time a slide will be displayed on the screen before PowerPoint moves to the next slide.

smart tag A flag that identifies a certain type of information, such as date and time, names, street addresses, or telephone numbers, so that you can perform actions associated with that type of information.

soft page break A page break that Word inserts when the text reaches the bottom margin of a page.

sorting Arranging information so that it is based on any field or combination of fields.

source file A file containing an object that is inserted in a destination file.

status bar An area across the bottom of the program window that gives information about the current document.

subpage In OneNote, a page that is subordinate to another page. Subpages are linked to the corresponding page and move with the page as a unit.

subpoint A subordinate item below a bullet point in a list.

syntax The required format in which expressions must be entered.

tab In the Microsoft Office Fluent user interface, a task-centric segment of the Ribbon containing groups of commands. In a document, a character with which you can specify the amount of space preceding or following a section of text, and its alignment.

tab leader A repeating character (usually a dot or dash) that separates text before a tab from text or a number after it.

tab stop A location in the text column where text will align after you press the Tab key to insert a tab character.

table style Predesigned combinations of font, color, lines, and shading that you can apply to a table.

tablet pen The electronic "pen" supplied with a Tablet PC, which you use to interact with items on the screen.

tabular list A list that arranges text in simple columns separated by left, right, centered, or decimal tab stops.

template In PowerPoint, a pattern used as the basis for creating the slides, handouts, and speaker notes in a presentation. In Word, a predefined set of text, formatting, and graphics, stored in a special type of document that can be used as the basis for or to style other documents.

text box A box drawn independently on a slide to contain text that is not part of any placeholder.

text wrapping break A manual break that forces the text that follows it to the next line. Also called a *line break*.

theme A predefined format consisting of fonts, colors, and visual styles that can be applied to an Office document.

Thesaurus A feature that looks up alternative words, or synonyms, for a word.

thumbnail A picture representation of choices available in a gallery; or of pages in a document.

title In PowerPoint, a name you designate for a slide in the Title placeholder.

title bar An area at the top of the program window that displays the name of the active document.

title slide In PowerPoint, the introductory slide in a presentation.

toolbar area In the traditional Office user interface (without the Ribbon), the area near the top of the program window, below the menu bar, in which docked toolbars are displayed by default.

typeface See *font*.

Unfiled Notes section In OneNote, the information storage unit that exists outside of any specific notebook. By default, OneNote saves screen clippings and Web notes to the Unfiled Notes section.

View toolbar A toolbar on the right end of the status bar that contains tools for adjusting the view of document content.

views Different ways in which the elements of the program window can be arranged for viewing messages, or different perspectives of document content.

Web Layout view A view that shows how a document will look when viewed in a Web browser.

widow At the top of a page, a single line of a paragraph that continues from the previous page.

wildcard characters A placeholder, such as an asterisk (*) or question mark (?), representing an unknown character or characters in search criteria.

Windows logo key Also know as the Start key, a key labeled with the Windows logo (a waving flag) located in the bottom row of a standard PC keyboard. Pressing the Windows logo key opens the Start menu. Many programs offer system-related keyboard shortcuts incorporating the Windows logo key and another key.

word processing The writing, editing, and formatting of documents in a word processor.

word wrap The automatic breaking of a line of text when it reaches the page margin.

Index

A

absolute references in Excel formulas, 188–189
active cells (Excel), 161, 423
Align Center button (Word), 108
Align Center Right button (Word), 109
Align Text Left button (PowerPoint), 285
aligning paragraphs, xxxii, 79
aligning text in PowerPoint presentations, li, 282
All Notebooks List window, 339
Apply To All button (PowerPoint), 313
arguments, 185, 423
arithmetic operators, 423
Arrange Windows dialog box (Excel), 147, 151
aspect ratio, 423
attributes, 423
audio notes, lxi, 391–392
Audio Search (OneNote), lxiii, 420
auditing Excel formulas, xliii, 195–202, 423
Auto Fill Options button (Excel), 158–159
AutoComplete (Excel), xxxix, 157–158, 423. *See also* Formula AutoComplete (Excel)
AutoCorrect dialog box (Excel), 174
AutoCorrect dialog box (PowerPoint), 271–272
AutoCorrect dialog box (Word), 57, 95
AutoCorrect (PowerPoint), 271
  adding entries to, xlix, 272
  defined, 423
AutoCorrect (Word), 56, 95. *See also* checking spelling (Word)
  customizing, 57
  defined, 423
AutoFill (Excel), xxxix, 157–158, 423
AutoFit Options button (PowerPoint), 273
AutoFit (PowerPoint), 271, 273
automatic saving, customizing, 29
AutoRecover, 29
AVERAGE function, 185
AVERAGEIF function, 191–193
AVERAGEIFS function, 192

B

backgrounds, slide
  customizing, 302–305
  defined, 423
  pictures as, liii, 302–305

backgrounds, worksheet
  customizing, 236
  deleting, 236
  pictures as, 234, 236
Backspace key, vs. Delete key, 37
bar tabs, 102
BE SURE TO paragraphs, xiv
blank documents, creating, 26
blank notebooks (OneNote), 423
blank presentations, opening, 242
Bold button (Excel), 209
Bold button (Word), 71, 103
bolding text, 71, 207, 209
book features and conventions, xiii–xiv
Border button (Excel), 210
borders
  for paragraphs, xxxiii, 86–87
  for tables, 115
  for text boxes in PowerPoint, xlix, 267
  for worksheet cells, xliv, 207–208, 210
Borders And Shading dialog box (Word), 86–87, 115
Borders button (Word), 86, 115
Breaks button (Word), 101
Browse by Page button, 16
building blocks. *See also* Quick Parts
  creating, xxxix, 42–43
  defined, 423
  inserting, xxix, 42–43
  saving, 44
Building Blocks template, 44
Bullet Library, 90
bullet points (PowerPoint), 258
  adding, xlviii, 261
  collapsing, lii, 293
  converting into slides, 261
  converting slides into, 261
  defined, 423
  selecting, 263
  subpoints, creating, xlviii, 262
bulleted lists. *See also* lists; numbered lists
  bullet symbol, changing, 89–91
  converting to normal paragraphs, 91
  creating, 88, 90
  multilevel, creating, 89, 93
Bullets button (Word), 90
Business Tools tab (Word), 5
buttons. *See also* specific buttons
  adding to Quick Access Toolbar, 148, 152
  arrows on, 6
  deleting from Quick Access Toolbar, 148
  displaying name/function of, 6
  ScreenTips, displaying, 6

C

E

F

What do you think of this book?

We want to hear from you!

Do you have a few minutes to participate in a brief online survey?

Microsoft is interested in hearing your feedback so we can continually improve our books and learning resources for you.

To participate in our survey, please visit:

www.microsoft.com/learning/booksurvey/

...and enter this book's ISBN-10 number (appears above barcode on back cover*). As a thank-you to survey participants in the United States and Canada, each month we'll randomly select five respondents to win one of five $100 gift certificates from a leading online merchant. At the conclusion of the survey, you can enter the drawing by providing your e-mail address, which will be used for prize notification only.

Thanks in advance for your input. Your opinion counts!

*Where to find the ISBN-10 on back cover

ISBN-13: 000-0-0000-0000-0
ISBN-10: 0-0000-0000-0

00000

ple only. Each book has unique ISBN.

Microsoft®
Press